Katherine Clyde
869 E 217th Street Apt. 1b
Bronx NY 10467

D1028258

THE SPLENDOR
OF THE CHURCH

HENRI DE LUBAC

THE SPLENDOR
OF THE CHURCH

Translated by
MICHAEL MASON

IGNATIUS PRESS   SAN FRANCISCO

This translation was originally published by
Sheed and Ward, New York, © 1956
and is from the second edition of
the French original:
Méditation sur l'Église
© 1953 Éditions Montaigne, Paris

Cover art:
The Holy Spirit
Alabaster window, detail of the Cathedra of Saint Peter
by
Gian Lorenzo Bernini

Photograph by Stefano Spaziani
Calligraphy by Victoria Hoke Lane
Cover design by Roxanne Mei Lum

With ecclesiastical approval
© 1986, 1999 Ignatius Press, San Francisco
All rights reserved
Reprinted in 2006

ISBN 978-0-89870-742-7
Library of Congress catalogue number 99-73012
Printed in the United States of America ∞

This re-edition is
dedicated to Cardinal de Lubac
in the year of his ninetieth birthday.

My personal debt of gratitude to this
extraordinary scholar, loyal churchman,
gracious and patient teacher, and fellow Jesuit
is but a small part of what is owed him
by the countless numbers of men and women of every land
whose faith has been so profoundly enriched
by his life's work.

Cardinal de Lubac is above all else
a man of the Church, *homo ecclesiasticus*,
such as he himself portrays in these pages.
He has received all from the Church.
He has returned all to the Church.

This book, which, characteristically, he so humbly describes
in its introduction, is a testament that will endure
to his lifelong love of his Mother and ours,
the Immaculate Bride of the Lamb,
Holy Church.

Joseph Fessio, S.J.
Editor, Ignatius Press

CONTENTS

INTRODUCTORY

THE subject matter of this book was, originally, that of various conversations I had with fellow priests at days of recollection, study weekends and retreats, and the like; so that the reader should not expect it to be "scientific". Still less should it be treated as a pocket treatise on the Church; I had no intention of doing original research, or doing yet again what has already been done quite satisfactorily by others. What I have done is meditate, in the light of faith, on certain aspects of the mystery of the Church, as an attempt to work myself into the very heart of that mystery. There are, I know, plenty of texts cited at the foot of each page—sometimes rather haphazardly, I am afraid—but that is only with the idea of giving the reader a direct line on the essential texts of Tradition; for my ambition is simply to be its echo—that is all. I want to share with others the recurrent thrill that comes from recognizing that impressive and undivided voice in all its modulations and all its harmonics.

That voice of Tradition has continually called on me to look up into the "Heavenly Jerusalem", whose beauty has taken a daily firmer hold upon me. But for all that I have not looked to the heavenly city as one does to a dream; for I have not been looking for a sort of refuge from everyday monotony and the burden of existence, in some airy mirage or other. On the contrary; to me, that mother-country of freedom, with all its royal majesty and heavenly splendor, is something to be seen at the very heart of earthly reality, right at the core of all the confusion and all the mischances that are, inevitably, involved in its mission to men. My love is for the Holy City not only as it is ideally, but also as it appears in history, and particularly as it appears to us at present; and I love it with an ever-growing affection. So, since that is where my heart lies, and since heart speaks to heart, my hope is that others—especially my fellow priests—will find helpful what has been of help to me. It may be that some of the reflections I put before them will seem out of date already; today situations change quickly, as do mental attitudes and key problems, particularly among those who are more hotly engaged than the present writer in the world of action. But I was not really aiming at topical application. We live in a particularly turbulent period, and it is impossible that its troubles should be altogether without repercussions in our souls. And if at such a time anything I have to say can help anyone to a clearer sight of the Bride of the Lamb, in all her radiant motherhood, my object will have been achieved and I shall be well satisfied.

PREFACE TO THE SECOND EDITION

THIS book had hardly been finished before there had appeared a whole series of further works that demanded to be taken into account in it—a demand met, as far as possible, in the second edition, which does not, however, otherwise make any substantial change from the first. In one or two places I have made further precisions, additional citations of traditional texts or documents of the Magisterium, or developments aimed at getting a closer view of this historical process or that linguistic fact—and that is about all. Though I have been able to take advantage, where various matters of detail have been concerned, of the helpful suggestions of several correspondents, the reviews I have seen so far have (I am glad to say!) been too kind to do much for me in that direction.

One of my reviewers—Fr. Georges Courtade—wrote: "This book is closely connected with several previous books by the same author", and he goes on to add that it even makes "numerous borrowings" from them. Leaving on one side the many things he had to say in praise of the book as well, I am glad to be able to confirm that statement. For my aim was not, in fact, to break new ground; all I was trying to do was to extend a little the effect of my own efforts—however insignificant these may have been—between the years 1945 and 1950 in particular, during which time I felt, too strongly for comfort, the gathering of those dangers which have in some cases, unfortunately, since become only too clear to all. It was something that I wanted to do without putting a damper on goodwill in any quarter. I went so far as to hope that even though some of the things I said might be clumsily put, the reader might still be able to see through them, in the last analysis, not the ideas or the arguments of an individual, let alone his prejudices and his limitations, but the authentic voice of our Mother the Church, which can never lack in power and sweetness to persuade where her own children are concerned. Granted, that is an ideal impossible of attainment. Yet I hope nevertheless that I have got near enough to it—or at least have given sufficient evidence of my desire to reach it—for the effect of my words to be in no instance contrary to this sole desire of mine.

In 1949 a certain theologian denounced, among the dangers of the time, "the spirit of faction" that had found its way into certain ecclesiastical circles in France; a taste for "daring innovations" in matters of doctrine, the use of principles that were "implicitly Modernist", adventurings on the slippery slope of esotericism, contempt for the hierarchy, and the like. Whether any clique so minded really did exist or not, I do not know; I sincerely hope not. But it does seem to be undeniable that the sense of the Church was sometimes threatened even in men of the utmost nobility of character and the profoundest loyalty—or that at any rate it ran much risk of being so threatened, existing as it did among so many adverse influences attacking it from all sides. Hence a sense of alarm on my part, which I could not but give expression to in discussions whose publication I could have wished to take place more speedily. Yet I must be quick to add that my expression of concern was at the same time and in a far deeper sense one of joy as well. It could not be otherwise for anyone able to realize, to some extent at least, the pricelessness of that good which consists, quite simply, in belonging to the Church at all. Once you have got your eyes in focus, you cannot miss the wonderful blossoming that goes on everywhere in her garden. And it does not matter where the causes of sorrow or worry throng in from, or how grave they are, or what their nature may be; joy is still triumphant, breaking through the most somber of appearances and flourishing on everything that should, humanly speaking, snuff it out. Joy is over everything and the foundation of everything.

So that the Church's children can boldly borrow the words of the Bridegroom in the Song of Songs (which, St. Bernard says, is "the Holy Spirit's masterpiece") and say to their Mother, with a depth of feeling born of ever-increasing conviction: "Thy voice is sweet and thy face is beautiful."

I hope that the reader will bear with these few words of explanation. Whatever he thinks of the book, may he remember the author before God.

I

THE CHURCH AS MYSTERY

M ORE than one man has noted that the most tradition-minded centuries did the least talking about Tradition. Rather, they lived it. They were soaked through with it. It was through the eyes of Tradition that they read the Scriptures themselves. Then, men were not in the habit of questioning themselves about Tradition, for to them it was the present rather than the past and less an object of study than the very form of their thinking. To them, the monuments of Tradition were not things to be examined minutely with all the resources of scholarship and the critical method; they were handled with a sense of possession and interpreted with a freedom that, far from being opposed to a deep faithfulness to their spirit, was, on the contrary, inclusive of it. Possessed as these men were of the thing-in-itself, they were to some extent freed from the need for conceptualizing it. All the richness of Tradition was theirs; they brought it to flower and handed it on without very much conscious reflection on what they were doing.

Now, reflection implies a pause, detachment, severance; initially, at any rate, a sort of question mark. Sooner or later it is of course bound to become necessary, and besides, it is something that has never, in any case, been entirely absent. One is even surprised, after its advent, to see how much of it there has been, in potentiality, from the very beginning—though it *has* been in potentiality and nothing more. But once circumstances suddenly make it imperative, this reflexive activity starts up everywhere. It fastens on the very heart of its object, explores every approach to it, rummages in its very foundations, and penetrates its remotest ramifications. It does not matter whether it be historical, critical, philosophical, or even grammatical; there is the same almost feverish intensity.

For the most part this sort of thing happens when the whole inheritance of Tradition, hitherto held without question, becomes, in one way or another, disputed territory. Doubts arise as to its value, and insidious comparisons are made between its original form and that which it has at the time; every element in it is put to the test, and there is as much criticism from the man of religion himself as there is from the scholar pure and simple. People begin to ask themselves whether the whole of this assemblage of beliefs and customs is really authentic, and whether there has not been, in the course of the centuries, a process of accretion that has also been one of corruption. The thing seems to have become a burden rather than a source of vitality and, thus, to constitute an obstruction of the very life it is supposed to feed and transmit.[1] And that is the situation in which it becomes imperative to reflect upon what one previously lived unthinkingly. The full-bloodedness of primitive naïveté becomes a thing of the past, and one has to stand back and "objectify". When something is called in question, you have to get down to its roots. If you are to meet the strategic demands of the situation, and if you are to be rational in retaining what others reject, the whole matter has to be studied from a new viewpoint. It is not so much a question of justifying as of elucidating; polemic is not the primary concern. Fundamentally, what you feel is a need to see straight; it is a time for stocktaking.

In this way it became necessary, from the time of the Reformation onward, to clarify our minds on the subject of Tradition; hence a flood of studies and definitions and distinctions and precisions (to say nothing of argument)—hence innumerable boldly novel systematizations and a great deal of first-rate work generally; yet in spite of it all, it is doubtful—unfortunately—whether the sense of Tradition is any more lively today

---

[1] See, for example, the lengthy—and odd—chapter 79 ("Contra Traditionum onerositatem et multitudinem") of Peter Cantor's *Verbum abbreviatum* (PL 205, 233–39).

than it was in the past. However, the doctrine of Tradition has been kept alive and consolidated, even if in a way decidedly different from the old one, and often, as it were, back-to-front.[2] And thanks to this reflexive renaissance, it has come victoriously through a crisis that did seem, humanly speaking, bound to destroy it.

In our own day a situation somewhat similar exists with regard to the Church. In the classic manifestations of the first centuries of the Christian era—to say nothing of Scripture—her self-expression has a superb vitality. From the very start you feel that she has an extraordinarily deep awareness of her own being; the idea of the Church is everywhere, and everywhere shapes the expounding of the faith. In addition, at a very early stage she is compelled to begin the process of reflection on herself. Every one of the great heresies that she has to fight forces this upon her: for it does not matter which direction the attack comes from—whether the Incarnation or the Trinity or grace is the subject of contention—in each case the thing threatened is something in the Church herself. All the mysteries that she examines, one by one, provide occasions for the same thing, for she is bound up with each and finds herself involved in all of them. Yet today we are at the beginning of an attempt at an unfolding that is at once analytic and generalized—an attempt to grasp the mystery in its totality; and circumstances have never before made necessary an effort of this kind.[3]

[2] Ever since the denials of Protestantism, Tradition has received—and rightly—an explicit emphasis it was not accorded by early theology. This last for the most part talks in terms of Scripture exclusively (though there are, certainly, texts on Tradition as well). But the Scripture it discusses is always Scripture read within the Church, as interpreted by the Fathers and as understood by Tradition; see Edmond Ortigues, S.M., "La Tradition de l'Évangile dans l'Église", *Foi et vie* (July 1951), and, for an example of the modern point of view, Bruno de Solages, "Le Procès de la Scolastique", *Revue thomiste* (1927), pp. 330–32.

[3] See J. A. Jungmann, S.J., "L'Église dans la vie religieuse d'aujourd'hui", in *L'Église est une: Hommage à Moehler*, ed. P. Chaillet, S.J., pp. 334–48; Msgr. Charles Journet, *L'Église du Verbe Incarné* (1951), 2:60. Msgr. Bartmann's *Lehrbuch der Dogmatik* says, somewhat exaggeratedly: "The Church was in

For some time there has, in fact, been a great deal of talk about the Church—much more than in the past, and about a much more comprehensive sense of the word. This much is common experience, and indeed some people find themselves tempted to say that there is altogether too much talk—and ill-considered talk at that—about it. Would it not be better perhaps to try, quite simply, to live the Church, as so many have done before us? It seems that by considering her from outside in order to discuss her, we run the risk of growing apart from her, in our heart of hearts. Surely there is a danger here of straining, if not actually snapping, the intimate bonds without which a man is not really Catholic? One wonders whether all these refinements and analyses and subtleties, with all the mental turmoil they involve, are not incompatible with that time-weathered simplicity and instinct of obedience which have always been the distinctive mark of a loyal member of the Church. And in addition to this, many will be quick to point out that the Church is not a this-worldly reality such as lends itself to exact measurement and analysis. "So long as the present existence lasts she cannot be perfectly known but remains hidden as under a veil":[4] the Church is a mystery of faith[5] and "surpasses the capacities and powers of our intellect no less than

---

existence for about fifteen hundred years without reflecting on her nature and trying to formulate it in the precision of a logical definition." It demands amazing prejudice, or at least astonishing ingenuousness, to find it a "curious thing" that "in his *De principiis*" Origen "devotes no chapter to the Church" (Eugène de Faye, *Origène* [1928], 3:275).

[4] Berengard, *Expositio super septem visiones libri Apocalypsis*: "Ecclesia, quamdiu in hac vita consistit, agnosci perfecte non potest, sed qui sub quodam velamine abscondsa tenetur" (PL 17, 947a).

[5] *Roman Catechism*, chap. 10, no. 21: "Cum igitur hic articulus non minus quam caeteri intelligentiae nostrae facultatem et vires superet, jure optimo confitemur, nos Ecclesiae ortum, munera, et dignitatem non humana ratione cognoscere, sed fidei oculis intueri." We may say of the Church what the encyclical *Mystici corporis* says of the dwelling of the Holy Spirit in our souls: "We are dealing with a mystery that during our exile on earth can never be completely unveiled, never altogether understood, nor adequately expressed in human language."

any other".[6] More than this, she is, as far as we are concerned, the meeting place of all mysteries; and mystery is something that is fitly believed in obscurity, something to be meditated in silence—"Seek not the things that are too high for thee."[7] It was this very fact which, in the past, called forth protest from many Christian writers: from St. Ephraem,[8] St. Basil,[9] and St. Hilary[10] in Christian antiquity, past William of Saint-Thierry[11] and Alain of Lille[12] up to Pascal[13] and beyond him, innumerable believers have felt the greatest reluctance in speaking of the Church. They have felt a sort of deep-seated resentment against those whose provocativeness has forced them to talk about something they simply want to adore, and to drag the sacred object of their faith out into the turmoil of theorizing and disputation. And after all, there does seem to be a special reason for reserve where the Church is concerned. As Christians we believe and hope—but that is, in itself surely, the Church's characteristic too? She is—as we shall see later—the assemblage

[6] *Roman Catechism*, chaps. 1, no. 4; 10, no. 21.

[7] Sir 3:22. The phrase has often been quoted since St. Augustine (*Ad Orosium*, chap. 11, no. 14 [PL 42, 678]). See my *Corpus mysticum: L'Eucharistie et l'Église au moyen âge*, 2d ed. (1949), pp. 268–69, and Prov 23:5.

[8] Hymn 79, strophe 10 (E. Beck, "Die Theologie des hl. Ephraem", SA 21 [1949]: 64).

[9] Homily 15, *On Faith* (PG 31, 464b). Cf. Diadocus of Photike, *A Hundred Chapters concerning Spiritual Perfection*, 22 (ed. E. des Places in the series *Sources chrétiennes*, no. 5, p. 88); *Clementine Homilies*, hom. 19, chap. 8; hom. 20, chap. 8, etc.

[10] *De Trinitate*, bk. 2, chap. 2 (PL 10, 51).

[11] *Aenigma Fidei* (PL 180, 194; cf. col. 409); *De sacramento altaris*, chap. 11 (PL 180, 359b).

[12] In the *Elucidatio in Cantica*, on the subject of the Assumption: "*Ne evigilare faciatis dilectam meam*. . . . Monet Christus filias Jerusalem, id est Ecclesias, quod de resurrectione gloriosae Virginis numquam deficient . . . quod a patriarchis, prophetis et apostolis distinctum non est" (PL 210, 74).

[13] When he speaks adversely of those who have "obliged him to speak of the depths of religion". One remembers also Joseph de Maistre's reflection, in his *Du Principe générateur des constitutions politiques*: "The faith would be more angelic if it had not been forced to evolve by the sophistical opposition [of innovators]."

of the faithful, that is, of believers, in the primary and fundamental sense of that phrase; the union of those who "call upon
the name of the Lord"[14] and await his second coming. As His
Holiness Pope Pius XII reminded us when speaking of the laity,
we are the Church ourselves,[15] and since this is so, it would
seem as if there were in this reflexive activity a danger such as
that which threatens the man who wants to be a spectator at his
own prayer. For if you turn back in contemplation of yourself
instead of contemplating the object of your faith and invoking
that of your hope, the recoil and self-regarding involved seem
likely to put a sort of filter between your spiritual vision and the
reality that is the object of the faith and hope alike.

* * *

The danger should not be underestimated. The business of
reflection is always tricky; powerful forces are brought into
play, and there is more than one misapplication of them that
can prove dangerous to us. The false way of subjectivism is
particularly hard to recognize, and there are innumerable approaches to it. In any case, danger lies on every side in the life of
the mind, and even more so in the life of faith; after all, it lies on
every side in life at the bodily level too. Yet forewarned is
forearmed; if we do nothing but brood over this danger we only
increase it and hypnotize ourselves helpless in the face of it. To
run away from all danger is to run away from all responsibility
and indeed from action itself; ultimately, it is the refusal of
vocation as such. To behave in such a way is often to accept
defeat in advance, much as we hate to admit to the fact. And all
the danger in the world cannot release us from a task that has
become necessary.

The historicity of man is something more than a mere
phrase; and similarly, there is a historicity of the Christian.
Even though faith has no history, substantially speaking—for

[14] Acts 2:21; Rom 10:13, 4:24–25. Cf. L. Cerfaux, *Le Christ dans la théologie de
St. Paul* (1951), pp. 260–61.

[15] Allocution of February 20, 1946 (*Documentation catholique* [1946], col. 176).

the eternal is not subject to becoming—"the man of faith and the world in which he dwells have one." [16] And it follows that we cannot run away whenever we feel like it into another age— not even if we do not actually intend a negative attitude in so doing. We cannot avoid the problems of our own day, any more than we can excuse ourselves from its tasks or run away from its battles. If we are to live in the Church, then we have to become involved with the problems she faces now, and the assent of our intelligence is owed to her doctrine as we find it set out today. It would be a big mistake for us to think that we could ever rediscover the faith of the past in its exact tenor and all its richness, at the expense of all that has been clarified since: a big mistake too, even granting that the thing were legitimate in itself. If you reject the fruit and blossom of the live branch, then it is, as far as you are concerned, a dead one. For time cannot be reversed; even error and revolt, however complete their over-throw, impose a new life-style and a different *emphasis* on the life of faith, as on the expression of truth. The need to face up to them stimulates the instinctive reaction of the intellect of the believer (which is always trying to achieve a greater articulate-ness with regard to the revelation received) and overcomes, if need arises, that intellect's own timidities.[17]

[16] Étienne Gilson, "La Sagesse et le temps", LV (1951), pp. 79–80: "Under the first and the most striking of its aspects, the substance of the faith presents itself to the Christian as of a rigorous stability not subject to time, and this down to the very letter of its expression. Yet . . . this stability itself is not of the temporal order. . . . Divine in essence though it be, the substance of the Christian faith is not immobile, but eternal. . . . In the eternal there is no becoming. God has no history, and neither has faith, since even in time faith is the grasping of a substance that is of eternity. But if faith itself has no history, nevertheless the man of faith and the world in which he dwells have one. They are history in their very essence just because everything save Him who Is is creaturely—that is, that mingling of being and non-being which we call becoming."

[17] Cf. William of Saint-Thierry, *De sacramento altaris*, chap. 11 (he is talking about heresy): "quod nisi coegisset necessitas de re qua quaerebatur, viros sanctos et eruditos aliquid sentire et proferre, semper timidae hominum mentes habuissent obscurum" (PL 180, 359b).

Admittedly, this is an entirely relative progress; there is no question of any change of substance, and it "introduces no invention";[18] rather, by means of a series of clarifications and precisions, it prevents the whittling away or disintegration of doctrine and stops it from withering up by virtue of the vitality it sustains, forestalling or correcting all deviation. Hence it can appear as some suspicious novelty only to those who have already begun to lose their understanding of the very thing whose name they are invoking. The truth of the matter is that it maintains against the hostile forces that are always at work the truth entrusted to the Church once and for all—maintains it "in its fullness, integrity, and authenticity", and makes it fruitful "in the same sense and with the same mind".[19] For the Church, "having custody of the deposit of divine revelation, will never suffer anything to be subtracted from the truths proposed to us by the faith, nor anything to be added to them"[20]—which

[18] Pius XI, encyclical *Mortalium animos*.

[19] Vatican Council I, constitution *De fide catholica*, chap. 4, quoting St. Vincent of Lérins, *Commonitorium*, chap. 28.

[20] Pius IX, encyclical *Nostris et nobiscum* (December 8, 1849); bull *Ineffabilis Deus* (1854); Pius XI, encyclical *Mortalium animos*. And É. Gilson also says ("Sagesse", p. 78): "Twenty centuries of philosophy, science and even theology have neither increased nor lessened by one iota the substance of the hope and faith possessed by all Christians in the word of God." See also my study "Le Problème du développement du dogme", RSR (1948), pp. 130–60. This study formed the subject of an astonishing criticism by Fr. F. Spedalieri, S.J., in *Selectae et breviores philosophiae ac theologiae controversiae* (Rome: Catholic Book Agency, 1940), pp. 85–122. The author attributes to me opinions on the most important issues that are diametrically opposed to those which I have always maintained, and that most explicitly, in that particular study as elsewhere. There does not seem to me to be any great point in explaining at length that I have not attacked the apostolicity of the faith, nor the unchangeable character of dogmatic concepts, nor the activity of theological reflection itself, nor the possibility of certain conclusions based on explicitly revealed truth, nor the value of analogical knowledge of mystery, nor the existence of truths of the faith formulated from the beginning—and so on. However, since the work in question has circulation in many quarters where *Recherches* does not, I am compelled to take this occasion of clearing myself of charges so unfounded. The reader may see for himself how very differently my work was interpreted

being so, we must not confuse this relative progress with progressive revelation. But we cannot reject it or systematically ignore it without corrupting the very thing it is designed to preserve.

Just as the faith is one in its formal principle, because the believer "adheres to all the articles of faith by reason of one means, that is, the First Truth",[21] so also the Christian mystery, which is the object or content of faith, is in itself one. It offers itself for our adherence, under the multiplicity of the formulae that have accumulated with the centuries, as the one total reality, which these formulae "enclose on all sides, without ever exhausting it or dividing it".[22] As St. Irenaeus said long ago, it is the "whole body of the work of the Son of God", which is made manifest by the Scriptures to those who read them with understanding; moreover, as the same writer says elsewhere, this unique body is so constituted that all its members are in continual interaction.[23] And the various sections of dogma are thus "involved one with another" so that error concerning one has its repercussions throughout the whole body, while in compensation one method of reaching that "understanding of faith", which is not a luxury but a necessity, is to consider them in their interconnection.[24] According to St. Thomas, all this stems from the term "article" (of faith) itself, which is applied to each one of these separately formulated

---

by Fr. Joseph Duhr, S.J., in "Le Développement dogmatique et l'Immaculée Conception", NRT (1951), pp. 1025–30, and in the supplement to Msgr. Bartmann's *Lehrbuch der Dogmatik* (1952), pt. 1.

[21] St. Thomas Aquinas, ST II-II, q. 5, a. 3 ad 2.

[22] Fr. Louis Bouyer, commenting on Newman in his *Newman: Sa vie, sa spiritualité* (1952), p. 239; cf. p. 288.

[23] *Demonstration of the Apostolic Faith*, chap. 1; *Adversus haereses*, bk. 1, chap. 8, no. 4 (PG 7, 584), etc. See also E. Mersch, S.J., *Le Corps mystique du Christ: Études de théologie historique*, 2d ed. (1936), 1:317.

[24] Vatican Council I, constitution *De fide catholica*, chap. 4: "Ac ratio quidem, fide illustrata, cum sedulo, pie et sobrie, quaerit, aliquam Deo dante mysteriorum intelligentiam eamque fructuossissimam assequitur, tum . . . e mysteriorum ipsorum nexu inter se" (Mansi, *Amplissima collectio conciliorum*, vol. 2, col. 433).

truths; etymologically speaking, it signifies the articulation of members of one single body.[25]

At a certain given state of crisis or point of maturation, one particular mystery—one particular part of the unique whole—comes, as it were, into the foreground of the reflective landscape. In consequence, it becomes a species of vital center round which, for practical purposes, all the others organically group themselves in a sort of genesis: and by the same token it is also the point of nervous sensitivity, error, or indecision that affects all the others in a doubly powerful reaction. It becomes the standard round which is fought out and decided the crucial battle for orthodoxy. The theology of the Trinity, Christology, the dogma of grace—all these have been, in succession, key positions of this kind. And as soon as that happens, the decisive point becomes the focal point of the best of our reflexive thought; our careful scrutiny of it will go on as long as the formulae that express it have not yet received the necessary revision, or at least been weighed, trimmed, adjusted, and reset "for the greater security of the faith".[26] We are not, of course, in ourselves fit for the business, but we can count on the guidance and reassurance of God.[27] On the development of doctrine Newman writes, "Wonderful it is to see with what effort, hesitation, suspense, interruption,—with how many swayings to the right and to the left—with how many reverses, yet with what certainty of advance, with what precision in its march, and with what ultimate completeness, it has been evolved." [28] Truth finds its own equilibrium, through ways that are often

---

[25] ST II-II, q. 1, a. 6: "Nomen articuli . . . significat quandam coaptationem aliquarum partium distinctarum; et ideo particulae corporis sibi invicem coaptatae dicuntur membrorum articuli"; see also L. de Grandmaison, *Jésus-Christ*, 15th ed. (1931), 2:214–17.

[26] See St. Hilary of Poitiers, *De Trinitate*, bk. 4, chap. 7: "Ad maximam fidei securitatem" (PL 10, 100b).

[27] 2 Cor 3:4–5.

[28] John Henry Newman, "The Theory of Developments in Religious Doctrine", 6, in *Fifteen Sermons Preached before the University of Oxford* (London: Longmans, Green, 1892), 317.

unforeseen. The risks and chances of the most unfavorable situations, the conjunction of efforts apparently entirely independent one of another, even mutually opposed—through the ebb and flow of all this, even through outright forgetting, or neglect at least, harmony is established. The human mind, brushing aside the constructions of overnaturalistic thought, resolving ambiguities and recasting, as it were, in the furnace of revelation the very molds of thinking itself, moves onward to the perfect development of a theory entirely without fuzziness at the edges, and with the help of the Holy Spirit "a mankind in labor" once more succeeds "in tearing from its heart a perfect naming".[29]

It certainly seems as if the present day has brought about the moment for carrying out a labor of this kind à propos that particular section or aspect of the total Christian mystery, that particular member of the "body of truth", which is the mystery of the Church.

To begin with, the Catholic consciousness of many who are worlds apart from any temptation to formal schism or heresy is sometimes threatened today by new errors and aberrations, which, coming as an addition to those of past centuries—themselves the source of so much schism, acrimony, and turmoil, and still alive among us—are more subtle yet than they. There are all sorts of failures in understanding, stemming from the individualism that was the order of yesterday and the false collectivisms that are the order of today.[30] There are the illusions, impatience, and criticism that are nearly always bound up

---

[29] Paul Claudel, L'Épée et le miroir, p. 65; cf. pp. 63–64: "Once introduced, an idea cannot be immobilized. It has to produce its consequences and its proper offspring. . . . The Gospel has not completed its mission. It has something new and old to teach each generation as it arises—something especially for our own ear, which our fathers never heard; an explanation, perhaps a way of looking at things, a task, fresh orders. And all the while the landscape of what is negative crystallizes line by line around our advance."

[30] Fr. Karl Rahner, S.J., has outlined some of the features of this false collectivism in his essay on the individual in the Church, in *Gefahren im heutigen Katholizismus* (Einsiedeln, 1950).

with some distortion of the faith; confusions of mode and an overnaturalistic type of thinking that modern apologetic has not always steered entirely clear of,[31] in the light of which the Church appears as if founded on human principles and directed to human ends or is explained by human analogies that have been insufficiently scrutinized. And all this all the more in proportion as the Church is not looked at as God made her, in the mystery of her supernatural being.[32] Thus arises the necessity of bringing out in bold relief not just this or that particular truth but the very center—the soul, if you will—of doctrine itself. But it is also true that—as if by a countermovement of the Holy Spirit—there has never been a more ardent effort toward the reintegration of Christians in Catholic unity. There has, perhaps, never been a time when nostalgia for the visible Church was so deep-seated in the heart of Protestantism, or when there was so strong an ambition among Christians to make the fullness of Christian living real in terms of a life of the Church. When—as happens, unfortunately—priests are moved to say, again and again: "These people of mine have no sense of the Church", the thing is something more than mere condemnation of a very real evil; it is the mark of an ecclesial[33] conscience

---

[31] See Pierre Charles, S.J., "Vicarius Christi", NRT (1929), pp. 449–50.

[32] See the shrewd reflections of A. Vacant in his *Études théologiques sur les constitutions du Concile du Vatican* (1895), 2:213, and L. Billot, *Tractatus de Ecclesia Christi*, 3d ed. (1909), p. 515: "Sic igitur fundamentalem tenes differentiam inter ecclesiasticum et politicum gubernium, ut neque ea quae ecclesiae constitutioni propria sunt ad civilia transferas, neque vicissim ex iis quae de civilibus naturalis ratio perspicit, genuinam rationem sacri principatus corrumpas." In 1885, Msgr. Mermillod lamented the fact that "the unfortunate demands of our time, the vested interests of some, and the petty devotions of others minimize and naturalize this holy Church, which, being one thing with Christ, and his body and fullness, is, together with him, the primordial and final consideration of God in all his works" ("Letter to Dom Gréa", in Gréa, *De l'Église et de sa divine constitution*, p. v).

[33] There has been some criticism of this neologism; and, of course, I have no special liking for it in principle. It is just that it seems handy in certain cases where the word "ecclesiastical" is rather ponderous, or overmuch worn by current usage (cf. the parallel case of *marial*), and also for denoting certain

become today, in the persons of its best embodiments, more sensitive and more exacting than before. The ecumenical movement, the liturgical movement, the sociological movement—all these are developing side by side; it is not a matter of the fantasies of the crank or the hothouse busyness of a clique but of a vast collective impulse. As always, there is the odd *faux pas* and the occasional unfortunate exaggeration. But the general advance is neither held up nor deflected. Thirty years ago Romano Guardini drew our attention to a fact that has asserted itself more and more strongly ever since—that the Church has reawakened in our souls.[34] The reality of the Church has, somehow, soaked itself deeper into the core of the Christian consciousness, and alongside that development has gone a general flourishing of ecclesiological studies—not, admittedly, altogether without misfires here, too. The needs of Catholic action, thought on the subject of our own missionary activities, and the meditation of Scripture have all made their contribution to these studies, and both the work and the aspirations behind it have been encouraged by authority itself, as witness in particular the encyclical *Mystici corporis Christi*, issued by His Holiness Pope Pius XII on June 29, 1943. In a word, it seems as if, as far as the development of doctrine is concerned, the twentieth century is destined to be "the century of the Church".

Still, we must remain careful not to exaggerate. Not only must we guard against thinking of progress in terms of innovation;

nuances called for by the context. It is used by a respectable number of theologians, and I believe (for example) that it is expedient to say, as one of them does, in an appropriate context, that Bible reading ought to be "ecclesial". "Ecclesiastical reading" would not be a very happy way of putting the thing, and, although one could doubtless do without an adjective altogether, this would mean putting the idea at greater length. What follows will, I trust, make it sufficiently clear that for my own part I have no prejudice against "ecclesiastical"—very much the contrary. See also my *Histoire et Esprit* (1950), pp. 61–68.

[34] Romano Guardini, *Vom Sinn der Kirche* (1923), p. 1. See also E. Przywara, S.J., "Corpus Christi mysticum, eine Bilenz", ZAM (1940), pp. 197–215, and A. Brien, "La Pédagogie du sens de l'Église", NRT (1952), pp. 561–79.

we must also remember that we are a long way from having either fully listed or completely explored the wealth laid down for us throughout the past. That past did not constitute our "pre-theological" stage, and likewise the future will not see us the possessors of a completed theology of the Church that leaves our successors nothing to do but repeat our formulations of it. However great the number and value of the theological tasks completed, there will be no closed circuit of doctrine that puts an end to discussion and reflection alike and discourages the raising of new questions. Such a Utopia fits in with neither the nature of revealed truth nor that of the human intelligence; the experience of history is incompatible with it, and the publication of *Mystici corporis Christi* dashed precisely those hopes that were set on it.[35] For the same holds good of this mystery as of all others—it stands wide open to us, but its depths defy our sounding;[36] it is intelligible, to be sure, but not "comprehensible"—"it is discovered in such a way that there always remains something to discover."[37] And for this reason, although the reflections of our predecessors must inevitably be our guide, they do not excuse us from making our own meditation. Even that meditation itself can never come to a close, as wholly satisfactory; without calling in question all over again its established results, we shall nonetheless have to say always, with the author of Sirach: "We shall say much, and yet shall want words."[38] Here, at any rate, my aim

[35] Karl Adam showed this, and the encyclical has confirmed his views. For one or two details, see Dom C. Lialine, O.S.B., "Une Étape en ecclésiologie: Réflexions sur l'encyclique *Mystici Corporis*", IK 19 (1946): 148–50, and 20 (1947): 13.

[36] J. Lebreton, "L'Église corps du Christ", RSR (1946), pp. 241–44.

[37] Andrew of Saint-Victor, *Prologue to the Explanation of Isaias*, in Beryl Smalley, ed., *The Study of the Bible in the Middle Ages* (1941), pp. 274–75. Cf. St. Augustine, *De Trinitate*, bk. 15, chap. 2 (PL 42, 1057–58); *Sermo* 169, no. 18 (PL 38, 926); A. Brien, "Pédagogie", p. 574: "Dogmas are not lifeless concepts, but the exact signs of a living reality the depths of which faith will never come to the end of plumbing."

[38] Sir 43:29. Cf. St. Augustine, *De Trinitate*, bk. 15, chap. 28, no. 51 (PL 42, 1098), and bk. 9, chap. 1: "Quaerentem nemo juste reprehendit, si tamen in fide firmissimus quaerat" (PL 42, 959).

will be a straightforward and sustained returning to the essential data of faith. I shall try to explore them from points of departure recently established and, even more than this, to discover in them, under the guidance of the living Magisterium, the permanent norm of all theological activity.

* * *

The mystery of the Church is already written into the first, most elementary and most popular of our creeds: *"Credo . . . sanctam Ecclesiam Catholicam."* It occupies a definite place, which was not chosen haphazardly and which is worth considering. Without becoming involved in the difficult problems relative to the origins of the Apostles' Creed,[39] we may easily establish one fact, which has been duly noted by many catechists:[40] its structure is in ternary form, since it is essentially a "symbol of the Trinity".[41] It is summed up in the threefold *credo*, the threefold response to the threefold questioning concerning the three Divine Persons: "Do you believe in God the Father Almighty? Do you believe in our Lord Jesus Christ and in his Cross? Do you believe in his Holy Spirit?"[42] The believer who recites the Apostles' Creed proclaims his faith in the three Persons of the one Trinity, made known to him in the Christian revelation by and through their works; as did before him candidates for baptism in the first centuries of the

[39] Cf. J. N. D. Kelly, *Early Christian Creeds* (1950); Joseph Crehan, S.J., *Early Christian Baptism and the Creed* (1950), chap. 6, "The Facts about the Holy Spirit", pp. 111–30; Joseph de Ghellinck, S.J., *Patristique et moyen âge*, vol. 1, *Les Recherches sur les origines du Symbole des Apôtres*, 2d ed. (1949); T. Camelot, O.P., "Les Récentes Recherches sur le Symbole des Apôtres et leur portée théologique", in *Mélanges Jules Lebreton*, vol. 1 (RSR [1951]), 323–37. See also LV (1952), no. 2, which is wholly devoted to the Apostles' Creed.

[40] Thus Luis of Granada, *Treatise on Christian Doctrine*, bk. 1, chap. 3.

[41] "Symbolum trinitatis"—so Firmilian of Caesarea, quoted by St. Cyprian, *Epist.* 75, chap. 11 (2:818, in Hartel's edition).

[42] St. Ambrose, *De sacramentis*, bk. 2, chap. 7, no. 20; Ivo of Chartres, *Decretum*, pt. 1, chap. 126 (PL 161, 90b–c), etc.

Christian era[43]—"In all three Persons there is one profession handed down by the Apostles, one individual personality of the word, to be professed by all in a clear voice." [44] First are mentioned the Creator Father and the Redeemer Son, then the sanctifying Spirit. The Church comes next; she is included in all the ancient formulae, more or less in the same place, and always associated with the Holy Spirit. Today she appears in the Creed as the first of that Spirit's works, before the Communion of Saints, the remission of sins, the resurrection of the body, and the life everlasting. In the so-called Nicae-Constantinopolitan Creed, the text of which is based upon the ancient baptismal Creed of Jerusalem, and which was likewise employed in the baptismal liturgy of Constantinople, [45] the essential structure and order are the same.

There is one more important detail to be noted. According to the text of these two creeds, as established for us since ancient times, [46] it is not said that we believe "in" the Church, any more than it is said that we believe "in" any other of the

[43] To use Scholastic terminology, which is of course founded on that of the Scriptures, we may say that the "processions" of the Persons within the Divinity are revealed by their "missions" without; see J. Lebreton, *Histoire du dogme de la Trinité*, vols. 1–2; T. de Regnon, *Études de théologie positive sur la Sainte Trinité*; M. J. Lagrange, *Saint Paul: Épître aux Galates* (1918), p. 104. For the trinitarian character of the Creed, see St. Thomas Aquinas' explanations, *In III Sent.*, d. 25, q. 1, a. 2.

[44] St. Paschasius Radbertus, *De fide, spe et caritate*, bk. 1, chap. 6, no. 1 (PL 120, 1402).

[45] Hence (in this creed as in the Apostles' Creed), the use of the singular: *credo*. See the catechetical homilies of Theodore of Mopsuestia, ed. R. Tonneau and R. Devreesse (1949), pp. 13, 21, 363, 365, etc.

[46] We do sometimes find εἰς τὴν Ἐκκλησίαν or "in Ecclesiam", but this variant is of the purely literary order and without doctrinal implications; it does not mean that the Church is thereby distinguished from the following articles, in the case of which we also find "in resurrectionem carnis", "in unum baptisma", "in vitam aeternam", and so on. In these cases the preposition has lost the weight of meaning we attribute to it when it is used for God only. See Kelly, pp. 83, 184, 187–89, 191, and compare St. Cyril of Jerusalem, *Catechesis* 18, chap. 26 (PG 33, 1048a), and St. Hilary of Poitiers' historical fragment in PL 10, 676a.

works of God. According to an ancient and well-attested formula, we "believe in" the Holy Spirit—or, more precisely, the
Trinity as a whole—"within the Church";[47] or, as St.
Thomas explains, "in the Holy Spirit unifying the Church",[48] or "sanctifying the Church".[49] In saying "I believe [in] the Holy Catholic Church", we proclaim our faith not "in" the Church but
"about" the Church—that is, in her existence, her supernatural
reality,[50] her unity,[51] and her essential prerogatives.[52] It is in the
same way that we have previously proclaimed our faith in the
creation of heaven and earth by God the Father Almighty and
in the Incarnation, death, Resurrection, and Ascension of
Christ our Lord. Here we profess that the Church is formed by
the Holy Spirit[53] and that she is "his own proper work",[54] the
instrument with which he sanctifies us; we affirm that it is in

---

[47] Camelot, p. 327; Pierre Nautin, *Je crois à l'Esprit saint dans la sainte Église pour
la résurrection de la chair*, in the series Unam Sanctam, no. 17 (1947); Dom B.
Botte, "Note sur le symbole baptismal de Saint Hippolyte", *Mélanges J. de
Ghellinck* (1951), 1:189–200 (this last being a critical appraisal of the work
previously mentioned); de Ghellinck, p. 190, quoting Jungmann, and the
quotation from Rufinus *infra*.

[48] *In III Sent.*, d. 25, q. 1, a. 2 ad 5: "in Spiritum sanctum unientem Ecclesiam".

[49] ST II-II, q. 1, a. 9 ad 5: "Si dicatur: 'in sanctam Ecclesiam catholicam', hoc
est intelligendum secundum quod fides nostra refertur ad Spiritum sanctum,
qui sanctificat Ecclesiam, ut sit sensus: 'credo in Spiritum sanctum sanctificantem Ecclesiam'. Sed melius est, et secundum communiorem usum, ut non
ponatur ibi 'in', sed simpliciter dicatur: 'Sanctam Ecclesiam catholicam', sicut
etiam Leo papa dicit."

[50] "Sanctam esse ecclesiam catholicam" (Bangor Antiphonary, PL 72, 597c).

[51] "Si credis unitatem Ecclesiae?" and "Subsequitur unius matris pia
confessio, dicens sanctam esse Ecclesiam" (*De controversia Paschali*, PL 87, 974).
See also J. E. L. Oulton, "The Apostles' Creed and Belief concerning the
Church", JTS 39 (1938): 241.

[52] See, for example, Rozaven, S.J., *L'Église catholique justifiée* (1822), pp.
280–81.

[53] Olier, *Catéchisme chrétien pour la vie intérieure* (1678), p. 217: "I believe
. . . that the Holy Spirit has formed the Catholic Church."

[54] St. Albert the Great, *De sacrificio Missae*, bk. 2, chap. 9, a. 9 (38:64–65, in
Borgnet's edition).

her and by the faith that she communicates to us that we have a part in the Communion of Saints, the forgiveness of sins, and the resurrection into life,[55] and we say that there is a vast assembly, "spread throughout the whole world, hoping by faith in love, and united with God by the bonds of a marriage which is eternal and indissoluble, and that no one can be saved if he does not remain faithfully in the bosom of its unity".[56] Last, we believe that this Church exists not for herself but for God; she is included together with all the rest in the well-chosen words that punctuate the Creed in the Bangor Antiphonary—"All these things I believe unto God. Amen."[57]

Here we are dealing with something more than a matter of detail or a mere nuance. In the full sense of the words we can in fact "believe in"—that is to say, have faith in—God and God alone, Father, Son, and Holy Spirit.[58] This was what St. Peter Chrysologus wanted to convey, or at any rate imply, when he explained to his hearers: "He believes in God who professes Holy Church unto God."[59] We cannot ponder this point too much; the Christian novelty of the formula "believe *in*" is something more than a mere item of information without any particular significance. It is unknown in classical Greek, as in the Greek of the Septuagint; we owe it to the Gospel according to St. John.[60] We can, of course, account for it in terms of Hebrew influence and explain its final persistence with reference to the evolution of the *koine*.[61] But it is certainly also

[55] William Durandus, *Rationale*, bk. 4, chap. 25, nos. 24–31 (ed. De Lyon [1672], p. 136).

[56] St. Helinand of Froidmont, *Sermo 27, In Dedicatione* (PL 212, 707c–d).

[57] PL 72, 597c.

[58] See St. Clement of Rome, *Epistle to the Corinthians*, chap. 58, no. 2: God, our Lord Jesus Christ, and the Holy Spirit are "the hope and the faith of the elect".

[59] *Sermo* 57 (PL 52, 360c).

[60] It has been the subject of brief studies by Hausleiter, Kattenbusch, and Bousset; see also de Ghellinck, pp. 109–10.

[61] See T. Camelot, O.P., "Credere Deo, Credere Deum, Credere in Deum: Pour l'histoire d'une formule traditionnelle", RSPT 30 (1941): 150. But the *koine*'s tendency to substitute εἴς with the accusative for ἐν with the dative

permissible to see in it the sign of a new development at a level deeper than this. A new idea very rarely emerges in a formula established on the spot, and both the Greek texts and the Latin translations show traces of hesitation and reversion; yet for all that, *"credere in* becomes, more and more, the usual phrase for expressing the Christian act of faith."[62] For the sense that attaches to it implies a revelation of God concerning himself—culminating in Christ—and suggests a corresponding attitude of soul. And both these things were unknown to the ancient world. Although "belief" and "faith" are, in current speech, both nouns corresponding to the verb "believe" and can be used interchangeably, the second can, in certain cases, imply an act that goes deeper than that implied by the first. And not only does it go deeper; its nature is different. One's faith commits one more deeply than a simple belief. You can believe in a lot of different things; but, strictly speaking, you can have faith only in a person. Again, you can believe in personal beings too, in the sense of believing in their existence, and it is in this sense that we speak of belief in angels; but faith in the full sense of the word can have only God as its object, and this is the sort of faith that is meant by the expression "credo *in*". In every other case one can say "I believe it", but only of God can one say "I believe in" him, for, in the first place, one speaks directly to him in the secrecy of the heart; faith, like hope and charity, is directed to someone. And whereas the Creed, which is a declaration of faith—*protestatio* or *confessio fidei*[63]—and thus a "symbol", says "I believe in God", the Act of Faith, as formulated for us by the catechism, says "My God, I believe in you." Understood in this way, faith contains in its "alpha" as in its "omega" a personal

---

merely explains the eventual disappearance of one of the two forms of the expression: it does not explain in any way the actual appearance of the expression itself nor its success.

[62] Christine Mohrmann, "Credere in Deum: Sur l'interprétation théologique d'un fait de langue", *Mélanges J. de Ghellinck*, 1:278.

[63] "Haec est confessionis nostris fides exposita", as the Council of Toledo was to say (J. Madoz, S.J., *Le Symbole du XIe Concile de Tolède* [1938], p. 26).

element distinguished by the characteristic that it can concern God alone. It is ecclesial in its mode (if one may put it so) but theological in object and principle.[64]

This linguistic analysis is nothing new. Let us listen for a moment to Blessed Marie of the Incarnation, as she teaches the elements of Christian doctrine to her young Ursuline sisters at Tours at the beginning of the seventeenth century:

> *I believe in God.* We add that particle *in*, which indicates a certain motion of the understanding which believes. Thus, when we say "I believe in God", it is as if we said "I do not only believe that there is a God, but I believe it in such a way that I try, with all the affection of my heart and with all my strength, to reach him as Sovereign Good and the End for which I have been created." Thus Christian hope is in a way enclosed within the faith which we profess.[65]

Eight centuries earlier, St. Paschasius Radbertus had put something similar in slightly greater detail:

> No one can say, properly speaking, "I believe in my neighbor" or in an angel or in any creature whatsoever. Throughout Holy Scripture you will find the correct use of this profession reserved to God alone. . . . We say, and rightly, "I believe concerning this man" as we say "I believe concerning God"; but we do not believe *in* this man, or any other. For they are not themselves truth, or goodness, or light, or life; they do no more than participate in these. And that is why, when in the Gospel our Lord wishes to show that he is of one substance with the Father, he says "You believe in God; believe also in me" (Jn 14:1). For if he were not God, we should not have to believe *in* him; by using this word he revealed himself as God to his chosen ones.

---

[64] This brief analysis—which it would be irrelevant to work out further here—links up with that made from another standpoint by Fr. Paul Demann, "Foi juive et foi chrétienne", in CS (1952). Fr. Demann makes a distinction between the two aspects, which he describes as theological and doctrinal, of the act of faith; these aspects are inseparable and complementary and may be further described as "personal" and "objective", respectively (pp. 94–95).

[65] *Explication des mystères de la foi*, 3d ed. (1678), p. 9.

> Therefore do not let us say "I believe *in* the holy catholic
> Church", but rather, cutting out the syllable "in", let us say "I
> believe the holy catholic Church" and "the life everlasting" and
> "the resurrection of the body". Otherwise we shall seem to
> "believe in" man, which is forbidden to us. We believe in God
> alone and in his unique majesty.[66]

One is struck equally by the power and the uniqueness of the
fundamental affirmation of our *Credo*. Faustus of Riez, in a
passage destined to be quoted and commented on more than
once, says: "To believe in God is to seek him in faith, to hope
piously in him, and to pass into him by a movement of choice.
When I say that I believe in him, I confess him, offer him
worship, adore him, give myself over to him wholly and transfer
to him all my affection."[67] A little before him, St. Augustine had
spoken in the same way, in a series of texts no less worthy of
study and commentary. Paschasius Radbertus derives from him
and from Faustus; and these two likewise form the source for the
great Scholastics in the more abstract analyses that they made
from a different standpoint—St. Albert talking about the "*tensio
fidei*"[68] or St. Thomas pointing out the movement of the will in
the theological act of faith.[69] From the Augustinian texts there

---

[66] *De fide, spe et caritate*, bk. 1, chap. 6, nos. 1–2 (PL 120, 1402–4).

[67] *De Spiritu Sancto*, bk. 1, chap. 1: "Credere illi cuilibet potes homini; credere vero in illum, soli te debere noveris majestati. Sed et hoc ipsum aliud est,
Deum credere, aliud in Deum credere. Esse Deum et diabolus credere dicitur.
. . . In Deum vero credere, nisi qui pie in eum speravit, non probatur. In Deum
ergo credere, hoc est fideliter eum quaerere, est tota in eum dilectione transire.
Credere ergo in illum, hoc est dicere; confiteor illum, colo illum, adoro illum,
totum me in jus ejus ac dominium trado atque transfundo" (p. 103 in Engelbrecht's edition; PL 62, 10c–d, under the name of Paschasius the Deacon).

[68] *In III Sent.*, d. 23, a. 7.

[69] *In Rom.*, chap. 4, lect. 1; ST II-II, q. 2, a. 2; q. 11, a. 1. St. Thomas also refers
to the definition of Isidore of Seville: "Articulus est perceptio divinae veritatis
tendens in ipsam" (*In III Sent.*, d. 25, q. 1; ST II-II, q. 1, a. 6). See also the two
complementary studies by Camelot and Mohrmann, quoted above, notes 61
and 62. The Scholastic *tendere* is the equivalent of the fifth-century *quaerere*; in
either case it figures as something essential to the theological act of faith—quite
apart from charity, of course.

emerges a threefold distinction that was destined to acquire classical status. There is simple belief in the existence of something or some being *(credere Deum)*, and then again there is simple faith—slightly more particularized, admittedly—in the authority of someone, in the sense of accepting some truth on his word *(credere Deo)*:[70] and these two are distinct. But, in distinction from both, faith in God *(credere in Deum)* is unique. It implies a search, an advance, a movement of the soul *(credendo in Deum ire)*; it implies a personal impulse and, last, an adherence, which cannot find the term of their action in anything created.[71]

The believer will see high value in everything that helps him to get a firmer grasp of a truth so simple and yet so profound. That is why there are so many among the early writers who make a point of emphasizing this linguistic detail when discussing the Church. There is, for example, Rufinus of Aquilaea, who says: "Wherever we are concerned, not with the Divinity, but with creatures or with mysteries, the preposition *in* is omitted. . . . So, by the syllable of this preposition, the Creator is set apart from creatures and divine things from human."[72] St. Maximus of Turin, St. Ildephonsus of

---

[70] See St. John Chrysostom, *In Joannem*, hom. 19, no. 1 (PG 59, 377).

[71] St. Augustine, *In Joannem*, tract. 29, no. 6; tract. 48, no. 3 (PL 35, 1631 and 1741); *In Psalm.* 77, no. 8 (PL 36, 988–89); *In Psalm.* 130, no. 1 (PL 37, 1704); *Sermo* 131, "Ad illum qui ubique est, credendo venitur" (PL 38, 730); *Sermo* 144, 3, no. 2 (PL 38, 788); *Sermo* 14, no. 2 (ed. Morin-Guelf [1917], p. 55). See also Hugo of Rouen, *De fide catholica* (PL 192, 1323c): "Attende quia credere Deum rationis est, credere Deo industriae, credere in Deum vita est." Also Luis of Granada, *Treatise on Christian Doctrine*, bk. 1, chap. 3.

[72] *Commentarius in symbolum apostolorum*, chap. 26: "Non dixit *in sanctam Ecclesiam* nec *in remissionem peccatorum*. . . . Si enim addidisset *in* praepositionem, una cum superioribus eademque res fieret. Nunc autem in illis quidem vocabulis, ubi de divinitate ordinatur fides, in Deo Patre dicitur, et in Jesu Christo Filio ejus, et in Spiritu Sancto. In caeteris vero, ubi non de divinitate, sed de creaturis et de mysteriis sermo est, *in* praepositio non additur, ut dicatur *in Sancta Ecclesia*, sed Sanctam Ecclesiam credendam esse, non ut Deum, sed ut Ecclesiam Deo congregatum. . . . Hac itaque praepositionis syllaba, Creator a creaturis secernitur, et divina separantur ab humanis" (PL 21, 373a–b); chap. 39: "Hi igitur qui semper in uno Deo credere edocti sunt sub mysterio Trinitatis,

Toledo,[73] Venantius Fortunatus,[74] and many others speak similarly. It matters little that in some cases the opportunity was provably occasioned by an error of transcription that had given food for thought[75] or by the desire to refute the error of the Macedonians, by distinguishing the divinity of the Holy Spirit from the humanity of the Church;[76] for none of this detracts in

---

credere etiam hoc debent, unam esse Ecclesiam sanctam, in qua est una fides, et unum baptisma, in qua unus Deus creditur Pater, et unus Dominus Jesus Christus Filius ejus et unus Spiritus sanctus. . . . De hac autem Ecclesia, quae fidem Christi integram servat, audi quid dicat Spiritus sanctus in Canticis Canticorum: Una est columba mea, una est perfecta genitricae suae" (PL 21, 375a, b). (We may note the ablative form, which was to disappear.)

[73] *De cognitione baptismi*, chap. 37 (PL 96, 127). The author of this treatise may in point of fact be Justinian of Valencia.

[74] *Explicatio symboli*: "Ergo *in* ubi praepositio ponitur, ibi divinitas adprobatur, ut est: credo in Patrem, in Filium, in Spiritum sanctum. Nam non dicitur *in sanctam ecclesiam*, nec dicitur *in remissionem peccatorum*" (MGH, *Auctores antiquissimi*, 4:252—bk. 11, chap. 1, of the *Miscellanea* in PL 88, 350—51). There are many other like-minded authors in the Middle Ages (see my *Catholicism* [San Francisco, 1988], p. 75), and we may add to the list St. Bede the Venerable (PL 93, 22), Ivo of Chartres (PL 162, 604), Abelard (PL 178, 840), Honorius of Autun (PL 174, 1025), and William Durandus (*Rationale*, bk. 4, chap. 25), among others.

[75] See Kelly. But this should not be exaggerated—see Crehan's remarks on the subject of the *canonica* of Faustus (*Early Christian Baptism*, p. 126).

[76] Thus Faustus of Riez, *De Spiritu Sancto*, bk. 1, chap. 2: "Dicis: Credo in sanctam Ecclesiam catholicam. Quid supponendo exiguam, id est *in* syllabam, ingentem caliginem subtexere conaris? . . . Cum in solam specialiter credi oportere Trinitatem, etiam memoratorum Patrum toto celebrata orbe doctrina confirmet, aut remove hanc de Ecclesiae nomine syllabam; aut certe credere te in Ecclesiam manifesta professione Scripturis assere, testimoniis doce, divinis oraculis convince. . . . Qui in Ecclesiam credit, in hominem credit. Non enim homo ex Ecclesia, sed Ecclesia cepit ex homine. Recede itaque ab hac blasphemiae persuasione, ut in aliquam humanam credere te debere aestimes creaturam. . . . Haec, enim, quae in symbolo post sancti Spiritus nomen sequentur, ad clausulam symboli remota *in* praepositione respiciunt . . . ut haec a Deo deposita et in Deo constare fateamur. Nam nonnullorum imperitis, *in* praepositionem hanc, velut de proxima vicina que sententia in consequentem traxit ac rapuit, et ex superfluo imprudenter adposuit. In nullis autem canonicis, de quibus symboli textus pendet, accipimus, quod in Ecclesiam credere sicut in Spiritum sanctum Filiumque debeamus . . ." (pp. 104—5 in

any way from the truth and importance of the doctrinal *exposés* concerned.

* * *

The Church, these writers explain, is not God, but she is "the Church of God".[77] She is his inseparable Bride, serving him in faith and justice;[78] she is the House of God, and it is in her that he welcomes us[79] to the forgiveness of our sins.[80] It is in this Church, "the pillar and firmament of truth", that we believe in him correctly,[81] and glorify him;[82] such is probably the original sense of its mention in the Creed, in which—so it appears—it first figured, not as an article of faith along with the rest, but as

---

Engelbrecht's edition; PL 62, 11). Cf. St. Paschasius Radbertus, *De fide, spe et caritate*, bk. 1, chap. 6, nos. 1–2 (PL 120, 1402–4).

[77] St. Ildephonsus of Toledo, *De cognitione baptismi*, chap. 37: "Credimus ergo in Deum. Credimus et sanctam ejus Ecclesiam esse. Non autem credimus in Ecclesiam sicut in Deum, quia Ecclesia non est Deus. Credimus autem singulariter in Deum. Credimus et sequenter Ecclesiam ejus esse" (PL 96, 127d).

[78] St. Helinand of Froidmont, *Sermo* 27 (PL 212, 707c–d).

[79] Tertullian, *De idololatria*, chap. 7 (PL 1, 669a); St. Augustine, *Enchiridion*, chap. 57 (PL 40, 258); *Missale Gallicanum vetus* (ed. Martène, 1:97); Pseudo-Alcuin, *Confessio fidei* (PL 101, 1072); Letter to Charlemagne (PL 97, 939).

[80] St. Fulgentius of Ruspe, *Contra Fabianum*, frag. 35: "Subjungitur autem et sancta Ecclesia, ut agnoscatur quae sit domus Dei conditoris, aeterna civitas redemptoris; sine cujus societate atque unitate remissio peccatorum non acquiritur" (PL 65, 826–27).

[81] 1 Tim 3:15; Pseudo-Augustine, *Sermo de mysterio baptismatis*: "Quod autem interrogavimus: Credis sanctam Ecclesiam . . . , non eo modo interrogavimus ut quomodo in Deum creditor, sic et in Ecclesiam sanctam et catholicam. Propterea sancta et catholica est, quia recte credit in Deum. Non ergo diximus ut in Ecclesiam, quasi in Deum, crederetis: sed intelligite nos dicere et dixisse ut in Ecclesia sancta et catholica conversantes, in Deum crederetis" (PL 40, 1210); Ivo of Chartres, *De baptismo*, chap. 194.

[82] Eph 3:21. Cf. the doxology of the *Apostolic Tradition*: "Tibi gloria et virtus, Patri et Filio, cum Spirito sancto, in sancta Ecclesia et nunc et in saecula saeculorum" (chap. 8; cf. chap. 6); and the Ethiopian text "In quo tibi laus et potentia in sancta Ecclesia": Serapion of Thmuis (Brightman, JTS, 1:103). Other examples are given in Jungmann, *Die Stellung Christi*, pp. 130–37.

the conclusion[83] of the whole "symbol", said after the exposition of the Catholic faith in the Trinity. Later, even though it was already followed, as it is today, by a further series of articles, it was still possible to say that the whole "symbol" terminated in it, for it was in it that that "symbol" found its authority, in the last analysis—"sancta Ecclesia, in qua omnis hujus sacramenti terminatur auctoritas".[84] Theodore of Mopsuestia, quoting the actual words of the liturgical text before commenting upon them, says: "Each of us confesses: I believe and I am baptized in the name of the Father and the Son and the Holy Spirit in one sole holy and Catholic Church."[85] It is the place chosen by God for the invocation of his name,[86] the temple in which we worship the Trinity and—as Pius IX was to make clear—"the unshakeable sanctuary outside which, save with the excuse of invincible ignorance, we cannot hope for salvation".[87] In order to explain the mention made of the Church at baptism, Tertullian went so far as to say that she is the body of the three Persons.[88] Again, she is the dwelling place prepared

---

[83] Dom B. Botte, O.S.B., "Note sur le symbole baptismal de saint Hippolyte", *Mélanges J. de Ghellinck*, 1:189–200. The "in" here has perhaps a sense akin to the instrumental sense that became current in the *koine*—"through the Church" (p. 198).

[84] St. Augustine, *De symbolo*, no. 14: "Sequitur post Trinitatis commendationem, sanctam Ecclesiam" (PL 40, 635); Pseudo-Augustine: "sacramenti hujus conclusio per Ecclesiam terminatur" (PL 40, 65; 660 and 668).

[85] *Tenth Catechetical Homily* (pp. 273–75 in the Tonneau-Devreesse edition).

[86] Rupert of Deutz, *In Deuter.*, pt. 1, bk. 2, chap. 1: "Locus quem elegit Dominus noster ut ibi invocetur nomen ejus, Ecclesia catholica est, estra quam nusquam prope est invocantibus eum, extra quam alibi nusquam invocatur in veritate nomen ejus" (PL 167, 957b).

[87] Encyclical *Singulari quidem* (March 17, 1856); St. Augustine, *De symbolo sermo ad catechumenos*, chap. 6, no. 14 (PL 40, 635); Pseudo-Augustine, *Sermo de symbolo*, chap. 12 (PL 40, 1196), etc.; St. Cyril of Jerusalem, *Catechesis* 6, chap. 35 (PG 33, 601a); St. Martin of Leon, *Sermo* 4 (PL 208, 316a–b). See also 1 Cor 3:17; Is 56:7; Ps 86:2.

[88] *De baptismo*, chap. 6: "Necessario adjicitur Ecclesiae mentio, quoniam ubi tres, id est, Pater et Filius et Spiritus Sanctus, ibi Ecclesia, quae trium corpus est"; see also *De oratione*, chap. 2, and *De pudicitia*, chap. 21.

on the mountaintops and foretold by the Prophets, to which, one day, all nations are to come to live in unity under the law of the one God.[89] She is the treasure chamber in which the Apostles have laid up the truth, which is Christ;[90] the one and only hall in which the Father celebrates the wedding of his Son; and since it is in her that we receive our forgiveness, it is through her that we have access to life and the gifts of the Holy Spirit.[91] We cannot believe in her as we believe in the Author of our salvation, but we do believe that she is the Mother who brings us our regeneration.[92]

The distinction is of primary importance, whatever the manner in which it be accounted for; it seemed sufficiently illuminating to be, for a long period, considered necessary in the baptismal catechisms of a whole section of Christendom.[93] The great theologians of the Middle Ages stressed its impor-

---

[89] Is 2:2–3.

[90] St. Irenaeus, *Adversus haereses*, bk. 3, chap. 4, no. 1.

[91] St. Cyprian, *Epist.* 69, no. 7, and *Epist.* 70, no. 2 (pp. 756 and 768 in Hartel's edition). The candidate for baptism is questioned: "Credis in vitam aeternam et remissionem peccatorum per sanctam Ecclesiam?" (St. Augustine, *Sermo* 215, no. 9; PL 38, 1076). Cf. the Preface for the dedication of a church according to the Use of Paris: "et Ecclesiam, quam ipse fundasti, incessabili operatione sanctificas. Haec est enim vere domus orationis, visibilibus aedificiis adumbrata, templum habitationis gloriae tuae, sedes incommutabilis veritatis, sanctuarium aeternae caritatis. Haec est arca, quae nos, a mundi ereptos diluvio, in portum salutis inducit. Haec est dilecta et unica sponsa, quam acquisivit Christus sanguine suo; cujus in sinu renati per gratiam tuam, lacte verbi pascimur, pane vitae roboramur, misericordiae tuae subsidiis confovemur. . . ."

[92] Faustus of Riez, *De Spiritu Sancto*, bk. 1, chap. 2: "Credimus Ecclesiam, quasi regenerationis matrem; non in Ecclesiam, quasi in salutis auctorem" (p. 104 in Engelbrecht's edition; PL 62, 11a).

[93] For example, a ninth-century catechism: "In Spiritum vero sanctum credimus quia Deus est, sicut Pater et Filius. Sanctam Ecclesiam catholicam, subauditur: Credo esse" (RBN [1947], p. 198). This catechism makes distinction between the three meanings of *credere*: "Credo in Deum, id est totam spem meam in illum colloco. Credo Deum, subauditur esse. Credo Deo, subauditur dictis ejus" (ibid., p. 197). Cf. St. Thomas, ST II-II, q. 2, a. 2.

tance in their turn,[94] and in the fifteenth century Cardinal Juan de Torquemada (who served as pontifical theologian at the Council of Basel) grew indignant at the memory of the way in which it had been misunderstood—for practical purposes at least—by the members of that gathering.[95] After the Council of Trent the *Roman Catechism* (1566) once more saw fit to make express mention of it,[96] and others were to follow suit; it still

[94] Thus St. Albert the Great, *In III Sent.*, d. 24, a. 6: "Quinque autem residui [articuli] pertinent ad Spiritum sanctum, tam in se quam in donis suis. . . . In donis autem primum est quo sanctificat et unit generaliter Ecclesiam. . . . 'Sanctam Ecclesiam catholicam' et est sensus: Credo in Spiritum sanctum, sanctificantem Ecclesiam catholicam, id est universalem Ecclesiam."

[95] *Summa de Ecclesia* (1448; Venice, 1615), bk. 1, chap. 20: "Necessarium nobis visum est declarare hoc loco qualiter accipiendum sit quod in symbolo sanctorum Patrum aliqui legunt: 'et in unam sanctam Ecclesiam'. Sunt enim nonnulli qui hoc perverse interpretantur. Vidimus enim nos in Basilea apud congregatos in concilio universali circa auctoritatem Ecclesiae ita deliros, ut ad hoc verbum ita genus flecterent et profunda humilitate articulum illum venerentur, sicut fidelis et devotus populus christianus solitus est ad verbum illud: 'et homo factus est'. Pro quo considerandum quod, ut ait Albertus magnus, dictum illud sanctorum Patrum non est ita accipiendum, ac si nos synodus jubeat credere in aliud quod non est Deus; quia hoc idolatria et non fides esset; cum enim id in quod credimus designetur finis fides nostrae." Torquemada was "acerrimus Pontificiae potestatis defensor contra Basileensem synodum" (Fénelon, *Memoir to Cardinal Fabroni* [1711]; quoted in Ernest Jovy, *Fénelon inédit d'après les documents de Pistoia* [1917], p. 349). His work, dedicated to Nicholas V, bore as its full title *Summa contra Ecclesiae et primatus apostoli Petri adversarios*. On this work and its author, see Ludwig Pastor, *Histoire des Papes*, trans. F. Raynaud (1888), 2:5–6 and 46–47.

[96] Pt. 1, chap. 10, no. 23: "Ecclesiam credere oportet, et non in Ecclesiam. Tres enim Trinitatis personas . . . ita credimus, ut in eis fidem nostram collocamus. Nunc autem, mutata dicendi forma, sanctam, et non in sanctam Ecclesiam, credere profitemur; ut, hac etiam diversa loquendi ratione, Deus omnium effector a creatis rebus distinguatur, praeclaraque illa omnia, quae in Ecclesiam collata sunt beneficia, divinae bonitati accepta referamus." Concerning the authority of the Catechism, see Moehler, *La Symboloques*, trans. F. Lachat (1836), 1:lv–lviii. Karl Barth is perhaps unaware that he is expounding a doctrine of so classical a status in Catholicism when he writes (*Dogmatics in Outline*, p. 141): "We cannot speak of the Holy Spirit without continuing *credo ecclesiam*, I believe in the existence of the Church. . . . *Credo in Spiritum Sanctum*, but not *credo in ecclesiam*."

figures in the *Catholic Catechism* edited by Cardinal Gasparri, though in the French version at least it does not seem to be understood in its full force.[97]

As we shall see, there is of course a legitimate sense in which the believer can say—indeed in which he ought to say—that he believes in the Church. It is simply that the formula should not be made to bear a "perverse interpretation" of the kind denounced by Torquemada. Strictly speaking, however, if we take "the Church" in the fullness of her reality, it is she who believes[98] and confesses the Trinity,[99] as it is also she who hopes, loves, and serves her Lord. It is she who was compassionately sought for by him in the suffering and inchoateness of her first state; she who is now reconciled in him to God, and whom he feeds daily with his sacraments, and who is faithfully united to him as wife to husband;[100] she who bears witness to him, prays to him, longs for sight of him, and waits for his second coming;[101] she, finally, who fights in this world and is to triumph in the next:

Haec fideliter in terris, Sponso adjuvante, militat, et perenniter in caelis, ipso coronante, triumphat.[102]

---

[97] In the 1932 translation, p. 156, where the "in" is rendered not by "*en*" but by "*à*".

[98] St. Ambrose, *De mysteriis*, 7, 35–41; and 9, 55: "His igitur sacramentis pascit ecclesiam suam Christos"; Berengard, *In Apoc.*: "Conjungitur namque Ecclesia quotidie Christo per fidem" (PL 17, 965b); St. Irenaeus, *Adversus haereses*, bk. 2, chap. 30, no. 9: " Ecclesia credit" (PG 7, 832a); also bk. 1, chap. 10, no. 2 (PG 7, 552a).

[99] St. Epiphanius of Salamis, *Expositio fidei*, chap. 15 (PG 42, 808–9).

[100] St. Ambrose, *De Abraham*, bk. 2, chap. 11, no. 79 (PL 14, 494c); Ambrose Autpert, *In Purif.*, no. 5.

[101] Haymo, *Expositio in Apoc.*, bk. 7: "Haec omnis Ecclesia loquitur in Joanne, optans ut veniat Christus ad judicium" (PL 117, 1220c).

[102] Preface for the dedication of a church according to the Use of Paris. See also the sixth and eleventh Councils of Toledo (638 and 675), in F. Cavallera, *Thesaurus doctrinae Catholicae* (1936), p. 149; St. Augustine, *In Psalm.* 36, no. 12 (PL 36, 362), etc.; Rupert of Deutz, *In Reg.*, bk. 1, chap. 10 (PL 167, 1077).

If she is holy and catholic, this is, precisely, because she has true faith.[103] She could scarcely declare that she believed in herself;[104] the earlier writers do, admittedly, talk about a *fides ecclesiastica*, but this has nothing in common with the concept of "ecclesiastical faith" that was worked out in more recent times and used for putting out of court certain sophistries employed by the Jansenists.[105] The ancient *fides ecclesiastica* was "the faith of the Church"[106] plain and simple. It was, in other words, the faith that was Christ's gift to her, to be a power glowing inside her, at once her origin and her sustaining[107]—a faith we profess individually only by associating ourselves with the whole Church[108]

[103] St. Maximus of Turin, *Tract.* 2 *de baptismo*: "Propterea sancta et catholica est, quia recte credit in Deum. Non ergo diximos, ut in Ecclesiam quasi in Deum crederetis, sed intelligite nos dicere et dixisse ut in Ecclesia sancta et Catholica conversantes, in Deum crederetis" (PL 57, 776b–c = Pseudo-Augustine, *Sermo de mysterio baptismatis*, PL 40, 1210). Ever since St. Cyprian (*Epist.* 73, chap. 2), "catholic" is often the equivalent of "orthodox".

[104] Faustus of Riez, *De Spiritu Sancto*, bk. 1, chap. 2: "Nam cum hoc de Spirito Sancto universa confiteatur Ecclesia numquid et in semet ipsam Ecclesia credere potest?" (p. 104 in Engelbrecht's edition; PL 62, 11a–b).

[105] Concerning the "problem of fact" or of "the infallibility of the Church concerning texts" (Fénelon's phrase). For the history of this concept, see A. Gits, *La Foi ecclésiastique aux faits dogmatiques dans la théologie moderne* (Louvain, 1940).

[106] St. Caesarius of Arles, *Libellus de mysterio sanctae Trinitatis*, in *Opera omnia*, ed. Morin, 2:176; see also the Ordinary of the Mass according to the Roman Rite: "Ne respicias peccata mea, sed fidem Ecclesiae tuae"; St. Augustine, *Sermo* 91, no. 2 (PL 38, 568); *Liber mozarabicus sacramentorum*, ed. M. Férotin (1912), col. 99; Rupert of Deutz, *In Matt.* (PL 168, 1328a) and *In Job* (PL 168, 1151a), where it may, objectively speaking, be equally taken as meaning "the dogma of the Church". Similarly, St. Hilary of Poitiers, *In Psalm.* 138, no. 30: "Omnia ecclesiasticae spei sacramenta" (p. 765 in Zingerle's edition).

[107] St. Irenaeus, *Adversus haereses*, bk. 3, chap. 24, no. 1; Origen, *In Exod.*, hom. 9, no. 3; St. Augustine, *Sermo* 246, no. 3: "Maximus ardor et intima vis fidei in Ecclesia" (PL 38, 1154).

[108] Origen, *In Levit.*, hom. 5, no. 3 (pp. 339–40 in Baehrens' edition); St. Thomas, ST III, q. 68, a. 9 ad 3: "[Baptizatus] huic fidei aggregatur, per fidei sacramentum". See also St. John Damascene, *De fide orthodoxa*, bk. 4, chap. 10, no. 23: "He who does not believe according to the tradition of the Church, that man is an infidel" (PG 94, 1128a); this is the only mention of the Church that the saint makes in his exposition of the *Credo*.

and that we can only participate in, no more, to a degree that always leaves something to be desired. This is the faith that feeds the Church and strengthens her. It is a faith that is perfect and unchangeable, always "in its plenitude",[109] "always the same and always serene", persevering,[110] as unshakeable as the Cross of Christ, "never hesitating and never doubting", never sleeping,[111] living and vivifying,[112] bearing fruit throughout the world;[113] a faith at which the faith of the individual is lit and in which it is rooted.[114] So that when any one of us says "I believe in God", he speaks in the Church and in dependence upon her. "Confession of faith in the Creed is always made as in the name of the whole Church"; that is why someone who has no more than an "unformed" faith can still truly say that he believes, however far he may be from having the dispositions that have been described for us by Faustus of Riez. The thing is possible because he is of the Church and is thus able to speak *in persona Ecclesiae*;[115] conversely, he who voluntarily separates himself from her no longer has a valid faith.[116] Similarly, our predestination in Christ is the predestination of the Church; St. Paul never envisages it

[109] *Liber mozarabicus sacramentorum*: "Da Ecclesiae tuae catholicae et sanctae fidei plenitudinem, quam illi dedisti semper perfecte tenere" (ed. Férotin, col. 637).

[110] St. Irenaeus, *Adversus haereses*, bk. 3, chap. 12, no. 7.

[111] Dom Anscar Vonier, *The Spirit and the Bride* (French trans., *L'Esprit et l'Épouse*, Unam Sanctam, 16 [1947], p. 96); Gregory of Elvira, *Tractatus* 11 (pp. 125–26 in the Batiffol-Wilmart edition).

[112] St. Irenaeus, *Adversus haereses*, bk. 3, chap. 3, no. 3.

[113] St. Augustine, *Sermo* 214, no. 11 (PL 38, 1071). See also Col 1:6, etc.

[114] Rémi of Auxerre, *In Michaeum*: "Donec Ecclesia mater gentilem populum spiritualiter ad fidem generet" (PL 117, 157d); Rupert of Deutz, *In Cantica Canticorum*, bk. 6: "Hierusalem liberam, quae est mater omnium secundum fidem . . . , generat enim secundum fidem" (PL 168, 941a).

[115] St. Thomas, *In III Sent.*, d. 25, q. 1, a. 2 ad 4; ST II-II, q. 1, a. 9 ad 3: "Confessio fidei traditur in symbolo, quasi ex persona totius Ecclesiae"; William Durandus, *Rationale*, bk. 4, chap. 25, no. 16.

[116] St. Augustine, *In Joannem*, tract. 80, no. 3 (PL 35, 1840); Ivo of Chartres, *Decretum*, pt. 1, chap. 122: "Verbum fidei valet tantum in Ecclesia Deo" (PL 161, 89d).

outside this framework of totality.[117] In everything he does on the supernatural level the Christian acts *ut membrum Ecclesiae, ut pars Ecclesiae*[118]—Christ loves us individually but not separately, saying to each of us, as he did to Moses, "I know thee by name";[119] he loves us in his Church, for which he shed his blood.[120] Our personal destiny can work itself out only in the common salvation of the Church,[121] who is the "Mother of Unity".[122]

Thus the Church is not only the first of the works of the sanctifying Spirit, but also that which includes, conditions, and absorbs all the rest. The entire process of salvation is worked out in her; indeed, it is identified with her. In consequence, something that may well have seemed a restriction at first glance turns out, on the contrary, to give us an opportunity of appreciating the scope of the truths concerning the Church, the strength of the bonds that hold us to her, and the depth of the part she plays in the economy of our life as Christians.

The chapters that are to follow will do no more than develop this initial sketch and fix more sharply certain of its outlines. Existing as she does by the will of God, the Church is necessary to us—necessary as a means. And more than this. The mystery of the Church is all Mystery in miniature; it is our own mystery par excellence. It lays hold on the whole of us. It surrounds us

[117] Rom 8:18–39 and 11:33. See also my *Catholicism*, pp. 275–81.

[118] Cajetan, *In II-II*, q. 39, a. 1, no. 11.

[119] Ex 33:12.

[120] Acts 20:28; Gregory of Elvira, *In Cantica*: "Quid enim carius Christo quam Ecclesia, pro qua sanguinem suum fudit?" (ed. Wilmart, BLE [1906], p. 240). See also Tertullian, *Adversus Marcionem*, bk. 5, chap. 19 (p. 645 in Kroymann's edition); St. Peter Canisius, *Summa doctrinae Christianae*, chap. 1, no. 16: "pro qua Christus in carne cuncta et fecit et pertulit" (*Catechismi Latini*, ed. Streicher [1933], p. 8).

[121] This gives us a measuring stick against which to see how far astray the later pseudo-Augustinians went. Even the wise and moderate Nicole echoed their views when he wrote, in his *Essais de morale*, vol. 5 (1730), pp. 310–11: "Man is created in order to live in an eternal solitude with God alone. . . . To prepare oneself for death is to accustom oneself to this solitude with God."

[122] St. Augustine, *Sermo* 192, no. 2 (PL 38, 1013).

on all sides, for it is in his Church that God looks upon us and loves us, in her that he desires us and we encounter him, and in her that we cleave to him and are made blessed by him.

* * *

This mystery has one aspect which is all light. The Catholic Church is a "standard raised among the nations", as the [First] Vatican Council puts it, following Isaiah.[123] She is a rallying point for all, "inviting those who as yet have no faith, and assuring her own children that the faith which they profess has the firmest of foundations".[124] She is the mountain visible from afar, the radiant city, the light set in a candlestick to illuminate the whole house.[125] She is the imperishable building of cedar and cypress,[126] which defies the passage of time in its awe-inspiring massiveness and gives to our ephemeral individualities their measure of confidence. She is the "continual miracle", always announcing to men the coming of their Savior and manifesting his liberating power in examples without number;[127] the magnificent vaulting under which the saints, like so many stars, sing together of the glory of the Redeemer.[128] Through the depth and cohesion of the doctrine she puts forward, her experience of men, and the fruits the Holy Spirit continually ripens in her, the Church exercises over people of spiritual integrity an attraction that is witnessed to throughout history by a vast number of conversions, which are, humanly speaking, startling in the extreme. As the deposi-

[123] Is 49:22; St. Ignatius of Antioch, *Smyrn.*, 1, 2.

[124] First Vatican Council, constitution *De fide catholica*, chap. 3; Leo XIII, encyclical *Caritatis studium*.

[125] St. Gregory Nazianzen, *Fourth Discourse*, chaps. 67–74 and 110–13 (PG 35, 588–600 and 645–52); St. Augustine, *Sermo* 45, nos. 5–7 (PL 38, 265–68); *In Joannem*, tract. 4, no. 4 (PL 35, 1407); *In Epist. Joannis*, tract. 2, no. 2 (PL 35, 1490), etc. See also Ps 86:1–3; Mt 5:14–15.

[126] Origen, *In Cantica*, bk. 3 (PG 13, 148–49).

[127] Cf. Rom 1:16; 1 Cor 2:4; Origen, *Contra Celsum*, preface (pp. 51–55 in Koetschau's edition); St. Augustine, *Sermo* 88, no. 3 (PL 38, 540), etc.

[128] Alain of Lille, *Sententiae* (PL 210, 259b).

tary and guardian of Scripture, she is the diffusion point for its illuminating power, which alone can make our history intelligible. And thus she leads us to Christ by many ways, all of which converge. In her, God makes himself continually visible to the eyes of those "who see wisdom";[129] anyone who has given himself to her with his eyes open proves it for himself again and again:

> Haec est cymba qua tuti vehimur,
> Hoc ovile quo tecte condimur,
> Haec columna qua firmi nitimur
> Veritatis! [130]

To a man who lives her mystery, she is always the city of precious stones, the Heavenly Jerusalem, the Bride of the Lamb, as she was to St. John; and seeing her thus, he feels that very joy which bursts through the light-split skies of the Apocalypse and glows in its visions of serenity. One begins to understand what makes him cry, like St. Augustine: "When I talk about her, I cannot stop." [131]

But the dark side of the mystery is there too, and just as surely; the heavens are not always rent.[132] For the unbeliever whom the Father has not begun to draw to him, the Church remains a stumbling block. And she can be a testing ground for the believer too, which is a good thing; perhaps the test is all the more strenuous in proportion as his faith is purer and more vital.

The mysteries of the Divinity are, in a way, more at a distance from us, and in virtue of that very fact less startling, since we are ready in advance, so to speak, to admit that God throws

---

[129] Pascal, *Pensées*, frag. 793; St. Augustine, *Sermo* 238, no. 3 (PL 38, 1126).

[130] Hymn for the dedication of a church according to the Use of Paris and Lyons.

[131] Cf. St. Bernard's phrase: "De Maria numquam satis!"

[132] Cf. Paschal Rapine, *Le Christianisme florissant dans le monde* (1666), vol. 2, treatise 2, chap. 4, p. 232: "The Catholic religion is a medal with two faces, charged respectively with shadow and light."

us off our balance. After all, he does transcend everything that we can understand about him,[133] and every time we are struck with some resemblance between ourselves and him, we realize that in the next breath we must affirm the greater dissimilarity,[134] for nothing could be more ridiculous than the demand for a God who is "our size". But by the time we have come to the Word Incarnate, the mysteries involved are already harder to believe. "God takes a form, a name is to be heard; a human being takes among us the place of the Most High." [135] "This is indeed an unheard-of commingling and a paradoxical fusion. He who is, becomes; the Infinite is created and contained in space. . . . The Word becomes reachable by the senses, the Invisible is seen, the Inaccessible touched, the Timeless steps into time, the Son of God becomes the Son of Man!" [136] Quite apart from the case of those who dream of a man-god, the idea of a God-Man is itself something that hits the mind head-on; even though we can see that there is no contradiction within the idea, the whole chain of realities associated therewith creates a mental atmosphere of bewilderment.[137] Stop to think for a moment: "He who is the Power and Wisdom of God himself, and in whom all things visible and invisible were created, was, we are to believe, narrowly circumscribed within the limitation of that Man who once appeared in Judaea—entered into the

[133] St. Augustine, *Sermo* 52, chap. 6, no. 16 (PL 38, 360), etc.

[134] Fourth Lateran Council (1215): "Inter Creatorem et creaturam non potest tanta similitudo notari, quin inter eos major sit dissimilitudo notanda."

[135] Karl Barth, *Esquisse d'un dogmatique*, trans. É Mauris and F. Ryser (1950), p. 65.

[136] St. Gregory Nazianzen, *Thirty-Eighth Discourse*, chaps. 2 and 13 (PG 36, 313b and 325c); Theophanes of Nicaea, *Sermo in sanct. Deiparem* (p. 20 in Jugie's edition); William of Saint-Thierry, *Speculum fidei* (PL 180, 388d).

[137] St. Irenaeus, *Adversus haereses*, bk. 1, chap. 11, no. 9; St. Athanasius, *Third Discourse against the Arians*, chaps. 32–33, 54, etc.; St. Theodore the Studite, *Antirrheticus* I (PG 99, 332a); Adam Scotus, *Sermo* 23, *In die natali Domini*, chap. 3: "Certe mihi triplex in hac nativitate sacrosancta consideratio ingerit stuporem" (PL 198, 220c), etc. Cf. Spinoza, *Epist.* 21 (to Oldenburg) and *Epist.* 73.

womb of a woman, was born a baby, crying as the newly born always cry. . . . The narrowness of the human understanding is at a loss and, overcome with the amazement of such great admiration, does not know where to withdraw, what to hold on to, or where to turn."[138] And the mention of the cross completes the mental checkmate. A God "born and crucified"![139] —it is "a sacredly terrifying mystery".[140] "Unto the Jews indeed a stumbling block, and unto the Gentiles foolishness",[141] it was an obstacle from the very start, and all who came to Christ were well aware of the startlingness of the paradox with which they had to come to grips. If we no longer experience the shock of the statement, may not the reason be that our faith has lost its cutting edge, however honest and firm it may be, and probably is? Its object has had the *mana* taken out of it, and habit has made us comfortable so that neither in prayer nor in the business of living are we able to achieve compassion, in its strict sense, any longer. Yet if all this is so, there is something yet more "scandalous" and "foolish" about belief in a Church where the divine is not only united with the human but presents itself to us by way of the all-too-human, and that without any alternative. For, granted that the Church is really Christ perpetuated among us, Christ "spread abroad and passed on",[142] still the Church's members, lay and clerical, are not the inheritors of the privilege that caused Christ to say so boldly: "Which of you shall convict me of sin?"[143] And their understanding of their own time—even of the things that stand outside it—may be unimpressive enough. Truth to tell, the Church is even

[138] Origen, *De principiis*, bk. 2, chap. 6, no. 2 (Koetschau ed., pp. 140–41).

[139] St. Justin, *Dialogue with Trypho*, chap. 88 (2:74, in Archambault's edition); St. Irenaeus, *Adversus haereses*, bk. 3, chap. 32, no. 6.

[140] The Ursuline Catherine Ranquet, *First Letter to Père de Bus*, quoted in G. Gueudré, *Catherine Ranquet: Mystique et éducatrice* (1952), p. 143.

[141] 1 Cor 1:23; cf. Phil 2:7.

[142] Bossuet, "Allocution aux nouvelles catholiques" (*Oeuvres oratoires*, ed. Lebarcq, 6:508). The phrase "the permanent Incarnation of the Son of God" has also been used.

[143] Jn 8:46.

more compact of contrast and paradox than Christ. We can say of the Church, as of Christ, "a great mystery and wonderful sacrament",[144] but we are driven to say of her even more than of Christ, *Avocamentum mentis, non firmamentum!*,[145] "A stone of stumbling and a rock of offense".[146] The former is the voice of faith triumphant, presupposing a victory over the astonishment of the "natural man" and the disinclination of the sophisticated mind. If a purification and transformation of vision is necessary to look on Christ without being scandalized, how much more is it necessary when we are looking at the Church! Here it will be even more essential—if we are to reach some understanding of her—to "cast far from us the darkness of earthly reasoning and the mists of the wisdom of this world".[147]

On top of all this, it must be confessed that we are so blind that we can sometimes imagine to ourselves—even if we cannot think it, properly speaking—that our belief in God hardly commits us at all. One does not run into God in the streets; one does not—now—run into Christ: but the Church is always there. There are so many who would be ready to admire her for some things at least, in spite of all the faults they find in her, so many who would be ready to "cooperate" with her, as they say—if only she were not what she is. She is the permanent witness of Christ and the messenger of the living God; his urgent and importunate presence among us. Let us within the Church, who speak of ourselves as being "of the Church", manage to grasp the fact as sharply as it is sensed by those who are afraid of her and those who run away from her.

[144] From the Christmas Liturgy according to the Roman Rite. See also St. Bernard, *Sermo 1, De circumcisione*, no. 2: "Divinis humana sociat, ima summis" (PL 183, 133c).

[145] See St. Augustine, *In Epist. Joannis*, tract. 1, no. 4 (PL 35, 1980).

[146] Is 8:14; Rom 9:33; 1 Pet 2:8.

[147] St. Leo the Great, *Sermo 7, De nativitate Domini*, chap. 1: "Abigatur procul terrenarum caligorationum, et ab illuminatae fidei oculo mundanae sapientiae fumus abscedat" (PL 54, 216c); Eph 1:17; Karl Adam, "Le Mystère de l'Église: Du scandale à la foi triomphante", in *L'Église est une*, ed. Chaillet (1939), pp. 33–52.

II

The Dimensions of the Mystery

Let us go back for a moment to the three words that are all the Apostles' Creed devotes to the Church—*sanctam Ecclesiam catholicam*.[1] We will leave out of it for the moment the adjective *sanctam* (although it is the older-attested of the pair) and concentrate on "the Catholic Church". Originally this meant simply "the universal assembly"—the perfect community, through space and time, of all those who unite themselves to Christ as their Savior and are united to God by him.[2] *Una fidelium universalis Ecclesia* is the way the Fourth Council of the Lateran was to put it in 1215; and St. Thomas[3] explains: *Ecclesia catholica, id est universalis*. And the second-century author of the *Martyrdom of Polycarp* calls Christ "the Shepherd of the universal Church throughout the earth".[4]

Following in the footsteps of St. Thomas, we can give the name "Church" to that gigantic organism which includes all

[1] The same formula appears in St. Cyril of Jerusalem, *Catechesis* 18, chap. 1: "The holy catholic Church" (PG 33, 1017a). Cf. F. Kattenbusch, *Das Apostolische Symbol* (Leipzig, 1900), 2:922–30.

[2] St. Ignatius of Antioch, *Smyrn.*, chap. 8, no. 2; St. Cyril of Jerusalem, *Catechesis* 18, chaps. 13 and 16 (PG 33, 1044a and 1048b). On the different meanings of the word "catholic", see also my *Catholicism* (San Francisco, 1988), pp. 48–55, 296–98.

[3] *Expositio in symbolum*; cf. St. Irenaeus, *Adversus haereses*, bk. 2, chap. 31, no. 2 (PG 7, 825a); *Demonstration of the Apostolic Faith*, chap. 98; St. Ildephonsus of Toledo, *Liber de virginitate perpetua S. Mariae*, chap. 6: "assumpturus illam sponsam ex omnibus nationibus, Ecclesiam universam" (PL 96, 74d); *De cognitione baptismi*, chap. 73 (PL 96, 138c); *Roman Catechism*, pt. 1, chap. 10, no. 17, etc.

[4] Chap. 8, no. 1; cf. chap. 19, no. 2.

the host of the angels as well as men, and even extends to the whole of the cosmos as well.[5] But even if we take it in a sense less wide than this, "the Church of God"[6] still knows, in principle, no limit of place or time. She is open to all; she draws her recruits from anywhere and everywhere and "embraces the whole of humanity".[7] Even when, at her beginning, she was containable in the upper room at Jerusalem, she had already reached out to all the people of the world by virtue of the miracle of the many tongues, and she knew that she had received these peoples as her inheritance.[8] She was, in fact, to appropriate to her own use the idea of the *oikoumene*[9] as soon as she came into contact with it. For she accepts no frontier, either geographical or social, as a check to her expansion; she does not stop short even at the frontier of the visible world, for, in accordance with a terminology long traditional, she is distinguished into three groups in ceaseless intercommunication— the Church Militant in this world, the Church Suffering in purgatory, and in heaven the Church Triumphant[10] (though

[5] St. Thomas Aquinas, *De veritate*, no. 29, a. 4, obj. 5; *In Ephes.*, chap. 1, lect. 8, etc.; so also Romano Guardini, *Vom Sinn der Kirche* (1922), p. 11. Opinion is divided concerning St. Paul's views on this subject (in the captivity Epistles); cf. L. Cerfaux, *La Théologie de l'Église suivant Saint Paul*, 2d ed. (1948), pp. 255–57. The reservations there made seem to me justified, as do those of Frs. Huby and Benoit in RB (1937), pp. 354–55. Cf. the Ambrosiaster, *In Eph.*: "Omnem Ecclesiam dicens, summatim totum comprehendit, quod in caelo est et in terra"; Heb 12:22–23 and 1 Tim 5:21; *Acta et decreta SS. Concilii Vaticani*, in *Collectio Lacensis*, vol. 7, cols. 326–27 (Bartolommeo d'Avanzo's report).

[6] 1 Cor 15:9; cf. below, p. 60, n. 37.

[7] Leo XIII, encyclical *Immortale Dei*.

[8] St. Augustine, *Sermo* 267, no. 3 (PL 38, 1231); cf. Ps 2:8.

[9] St. Ambrose, *In Psalm.* 118, *sermo* 12, no. 25: "Orbis terrarum Ecclesia. . . . Et vere orbis terrarum in Ecclesia" (PL 15, 1369c–d); St. Augustine, *In Psalm.* 7, no. 7 (PL 36, 101); Alain of Lille, *Sermo* 1 (PL 210, 221–22).

[10] Cf. Garnier of Rochefort, *Sermo* 26 (PL 205, 746a): "Triumphans, dormiens et militans", as Nicholas of Cusa was to put it in the preface to his *De concordantia Catholica* (*Opera omnia*, ed. Kallen, p. 5; cf. chap. 5 of the same work, pp. 52–53, etc). On the distant origins of this terminology, see my *Corpus mysticum*, pt. 2, on the *Corpus triforme* of Amalarius and its fate.

the triumph is not yet complete, since it awaits the day of days when the Church will be totally victorious after the glorious coming of her Savior).

It is vitally important that we should all become aware of these "dimensions" of the Church.[11] For the more lively our sense of them, the greater will be the amplification of our own existence; and this is the way in which we shall realize fully in ourselves and for ourselves the title of "Catholic" which we bear as individuals.

The real believer is not alone in his faith. His dependence on other men can be a trial to him, but his solidarity with them is a strength that more than compensates for it. He has made his entry into the great Catholic family by baptism and shares one and the same hope with its members; he has responded to the same call and is a part of the same body.[12] He is enrolled in the "army that marches on the road to salvation—Jesus Christ",[13] and integrated with the "universal assembly" made up "from every nation, tribe, people and language"[14]—this assembly being at the same time a clear-cut tradition and a well-defined power. It is a concrete reality living and developing in the conditions of the world we know, "a common vocation served by an organization that is infinitely complex and detailed",[15] a bond visible everywhere. The richness of the thing is unique; nothing comparable has ever been thought up by men, let alone realized. If, for example, one were to speak of a Buddhist or a Taoist Church, it would only be in virtue of a very distant analogy. And this

[11] Cf. the famous phrase of St. Fructuosus, bishop of Tarragona and martyr: "In mente me habere necesse est Ecclesiam catholicam, ab Oriente usque ad Occidentem diffusam."

[12] Cf. Eph 4:4–6; St. Paschasius Radbertus, *De fide, spe et caritate*, bk. 1, chap. 13, no. 1: "Una eademque in omnibus jure creditur (fides), ex qua unum corpus in Christo efficimur, per quam uno baptismo consecramur, et in una spe vocationis nostrae, una et sola fides est qua renascimur" (PL 120, 1425b).

[13] Clement of Rome, *Corinthians*, chap. 36, no. 1.

[14] Rev 7:9.

[15] Paul Claudel, *Un Poète regarde la croix*.

richness is marvelously multiform. If we wanted to explore every aspect of it there would be no end to the business. But let us look for a moment at the whole great panorama of the twenty centuries. It begins in the wounded side of Christ on Calvary,[16] goes through the "tempering" of the Pentecostal fires[17] and comes onward like a burning flood to pass through each in his turn, so that fresh living water springs up in us and new flames are lit. By virtue of the divine power received from her Founder, the Church is an institution that endures; but even more than an institution, she is a life that is passed on. She sets the seal of unity on all the children of God whom she gathers together.

It happens that sometimes we do really get a sense of this mystery of unity and life that the faith brings before us. Mankind is diverse in the extreme, divided up by period, climate, culture, environment, and innumerable other things: its problems, anxieties, tastes, and modes of expression are correspondingly diverse, and the differences are irreducible. It is not just that there can be an opposition of mentalities—for this would be a meeting, of a kind—but that often they are total

[16] Council of Vienne (DR, no. 480); St. Hilary of Poitiers, *Treatise on the Mysteries*; St. Ambrose, *In Lucam*, bk. 2, chaps. 85–89 (PL 15, 1585); St. Augustine, *In Joannem*, tract. 120, no. 2 (PL 35, 1953); *In Psalm*. 103, s. 4, no. 6 (PL 37, 1381); *In Psalm*. 138, no. 2 (PL 37, 1785); *Sermo* 120 (PL 38, 1987); *Contra Faustum*, bk. 12, chap. 8 (PL 42, 258); Gregory of Elvira, tract. 15 (p. 165 in the Batiffol-Wilmart edition); St. Ildephonsus of Toledo, *De cognitione baptismi*, chap. 7: "De Christi latere sanguis et aqua producitur, et his sacramentis Ecclesia sancta formatur" (PL 96, 114a); Rhabanus Maurus, *De laudibus Sanctae Crucis*, bk. 1 (PL 107, 170b); Pseudo-Bonaventure, *Ligno Vitae*, no. 30 (on the wedding of the Heavenly Jerusalem and the Lamb on Calvary: 8:79–80, in the Quaracchi edition). Many other texts are given in S. Tromp, S.J., "De nativitate Ecclesiae e Corde Jesu in Cruce", GR 13 (1932): 482–527.

[17] Pius XII, encyclical *Mystici corporis Christi*: "Having established the Church in his blood, he fortified it on the day of Pentecost"; Leo XIII, encyclical *Divinum illud*: "The Church, which had already been conceived and which issued, as it were, from the loins of the New Adam when he slept on the cross, was dazzlingly manifested to men for the first time on the solemn day of Pentecost."

strangers one to another. One of the historian's jobs is to bring out these differences, and when he devotes himself to it time ends up by seeming to him, in and through its very continuity, to be something that separates and obscures. Sharers in human solidarity though they are, succeeding generations are isolated from one another nonetheless for that. The common human nature in which all men participate does not stop them from reacting with repulsion and bewilderment to the encounter with themselves that they experience in the very creations of their own genius. And the permanent bond of that nature only serves to emphasize by contrast the separation that is so contrary to its own demands. Any historian who retains the distinctively human hunger for communion with his fellow men cannot help feeling continually the pathos of this situation. Yet that pathos leaves the Church out of account. And there, startlingly, is the wonderful phenomenon: a sudden closeness of those very men who seemed to have least in common and to be doomed, on every account, to irremediable separation. There is a brotherhood of common responses; they answer the same appeal and enjoy the same communion in the same love; it is as if one and the same blood flowed in their veins. They are children of the same Church and have all had from her the inheritance of the same Christ; fed by the same faith, they are "given to drink by the same Spirit", who produces in them one and the same spontaneous reaction, and thus provides the sign by which they recognize one another.[18]

To take an example: it would be hard to imagine people more remote from us than the Alexandrians of the third century or the Africans of the fourth, in spite of the fact that

---

[18] Cf. the beautiful words of St. Victricius of Rouen, *Liber de laude sanctorum*, chap. 7: "Scire debemus homines inter se . . . loco et tempore et opere et cognitatione distare. . . . Quod Si omnium hominum unum corpus esse rationis oculi perviderunt, sequitur ut in Christo et in Ecclesia viventibus pari argumento unam, beneficio adoptionis, et carnis et sanguinis et Spiritus credamus esse substantiam. . . . Ait enim Apostolis: 'Vos estis corpus Christi et membra, et Spiritus Dei habitat in vobis' " (PL 20, 449).

certain elements of our culture have come down to us by way of them. From us to them is a step into a different world. Granted, a scholarly curiosity and its associated methods of study do, over a considerable period, get us acclimatized a little; but if this were not so, how strange we should find the intellectual achievement mirrored for us in their works, and how unreal and hairsplitting most of their problems! Today we are left indifferent by things in which they were passionately interested, and the indifference is, paradoxically, a burden to us, if we stop to think about it; for it arises (as one becomes aware) because between us and them something has gone dead, and we cannot bring it alive. We set ourselves to read them because it is our business rather than because we want to—or rather, if we want to, that is because it is our business. We move among signs that are cold in their abstractness, deciphering, analyzing, reconstructing—without really understanding. One begins to wonder whether there will ever be anything more to show than the extinct ashes that are the stock-in-trade of archaeology. And then, at the turn of a page, there is the name of God; and the mists are gone as in a shaft of light. Detail after detail gathers round it in a hierarchy of order, and before long everything has a share of its illuminating power, and everything comes to life again. And it is more than the historian in us that understands and is moved. One becomes aware of fine shades of response that parallel our own for us, down to the subtlest nuance: in love for Christ, Origen and Augustine are really our contemporaries,[19] our fathers and brothers.[20] And the experience continues, however far we push our researches, and whatever their direction. Everywhere one and the same direction of attention pulls everything to-

---

[19] For Origen the reader should consult the work of Frédéric Bertrand, S.J., *La Mystique de Jésus chez Origène*, in the series Théologie (1951). It contains a delicate and penetrating analysis of the attitude of Origen toward the Person of the Savior, as shown in his commentaries on the Gospels.

[20] J. A. Moehler, *Athanasius der Grosse*: "The hearts of our forefathers were full of Jesus Christ" (1:199, in Cohen's French translation of 1840).

gether, and if it is true that a society is "a group of reasonable beings united among themselves by a love having the same object",[21] the Christians of every age and country, every race and culture, do indeed form one single whole, united by the love of Christ. Everywhere you meet the witnesses of our Lord who love him without having seen him.[22] Père de Grandmaison made a place for them at the close of his great work on Christ and showed a very true sense of Catholic community in doing so.[23] It does not matter whether it be Bernard of Clairvaux speaking, or St. Francis of Assisi, or St. Ignatius Loyola, or, nearer to our own time, Charles de Foucauld or Pierre Lyonnet;[24] they speak the same language. There may be something like an infinite variety of harmonics in the sound, but it is always the same "new song" learned from the same Mother after the "new birth": "How many souls made new today have loved the Lord Jesus."[25] The name of Christ is a serene light to the eyes of these men and the very sound of life to their ears;[26] they are all agreed that to lack in the love of Christ is not just weakness, but death.[27] They all find in that love a "sort of bloom and comeliness" and youthfulness in

[21] St. Augustine, *De civitate Dei*, bk. 29, chap. 24 (PL 41, 655).

[22] I Pet 1:8.

[23] *Jésus-Christ*, 2:631–60, "Witnesses to Jesus Christ in History".

[24] Pierre Lyonnet, S.J., *Écrits spirituels*, 2d ed. (1951). See in particular the account of his last moments at the end of the book.

[25] St. Ambrose, *De mysteriis*, 6, 29; cf. Pseudo-Anselm (Ekbert of Schoenau), *Meditatio* 13: "Verbum secretum mihi est ad te, Domine mi Rex saeculorum, Christe Jesu" (PL 158, 733b).

[26] St. Paulinus of Nola, *De nomine Jesu* (PL 61, 741a).

[27] St. Augustine, *De diversis quaestionibus* 83, q. 71, no. 7; cf. the *Confessions*, bk. 3, chap. 4, à propos the *Hortensius*: "The name of Christ was not there. For with my mother's milk my infant heart had drunk it in, and still held deep down in it, that name . . . and whatever lacked that name, no matter how learned and excellently written and true, could not win me wholly"; *De civitate Dei*, bk. 18, chap. 32, on the subject of Habakkuk: "*Gaudebo in Deo salutari meo*. . . . Melius autem mihi videntur quidam codices habere, *Gaudebo in Deo Jesu meo*, quam hi qui volentes id latine ponere, nomen ipsum non posuerunt, quod est nobis amicius et dulcius nominare" (PL 41, 591).

spirit[28] and know that, giving them Christ, "as brother, master, companion, ransom and reward", God has answered in advance every request they can make, since in Christ he has revealed all and given all.[29] All the members of the great "family of Christ" recognize one another and call to one another. This is the common ground for the illiterate and the philosopher; here, there is no essential difference between the monk in his cloister and him who bears "the care of all the Churches", and the voice of the twentieth-century martyr in China becomes one with that of the second-century martyr in Syria. It is the Church's tradition that sustains this tremendous harmony and her operative power[30] that directs it. Yet it is not the result of a sort of biological mimicry or of an agreement laboriously reached. The voice of the one Spirit, speaking to his Bride, finds an echo in the depths of each individual consciousness, and correspondingly, it is the same faith, hope, and charity everywhere; the outward expression of a unity that goes down to the roots, and the blazing up of one single flame.

* * *

But when we have said "twenty centuries"—of a duration which, as it were, winds itself up as fast as it winds itself out— we still have not said enough. Père Sertillanges, writing on the Catholic Church, headed one of his chapters "The Church before the Church",[31] and in so doing he was doing no more than expounding a well-established tradition. Some theologians have even gone so far as to say that failure to recognize a

[28] John Henry Newman, "The Crucifixion", sermon 10 of vol. 7 in *Parochial and Plain Sermons* (San Francisco, 1997), 1497; cf. *Callista*, p. 171. These texts are quoted and commented on in Henri Bremond's *Newman*, pp. 243–45.

[29] St. John of the Cross, *The Ascent of Mount Carmel*, bk. 2, chap. 22.

[30] St. Irenaeus, *Adversus haereses*, bk. 1, chap. 10, no. 2 (PG 7, 552b).

[31] *Le Miracle de l'Église*, chap. 1. Cf. Paul Claudel's letter to Gabriel Frizeau of January 20, 1904: Jesus did not "create the Church, which is as old as the first man, but he did confirm her in her indefectible Magisterium, giving to it the power to be her permanent form on earth" (Paul Claudel, Gabriel Frizeau and Francis Jammes, *Correspondance*, ed. André Blanchet [1952], p. 34).

first stage of the Church's existence, before the Incarnation, is an indefensible error;[32] and for a long time past we have been accustomed to distinguish in the Church, as in the whole economy of salvation, two regimes—those of the Old and the New Law, respectively.[33] From their first generation onward Christ's followers, however thrilled by the newness of Christianity, were also aware of their ancient titles to spiritual nobility. They realized that the salvation so recently announced to them was not the outcome of some "sudden improvisation",[34] as some among the heretics were soon to suppose. And the very word "Church", which described their community in the Gospels, the Acts, and the Pauline Epistles, bore witness to the fact. It was the word that, in the Greek translation of the Bible, was applied in particular to the assembly of the Israelites round Moses in the far-off days of Exodus.[35] "The Church of God"—the term applied first to the Christian community of Jerusalem and then by extension to other local communities, and, eventually, to the universal Church[36]—is,

[32] Torquemada, *Summa de Ecclesia* (Venice, 1651), bk. 1, chap. 22, p. 26: "error quorumdam haereticorum asserentium, quod ante adventum Christi non fuit fides apud antiquos, et per consequens nec Ecclesia"; chap. 51: "Surrexit diebus nostris opinio, si opinio et non error dicenda sit, quorumdam dicentium . . . quod Christus ante incarnationem non fuerit caput Ecclesiae, nec per consequens ante incarnationem inceperit Ecclesia, secundum suam formalem denuntiationem. . . . Opinio istorum nostro judicio sustineri non potest. . . . Fundamenta praefatae propositionis falsa esse videntur, cum a communi doctrina illuminatissimorum doctorum aliena sint et separata . . . [et] contra sanam doctrinam Patrum Ecclesiae" (ibid., pp. 59 and 60); etc.

[33] Cf. the texts quoted by Yves Congar in "Ecclesia ab Abel", *Abhandlungen über Theologie und Kirche: Festschrift für Karl Adam* (1952), pp. 94–95. Hence the expression "The Church of the New Testament", as that of the "sacraments of the New Law". Cf. Garnier of Rochefort, *Sermo* 28: "In Ecclesia primitiva" (which means "under the Old Law") (PL 205, 752c).

[34] Cf. St. Irenaeus and Tertullian, refuting Marcion.

[35] The Greek ἐκκλησία is a translation of the Hebrew *Qahal* (and of the Aramaic *Qehilla*). Cf. M. Braun, O.P., *Aspects nouveaux du problème de l'Église* (1942), pp. 33–37; Acts 7:38: "This is he [Moses] who was in the church in the wilderness."

[36] Joseph Bonsirven, *Théologie du Nouveau Testament* (1951), pp. 89–90.

precisely, the *Qehal Yahweh*, the desert community so often alluded to in the Gospel according to St. John: and Christ himself doubtless wished to show the continuity between the two by using the Aramaic equivalent *Qehilla* to describe his Church.[37] To be received into the Church was thus to be introduced into this time-honored assembly and admitted to "the dignity of an Israelite".[38] The Christian people, the people of the "New Covenant", is drawn from every quarter, chosen from among the infidel peoples to worship and serve God; and in virtue of that fact it steps into the place of the ancient Israel, as God's chosen race.[39] Or rather, from that point onward it is made one with that section of the old Israel which recognized the Messiah—like a wild shoot grafted into the good olive tree.[40] Here, in its definitive form, is the people of the "new Covenant", the "people of the inheritance",[41] proclaimed by the Prophets.[42] This is the "true Israel"—its race the true seed of Judah, Jacob, Isaac, and Abraham.[43] It is the fine flower of the "remnant" spoken of by these same Prophets, the remnant of "the fewest of any people", which Yahweh had promised to bring together again after its scattering[44] and

[37] Acts 5:11, 9:31; 1 Cor 15:9; Gal 1:13; 1 Th 2:14. Cf. L. Cerfaux, *La Théologie de l'Église*, pp. 78–88.

[38] The prayer after the fourth prophecy on Holy Saturday: "Praesta, ut in Abrahae filios et in israeliticam dignitatem totius mundi transeat multitudo." Cf. St. Thomas, *In IV Sent.*, d. 27, q. 3, a. 1, q. 3: the Synagogue was not a concubine, but the Bride.

[39] 1 Pet 2:10: "[You] who in time past were not his people: but are now the people of God"; Heb 8:10; Rev 21:3. St. Paul says the same (Phil 3:3)—"We are the circumcision."

[40] Rom 11:16–24. It is only "some of the branches" that have been broken.

[41] *Epistle of Barnabas*, 14:4; St. Justin, *Dialogue with Trypho*, chap. 119 (vol. 2, p. 211, in Archambault's edition).

[42] Jer 31:31–34; Ezek 11:17–20, 36:26–28.

[43] St. Justin, *Dialogue with Trypho*, chap. 11, no. 5 (1:55, in Archambault's edition); St. Augustine, *Quaestiones in Heptateuchum*, bk. 6, chap. 25: "Quod certissime futurum in Christo et in Ecclesia praenuntiabatur, quod est verum semen Abrahae; non in filiis carnis, sed in filiis promissionis" (PL 34, 789).

[44] Jer 23:3; Dt 7:7.

which had just been focused, in its entirety, in Christ.[45] The Church, which is the locus of this concentration of the people of God, is always "God's Israel".[46]

If we are to survey all its dimensions, in the focus of faith, we must go even deeper into the past. "The ancient Patriarchs [already] belonged to that same body of the Church which we constitute";[47] we have to look beyond Moses and the covenant of Sinai and beyond the promises made to "our father Abraham"[48] into the dawn of time. The Church, "the sacrament of man's salvation", is not the result of some fresh plan, as it were, on the part of God, nor of any "belated pity"; it does not matter how far back you go, you still find her.[49] Before the Law of Moses, the Church existed under the "law of nature";

[45] Gal 3:16, 26–29, etc. Cf. St. Leo the Great, *Sermo* 26, chap. 2: "Dum Salvatoris nostri adoramus ortum, invenimur nos nostrum celebrare principium. Generatio enim Christi origo est populi christiani, et natalis capitis est corporis" (PL 54, 213b).

[46] Gal 6:16, 3:29; Rom 9:6; Acts 13:17. Israel appears as the People of God and the holy nation in Ex 19:6; Dt 4:20, 7:6, 26:19; Is 4:3; Jer 2:3, 31:31–34; Ezek 37:11–14; Dan 7:27; Jg 20:2; etc. On all this, see L. Cerfaux, *La Théologie de l'Église*, pp. 38–57; A. Chevasse, "Du Peuple de Dieu à l'Église du Christ", *Maison-Dieu* 32 (1952): 40–52.

[47] St. Thomas, ST III, q. 8, a. 3 ad 3, etc. Cf. *Commentarii Michaelis Ghislerii Romani in Canticum Canticorum Salomonis*, 4th ed. (Venice, 1617), p. 4 (on Song 1:2): "Arguit profecto perpetua divine Numinis unitas unam eamdemque et esse et fuisse Ecclesiam, dispensatam Deo sive per legem naturae quae insita in singulorum est cordibus; sive per legem Moysis, quae Dei digito lapideis insculpta est tabulis; sive per legem gratiae, quae per Christi Domini incarnationem fidelium infusa est mentibus; unde et ab ipsomet Domino in praesenti libello de ea pronunciatum legimus: Una est columba mea, perfecta mea, matri suae. Nihilominus haud certe a veritate aberrare censendi ii sunt, qui hanc ipsam distinguunt in duas, ita tamen ab invicem dispertitas, ut a perfecta, quam ostendimus, unitate minime recedant."

[48] Lk 1:55; Rom 4:12–18 (cf. 9:6–13); St. Ambrose, *De sacramentis*, bk. 1, chap. 4, no. 27; Canon of the Mass (Roman Rite): "sancti patriarchae nostri Abrahae". Cf. the pamphlet issued in 1951 by *Cahiers sioniens* on the subject of Abraham as the father of believers, especially Paul Demann's "Le Signification d'Abraham dans la perspective du Nouveau Testament" (pp. 44–67); L. Cerfaux, *La Théologie de l'Église*, pp. 59–68.

[49] St. Leo the Great, *In nativitate Domini sermo* 3 (PL 54, 201–3).

she exists *ab exordio saeculi*.[50] There has always been a people of
God and a vine that the Father tends unceasingly;[51] the union
of Christ and his Church is prefigured in the union of Adam
and Eve. Here, says St. Paul, is a "high mystery",[52] that very
mystery which was to be revealed in its fullness "in the fullness
of time". But the idea of a prefiguring of the Church and that of
her effective commencement in Adam[53] are neither of them
entirely adequate. For though Christ was not to appear in the
humility of our flesh until long after these things, he is nonetheless "the first-born of every creature", as St. Paul teaches;[54] so
that whatever is true of him is also true of his Bride the Church.
She was certainly prepared for over many years, as he was, by the
history of the Jewish people[55] and prefigured in the earthly
paradise; but in reality she is older than all this, as he is. She must
be seen as in God before the beginning of the world[56]—"she
flowered there with Christ by the will of the Father, the Son,
and the Holy Spirit" [57]—and recognized in the mysterious Wis-

[50] Nicetas of Remesiana, *Explanatio symboli*, no. 10 (PL 52, 871); cf. the *Liber
quaestionum*, q. 3, no. 4: "itaque, semper christianismus" (p. 24 in Souter's
edition).

[51] St. Gregory the Great, *In Evangelia*, hom. 19, no. 1 (PL 76, 1154b); St.
Paschasius Radbertus, *In Matt.*, bk. 9, chap. 20 (PL 120, 674–75); Rupert of
Deutz, *In Genesim*, bk. 9, chap. 30 (PL 167, 554–55); Alain of Lille, *Sermo* 5 (PL
210, 211–12); etc. In 1625 a Franciscan published a work entitled *Ecclesia ante
Legem*. Cf. Msgr. Berteaud, *Oeuvres pastorales*, vol. 2 (1872), pp. 34–37: "The
Church covers all time. . . . she spreads out like a noble vine into all places and
all ages. The penitent Adam and Eve were her first roots; Abel blossomed on her
trunk."

[52] Eph 5:32 [Knox version—TRANS.].

[53] Cf. Suarez, *De fide*, disp. 9, s. 2 (*Opera* [1868], 12:253–55).

[54] Col 1:15.

[55] St. Ambrose, *In Psalm.* 118, *sermo* 1, no. 4: "Et in primordiis mundi
desponsata in paradiso, praefigurata in diluvio, annuntiata per Legem, vocata
per prophetas" (PL 15, 1201a–b), etc.

[56] St. Epiphanius of Salamis, *Expositio fidei* (PG 42, 784c–d).

[57] Prayer from Leonian Sacramentary: "Quae Ecclesia ante mundi principium in tua semper est praesentia praeparata" (PL 55, 111); St. Augustine, *De
civitate Dei*, bk. 16, chap. 2, no. 3 (PL 41, 479); St. Thomas, ST III, q. 8, a. 3; St.
Robert Bellarmine, *De Verbo*, bk. 4, chap. 4.

dom that, with the Creator, presides over the first creation itself.[58]

Hermas was right, then, when he saw her in his vision as an old woman; for, as his guide the Shepherd explained to him, "she was created first, before all things." That is to say, the world "was made for her".[59] "The God who drew creatures out of nothing and made them multiply and increase" did it all "for the Holy Church".[60] When he talks in this way, Hermas is merely applying to the Church, in accordance with the great law of Christian transposition, what Israel thought about itself.[61] Origen was soon to say the same thing, basing his thought on St. Paul and the Psalmist:

> Do not believe that the Bride—that is, the Church—has existed only since the Savior's coming in the flesh; she exists since the beginning of the human race and even since the creation of the world: even—I call St. Paul to witness—since before the creation of the world. For the Apostle said: "Since he has chosen us in Christ since before the creation of the world, that we might be holy and immaculate before him, predestining us in love to the adoption of the Son." And it is written in the Psalms: "Remember, Lord, thy Church, which thou hast gathered together from the beginning." So, the foundations of the Church have been laid from the beginning. And that is why the Apostle also says that the Church is founded not only on the Apostles but also on the Prophets, and Adam himself is reckoned among the number of the Prophets.[62]

[58] Both the Greek and the Latin branches of tradition effected this assimilation early on. Or rather, the Church is the House that Wisdom (that is, our Lord) has built for himself from all the ages; cf. Prov 9:1: "Wisdom hath built herself a house"; thus Berengard, *In Apoc.* (PL 17, 775a).

[59] Hermas, *The Shepherd*, vision 2, chap. 4, no. 1; cf. St. Epiphanius of Salamis, *Haeres.*, bk. 1, vol. 1, chap. 5 (PG 41, 181b).

[60] Hermas, *The Shepherd*, vision 1, chap. 1, no. 6.

[61] *Assumption of Moses*, 1, no. 12 (p. 58 in Charles' edition).

[62] Origen, *In Cant. comm.*, bk. 2 (p. 157 in Baehrens' edition); translated in G. Bardy, *La Théologie de l'Église de saint Irenée au concile de Nicée*, p. 146. Cf. *In Numer.*, hom. 3, no. 3.

But all this does not bring our exploration to an end. Having looked deeper and deeper into the past, we now have to look deeper and deeper into the future, to the very end of time— "from the time of Abel the just unto the last elect,[63] from the beginning of the world to the end".[64] Tradition is full of these formulas, and if they are made a pretext for making the true Church consist of the invisible fellowship of the fully initiated or the predestined, that is a misinterpretation; but this particular abuse of them ought not to blind us to the truths they contain.[65]

We should break through the very limitations indicated by them, as we did through that of the world's beginning—*novissima prima*. The definitive reality is that which comes first in the plan of God. As Clement of Alexandria said (and said superbly): "Just as the will of God is an act and is called the world, so also

[63] On this formula, see Y. Congar, "Ecclesia ab Abel", pp. 94–95.

[64] Hugh of Saint-Victor, *De arca Noë morali: De arca Noë mystica*, chap. 3 (PL 176, 625 and 688); St. Thomas, ST I-II, q. 8, a. 3: "Corpus Ecclesiae constitutur ex hominibus qui fuerunt a principio mundi usque ad fidem ipsius"; *Roman Catechism*, pt. 1, art. 9, no. 17: "Qui ab Adam fuerunt, quive futuri sunt, quamdiu mundus exstabit, veram fidem profitentes, ad eamdem Ecclesiam pertinent"; Suarez, *De fide*, d. 9, s. 2; d. 12, s. 4, no. 22.

[65] An abuse of this kind had been noted and resisted by Torquemada (*Summa de Ecclesia*, bk. 1, chaps. 54–59, pp. 62–72). In his *De Ecclesia Christi* (1887; posthumous and unfinished), J. B. Franzelin shows how it is possible to maintain a wide view of the Church without, however, falling into that particular error: "Ecclesia Dei secundum amplissimam notionem spectata est supernaturalis societas seu civitas eorum omnium qui sive angeli, sive homines ab Adam usque ad consummationem sub capite Christo fide in via, visione beatifica in termino, adhaerentes Deo uniti sunt ad communionem sanctorum" (*Thesis secunda*, p. 8). On the other hand, a number of traditional texts (without implying any meaning in the phrase contrary to Catholic truth) do speak of the "sancta electorum Ecclesia" or—referring to Heb 12:22–23—of the Church of the predestined; thus, among others, Berengard, *In Apoc.* (PL 17, 775a); Adam Scotus (PL 198, 368b, 690, 691, 792d); cf. St. Augustine, *Sermo* 4, no. 11 (PL 38, 39); St. Gregory, *In Ezechielem*, bk. 2, hom. 3, no. 15: "Et quidem ab Abel sanguine passio jam caepit Ecclesiae et una est Ecclesia electorum, praecedentium atque sequentium" (PL 76, 966c); *Epist.* 1, 5, no. 18 (PL 77, 740); Hugh of Saint-Victor, *In Col.* (PL 175, 583a); etc. Cf. Koster, *Ekklesiologie in Werden* (1940), chap. 1.

his intention is the salvation of men and is called the Church":[66] and we should say of the Church, as of Christ, that her kingdom "shall be without end", for the "nuptials of the Lamb" are eternal. We have already noted that for the elect salvation consists in being welcomed, for good and all, into the heart of the Church for which they were created, in which they have been predestined and are loved. For Christ loved his Church and delivered himself up for her:[67] he redeemed her with his blood,[68] and we ourselves are loved and saved by participating in this mystery of love and the unity that is its consummation.

Insofar as we consider only the Church's visible and terrestrial aspect, instituted by God for the purpose of our salvation, we can of course say truly that she is something transitory; she will not outlast the faith that is her foundation or the "sacraments of the faith",[69] and she passes away as "the fashion of this world"[70] passes away. She is transitory as Christ himself willed to be transitory in his mortal individuality, bounded as he was by location in space and time—more than this, transitory as he always wishes to be inasmuch as he is the Way for us.[71] We say of the Church as of him—though from the opposite direction, as it were—"for us men and for our salvation"; adding, in the words of Pius XI: "Men are not made for the Church but the Church for men."[72] In her we see a means

[66] *Paedagogus*, bk. 1, chap. 6 (1:106, in Staehlin's edition).

[67] Eph 5:25.

[68] Acts 20:28; cf. Rev 1:5.

[69] When St. Thomas defines the Church thus, "Ecclesia, id est fides et fidei sacramenta", he is defining her, "not in her spiritual substance . . . , but in her condition as a society founded by Christ . . . , in her institutional and visible reality", although the two things are not, of course, to be separated; see Y. Congar, *Esquisses du mystère de l'Église* (1941), with the references there.

[70] 1 Cor 7:31.

[71] St. Augustine, *De doctrina christiana*, bk. 1, no. 38: "Nec ipse Dominus, in quantum via nostra esse dignatus est, tenere nos voluit, sed transire" (PL 34, 33). However, St. Augustine's thought must not be twisted out of true; we must remember also that precisely inasmuch as Christ is our Way, he never comes to an end of "passing"; cf. Heb 10:20, 7:15–23.

[72] Allocution to the Lenten Preachers of Rome, February 28, 1927.

that is, like all means, something provisional; which fact is also, incidentally, useful as providing a method of demonstrating that in Christianity the person is never subordinated or sacrificed to some collectivism, as the individual is to society according to so many theories of purely human inspiration. Far from being absorbed, he is, in fact, exalted. Yet in reality it is not the Church that passes away, but her "fashion"—the form in which she is at present visible to us. For her end is the end of the persons who constitute her, and it is in her alone that they find their fulfillment.[73] So we cannot stop short with this incomplete view of her.

If we are to go beyond it while still giving it its proper place, we have to distinguish three main epochs and three successive conditions of the Church.[74] The first transformation is accomplished when the Israel of the flesh gives place to the Israel of the spirit. This is the transition from the first stage to the second, and a prefiguring of the other transformation, which is the glorious transfiguration at the end of time, when the earthly Church enters upon her definitive status as the heavenly Church.

By this she will "become what she is"; for she is always that heavenly kingdom in embryo,[75] and she always has

[73] Cf. my *Catholicism*, chap. 11; Msgr. Berteaud, *Oeuvres pastorales*, 2:8–9, considering in turn both aspects: "The Church has been created to help in . . . the building up of this perfect man, who has as his mystical Head the Word incarnate. . . . Heaven is for the Church and not the Church for heaven; the former is thus the ultimate goal."

[74] Cf. St. Methodius of Olympus on the actual Church—as intermediate between the "shadows" of the Law and the "truths" of the future (*Banquet*, bk. 5, chap. 7; PG 18, 109), etc.; St. Thomas, *Quodl.* 7, a. 15. Similarly, St. Thomas, in ST I-II (q. 103, a. 3), makes distinction between the three successive stages of the interior *cultus*—this, of course, in accordance with Tradition as a whole; cf. *Acta et decreta SS. Concilii Vaticani, Collectio Lacensis*, vol. 7, col. 318 (Bartolommeo d'Avanzo's report): "In Ecclesia, ut probe noscitis (estis enim magistri in Israel) duo distinguenda sunt, substantia et modus seu forma externa regiminis."

[75] St. Augustine, *De civitate Dei*, bk. 20, chap. 9, no. 1: "Ecclesia *et nunc* est regnum Christi regnumque caelorum" (PL 41, 67). We may compare this with

been,[76] considered under the aspect of her substance. She bears the eternal promise of that kingdom just as she is today;[77] she is its inauguration[78] and ensures its actual and active presence among us. At this very moment her "foundation is in heaven",[79] although she is "a pilgrim upon earth"; if we consider her, in her totality, according to her present condition, we can say of her what St. John said of each one of us in a phrase that conveys excellently the paradox inherent in the Christian situation (what has been called "eschatological tension"):

the *et nunc* of St. John. St. Gregory the Great, *In Evangelia*, bk. 1, hom. 12, no. 1: "Quid itaque per hanc sententiam nisi praesens Ecclesia regnum caelorum dicitur?" (PL 76, 1119): "Sciendum nobis est, quod saepe in sacro eloquio regnum caelorum praesentis temporis Ecclesia dicitur."

[76] Though pure and simple identification of the one with the other is of course not possible. The Church and the Kingdom are distinct in several passages of the New Testament, particularly in Acts; cf. A. Wikenhauser, "L'Instruction des Apôtres par le Ressuscité d'après Act. i. 3", *Vom Wort des Lebens: Festschrift für Max Meinertz* (Munster, 1951), pp. 105–13; M. Braun, O.P., *Aspects nouveaux du problème de l'Église* (1942), pp. 109–11, 161–70: "The Church is the Kingdom insofar as she is penetrated by the power of the Kingdom in this world; inasmuch as she moves with all her being toward the glorious and consummated Kingdom of the age to come. And vice versa: the Kingdom is the Church inasmuch as the power of the Kingdom, which has come down into this world through Jesus under the form of grace and eternal life, is exercised principally and normally, though not exclusively, in the community of the faithful founded on the Twelve" (pp. 166–67); L. Cerfaux, *La Théologie de l'Église*, pp. 293–98; H. N. Ridderbos, *De Komst van het Koninrijk* (1950; reviewed by D. Hendrikx, RB [1952], pp. 1264–67); J. Bonsirven, *Théologie du Nouveau Testament* (1951), p. 91; S. Tyszkiewicz, S.J., *La Sainteté de l'Église Christo-conforme* (1945), pp. 86–87: "The Church in this world cannot be adequately identified with the Kingdom of God."

[77] St. Augustine, *De sancta virginitate*, chap. 24: "Nam etsi regnum caelorum aliquando Ecclesia etiam quae hoc tempore est appellatur, ad hoc utique sic appellatur, quia futurae vitae sempiternaequae colligitur" (PL 40, 409); cf. *De civitate Dei*, bk. 20, chap. 9, no. 1 (PL 41, 673); *Sermo* 251, chap. 4, no. 3 (PL 38, 1169).

[78] Joseph Huby, *Évangile selon saint Luc* (1941), p. 403.

[79] St. Augustine, *Sermo* 105, no. 9: "Civitas in terra peregrina, in caelo fundata" (PL 38, 622); *In Psalm.* 86, no. 3: "Fundamentum spiritualis fabricae in summo est" (PL 39, 1103); Alain of Lille, *Sermo* 5 (PL 210, 24c–d).

"What we shall be [which is already realized as far as God's vision is concerned] hath not yet appeared." [80] Although we are still on our journey, searching and expectant, we have also already found a way to the Mountain of Sion, the City of the Living God, the Heavenly Jerusalem of which we are fellow citizens with the angels;[81] the Epistle to the Hebrews is our surety for the fact. Or you can put it the other way around and say that the Heavenly Jerusalem has come from heaven into our midst; she is, in fact, "our Mother"[82] here and now. Yet at the same time a whole labor of consolidation and discovery waits to be carried out, since "the vanity of this world" still hangs thick about us and we are still lamenting pilgrims,[83] as St. Hilary puts it—though again there is, substantially, nothing left that we really have still to wait for in the strict sense. The sacramental element in the Church, being adapted to our temporal condition, is destined to disappear in the face of the definitive reality it effectively signifies; but this should not be thought of as one thing's effacing of another. It will be the manifestation of sacramentality's own proper truth;[84] a glorious epiphany and a consummation.

* * *

It will perhaps be as well to pause for a moment in consideration of the exact nature of this necessary transfiguration. It is

[80] 1 Jn 3:2. The Apostle has just said: "we are God's children now."

[81] Heb 12:22: "But you are come to Mount Sion and to the city of the living God, the heavenly Jerusalem, and to the company of many thousands of angels"—but see also 11:8–10 and 13:14. Cf. Erik Peterson, *Das Buch von den Engeln* (1935), p. 13; and Eph 2:6—we are already seated in heaven with Christ.

[82] St. Augustine, *Sermo* 214, no. 11 (PL 38, 1071).

[83] St. Hilary of Poitiers, *Tract. super Psalm.* 148 (PL 9, 879; à propos Rom 8:23); St. Augustine, *In Psalm.* 148, no. 4 (PL 37, 1940).

[84] This point is in the mind of Theodore of Mopsuestia when he says (in his *Tenth Catechetical Homily*, no. 17) that the Church bears the name "Body of Christ" today because she has "his likeness" and that in the world to come she will be the Body of Christ "effectively and in truth" because she will receive "the glory of the likeness". For a correct understanding of texts of this kind one must bear in mind the shades of meaning of the old terminology.

here that St. Paul's phrase "the figure of this world passeth away" has, *mutatis mutandis*, its point of application. "We shall all be changed", he says.[85] Our own day has—happily—reacted against that particular kind of emphasis on the spirit which had in its ancestry more of the dualism of Plato than that of the Gospels. We have found our way to a better understanding of the dogma of the resurrection of the dead and are no longer inclined to see in it nothing more than a revealed complement (and one of no great importance, either) to the doctrine of immortality presented to us by natural theology. All that is to the good; though even so we must take care to preserve moderation and not to be blind followers of a merely fashionable anti-Platonism that does not take into account all the scriptural data.[86] But the tendency constitutes a poor safeguard against another kind of temptation. There has recently been criticism, in principle justified, of the "passionate attempt" of some contemporary Christians to "satisfy all human aspiration, even as illuminated by the Gospel, within the *flammantia moenia mundi*". "If they still claim the title of 'sons of the resurrection', these Christians seem to understand it in a sense that ought to make them 'sons of this world' for a second time over, and not sons of heaven." [87] We should not lightly accuse people of such an attitude, and it is not always easy to disentangle therein what would be a serious deficiency in the spirit of faith from something that may well be no more than fantasy of the immature— something that can indeed reproduce today a confusion of modes known also to the past[88] but that does not involve the

[85] I Cor 15:51.

[86] In the case of St. Paul, for example, we may consult the literary analyses of Dom Jacques Dupont, O.S.B., " 'Avec le Christ' dans la vie future" (pt. I of *Sun Christoi: L'Union avec le Christ suivant saint Paul* [Bruges, 1952]).

[87] Louis Bouyer, *Le Sens de la vie monastique*, p. 46: "It must be stated that the witness of the Catholic tradition is all in the opposite direction."

[88] Cf. Guillaume Postel, when he says in *La Vergine Venetiana*: "In view of the fact that heaven is a transparent body, we need not be astonished . . . that she has seen the heavenly Jerusalem" (pp. 13–14 in Henri Morard's translation of 1928).

same danger at all. It offers a strange common ground, on the one hand, to those who dream of a future Utopia with many of the features of heaven and, on the other, those who—from the opposite end of the stick but in virtue of a similar contradiction—want to retain features very much of this world in an other-worldly happiness. Our last end is something transcendent, and its good things, prepared by God for those who love him, are all what "eye hath not seen, nor the ear heard", what "hath [not] entered into the heart of man".[89] But here and there the sense of this transcendence seems lost or at least dormant; as is that of the scope of the *renovatio* that the Day of the Lord is to bring about.[90] Above all, this attitude sometimes makes itself felt as a refusal, or at least a fear, to go through the great furnace of the Judgment that is to carry out the necessary purification; it seems as if, in their fascination with a future that demands for its building all their vitality, people can no longer face the changing of human hopefulness into the virtue of hope, so that the whole of Christian eschatology is degraded into one vast Utopianism.[91] Sometimes this takes the form of an inability to reject the more grossly concrete kinds of conception without a loss of mental equilibrium; sometimes, again, a certain scrupulosity about rejecting them, as if one had to believe in the eternal permanence of animal functions and pleasures in order to make sure of believing in the resurrection of the body—indeed, as if liberation from subjections of this kind, involved as they are with the weakness and corruption of our mortal flesh, were not, precisely, "the glory of this bodily resurrection".[92] Sometimes it seems as if these things are held on to

[89] 1 Cor 2:9; cf. 15:35–57; 2 Cor 4:18; St. Irenaeus, *Adversus haereses*, 1, 5, chap. 36, no. 3 (PG 7, 1224b).

[90] 2 Pet 3:7–13.

[91] Cf. my *Affrontements mystiques* (1950), pp. 52–65.

[92] St. Hilary of Poitiers, *Tractatus de titulo Psalmi* 91, no. 10: "ut, corruptionis nostrae infirmitate in caelestem gloriam transformata, nec vitium voluntas, nec ambitio gloriam, nec honorem superbia, nec otium labor, nec cibum corpus, nec somnium noctis diei lassitudo desideret. . . . Hoc fidei praemium, haec corporae resurrectionis est gloria, in qua nihil desiderandum est, quia nulla

as one of the privileges of the beatific life of the resurrected body; people seem to want to take the imagery of the eschatological feasting literally,[93] as if such things did not come high on the list of the *terrena* the power to despise which we ask constantly of God,[94] and as if the table of the Kingdom of Heaven ought not to wipe out our memories of all earthly food.[95] Yet people bring themselves to believe that we should not be able to come by that perfect knowledge of the universe which is to delight the elect if taste were not materially present to our sense in the act of eating. They take exception to the clear and well-founded teaching in which St. Thomas sums up the commonly received doctrine and interpret it—in the teeth of the evidence—with reference to a physique that will then, in point of fact, have been superseded.[96] They forget about St. Augustine's efforts to drive home to the worldly mind the fact that its longing to eat and drink is the longing of a sick man,

---

egendum est" (p. 354 in Zingerle's edition); cf. *In Psalm.* 1, no. 12 (ibid., p. 27); St. Basil the Great, *In Psalm.* 114, v. 5 (PG 29, 493); Theodore of Mopsuestia, *Catechetical Homilies*, 12, no. 5, and 16, no. 32; we must not figure out for ourselves a "base" and "judaic" idea of the resurrection; there will no more be "eating and drinking" in the Kingdom of God than there will be marriage.

[93] Cf. Lk 14:15, 22:30; Mt 25:10, 26:29; Rev 3:20. Cf. the Book of Enoch, 62:14.

[94] Cf. the Roman Missal's phrase: "Fac nos . . . terrena despicere et amare caelestia."

[95] Cf. St. Ephraem the Syrian, *Eleventh Hymn on Paradise*, strophe 15: "Paradisus est odor nutriens omnia omni tempore, et is cui spirat, gaudio exultat, oblitus panem suum. Mensa regni est. Benedictus, qui paravit eam in Edem" (Dom Edmund Beck, O.S.B., "Ephraems Hymnen über das Paradies", SA 26 [1951]: 127). It is worthwhile reading these hymns, in which an extremely concrete imagination is wholly at the service of a particularly strong consciousness of what is meant by transcendence. There is mention on several occasions of the fruits of the Tree of Life in the spiritual Paradise; cf. St. Irenaeus, *Adversus haereses*, 1, 5, chap. 36, no. 2 (PG 7, 1223b).

[96] St. Thomas, indeed, shows, precisely, how the joys of eternal life transcend all the joys of this world (*Summa contra gentiles*, bk. 3, chap. 63). We must not think in terms of animal functions any more (*Compendium theologiae*, chap. 158: "Quod post resurrectionem usus cibi et generationis cessabunt"); the same point is made in chap. 191, and we may also note the general principle

which holds it back from the joy that is God,[97] and his warning against rash curiosity where the state of the resurrected body is concerned.[98]

Whatever the finer points of these views may be, interlaced as they are in the opposition common to all of them, in each case the fact remains that, under the influence of a temptation never totally extinguished and recently accentuated—a temptation sometimes camouflaged with an appearance of a claim to "true orthodoxy", as in the distant age of St. Justin—our age is witnessing more than one resurgence of the old millenarian visions[99] in new forms, some of which are dangerous and some

---

enunciated in chap. 172: "Et sic totum universum corporeum habebit aliam dispositionem et formam, secundum illud 1 Cor. vii. 31: 'Praeterit figura hujus mundi'." Cf. 1 Cor 6:13, 15:30; A. D. Sertillanges, *Catéchisme des incroyants*, 2:252; Jean Mauraux, *Sens chrétien de l'homme*, p. 102; L. Billot, *Quaestiones de novissimis*, 3d ed. (1903), p. 164; A. Tanquerey, *Synopsis theologiae dogmaticae*, 19th ed., 3:614, etc.

[97] *Sermo* 255, no. 5: "In via fames, in patria satietas. Quando satiabimur? Satiabor cum manifestata fuerit gloria tua"; no. 7: "Quando ergo dicitur quia cetera subtrahuntur et solus Deus erit quo delectemur, quasi angustatur anima, quae consuevit multis delectari; et dicit anima carnalis, carni addicta, carnalibus cupiditatibus implicita, visco malarum cupiditatum involutas pennas habens ne volet ad Deum, dicit sibi: Quid mihi erit, ubi non manducabo, ubi non bibam, ubi cum uxore mea non dormiam, quale mihi gaudium erit? Hoc gaudium tuum de aegritudine est, non de sanitate." On the subject of the millennium, see *De civitate Dei*, bk. 20, chap. 7, no. 1 (PL 41, 667).

[98] *De civitate Dei*, bk. 22, chap. 21: "quae sit autem, et quam magna spiritualis corporis gratia, quoniam nondum venit in experimentum, vereor ne temerarium sit omne quod de illa profertur eloquium" (PL 41, 784); cf. Pseudo-Augustine, *De symbolo*, chap. 12, no. 23 (PL 40, 652).

[99] *Dialogue with Trypho*, chap. 80, no. 5 (2:37, in Archambault's edition). See also St. Thomas, *Suppl.*, q. 84, a. 4.: "Utrum omnes resurgent in vita animali"; "quia comedere, bibere et dormire, generare, ad animalem vitam pertinent, cum sint ad primam perfectionem naturae ordinata, ideo in resurrectione talia non erunt"; and ad 4: "Delectationes corporales, sicut dicit Philosophus in vii et x Ethic., sunt medicinales, quia adhibentur homini ad tollendum fastidium, vel etiam aegritudinales. . . . Et ideo non oportet quod tales delectationes sint de perfectione beatitudinis, ut Judaei et Saraceni ponunt, et quidam haeretici posuerunt, qui vocantur Chiliastae; qui etiam secundum doctrinam Philosophi non videntur sanum habere affectum."

harmless. Christian hope has suffered a renewed attack from more than one variety of devitalization.

Now, a similar illusion can find its way into some minds where the Church is concerned. Those in question, "anxious to turn to full account" her "visible organism" and "whatever in her is an institution or means of grace", end up (for example) by making the sacramental cultus "a sort of end in itself".[100] They are unwilling to admit that on the day of her triumph the Church will abandon "her mortal and historical clothing"— that is, "all that aspect of herself by virtue of which she is actually . . . the instrument of her own growth and a partaker in the earthly condition of her members".[101] With the idea of strengthening the authority of those who are in this world Christ's representatives and the Apostles' successors, they sometimes go so far as to want to make eternal not only the imprint of the sacred character such men have received—which would be legitimate—but the exercise of their power (under some form that cannot be exactly described).[102]

It must be admitted that there are plenty more this-worldly ways of conceiving the realities of the faith. They are all so many products of an illusion that cannot but affect its purity; one cannot, in fact (as St. Bonaventure said so bluntly), make an analogy between the polity of this world and that of the Heavenly Jerusalem—"it must be said that they are not alike"[103]—and as St. Thomas expressly teaches, the whole order of the sacraments and their "characters" is bound up with

[100] Yves Congar, "Structure du sacerdoce chrétien", MD 27 (1951): 77.

[101] A. Liégé, O.P., *Le Mystère de l'Église* (1950), p. 20 (unpublished lecture).

[102] Hence certain overbold exegeses of Mt 19:28: "Amen, I say to you that you, who have followed me, in the regeneration when the Son of Man shall sit on the seat of his majesty, you also shall sit on twelve seats judging the twelve tribes of Israel." A similar exaggeration has been noted in the extension of the pontifical power to the Church Suffering and Triumphant; but in that particular case the exaggeration lay in the vocabulary rather than in the thought itself; see also George Phillips, *Du droit ecclésiastique dans ses principes généraux*, trans. J. P. Crouzet, 2d ed. (1855), 1:162.

[103] *De perfectione evangelica*, q. 4, a. 3 ad 16 (5:198, in the Quaracchi edition).

"the cultus of the Church in her present condition"; so much so that if we had a mind to the future glory only and not to the actions that fit in with that present condition, the sacramental "character" would not make sense. Its mode is that of the "exterior cultus", which will subsist no longer in the Kingdom of Heaven, where nothing will take place in symbol, but all in naked truth.[104] To determine the exact nature of that cultus and the proper field covered by it is not to belittle the part it plays or take away from its grandeur; there is no question of challenging the title-deeds of legitimate authority or shaking its foundations, if we say that it is relative to our pilgrim status as *viatores*. After all, it can scarcely have any function left when "God [is] all in all".[105] God has set it up as a power over the body of the Church Militant,[106] and if there is any calling in question of the hierarchic principle, that is the work of those who, though inside time themselves, claim to be emancipated, in one way or another, from the conditions of time—not of those who emphasize that these conditions have the same limits as time itself. For "the possession of the ecclesiastical ministry which makes her visible is of the essence of the Church *until the resurrection*."[107] When Christ promised those who had left everything for him that in the Kingdom of Heaven they should sit "on twelve seats, judging the twelve tribes of Israel" with him, he did not extend the ecclesiastical hierarchy of this world into eternity, although he was talking to those whom he had chosen to found that hierarchy. Exegetes and theologians debate whether this phrase conferred a privilege on the twelve Apostles only or whether they were the first recipients of the privilege of the saints in

[104] Or again, "the cultus of God according to the rites of the Christian religion". See ST III, q. 63, a. 1, c. and ad 1; a. 2, c. and ad 2; a. 5, obj. 3.

[105] 1 Cor 15:28. Cf. Charles Journet, *The Church of the Word Incarnate* (1955), 1:15: "The visible hierarchy will not then be needed any more."

[106] Cf. Clement VI, *Epist. super quibusdam*, September 29, 1351, on the subject of the Roman Pontiff "super totum et universum corpus Ecclesiae militantis".

[107] Bossuet, *Réflections sur un écrit de M. Claude* (1727), p. 260.

general;[108] and again it may be debated whether it refers directly to the next world or to the this-worldly situation of a new order coincident with the founding of the Church.[109] Whatever the answer to these questions may be, the words did not set up a power that was to be analogous, in heaven, to that wielded by the hierarchy on earth. In the promise made to the Twelve we can see, at least, the symbol or extreme case of that promise which is made, in the same passage, to whoever leaves all for the love of Christ. Tradition is unanimous in seeing the matter so,[110] and that is how the Church sees it today. Her liturgy extends the Apostles' prerogative to all the just, following St. Paul's words to the Corinthians: "Know you not that the saints shall judge this world? . . . Know you not that we shall judge angels?"[111] and she relates it to the passage about them in the Book of Wisdom: "They shall judge nations, and rule over people: and their Lord shall reign for ever."[112] Revelation calls Christ's followers "victors", and the

---

[108] Mt 19:27–30. Cf. the commentaries by J. Knabenbauer (1893), pp. 162–70, and A. Durand (1924), pp. 324–26; C. Pesch, *Praelectiones dogmaticae* (1899), 9:353–54.

[109] Cf. M. J. Lagrange, *Évangile selon saint Matthieu*, p. 381: "Matthew was thinking of a new order, but we are not obliged to see in it . . . the complete renewal of eternal life. . . . McNeile refers the passage to Pentecost. This is to be over-precise. All we can do is to speak in terms of the assumption of office by the Son of Man, which coincides with the foundation of the Church."

[110] Origen, *In Matt.*, 14, 22–23 (pp. 416–18 in Klostermann's edition); St. Jerome, *In Matt.*, 19, 27–29 (PL 26, 138–39); St. Augustine, *In Psalm.* 86, no. 4 (PL 37, 1104); *De civitate Dei*, bk. 20, chap. 5 (PL 41); St. Gregory the Great, *In Ezech.*, bk. 1, hom. 2, no. 18 (PL 76, 803b); *Moralia in Job*, bk. 6, nos. 23–24 (PL 75, 741–42), bk. 10, no. 52 (ibid., 950), bk. 20, no. 41 (PL 76, 162a); bk. 26, nos. 31 and 51 (cols. 266 and 379–80); St. Bede the Venerable, *Homilia* 17, *In die natali Sancti Benedicti* (PL 94, 224–25); Alexander of Hales, *Summa*, bk. 3, pt. 1, tract. 8, no. 5, c. 1 ad 3, and c. 2 (4:308 and 309, in the Quaracchi edition); St. Bonaventure, *De sanctis apostolis Petro et Paulo, sermo* 3 (ibid., 9:552–54); St. Thomas, *Suppl.*, 2, 89, a. 2, etc.

[111] 1 Cor 6:2–3.

[112] Wis 3:8; Roman Missal, Introit for the Vigil of All Saints. Cf. Rupert of Deutz, *In Matt.* (PL 168, 1577a). We may, however—following the liturgy—speak of a jurisdiction of the hierarchy on the Day of Judgment in the sense that

"true and faithful witness" promises all such that Christ will give them to sit with him on his throne.[113]

To sum up: without going so far as to say, like Cajetan, that the whole social aspect of the Church and all that makes up her present structure will simply be "consumed with fire", we may believe, with Fr. Liégé, "that the Church's process of becoming and the structures that have built up her eternal reality will be taken up—together with our personal histories—into the community of glory under a new and wholly interiorized form".[114] To quote Fr. Humbert Bouëssé: "Since it is immutable in its essence, his 'character' sets a mark on the soul of the priest for ever; but the sacramental priesthood will pass away like the earthly Church. . . . Signs will have no place in the glory of the Heavenly City." [115] As Newman puts it in the *Apologia*, just as the visible world is at present—to our eyes—not completed by

---

the power exercised by the hierarchy in this world has effects that are ratified in heaven; cf. the Roman Breviary hymn:

> Quodcumque in orbe nexibus revinxeris
> Erit revinctum, Petre, in arce siderum,
> Et quod resolvit hic potestas tradita,
> Erit solutum coeli in alto vertice:
> In fine mundi judicabis saeculum.

[113] Rev 3:21: "To him that shall overcome, I will give to sit with me in my throne." Lagrange (*Saint Matthieu*, p. 382) says: "All those who are victors will sit in judgment with the Twelve, just as all those who achieve detachment will share their reward." Cf. the Book of Enoch, 108:12–15.

[114] *Le Mystère de l'Église*, p. 20. This does not mean that the sacramental character does not subsist in the soul. Derived as it is from the eternal priesthood of Christ and imprinted on a soul that is incorruptible, it cannot be lost: "Indebiliter inest animae, non propter viri perfectionem, sed propter perfectionem sacerdotii Christi, ex quo derivatur caracter, sicut quaedam instrumentalis virtus" (ST III, q. 63, a. 5, c. and ad 1). The soul remains marked with it for all eternity, but not as with a power it will have to use: "Quamvis post hanc vitam non remaneat exterior cultus, remanet tamen finis illius cultus. Et ideo post hanc vitam remanet caracter, et in bonis ad eorum gloriam, et in malis ad eorum ignominiam: sicut etiam militaris caracter remanet in militibus post adeptam victoriam, et in his qui vicerunt ad gloriam, et in his qui sunt victi ad poenam" (q. 63, a. 5 ad 3).

[115] *Théologie et sacerdoce* (1938), p. 117.

its "divine interpretation", so "Holy Church in her sacraments and her hierarchical appointments will remain, even to the end of the world, after all but a symbol of those heavenly facts which fill eternity." [116]

> What is the holocaust? The divine Fire that comes to set everything ablaze. The Church, Christ's Body and Christ's unity, catches a glimpse of this holocaust when she says: "By the holocaust I will enter into thy house." May I be burnt up wholly by thy flame! May nothing of my own proper being be left to me! May everything in me be thine! That is what will be made a reality in the resurrection of the dead. Then Scripture will be fulfilled: "Death has been swallowed up in victory." The Victory is the divine Fire. All that has to do with mortal life will be consumed, so that it can find its consummation in eternal life. . . . That is what the holocaust will be.[117]

* * *

"When the consummation comes, the sacraments will be employed no more." [118] That axiom must be given all the breadth of meaning that Tradition permits. Human mediation, now indispensable and of primary importance, will have no *raison d'être* in the Heavenly Jerusalem; there, everyone will hear God's voice directly and everyone will respond to it spontaneously,[119] just as everyone will see God face to face.[120] And more than this; in this "regime of perfect inwardness" the perfect and glorious knowledge of God will fill the elect "as the covering waters of the sea". The Source of Life will spring up in each one of them: "The whole city shall be one with the temple", and the only temple will be God himself, and its only lamp the

[116] He adds that her mysteries "are but the expression in human language of truths to which the human mind is unequal".

[117] St. Augustine, *In Psalm.* 65, no. 18 (PL 36, 798); cf. *De diversis quaestionibus 83,* q. 69, no. 7.

[118] *The Imitation of Christ*, bk. 4, chap. 2.

[119] See Is 54:13; Jer 31:34.

[120] Rev 22:4.

Lamb.[121] The altar will be an altar of incense and not of holo-
causts,[122] and the whole Church will be one single sacrifice of
praise in Christ.[123] At the Day of the Lord when the *catholica
societas* will be realized in its perfection, everything will be at
once unified, interiorized, and made eternal in God, because
"God [will be] all in all." [124]

We should, therefore, be on our guard against cramping
within concepts that are inadequate to it God's power to trans-
figure his Bride. Far from struggling against belief in something
our imagination cannot picture, we ought to let the daring of
faith sweep us off our feet. Here the mortification of our desires
comes by way of reflecting that they are in themselves inadequate; for "the eye hath not seen, nor ear heard: neither hath it
entered into the heart of man, what things God hath prepared
for them that love him." [125] The fact that we have taken seriously the Epiphany of Palestine or Pentecost should not stop us
from taking the coming Parousia equally seriously.[126] When we
sing in praise of the first great transition:

> Et antiquum documentum
> Novo cedat ritui!

we should be singing it, too, in advance celebration of the
second.

---

[121] Rev 21:22–23: "And I saw no temple herein. For the Lord God Almighty
is the temple thereof and the Lamb. And the city hath no need of the sun, nor
of the moon, to shine in it. For the glory of God hath enlightened it: and the
Lamb is the lamp thereof"; Is 11:9; Jer 31:33–34; Heb 8:10–12; see also Yves
Congar, *Le Christ, Marie et l'Église* (1952), pp. 39–40.

[122] Rev 8:3–5. To put it another way: the cultus of heaven will no longer
include a sacrifice properly so-called. See also Dom Anscar Vonier, *A Key to the
Doctrine of the Eucharist* (French trans., *La Clef de la doctrine eucharistique* [1914],
pp. 271–72).

[123] Jean-Jacques Olier, *Explication des cérémonies de la grand' messe de paroisse*
(1689), p. 142.

[124] 1 Cor 15:28.

[125] 1 Cor 2:9.

[126] Msgr. R. Grosche, *Pilgernde Kirche* (Freiburg, 1938), pp. 41–42.

"The holy Church has two lives: one in time and the other in eternity." [127] We should not separate them, as we should do were we to consider the *Ecclesia deorsum* as a stranger to the *Ecclesia sursum*.[128] We must always keep a firm hold on the continuity of the one Church in and through the diversity of her successive states,[129] just as we see the unity of Christ in his life on earth, his death, and his glorious Resurrection.[130] Prior to the Incarnation, before she had become the Bride, she was the Betrothed only; and that remains true to a certain extent right up until the end of time,[131] in that the mystical marriage of Nazareth and Calvary still needs the last Parousia as a

[127] St. Gregory the Great, *In Ezech.*, bk. 2, no. 10 (PL 76, 1060).

[128] St. Augustine, *Sermo* 181, no. 7 (PL 38, 982–83).

[129] St. Augustine, *De civitate Dei*, bk. 20, chap. 9, no. 1, concerning the Church "qualis nunc est" and "qualis tunc erit" (PL 41, 673); Richard of Saint-Victor, *Sermones centum*, s. 44: "Et licet sanctam Ecclesiam ita secundum status diversos, credulitatis scilicet et visionis, spei et rei, justificationis et beatitudinis, gratiae et gloriae, distinguamus, ut in exsilio sit filia, in regno mater . . . una est tamen uxor Agni, sponsa Christi. . . . Et ipsa quidem sancta Ecclesia est in caelo, partim in mundo. Ibi velut in patria, hic ut in exsilio. Ibi regnans, hic peregrinans. Et celebrantur nuptiae utrobique: hic in fide, ibi in contemplatione; hic in spe, ibi in re" (PL 177, 1016a–b and 1015d). Cf. the unpublished passage by Condren quoted by Jean Galy in his *Le Sacrifice dans l'école française de spiritualité* (1951), p. 220: "There are three churches in the unity of the Church: the Church of the Jews, which has no more than figures and understands in riddles; the Church of the Saints, which sees only the truth and things themselves; and the Church of Christians, which has the truth but with figures." See again p. 244 of the same work: "The Church of Jesus Christ that is on earth and that which is in heaven are not two Churches but one sole Church."

[130] St. Augustine, *Brevis coll. contra Donat.*, chap. 10, no. 20: "Eamdem ipsam unam et sanctam ecclesiam nunc esse aliter, tunc autem aliter . . . , sicut non ideo duo Christi, quia prior mortuus, postea non moriturus" (PL 43, 635). Cf. Lagrange, *Saint Matthieu*, pp. clxi and clxvi.

[131] Haymo, *Expositio in Apocalypsin*, bk. 7: "Sponsa itaque nunc est sancta Ecclesia, per fidem, spem et dilectionem; sed tunc erit uxor quando ad amplexus viri, id est ad contemplationem Dei omnipotentis pervenerit" (PL 117, 1193a). The rabbinic texts make a similar distinction concerning the union of Yahweh with the Jewish community (*Schemoth Rabb.*, 16, 30).

complementary:[132] "That is the wedding of the Lamb, when the Church shall be united with the Lord in the bridal chamber of the heavenly kingdom." [133] All the same, the Church has already received an incomparable betrothal gift, since her Bridegroom-to-be has given her his very blood.[134] We must of course make due distinction between the way and its goal, for a confusing of the two would be dangerous in the extreme;[135] but we should also be aware of the deep-rooted continuity between them and see how the latter is immanent in the former—the Temple of Solomon in the Tabernacle of Moses.[136] The Church at once passes away and remains, as does the universe[137]—and what remains of the universe for eternal life is what she has taken to herself.

Of course it is equally legitimate to say, like St. John Chrysostom, that our business is to pass from this present Church to

---

[132] Cf. E. B. Allo, *L'Apocalypse* (1933), p. 360; Louis Bouyer, *Vie monastique*, p. 160; Wilhelm Koester, S.J., "Agneau et Église dans l'Apocalypse", in *Vom Wort des Lebens* (1951), pp. 152–64.

[133] St. Bede the Venerable, *Explanatio Apocalypsis*, bk. 3 (PL 93, 188c); cf. Methodius, *Banquet*, 11 (p. 135 in Bonwetsch's edition).

[134] St. Augustine, *In Psalm.* 122, no. 5 (PL 37, 1634–65).

[135] S. Tyszkiewicz, S.J., *Sainteté de l'Église christo-conforme*, pp. 98–99.

[136] Cf. Honorius of Autun, *De offendiculo*, chap. 14.

[137] Here we may remember the reflections of St. Gregory the Great in his *Moralia in Job*, bk. 17, chap. 9, no. 11: "Terra et caelum, vel qualiter transeat, vel qualiter maneat, distinguamus. Utraque namque haec per eam quam nunc habent imaginem transeunt, sed tamen per essentiam sine fine subsistunt. *Praeterit figura hujus mundi. . . . Erit caelum novum et terra nova.* Quae quidem non alia condenda sunt, sed haec ipsa renovantur. Caelum igitur et terra, et transit et erit, quia ab ea, quam nunc habet specie, per ignem tergitur, et tamen in sua semper natura servetur" (PL 76, 16c–d). Cf. St. Hilary of Poitiers, *Tractatus super Psalm.* 55, no. 12 (PL 9, 362; cf. 285–86); St. Jerome, *In Amos*, bk. 2, chap. 5 (PL 25, 1043a–b); St. Prosper of Aquitaine, *In Psalm.* 101, vv. 26–28 (PL 51, 283–84); Ambrose Autpert, *In Apocalypsin*, bk. 9 (*Bibliotheca Maxima Patrum*, 13:628 and 630g–h); Haymo, *Expos. in Apoc.*, bk. 7: "Abiit primum caelum et prima terra, hoc est per innovationem immutata sunt, et a pristina figura recesserunt" (PL 117, 1192a); Cardinal Humbert, *Adversus Graecorum calumnias*, chap. 42 (PL 143, 959c–d), etc. Other texts can be found in my *Catholicism*, chap. 4.

that of the blessed, from the city that we build up in this world to the city that is in heaven.[138] This way of speaking is both fitting and natural and, in addition, well calculated to emphasize the radical change we have just been discussing. There is nothing wrong with looking at one truth from two opposite viewpoints; on the contrary, it may be both useful and necessary. After all, St. Paul himself says—comparing our bodies to dwellings—that "if our earthly house of this habitation be dissolved . . . we have . . . a house . . . eternal in heaven";[139] and other inspired texts speak of a "new heaven" and a "new earth".[140] Yet expressions of this type should not be allowed to mislead us; they carry their own corrective. St. Irenaeus makes the appropriate distinction: "Neither the substance nor the essence of creation is to be annihilated"; what will pass away is its "temporal form".[141] "Behold I make all things new"—it is a matter, not of novelty pure and simple, but of something more than that; a total renewal within the limits set by an underlying continuity,[142] in such a way that all aging is henceforward excluded,[143] a "regeneration"[144] and a "restitution of all things".[145] And something that is true of our fleshly bodies and of the whole of creation is no less true—at the appropriate level—of the

---

[138] St. John Chrysostom, *Sermon for the Feast of St. Philogonius* (Roman Breviary, Common of Confessors not Pontiffs, Sixth Lesson).

[139] 2 Cor 5:1.

[140] Rev 21:5; 2 Pet 3:13. Cf. Is 52:6, 66:22; 2 Cor 5:17: "If then any be in Christ a new creature, the old things are passed away. Behold all things are made new." In these texts, the Greek word is not νεός (which means new as to time) but χαινός (which means new as to mode of being). Cf. Behm, art. "χαινός" in Kittel's *Wörterbuch*; see also A. Viard, O.P., "Expectatio creaturae", RB (1952), p. 345, no. 2.

[141] *Adversus haereses*, bk. 5, chap. 36, no. 1 (PG 7, 1221b–c).

[142] Rev 21:1; 2 Pet 3:10 and 13. See also Is 65:17 and 66:22; Mt 19:28. The "new law" is something different from, and much more than, a "law that is a new one"; cf. St. Bonaventure, *Dominica prima Adventus, sermo* 19 (ed. Quaracchi, 9:41–42).

[143] St. Irenaeus, *Adversus haereses*, bk. 5, chap. 36, no. 1 (PG 7, 1222a).

[144] Mt 19:28.

[145] Acts 3:21.

Church, which is a second Creation and Christ's own body. Let me repeat again that there is one single Church, *una eademque Ecclesia*;[146] we shall see in the following chapter the foundation for this assertion. It is one and the same Church that is to see God face to face, bathed in his glory,[147] and yet is our actual Church, living and progressing laboriously in our world, militant and on pilgrimage, humiliated daily in a hundred different ways. In the depths of her being she is already the City of God;[148] through the anticipatory virtue of faith, she has already been "brought . . . into [the] storerooms [of the king]".[149] "Such is her present hope. She will live for eternity; the Holy City now visible on earth is to be snatched up into heaven; as Elijah was carried up in a fiery chariot, so also she will be carried away; glorious bride that she is, she will be raised up higher than Elijah."[150] This Holy Jerusalem is, mysteriously[151] and "in

---

[146] St. Thomas, *Quodl.* 13, q. 13, a. 19 ad 2: "Est alius status Ecclesiae nunc et tunc, non tamen est alia Ecclesia" (he is here speaking of the Church's first two states); Rupert of Deutz, *In Zachariam*, bk. 2: "Una eademque Ecclesia et in praesenti saeculo aedificatur dum gentes convertuntur, et in futuro exstruetur dum omnes resurgemus" (PL 168, 748c).

[147] St. Gregory the Great, *In Ezechielem*, bk. 2, hom. 1, no. 5 (PL 76, 338d); Haymo, *In Apoc.* (PL 117, 1004b–c); Rupert of Deutz, *In Zachariam*, bk. 5 (PL 168, 791d), etc. See also the traditional symbol of the moon—in St. Augustine, for example: *In Psalm.* 71, no. 10 (PL 36, 908); *Epist.* 55, no. 10 (PL 33, 209), etc.

[148] St. Ambrose, *In Psalm.* 118, *expositio, sermo* 15, no. 35 (PL 15, 1422c); St. Augustine, *De civitate Dei*, passim (PL 41, 251, 387, 479, 657, 674), etc. In his *Introduction à l'étude de saint Augustin*, 2d ed. (1943), p. 238, Étienne Gilson says shrewdly: "However surprising it may seem, the Church is not the City of God"; but this is because he is thinking of the Church in terms of her correlation with the State; in the index we find, under the heading "Church", "senses in which she is and is not the City of God". There is thus no real disagreement here. See the same author's *Métamorphoses de la Cité de Dieu* (1952), pp. 73–74.

[149] Song 1:3; Pseudo-Alcuin, *Compendium in Cant.*: "Cellaria regis aeterni gaudia sunt caelestis patriae, in qua nunc Ecclesia introducta est per fidem, introducenda plenius per rem" (PL 100, 643b–c).

[150] St. Ambrose, *In Lucam*, bk. 2, chaps. 87–88 (PL 15, 1585b–c); bk. 7, chap. 91: "Regnum Ecclesiae manebit in aeternum" (col. 1722c).

[151] St. Augustine, *In Psalm.* 148, no. 4 (PL 37, 1940).

hope",[152] the Heavenly Jerusalem; our earthly Mother—*Ecclesia mater super terram*—is already our heavenly Mother, *Mater caelestis*, and the doors she opens to us are already the "heavenly gates".[153] There will be one more changing yet of brass into gold and iron into silver; but in and through this further transmutation it will always be the same City of Yahweh, the Sion of Holy Israel:[154] "This is heavenly and that is heavenly, this is Jerusalem and that is Jerusalem."[155] We ought, indeed, to love that very element in the Church which is transitory—but we ought to love it as the one and only means, the indispensable organ, the providential instrument, and at the same time as "the pledge, the passing image, the promise of the communion to come".[156]

---

[152] Rupert of Deutz, *In Zachariam*, bk. 5: "Hierusalem hic, sicut et in plerisque Scripturarum locis, Ecclesiam significat in hoc mundo peregrinatem, quae quamdiu peregrinatur, etsi nondum re, tamen spe jam est caelestis Hierusalem" (PL 168, 791d).

[153] Origen, *In Levit.*, hom. 12, no. 4 (p. 46 in Baehrens' edition); hom. 11, no. 3 (ibid., p. 43). St. Zeno of Verona, *Paschal Allocutions* 1 and 2: "This heavenly Mother joyfully brings you forth in joy; brings you forth free and sets you in the world freed from the bonds of sin" (trans. H. Chirat in VS [April 1943], p. 327); Tertullian, *De baptismo*, chap. 15: "Una Ecclesia in caelis . . ."; cf. Rev 21:2.

[154] Is 60:14 and 17.

[155] St. Hilary of Poitiers, *In Psalm.* 124, no. 4 (p. 600 in Zingerle's edition).

[156] D.C.L., IK (1949), p. 444; Jacques Dournes, "Sagesse chrétienne", *France-Asie*, vol. 6, no. 54, p. 509; St. Clement of Alexandria, *Stromata*, bk. 4, chap. 8: "The Church of this world is the image of the heavenly Church" (PG 8, 1277b); Origen, *De principiis*, bk. 1, chap. 6, no. 2 (p. 82 in Koetschau's edition); the *Book of Degrees*, sermon 12, "De ministerio Ecclesiae occulto et manifesto": "Let us not despise the visible Church, for she it is who teaches our childhood; neither [let us despise] the Church of the heart, since she it is who strengthens our weakness; and let us live in the hope of that heavenly Church, for it is she who fulfills us all in sanctity" (PS 1, vol. 3, col. 294); Grosche, *Pilgernde Kirche*, pp. 23–76; also St. Thomas, *In Ephes.*, chap. 3, pt. 3: "Ibi est vera Ecclesia quae est mater nostra, et ad quam tendimus, et a qua nostra Ecclesia militans est exemplata." There are further reflections concerning the two complementary aspects here touched upon in *Beiträge zur Kontroverstheologie*, vol. 1, *Die Kirche in Epheserbrief*, by Heinrich Schlier and Victor Warnach (Münster, 1949), pp. 68–69; see also St. Augustine, *De diversis quaestionibus* 83, q. 69, no. 7, and q. 75, no. 1 (PL 40, 77 and 87); St. Cyril of Jerusalem, *Catechesis* 18, chap. 26.

III

THE TWO ASPECTS OF THE ONE CHURCH

WHAT has gone before has already made the point that in the process of reflection on the Church it is important to avoid certain dangerous dissociations. One we have already dealt with; others remain to be indicated.

There have always been visionaries and rebels against the burdensome conditions of Catholic unity who have made a distinction between the visible, temporal, hierarchic Church that exists among us and a sort of invisible Church—wholly "interior", wholly "spiritual", "the luminous community of God dispersed throughout the universe".[1] In such a view, the title "Church of God" could only be applied, properly speaking, to this vast *communio sanctorum*, the theoretical common ground of all Christian communities and all good men. It alone would be divine; the first Church, the "bodily" Church, would be a "human creation"[2] and no more. She is, after all, always and inevitably limited and infected with impurities; over the years she has undergone a fatal division into separated

---

[1] Eckharthausen, in his *The Cloud upon the Sanctuary*.

[2] Luther, *Treatise on the Papacy* (May 1520): "The first [reality] which is essentially, fundamentally, and truly the Church, we name spiritual and interior Christianity. The other, which is a human creation and an exterior phenomenon, we shall call corporeal and exterior Christianity" (quoted by Henry Strohl, *La Pensée de la Réforme* [1951], p. 178). See also *In Psalm.* 16 (1519); *Responsio ad Cathar.* (1521), in *Opera* (1600), 2:166, 356–65. For the ecclesiology of the first Reformers, see Strohl, pp. 173–224; for that of Calvin, see the second volume of Msgr. Journet's *L'Église du Verbe incarné*, pp. 977–87, and Yves Congar, *Vraie et fausse réforme dans l'Église* (1950), pp. 368–538. For the Lutheran doctrine of the mystical body, see Wilhelm Wagner, ZKT (1937; summed up by Journet, pp. 340–57).

groups often in opposition one to the other. And surely the demands of order impose on her an entire human governing apparatus that has nothing at all to do with the sanctity of the Gospels.

Roughly speaking, those are the Lutheran objections, and they are still to be found underlying, to a greater or lesser extent, certain types of "ecumenical" thought outside Catholicism. From the standpoint of a purely natural wisdom, they would be by no means without weight.[3] Yet if you do in fact think in this way—if, like Leibniz, you dissociate "the temple of God" and "the temple of men"[4] or, like Calvin, you maintain that the Church "is the company of the faithful whom God has ordained and elected to eternal life"[5] and that she can "exist without visible appearance"—if you do this, then you are giving a dream the status of an extra-mental entity and trying to separate what God has united. You are not only opening the door to general doctrinal anarchy,[6] as Melanchthon was rapidly obliged to admit and to deplore;[7] you are shutting out all understanding of the "eternal purpose" that God "realized in Christ Jesus our Lord".[8] You are denying all Scripture for the sake of human considerations.

[3] Very cogent reasons can be brought forward at the natural level against each one of the mysteries of faith, when the "ratio" concerned is not "fide illustrata". There is surely something instructive in the fact that it should be Catholicism, which is considered too much of a slave to natural reason, that has to remind Lutheranism of the paradox of faith in this matter of ecclesiology. Doubtless Luther himself would not have gone wrong on this point if he had not found himself bound to justify the schism into which he had allowed himself to be carried away by a new ecclesiology formulated after the event.

[4] Foucher de Careil's edition, 4:339–40.

[5] Catechism of the Church of Geneva.

[6] *Letter to the King of France*: "[Some] always demand a visible and apparent form of Church. . . . We, on the contrary, affirm that the Church can subsist without visible appearance" (*Opera omnia*, vol. 3, Corpus Reformationum [1844], pp. 26–27).

[7] Ibid., 12:365–71. However, Melanchthon sets aside the "regnum pontificium" in favor of an "honesta aristocratia".

[8] Eph chaps. 3 and 2.

It is true that "the social structure of the Christian community, which moreover proclaims the wisdom of its divine Architect, is nevertheless seen to be of an entirely inferior order when compared with the spiritual gifts with which it is ornamented and by which it lives." [9] Yet that structure is nonetheless of divine institution, at any rate in its essentials. When we recite the Credo we profess our belief in the Church; and if we believe that that Church is both a universal and a visible community, then we cannot—without betrayal of our faith—be content to grant that the universal Church is made visible and concrete to the individual by that particular community which is his, regardless of the separation of these communities one from another.[10] This would only be another way of resolving the problem of unity by appeal to an "invisible Church"; it would still be a case of "Platonizing" rather than listening to Christ.[11] "From the very morrow of Christ's death" a Church was in existence and living, just as Christ had constituted her;[12] the Church as she is should be in verifiable continuity with the community of the first disciples, which was in turn, and from the beginning, a clearly defined group, social in character, organized, and having its heads, its rites, and—soon—its legislation. She should be united to the "root of Christian society" [13] by a

[9] Encyclical *Mystici corporis Christi*.

[10] After having proclaimed, in *Dogmatics in Outline* (pp. 139–42 of the French ed.), "The apostolic confession of faith does not mean to speak of an invisible society but of a fundamentally visible assembly" and also: "*Credo Ecclesiam* means: I believe that the community to which I belong is the one, holy, universal Church", Karl Barth ends by saying, "I testify in faith that the concrete community to which I belong . . . is intended to make visible, here, in the form proper to it, the one, holy, and universal Church"; which is, obviously, no longer the same thing. Still another formula betrays his predicament: "There are not multiple Churches, but one Church, this *concrete* Church which should be able to recognize itself in all the others" (p. 140).

[11] Karl Barth, "L'Église et les Églises", trans. Moobs, OA, 3:141.

[12] L. de Grandmaison, *Jésus-Christ*, 15th ed. (1931), 1:407–10.

[13] St. Augustine, *Epist.* 232, no. 3: "Videtis certe multos praecisos a radice christianae societatis, quae per Sedes Apostolorum et successiones episcoporum certa per orbem propagatione diffunditur" (PL 33, 1028); *Contra*

real and uninterrupted succession; the need for that cannot be got rid of by treating it as something "profane", "mechanistic", or "legalistic". And if anyone can extract a clear-cut meaning from the term "apostolicity of the spirit"—as opposed to any idea of historic succession—he is welcome to do so.[14] The matter has, in any case, never been viewed thus, from the very first. And it seems preferable by far to believe St. Irenaeus when he depicts the Apostles as entrusting to bishops the Churches that were entrusted to themselves.[15] If the Church today is not the apostolic Church, she is not really carrying on Christ's mission and is not his Church.[16]

Besides, "if there is only one soul, there can only be one body."[17] Many divided bodies cannot constitute one single Church. The supposition that there could be several independent Christian societies with a "spiritual unity" is "totally alien to the thought of St. Paul"[18] and contrary to the whole of the history of primitive Christianity. If the Church is real, she must be an organism that we can in some sense "see and touch",[19] just as we could have seen and touched the God-Man during

---

Faustum, bk. 11, chap. 2 (PL 42, 246); bk. 28, chap. 2 (PL 42, 486), etc. See also Dom T. Belpaire, O.S.B., "Autonomie et unité ecclésiologique", IK (1949), p. 58.

[14] See Karl Barth, *Dogmatique*, French trans. (1953): 99–100.

[15] *Adversus haereses*, bk. 5, chap. 20, no. 1: "Episcopi, quibus Apostoli tradiderunt ecclesias" (PG 7, 1177a), etc.

[16] On the apostolic succession, see Batiffol, *L'Église naissante et le catholicisme*; Braun, *Problème de l'Église*, pp. 171–209; Damien Van den Eynde, *Les Normes de l'enseignement chrétien* (1933), pp. 67–76.

[17] Paschal Rapine, *Le Christianisme fervent* (1671), vol. 1, *La Face de l'Église universelle*, p. 45.

[18] Armitage Robinson, *Ephesians*, 2d ed., p. 93; Joseph Huby, *Saint Paul: Épîtres de la captivité*, p. 196.

[19] Leo XIII, encyclical *Satis cognitum*, quoted in the encyclical *Mystici corporis Christi*, with the comment: "It is therefore an aberration from divine truth to represent the Church as something intangible and invisible, as a mere 'pneumatic' entity joining together by an invisible link a number of communities of Christians in spite of their difference in faith." See also Pius XI, encyclical *Mortalium animos* (1928).

his life on earth. Christ's Bride is unique, and it is one Church "which we see, we hear, which we believe, which teaches, which gives judgment and which baptizes".[20] Everything points to it. To quote Fr. Louis Bouyer's blunt words (based on a formula of St. Ignatius of Antioch), "an invisible Church is the same thing as no Church at all"; without the hierarchy, which is her point of crystallization, her organizer, and her guide, "there can be no talk of the Church." And if a man refuses to follow the paradoxical logic of the Incarnation on this point, it is hard to see how he can follow it in the matter of the sacramental economy. Indeed, he will surely run the risk of abandoning it even in what concerns the very Person of Christ himself.[21]

Granted, on the other hand, that the Church shows in her visible aspect "evident signs of the condition of our human weakness", this should not be attributed to her juridical constitution, "but rather to that tragic leaning toward evil on the part of the individual which her divine Founder suffered from even in the most highly placed members of his Mystical Body, with the aim of testing his sheep and causing the merits of Christian faith to grow in all".[22] In her structure the Church shows not only a mixture of visible and invisible but also a mixture of the divine and the human within the visible alone: "Christ has wrought our salvation, inasmuch as he was God and man . . . therefore the ministers of Christ too should be men, and have some participation in his divinity by means of a special spiritual power." [23] I must emphasize once again that this law constitutes a fundamental aspect of the mystery of the Church. Indeed, we do not really pay enough attention to its importance for us. St. Paul, in his Epistle to the Hebrews, exhorts us to be mindful of our dead leaders, through whom the word of God was passed

---

[20] Fénelon, *Lettres sur l'autorité de l'Église*, 1 and 5, 3.

[21] Louis Bouyer, *Dieu Vivant*, 2:140; St. Ignatius of Antioch, *Epistle to the Trallians*, 3.1 (p. 112 in Camelot's edition). Cf. Vladimir Soloviev, *La Russie et l'Église universelle*, 3d ed., pp. xxv and xxix.

[22] Encyclical *Mystici corpori Christi*.

[23] St. Thomas Aquinas, *Summa contra gentiles*, bk. 4, chap. 74.

on to us, and it is with good reason that he adds immediately:
"Jesus Christ yesterday and today; and the same for ever." [24] It
is by way of men who teach us and guide us with a divine
authority that we are made sure of that most precious thing,
unimpairable unity in faith in Christ and participation in his
life. But this same law, by way of evening the score, has, for
those who do not try to evade it by a kind of indifference, a
side often painful enough. History rubs in the obvious truth
that there are able pastors and incompetent ones, good pastors
and bad.[25] Whether he be a member of the hierarchy or not, a
zealous Catholic can still be no more than a mediocre Christian; that use of those terms may be debatable, yet it is forced
on us by an experience only too common. The very thing that
makes sanctity possible is also what opens the way to fakes of
the most horrible kind. It is the fate of men to make one
another suffer even while they help one another—that is,
whenever they are united; and all the more so when they are
united by a bond as deeply rooted as this. All kinds of human
malice, both the self-aware and the self-deceiving, draw from it
that much greater a degree of repulsiveness. There are some
milieux in the Church that furnish a particularly favorable
breeding ground for calumny, and once it has taken root there,
it feeds not only on the worst but also on the best. Even a
sincere and mutual desire for the good—even for the same
good—does not prevent tragic clashes; it can even provoke
them, as can be seen from the lives of the saints. And the
strangest and deepest of hurts, without parallel in purely human experience, become possible when, within this unique
form of association, some men possess the awe-inspiring power
of exercising pressure upon others at that most deeply personal
point of linkage where soul and intellect divide; when there

[24] Heb 13:7–8.

[25] Cf. the explanations given by St. Augustine, *Epist.* 208, nos. 2–5 (PL 33,
950–53), and St. John Chrysostom (PG 56, 126; 61, 180), quoted by Journet in
The Church of the Word Incarnate, 1:95–98; St. Peter Damian, *Epist.*, bk. 1, ep. 20
(PG 144, 245a).

even exists a power so strong and deep-reaching that merely to submit to it, even with patience, is simply not enough—that we have to consent personally and willingly to what would be a violation at the hands of any other power. For this is precisely the situation into which Catholic obedience, in its most common form, takes us.

Far from being something out-of-the-way, this sort of suffering is normal. In ordinary circumstances (I am of course thinking here of Christians anxious to live the Church's life properly), it is certainly more frequent in occurrence than that which is occasioned by men outside the Church, even though it may not always take its severest form. In any case, its inevitably paradoxical character makes it harder to accept willingly, and it inflicts its pain on us at a far deeper level of our being. Yet it is at the same time a source of joy. By humbling us "under the mighty hand of God", it prepares us for the "time of visitation";[26] and it may, too, be the occasion of duties so important and so delicate that they can be recognized only through many a process of trial and error.[27] It may be something that rends; yet that very rending is turned to account by the action of the Holy Spirit in the service of a unity better realized and better loved. And finally, it is surely indispensable if we are to enter a little deeper into understanding the mystery of the Church than our speculation and our talking will ever take us.

* * *

We may avoid making a fatal dissociation of the visible and the invisible (as schism or spiritual anarchy so often do); we may be

[26] 1 Pet 5:6.

[27] The point is that, where Catholic obedience is in question, we are concerned with something quite different from an instruction or word of command, quite different from military uniformity or social conformity. "The conformist looks at things—even things of the spirit—from the outside. The obedient soul sees things—even things of the letter—from the inside" (de Lubac, *Paradoxes of Faith*, trans. P. Simon et al. [San Francisco, 1987], p. 28–29). This is all the more so in the case under consideration, where the "things of the spirit" are always, in some sense at least, those of the Holy Spirit.

far from adopting the blurred concept of "evangelical catholic-ity" [28] put forward by ecumenicism of the liberal type; we may be equally disinclined to set in mutual opposition charismata and the hierarchy, or spirit and authority. We may do all this, and yet still sometimes get onto the slippery slope—if we are not care-ful—via a dangerous distinction between the "visible Church" and the "Mystical Body" of Christ. Some thinkers have even found themselves led into this situation, without actually so intending, through the undisciplined state of their theological reflection.

On the one hand, the Church would indeed seem to have defined herself adequately, or at least to have described herself adequately, without habitual recourse to the idea of the Mysti-cal Body,[29] for she has so stated and detailed in a series of solemn texts both her divine institution and several of the essential characteristics of her external structure (though even this task was not completed in her Councils).[30] Even the major

[28] In 1911, Nathan Söderblom wrote that the Roman Church "has relegated herself to the status of a sect and placed herself outside evangelical catholicity"; quoted by J. G. H. Hoffmann in *Nathan Söderblom: Prophète de l'oecuménisme* (1948), p. 152.

[29] The first document that describes the Church as the Mystical Body would appear to be the bull *Unam Sanctam* of Boniface VIII. But in a number of doctrinal and official texts of later date the "body of the Church" and the Church's unity are mentioned more often than the "body" or "mystical body" of Christ.

[30] On the First Vatican Council, see the historical summary given by Dom Lambert Beauduin, O.S.B., "L'Unité de l'Église et le Concile du Vatican", *Église et unité*, in the series Catholicité (Lille, 1948), pp. 13–16. A schema *De Ecclesia Christi* had been prepared in advance by theologians gathered from all over the world. This projected schema "was printed and distributed to the Fathers of the Council. As is known, for lack of time the Council was only able to discuss one chapter—the eleventh, on the Primacy of the Roman Pontiff . . . out of the fifteen that made up the schema. Thus, the constitution *De Ecclesia Christi* is far from giving the whole of the Church's doctrine on her own constitution. As a crowning indignity, the general title of the schema was preserved—'Constitutio dogmatica prima de Ecclesia'—which title cov-ered the whole fifteen chapters. The addition 'prima' easily passed un-noticed" (pp. 20 and 22). Msgr. Batiffol wrote: "There is no doubt that the

treatises *De Ecclesia* that were current in the past usually kept to that aspect of the subject, being, as they were, concerned chiefly to put the grounds of belief and the prerogatives of the Catholic hierarchy on a solid foundation, and then to defend their rights against denial or the encroachments of secular society. Even doctrinally, the viewpoint was throughout apologetic rather than mystical: the authors of these works were more concerned with manning and strengthening the walls of the Heavenly Jerusalem than with showing the faithful the way to its heart.[31] As far as the essentials were concerned, most of them stuck to the route mapped out in the seventeenth century by St. Robert Bellarmine in his famous *Controversies* and to the scholastic tradition created in the eighteenth by the first manuals.[32] And the same is of course true, to an even greater degree, of the authors of catechisms and treatises on pastoral theology.

Yet a great traditional path was reopened at the beginning of the last century by Johann Adam Möhler—the Möhler of not only *Die Einheit in der Kirche* but also the *Symbolik*. Möhler drew most of his inspiration from the Fathers, though he also owed

---

setting forth of the universal and immediate jurisdiction of the Pope gains from being completed by the setting out of the divine rights of the episcopate" (*Réponse au mémorandum du Dr. Gore* [Malines, May 1925]), quoted in Jacques Bivort de la Saudée, *Anglicans et Catholiques* (1949), vol. 2, *Documents*, p. 248.

[31] In the preface to his work *De l'Église et de sa divine constitution* (1885), Dom Gréa thus described the numerous modern treatises: "The Doctors raised up by God to defend the walls of Jerusalem . . . set themselves as their principal aim the establishment of the Church's authority as against rationalism. They affirmed her essential notes, and they set out in opposition to the errors given rise to by Protestantism and Gallicanism an exact knowledge of the powers which rule her, the elements which go to make her up, and the principles of her government."

[32] Cf. the treatises of Claude Regnier (*De Ecclesia*, 2 vols. [1789]) or L. Bailly (*Tractatus de Ecclesia Christi*, 2 vols. [1783]), 1:8: "Ecclesia, quae militans appellatur, et de qua agitur in hoc tractatu, est totum constans anima et corpore, ut notat Bellarminus. Anima Ecclesiae sunt ipsa dona Spiritus sancti. . . . [C]orpus Ecclesiae nihil aliud est, quam externa et vera Christi religionis professio."

something to Fénelon.[33] He rapidly obtained a following among the Jesuits of the Roman College, and Perrone, who had defended him in 1841,[34] introduced him to the attention of his students. In 1853–1854 Carlo Passaglia gave the "mystical body" a central place in his treatise *De Ecclesia Christi*, a massive and ponderous work somewhat overloaded with an insufficiently digested patristic learning. Clement Schrader, who was for a time his close collaborator,[35] and Jean-Baptiste Franzelin, who was the greatest of his disciples,[36] followed in his steps; and one of their pupils, Matthias Joseph Scheeben, a "man of genius"[37] who, like Möhler, died too young to give all that he had in him, produced in his work *Die Mysterien des Christentums* (1885) a deep-reaching exposition of the mystery of the Church as Christ's body.[38] Later on his book was to be criticized as having "an insufficient theological clarification of the relation between the mystery of the Body of the Church and her hierarchic structure",[39] but nonetheless this work, taken as a whole, stood for a tendency in the right direction. Yet it must be admitted that the lead was not very much followed. Confronted with the *schema* (doubtless originally drafted by Schrader), whose first chapter was entitled "Ecclesia est Corpus Christi Mysticum", a certain number of the Fathers of the First Vatican Council were astonished by the phrase, and several of them declared themselves

[33] Stephan Loesch, *Möhler*, 1:223–24, 290; Pierre Chaillet, *L'Église est une*, pp. 219–20.

[34] *Praelectiones theologicae*, 2:32–33.

[35] *Theses theologicae*, series 7 (1869).

[36] *De Ecclesia Christi* (1887; posthumous work, unfinished). Cf. Georges Courtade, S.J., "J. B. Franzelin, les formules que le Magistère de l'Église lui a empruntées", in *Mélanges Jules Lebreton*, vol. 2 (RSR 90 [1952]): 323–25. It was Perrone who advised Franzelin to study Möhler; see E. Hocedez, S.J., *Histoire de la théologie au XIXe siècle* (1952), 2:358.

[37] Pius XI, addressing the pupils of the German College, March 9, 1935 (reported in *L'Osservatore Romano*, March 11).

[38] See Dom Augustine Kerkvoorde, O.S.B., "La Théologie du Corps mystique au XIXe siècle", NRT 67 (1945): 415–30.

[39] See Dom C. Lialine, O.S.B., "Une Étape en ecclésiologie", IK 19 (1946): 138.

opposed to it. Some, recalling the abuse made of it by the Jansenists at the Synod of Pistoia,[40] even went so far as to fear that it would lend itself to heresy.[41]

For a time immediately after the Council the situation remained the same. In 1873 the Sulpician Brugère, having described the Church *ab extra*, did indeed say that the next thing to be done was to consider her "from within and in her relation to Christ";[42] but out of the 434 pages of his treatise, half a page seemed sufficient to him for outlining this new program. The later efforts of Dom Gréa (1885) and certain others did not have any better success to begin with than had those of Scheeben; and it was the same with the posthumous publication of Franzelin's lectures in 1887. At the beginning of the present century the Thomist movement, handicapped by a limited sense of Tradition and a too fragmentary knowledge of St. Thomas' work itself, was hardly likely to be favorable to the tendency,[43] and the reminders of Leo XIII in 1896 (in the encyclical *Satis cognitum*) and in 1897 (in the encyclical *Divinum illud*) received somewhat distracted attention. Admittedly, the *Corpus Christi mysticum* was no more totally without mention in the new treatises than it had been in the old ones, or in those of Bellarmine himself.[44] But normally it was the object of passing mention only, and the idea did not get its full emphasis. It played no fundamental part in the structure of the works concerned; sometimes it figured therein merely as corollary, or in an appendix,[45]

[40] See Pius VI, bull *Auctorem fidei*, prop. 25.

[41] The reason was that they more or less shared the idea that the "mystical body" comprises only members who are in a state of grace.

[42] "Jam ad altiorem quamdam concipere est Ecclesiae notionem, illam, scilicet considerando jam non ab extra et relate ad genus humanum, sicut antea fecimus, sed ab intra et relate ad Christum, quemadmodum nos docuerunt sancti Dei homines atque imprimis Sanctus Paulus."

[43] See Kerkvoorde, pp. 415–30.

[44] On the "mystical body" in Bellarmine, see S. Tromp, S.J., "Bellarmini duplex conceptus corporis mystici", GR (1942), pp. 279–90.

[45] As in the instances of A. Straub, *De Ecclesia Christi* (1912), 2 vols. Cf. R. M. Schultes, O.P., *De Ecclesia catholica* (1926), pp. 754–55, etc.

or was swamped in the enumeration of the "figures" of the Church contained in Scripture. Contrary to the desire of the theologians concerned in the *schema* "De Ecclesia" of 1870,[46] recourse was not had to it when there was question of determining "the Church's own innermost nature".[47] In more than one instance it may have been purely a question of presentation; but the general tendency was to emphasize the metaphorical character of the expression, to the point of watering down the realism of the doctrine it contained. The biblical image was viewed as fitted only to put across an idea that remained that of a society undoubtedly supernatural in its origin and end, and with equally supernatural means at its disposal, but without mystical unity in the true sense of the words. It seems as if we must diagnose as a symptom of this state of mind—in some cases at least—the open refusal (in the teeth of a solid tradition, both patristic and Thomist) to grant that the Holy Spirit was himself the Soul of this Body.[48] Even in 1934 Fr. de la Taille wrote: "However familiar this view [of the Church as Christ's body] was to the Fathers, and however central its place in St. Thomas, it is not necessary that it should hold the same place in the scholastic theology of today." [49] One may well feel that there had been a decisive breakdown in the plan that Schrader had in mind when he closed one of the paragraphs of his dissertation on the

[46] Cf. Mansi, vol. 51, col. 553.

[47] Cf. L. Billot, S.J., *Tractatus de Ecclesia Christi*, 1:49–50.

[48] As, for example, F. M. de Brouwer, *Tractatus de Ecclesia Christi* (1882), pp. 202–3, or G. Wilmers, *De Christi Ecclesia* (1898), p. 88. The Fathers spoke of the Holy Spirit "dum causa videlicet ponitur pro effectu", etc.; Cardinal Gasparri, *Catholic Catechism*, p. 99: "By the 'soul of the Church' is meant the invisible principle of the spiritual and supernatural life of the Church—namely, the ever-present assistance of the Holy Ghost, the principle of authority, inward obedience to rule, habitual grace and the infused virtues." There is a good critical appraisal and summing up of the whole matter (following on the lines indicated by M. d'Herbigny) in T. Zapelena, *De Ecclesia Christi* (1940), 2:125–36. Since then, the encyclical *Mystici corporis Christi* has, of course, ratified the traditional doctrine; see the commentary in L. Malevez's "L'Encyclique *Mystici corporis*", NRT (1945), pp. 394–405.

[49] Preface to J. Anger's *La Doctrine du corps mystique de Jésus-Christ*, 5th ed., p. 8.

Mystical Body of Christ with this exhortation: "Such is the sublime character of the Church, and it should be presented to the
minds of the faithful so that it may be deeply imprinted there; it
cannot be overemphasized." [50] To more than one theologian of
yesterday, as to more than one of the Vatican Fathers,[51] such a
conception would have appeared as apt to encourage a dangerous "imaginative exuberance" from which the hard-edgedness
of doctrine might well suffer; it was repellent as something "abstract and mystical".[52]

Yet more or less at the same time a considerable effort was
being made to give greater depth to the treatise *De gratia* by
giving greater prominence in it to the grace termed "habitual"
and freeing it from the over-individualistic viewpoint that had
for a long time been customary. A whole body of spiritual
writing expounded and developed the results of this effort in
their application to the Christian life; and thus theologians
were led to bring into the foreground—often, admitted, somewhat confusedly—the idea of a single Life, a single organism of
grace, and a communion of all with all in Christ. To this end
Tradition, both Greek and Latin, offered a wealth of material
for development, particularly in its commentaries on the
Pauline concept of the "body of Christ"; but very often these
commentaries contained no explicit reference at all to the visible Church.[53] The introduction of the phrase "mystical body",
whose precise significance was not always clearly grasped, contributed in many cases to a direction of attention toward the
spiritual and interior character of the great mystery expounded

---

[50] *Acta et decreta sacrorum conciliorum recentiorum, collectio lacensis* (1890), vol. 8,
col. 567; cf. cols. 301–2.

[51] For example, Msgr. Ramadie, bishop of Perpignan (ed. Mansi, vol. 51, col.
741).

[52] It has even been supposed that the theology of the "mystical body" had been
disavowed by the Council: see Lialine, "Une Étape en ecclésiologie", pp. 148–49.

[53] As early as with the Fathers (notably in a whole section of the work of St.
Augustine, but also in the cases of SS. Athanasius and Cyril), a number of texts
concerning the *Corpus Christi* have no explicit reference to the visible structure
of the Church.

by St. Paul,[54] and this being so, it is not surprising that it did not always occur to people to put together these two great doctrinal themes, which were studied in two separate treatises. When they did think of it, they were not always very clear as to how it was to be done. On the one side, there was "juridicalism", and, on the other, "mysticism"; the ecclesiological synthesis was sought for but not found.

In addition to this, some theologians, seriously preoccupied by the problem of the salvation of those outside the faith, believed that a solution could be found in this direction. They proposed to make use of the traditional distinction between the "body" and "soul" of the Church—but in a way that was imprudent and sometimes inaccurate and that even went so far as to separate them; or, again, to distinguish between the "juridical Church" and the "Church of charity",[55] or between the *Geistkirche* and the *Leibkirche*, or the "hierarchic society" and the "community of grace", or again (it all comes to the same thing), the visible reality of the institutional Church and that of the Mystical Body, which, in its "secret" mode of being, possessed a greater extension. The latter was sometimes placed, in one way or another, in a relation of dependence on, or even of "mystical identity" with, the first. Distinctions of this kind were not, of course, put forward as absolute; they were not intended as dissociations, and the mental attitude that lay behind them had nothing whatsoever in common with that

[54] Émile Mersch, *La Théologie du corps mystique* (Paris, 1944), 2:8: The idea of the mystical body in Western tradition "developed particularly around a question of practical order, the question of grace". Lialine, p. 134: "It may be said that the visible elements in the notion of the Body of Christ have receded in order to give an ever greater place to the invisible elements—the union of men with Jesus Christ either by sanctifying grace or by the grace of predestination."

[55] Cf. the allocution of Pius XII to Roman seminarians, June 24, 1939: "The distinction between the juridical Church and the Church of charity is an erroneous one. Things are not thus; rather, this juridically founded Church, whose head is the Sovereign Pontiff, is also the Church of Christ, the Church of charity and the universal family of Christians." The phrases "historical Church" and "mystical Church" have also been used.

which had set an invisible Church in opposition to the ecclesiastical society, as the divine is opposed to the human. The most
important among them had their place in the recent past in
treatises of the most widely accepted authority[56] and appeared,
even with considerable emphasis, in some of our catechisms.[57]
But they were put forward in consequence of a genuine problem, which theologians are obliged neither to dodge nor to
resolve in a merely negative fashion; and in point of fact the
solution aimed at in them was, more often than not, fundamentally right—even the only right one; sometimes minor
corrections only in the wording were sufficient to make them
acceptable, without any essentials being changed. Yet for all
that, they were still ill-adapted. Their terminology was not
sufficiently traditional, and the viewpoint that dominated them
was too subjective;[58] they were not sufficiently proof against
overemphasis both in interpretation and in use. Even considered from the most favorable standpoint, they occasioned a
danger of devitalizing—if no worse—the primary truth that St.
Paul so forcibly expressed in words as simple as they are mysterious—"his body, which is the Church".[59] And one of the

---

[56] Thus Schultes, De Ecclesia Catholica (1926), p. 98. Certain reservations are
made on this point by J. de Guibert, S.J., De Christi Ecclesia, 2d ed., p. 133.

[57] See the Catechism prescribed for use in the dioceses of France, nos. 166
and 174–78. Referring to these texts, M. Pierre Michalon, P.S.S., writes: "One
gets the impression that this distinction between the "body" and the "soul" of
the Church, far from clarifying the problem, raises several further problems"
("L'Étendue de l'Église", in L'Église et unité [1948], pp. 95–97). See also Journet,
The Church of the Word Incarnate, 1:72–73. The preparatory commission of
dogma for the [First] Vatican Council set aside the expression "utpote scolas-
ticam et novam omnino in modo loquendi conciliorum" (ed. Mansi, 49:624–
25). Guillaume Postel made use of a better terminology (I am not discussing his
doctrine) when he wrote, in his Absconditorum clavis, chap. 11, no. 4: "There is
no doubt that the body of the Church should possess many more members
hidden from our eyes than she does visible members who reveal themselves by
exterior worship."

[58] I have drawn attention to this in several places in my Catholicism, especially
in chap. 7.

[59] Col 1:24; cf. Eph 1:22.

consequences of this truth is that all salvation, without exception and whatever the appearances may be, comes by way of the Church.[60]

It was this fundamental truth to which the minds of Christians were recalled in 1943 by the encyclical *Mystici corporis Christi*, the publication of which had been prepared for by a whole series of valuable works[61] appearing in ever-increasing numbers over the previous fifteen years or so.

> The doctrine of the Mystical Body of Christ, which is the Church, a doctrine received originally from the lips of the Redeemer himself, and making manifest the inestimable boon of our most intimate union with so august a Head, has a surpassing splendor which commends it to the meditation of all who are moved by the divine Spirit, and with the light which it sheds upon their minds, is a powerful stimulus to the salutary conduct which it enjoins.[62]

This is therefore the doctrine and this the primary truth which should be the key point of theological reflection on the Church of Christ.[63]

---

[60] St. Ambrose, *In Psalm.* 39, no. 11: "Sola Ecclesiae gratia, qua redimimur" (PL 14, 1061b), etc.

[61] Among them those of Michel d'Herbigny, S.J., *Theologica de Ecclesia*, 2d ed. (1920); followed by H. Dieckmann, 1925; Msgr. F. Grivec, *De corpore Christi mystico quaestiones methodicae* and *Controversia de corpore Christi mystico*, in *Acta Academiae Vilebradensis* (1937, 1941); also Karl Adam, Fr. Erich Przywara, S.J., and Fr. Sebastian Tromp, S.J.

[62] From the opening of the encyclical. The same teaching is recalled, with some criticism of those who do not fully conform their thought and their terminology to it, in the encyclical *Humani generis* of August 12, 1950: "That the Mystical Body of Christ and the Catholic Church in communion with Rome are one and the same thing is a doctrine based on revealed truth and, as such, was set forth by us in an encyclical a few years back; some imagine, nevertheless, that they are not bound to hold it."

[63] The encyclical *Mystici corporis Christi* both rounds off the theological movement stemming from the reaction against the Reformation and also—by bringing us back to the Pauline conception taken at its broadest—can help us to make better use henceforth (within the framework of the present situation) of the ecclesiological riches of patristic and medieval Tradition. See Origen,

There are, however, some who, without in any way contesting this, and without wishing to deviate in any way from an accurate theology, still continue to distinguish from the supernatural reality of the Catholic Church what they call her "sociological reality" or "sociological situation".[64] They are for the most part laity, observers of the contemporary scene and anxious for social reform. The distinction is entirely sound in theory and sometimes extremely useful in practice; the only criticism to be levelled against those who make it is that sometimes, perhaps, they display an orthodoxy so complete and so easy of decision that it looks rather like indifference toward everything in the Church that does not fall under the aspect of their "sociology". There *is* a way of "submitting to dogma", in principle and in advance, which is little more than a refusal to take any interest in its content—that is, in revealed truth. Those who behave thus are "too indifferent concerning religion to want to give themselves the trouble" of forming any idea of what it teaches; for them, the essence of faith becomes reduced to "not daring to contradict certain incomprehensible mysteries, a certain vague submission with regard to which costs nothing". Where matters of this sort are concerned they place their reliance once for all on "those who claim to know what is what"[65] and announce that they "set respectfully on one side the deposit of dogmatic truths, and would not dream of discussing them". As the last phrase shows clearly enough,

Contra Celsum, bk. 6, no. 48, "Dicimus ex divinis Scripturis, totam Dei Ecclesiam esse Christi corpus, a Dei Filio animatum; membra autem illius corporis, ut totius, eos esse omnes qui credunt."

[64] Fr. Vivier, S.M., has published in IK 21 (1948): 274–84, an interesting study on the sources of the sociological body of the Church. This body he likens to the *sacramentum tantum* of Scholasticism and describes as "the sociological formation which appeared in the Mediterranean basin two thousand years ago". Formal distinctions of this kind are illuminating from the methodological standpoint, provided they are not allowed to petrify.

[65] Fénelon, *Mandement pour le Jubilé de l'année sainte* (1701); *Lettre à l'évêque d'Arras sur la lecture de l'Écriture sainte en langue vulgaire* (1707); François d'Argentan, *Grandeurs de Dieu* (1838), 1:157–58.

this attitude at the practical level tends, by its own gravitational pull, toward that doctrinal error which relegates all the mysteries of the faith to a region that has no connection with the intellect—a sort of exile in which they have no chance to be—as they ought to be—the light of our living.[66] However this may be, the "sociology" in question does of course find a vast and constantly changing field of study in the intensely complex and sensitive web of ecclesiastical affairs—the activities of churchmen, the customs and behavior patterns of the various Catholic milieux—in a word, in everything that Dom Gréa called "the varied clothing of accidentals and institutions".[67] Just as the Word, in his Incarnation, submitted a whole part of himself to the scrutiny of the most secular history imaginable (from the viewpoint of method), so also his Church offers herself to the analysis of sociology.

But this sociology, not content with analysis, readily assumes the critical role. There is nothing unsound about that, in principle; sometimes, nothing can be more healthy. But the union between the human and the divine is a very subtle one; so delicate that if we push ahead with our critique without due caution, we very often run grave risk of behaving like the son who insults his mother. If we talk of a "sociological Church", we only accentuate a dichotomy already suspect, without avoiding anything unpleasant in so doing. We must remember that the human element itself, as something essential to the structure and life of the Church as Christ willed her to be, is divine in its foundation; or, as one theologian has put it in a formula that is not particularly neat but has the advantage of including the disputed word—there is "a sociological incarnation of the Body of Christ" that is a part of its essence.[68] If we

[66] This is the noetic aspect of that error which goes as far as separating the natural and the supernatural orders; carried to its limits, it would be that very *incrédulité soumise* which Voltaire and Renouvier made the object of their mockery (*Second Essai de critique générale*, 2d ed., 3:154).

[67] *De l'Église et de sa divine constitution*, pp. 316–17.

[68] Fr. George Tavard, A.A., "Sens de l'Unité", *La Croix* (January 15, 1952).

lose sight of this, we shall introduce a fatal dissociation, through
a bias that is this time not theological but scientific.

* * *

There, then, is the Church—human and divine at once even in
her visibility, "without division and without confusion", just
like Christ himself, whose body she mystically is.[69] It is not
even necessary to say, as Schrader did,[70] that she has a visible
and social aspect inasmuch as she is a hierarchical society, and a
mystical aspect inasmuch as she is the body of Christ. We must
look for the multiple elements of which she is composed and
the many aspects under which she may be considered, in the
interior of the Church herself considered in her unimpairable
unity—that is, in the interior of the Mystical Body. For her
unity is complex and her riches are varied—*circumdata varietate*.
Such an undertaking should really end up as a complete treatise
on the Church; other such treatises have taken it for granted,
either in whole or in part. Here I shall attempt no more than to
draw attention to what seems to me a fundamental duality of
aspect; this once seen, many other distinctions are clarified and
rectified, many apparent anomalies disappear, and many traditional texts, which at first seem contradictory, fall into harmony. It is to be read in the very word "Church", "a word full
of mysteries".[71]

The word "Church" can in fact be understood in either an
active or a passive sense. When we are concerned with that
great "assembly" which is the Catholic Church, we can consider her under two aspects. We can think of the voice that

[69] In ecclesiology as in Christology, we may distinguish two opposite errors,
"Monophysite" and "Nestorian", respectively. The encyclical *Mystici corporis Christi* condemns certain forms of both. The first kind is concerned
particularly with our union with Christ within the heart of the Church; the
second kind attacks the very idea of the Church. But see also below, p. 104,
n. 79.

[70] *Theses theologicae*, pp. 1–3: "Pars prior, de Ecclesia ut corpore Christi
mystico"; "Pars secunda, de Ecclesia Christi ut societate visibili".

[71] *Roman Catechism*, pt. 1, chap. 10, no. 4.

calls her together, or the power that assembles, together with all the organs and all the "instruments" that are at its disposal for that purpose;[72] or again, we can consider the assembly once constituted—the totality of those thus assembled, with all their different characteristics. History shows us in fact that from the beginning both these approaches were made and that both alike were considered essential. Their duality materializes in the twofold Latin translation of the Greek ἐκκλησία: *convocatio* and *congregatio*. St. Cyril of Jerusalem, for example, says: "The Church is thus properly so called because she calls together all men and unites them in one single whole";[73] Theodore of Mopsuestia sees in the Church "the whole assembly of the faithful who serve God in orthodox fashion";[74] while St. Ambrose views her as the multitude "gathered in from the pagan peoples",[75] and St. Augustine describes the Churches that cover the earth as "the assembly of the peoples and nations".[76] "What is the Church," said Hugh of Saint-Victor, "but the multitude of the faithful, the totality of Christians?"[77] Both definitions appear in the writings of St. Isidore of

---

[72] Putting it this way does not, of course, mean that I have forgotten the fact that the voice that calls together, the power that assembles, is in the first place the Word of God itself (see chap. 6, below). But it effects its purpose through the voice of the Apostles and their successors, as also through those of the preachers and pastors whom the Church has raised up for herself. See L. Cerfaux, *Théologie de l'Église*, p. 76, on the vocabulary of the Septuagint.

[73] *Catechesis* 18, chap. 24 (PG 33, 1044b).

[74] *Tenth Catechetical Homily*, no. 16 (pp. 269 and 271 in the edition of Tonneau and Devreesse).

[75] *In Lucam*, bk. 2, chap. 86: "Ecclesia, quae de gentilibus populis congregata est" (PL 15, 1584c); bk. 3, chap. 32 (1602c); *De Tobia*, chap. 22, no. 86 (PL 14, 791b); St. Jerome, *In Ephes.*: "Ecclesia de cunctis credentibus congregatur" (PL 26, 534c); St. Hilary of Poitiers, *In Psalm.* 67, no. 12: "Ecclesiae congregatio"; *In Psalm.* 68, no. 32: "Ecclesiam vero ex conventu plebium effici notum est."

[76] *In Psalm.* 7, no. 7: "In ecclesiis, hoc est in illa congregatione populorum atque gentium" (PL 36, 101); Gregory of Elvira, *In Cantica*, hom. 5: "A tempore autem dominicae resurrectionis missi sunt Apostoli ut ex gentibus Ecclesiam congregarent" (ed. Wilmart, BLE [1906], p. 259).

[77] *De sacramentis*, bk. 2, pt. 2, chap. 2 (PL 176, 417a).

Seville,[78] who gave them classical status as far as the West was concerned. St. Paul himself may be cited as an authority for the two senses of "*Ecclesia convocans et congregans—Ecclesia convocata et congregata*", the "divine calling-together" and the "community of the called-together". St. Augustine has both in one and the same passage.[79] The active sense is primary, but the passive is no less necessary and no less important; St. Thomas employs it in most cases,[80] and Franzelin, for instance, takes it first.[81] To forget it or allow it to blur in the mind would be to enter on the dangerous path of a "practical-purposes monophysitism".[82] And there would be serious inconveniences

[78] *De ecclesiasticis officiis*, bk. 1, chap. 1 (PL 83, 739–40); *Etymologiae*, bk. 8, chap. 1 (PL 82, 293–95); St. Ildephonsus of Toledo, *De cognitione baptismi*, chap. 73 (PL 96, 138c) and chap. 76 (739b); Rhabanus Maurus, *De clericorum institutione*, bk. 1, chap. 1 (PL 107, 297a); Rémi of Auxerre, *In Joel*: "Congregatio populi collectio est in Ecclesia fidelium per Christum" (PL 117, 102d); Ivo of Chartres, *Decretum*, pt. 3, chap. 3 (PL 161, 200b–c); St. Bernard, *In Cantica, sermo* 77, no. 7; "Quamobrem si collectam, si certe, quod magis vocabulo Ecclesiae competit, convocatum a praedicatoribus se dixisset" (PL 183, 1158c); St. Martin of Leon (PL 208, 45c, 48c), etc.; *Roman Catechism*, pt. 1, chap. 10, nos. 3–5. The Church is also often described as "convocatio" (or "convocata") in opposition to the Synagogue, which was "congregatio", and it is noted that the first word is applied to men, while the second is applied to animals.

[79] L. Cerfaux, *Théologie de l'Église*, pp. 133–41; St. Augustine, *Contra Faustum*, bk. 12, chap. 16: "Ex omnibus gentibus multitudinem congregat Ecclesia"; "Ecclesia corpus Christi in unitatem collecta" (PL 42, 263).

[80] St. Thomas Aquinas, *Expositio in symbolum*: "Sciendum est quod Ecclesia est idem quod congregatio; unde Ecclesia sancta est idem quod congregatio fidelium" (ST I, q. 117, a. 2 ad 1; *In IV Sent.*, d. 20, q. 1, lect. 4; *Summa contra gentiles*, bk. 4, chap. 78; *In I Cor.*, chap. 12, lect. 3, etc.). We may make a comparison with "regnum" (βασιλεία, *Malkuth*), which signifies primarily "reign" (that is, royal government) and also "kingdom".

[81] *De Ecclesia Christi* (1887), p. 1: "Ἐκκλησία significatione concreta sunt collecti illi ipsi, qui evocatione in quandam unitatem convenerunt." Further references and quotations are given in my *Catholicism* and in Congar, *Esquisses du mystère de l'Église*, p. 69.

[82] In the case of the Church, as in that of Christ, this may be "the temptation for pious souls who are, for all their piety, insufficiently formed, and who preserve within their piety itself infantile ways of looking at things" (Congar, *Le Christ, Marie et l'Église* [1952], p. 68); see the whole chapter that discusses

involved in restricting the term "Church" to one or the other of these two meanings. Apart from the fact that there is the whole weight of a living and essentially secular usage against it, both meanings are in any case equally demanded by all that the Church teaches us about herself. Both unite in rounding out the concept of the Church; both are contained, more or less explicitly, in the classical definitions. The *Ecclesia de Trinitate*, whose hierarchic mission has its origin in the divine processions themselves, is also, under the other aspect, the *Ecclesia ex hominibus*, and this indissolubly so.[83]

We say that we believe our Church is *holy*—*credo sanctam Ecclesiam* [84]—and that she is the Church of the holy—*Ecclesia sanctorum*. This last does not mean that all her leaders are themselves among the just or that she has no sinners in her midst. But it does mean that she is both the sanctifying Church[85] and the Church sanctified by the Holy Spirit, the Church of the sanctified—that is, of those who are "called to be saints" and have in fact become such in Christ;[86] all this always by reference to him who alone is "the holy one".[87] She is the Church that

---

whether Catholic piety toward Christ, the Church, and our Lady always avoids the temptation toward a Monophysite tendency.

[83] The analogy of the Trinity is also sometimes developed with reference to the "Ecclesia ex hominibus"—for example, in Bossuet's *Sur le mystère de la Sainte Trinité* (1655), in *Oeuvres oratoires*, ed. J. Lebarcq, 2d ed. (1914), pp. 52–53, 56. Cf. Passaglia, *De Ecclesia Christi*, 2:354, commenting on John 17 (Christ's priestly prayer): "Non aliud his formulis Ecclesiae exemplar sistitur atque inculcatur, quam quod Trinitatis unitate comprehenditur. Haec igitur Trinitatis unitas et indivisa conjunctio paradigma est, quod in Ecclesia pariter ejusque ministerio eminere debet."

[84] Cf. the opening of the *Martyrdom of Polycarp*: "to all the communities of the holy Catholic Church" (p. 242 in Camelot's edition). Also see Tertullian, *Adversus Marcionem*, bk. 5, chap. 4 (p. 581 in Kroymann's edition; the text is Marcion's).

[85] See the encyclical *Mystici corporis Christi*.

[86] 1 Cor 1:2: "sanctified in Christ Jesus, called to be saints". See Rom 1:7; Eph 5:27; 1 Th 4:7; 2 Th 2:13–14, etc.; Cerfaux, *Théologie de l'Église*, pp. 89–108, 137–38. See also F. Prat's *Théologie de saint Paul*, 2d ed. (1912), 2:425–26.

[87] Lk 2:2; 1 Jn 2:20, 3:3; 1 Pet 1:15–16; cf. Lev 11:44, 19:2; Is 40:25, 54:5; Ps 20:22, etc.

gives the baptism of regeneration and the Church that receives it; a hierarchical society of which certain members are put "in possession of sacred powers",[88] by a choice which is not that of God alone, so that they may perpetuate among us the very functions of Christ, but also a community of grace in which exists another "hierarchy", this time wholly interior and the result of divine choice alone—the hierarchy of sanctity. She is a reconciling power and the family of all the reconciled;[89] a double mystery of communication and communion, since by the communication of the sacraments—holy things *(sancta)*— she is a communion of holy ones *(sancti)*.[90] She is sheepfold and flock,[91] mother and people; the mother who bears us into divine life[92] and the reunion of all those who, by participating in this life to varying degrees, make up the "People of God".[93] The

[88] Encyclical *Mystici corporis Christi*.

[89] St. Augustine, *De civitate Dei*, bk. 1, chap. 35: "Redempta familia Domini Christi" (PL 41, 46).

[90] Hence, frequently, the equivalence, for practical purposes, with the *communio sanctorum*. The *Roman Catechism* says that this article is a sort of elucidation of the preceding one (pt. 1, chap. 10, no. 24); cf. Nicetas of Remesiana, *Explanatio symboli*, no. 10 (PL 52, 771); St. Augustine, *Epist.* 149, chap. 1, no. 3 (PL 33, 641); P. Batiffol, *Le Catholicisme de saint Augustin* (1920), 1:266–68. See below, p. 109, n. 107.

[91] 1 Cor 9:7; Jn 10:16; Lk 12:32; Acts 20:28, etc.

[92] St. Jerome, *In Ephes.*, bk. 3, chap. 5, no. 21: "Et quomodo de Adam et uxore ejus omne hominum nascitur genus, sic de Christo et Ecclesia omnis credentium multitudo generata est" (PL 26, 525); St. Augustine, *Sermo* 44, *De verbis Domini*: "De hominibus in spiritu quotidie suscitatis gaudet mater Ecclesia", etc.

[93] Cf. Rhabanus Maurus, *In Genesim*, bk. 2, chap. 19: "Populo credentium, quem mater Ecclesia per fidem et baptismum generavit" (PL 107, 548b); or again, in the inverse sense, Haymo, *Enarratio in Cantica*: "Ecclesiam Dei, plebem videlicet fidelium" (PL 117, 307d). While there is certainly cause for rejoicing in the present-day return to favor of the title "the People of God" and in the response it shows itself capable of arousing, and while we must of course recognize the importance of the place it occupies in Scripture, it would appear that we should not choose it as our central concept in ecclesiology, as has been sometimes suggested. It expresses directly one aspect of the Church only, and this, moreover, only from a more or less external point of view—at any rate, as

Church is at once our mother and ourselves;[94] a maternal breast and a brotherhood.[95]

According to several of these twofold interpretations, it would be possible to say in either case that we are members of the Church; but in the first case it should also be said that we are her children or her subjects. Her very title of Bride, which always signifies her intimate union with Christ, can mean two things, according to circumstances. It can signify that power which participates in the majesty and sanctity of Christ alike, wielding his authority and distributing his graces;[96] or again, correlatively, it can signify the lost sheep that the Good Shepherd carries on his shoulders. And this second meaning has many further levels, involving a humanity once sinful, wretched, and disintegrated but now freed by Christ from its "tortuous ways",[97] made virginal by his kiss[98] and made the chaste Bride of his Spirit;[99] a humiliated captive whom he has

far as the primary meaning is concerned. This view will also have the advantage of keeping us clear of the danger involved in all those tendencies that wish to make of the Church the invisible society of the saints and the elect (see Dom Vonier, *The People of God* [French trans., *Le Peuple de Dieu* (1943), p. 10]).

[94] Origen, *In Isaiam*, hom. 2, no. 1: "Nos sumus Ecclesia Dei" (p. 250 in Baehrens' edition); *In Cant.*, hom. 2, no. 3: "Ecclesia . . . nos sumus de gentibus congregati" (ibid., p. 45), etc.; St. Peter Damian, *Liber qui appelatur Dominus vobiscum*, chaps. 5–10 (PL 145, 235–40).

[95] St. Cyprian, *Epist.* 46, no. 2: "Ad Ecclesiam matrem et ad vestram fraternitatem revertamini" (p. 605 in Hartel's edition).

[96] Bossuet, *Quatrième Lettre à une demoiselle de Metz*; St. Ambrose, *In Lucam*, bk. 3, chap. 38: "David enim vocatus est Christus . . . juxta quod scriptum est: *Inveni David servum meum*; cui nupsit Ecclesia, quae Verbi semine et Spiritu Dei plena, Christi corpus effudit, populum scilicet christianum" (PL 15, 1605b).

[97] St. Gregory the Great, *Moralia in Job*, bk. 1, no. 21: "Ad Christum ex gentilitate Ecclesia properans, in tortis vitiosisque vitae veteris conversationibus invenitur."

[98] St. Augustine, *Sermo* 213, no. 7 (PL 38, 1063).

[99] Gregory of Elvira, *Tractatus* 12 (pp. 129–31 in the Batiffol-Wilmart edition); *In Cantica*: "ut quae quondam fuerat popularis, fieret unius sancti Spiritus conjunx pudica" (ibid., p. 246). Cf. St. John Chrysostom, *Hom. de Eutropio secunda*: "In its union with Christ humanity becomes virgin" (PG 52, 402).

released from the haunts of the devil for entry into a real Promised Land.[100] This is the Bride whose frailty is continually manifested in the spiritual prostitution from which he as continually liberates her, purifying her by his union,[101] as we sing in the liturgy of the Epiphany: "Today is the Church united to her heavenly Spouse, for Christ has washed her stains in Jordan's waters."[102] As becomes immediately clear, these two aspects, neither of which can be reduced to the other, are, nonetheless, closely connected. The one implies the other, and this identity of substance in otherness of aspect is often expressed by paradoxical formulae.[103] For example, it is said that the one same Church is both Bride and Daughter of Christ; or again, as is the case when St. Ambrose develops the thought of Origen, that the Church, which was originally fallen, is rescued by the sons

---

[100] Haymo, *In Cantica*: "Ecclesia gentium, per baptismum de diaboli servitio liberata, et ad veram repromissionis terram et evangelicam libertatem introducta" (PL 117, 298d); Origen, *In Cantica*, bk. 2 (p. 157 in Baehrens' edition).

[101] St. Ambrose, *De mysteriis*, nos. 18, 35, 39; *In Lucam*, bk. 4, no. 60 (PL 15, 1632b–c), and bk. 1, no. 17 (PL 15, 1540–41); St. Martin of Leon, *Sermo* 32: "Baptismus, in quo sancta Ecclesia . . . abluitur et a peccatorum nigredine dealbatur" (PL 208, 1207a); Origen, the texts collected by Karl Rahner in RSR (1950), p. 253, etc.

[102] Antiphon for the Benedictus, Feast of the Epiphany. Cf. Dom Hieronymus Franck, O.S.B., " 'Hodie caelesti sponso . . .', Ein Beitrag zur Geschichte und Idee des Epiphaniefestes", in *Vom Christliche Mysterium: Gesammelte Arbeiten zum Gedächtnis von Odo Casel* (1951), pp. 192–226. See also St. Augustine, *Sermo* 364, no. 2: "Meretrix quam Samson in conjugium sumit Ecclesia est, quae ante agnitionem unius Dei, cum idolis fornicata fuit, quam postea sibi Christi adjunxit" (PL 39, 1640); *Tractatus I de symbolo* (p. 6 in Morin's edition of 1917); *In Joannem*, tract. 9, no. 2—Christ is the Spouse of the whole Church, *tota Ecclesia* (PL 35, 1459); St. John Chrysostom, *Homilia de capto Eutropio*, chap. 6: "How new and wonderful a thing! With us, weddings are the destruction of virginity; with God, they raise it up again" (PG 52, 402).

[103] Haymo, *Enarratione in Cantica*, chap. 6: "Praedicant Ecclesiam et laudant, quia universitas fidelium catholicam admiratur Ecclesiam. Ipsa enim Ecclesia, quae ex multis fidelibus constat personis, catholicam Ecclesiam conficit" (PL 117, 339–40).

which she conceives chastely in faith and charity.[104] The Venerable Bede writes: "Every day the Church brings forth the Church";[105] St. Cyril of Alexandria defines the Church, successively and within the space of a single paragraph, as "the Mother of believers" and the "multitude" or "flock" of believers.[106] On similar lines the Dedication hymn according to the Use of Paris sings of the maternal authority of her whom her Bridegroom has set free from her former misery:

> Christus enim, norma justitiae,
> Matrem nostram desponsat hodie,
> Quam de lacu traxit miseriae,
>   Ecclesiam!

It is equally clear that this mutual implication involves a meaning that is not interchangeable. No children without a mother; no people without leaders; no acquired sanctity without a sanctifying power and a labor of sanctification; no effective union in divine life without a passing on of that life; no "communion of saints"—that is, of holy ones—without a communication of holy things.[107] And similarly, no constituted assembly

---

[104] Haymo, *In Cantica*, chap. 7 (PL 117, 342a); St. Ambrose, *De Cain et Abel*, bk. 2, chap. 14, no. 72; "Haec enim vere in praevaricatione ante fuit, sed salva erit per filiorum generationem in fide, et caritate, et sanctificatione, cum castitate" (PL 14, 311b–c); Origen, *In Cant. comm.*, prologue: "Ecclesia sponso caelesti Christo conjungitur ac sociatur, desiderans misceri ei per verbum, ut concipiat ex eo salvari possit per hanc castam filiorum generationem" (p. 74 in Baehrens' edition).

[105] St. Bede the Venerable, *Explanatio Apocalypsis*, bk. 2: "Nam et Ecclesia, quotidie gignit Ecclesiam" (PL 93, 166d). Cf. St. Hildegarde of Bingen, *Scivias*, bk. 2, visio 5: "Fidelibus suis, qui et Ecclesia et filii Ecclesiae sunt" (PL 197, 510d).

[106] *Glaphyra in Genesim*, bk. 4 (PG 69, 221c, 224–25a–b), etc. See also above, p. 106, n. 91.

[107] Hence the twofold meaning of the phrase "communio sanctorum" (whatever its original meaning may be), according as one takes the second word as neuter or masculine; St. Augustine, *De civitate Dei*, bk. 1, chap. 35: "connexos communione sacramentorum" (PL 41, 46); *Sermo* 15, no. 2: "participationem et communionem sacramentorum" (PL 38, 116); *Contra Faustum*,

without a constitution, which includes a hierarchy. And we may end with the antithetical phrase which has won such favor in social philosophy and which, though sometimes abused, is adaptable to the Church's case, given the necessary adjustments: no realized community *(Gemeinschaft)* without a society *(Gesell-schaft)* in which and through which it is realized.[108]

The relation of these expositions to the classical distinctions taught by our catechisms now becomes apparent. These distinctions concerned two categories of persons within the society of the Church, and without all covering the same ground they all convey one and the same fundamental duality that is essential to the structure of that society—pastors and flock,[109] Church teaching and Church taught, Church ruling and governed, clergy and laity, hierarchy and faithful, ministers and subjects of sacraments—or, as was once said, *sacerdotes* and *idiotes*.[110] What I have said above was, precisely, intended to justify and consolidate distinctions such as these; but always within unity; for "the integrity of Christ signifies the indivisible unity of the Head and the body, *in plenitudine*

---

bk. 19, chap. 11 (PL 42, 355); St. Bede the Venerable, *Expl. Apoc.* (PL 39, 131c); St. Ambrose, "Communionis consortium" (PL 15, 1305a), etc.; Olier, *Catéchisme chrétien pour la vie intérieure*, p. 228: "communion in the holy things which are in the Church". Cf. F. J. Badcock, "*Sanctorum Communio* as an Article in the Creed", JTS (1920), pp. 106–26.

[108] Fr. Yves de Montcheuil performed the important service of re-emphasizing this indissoluble unity in the strongest terms (and that before an audience who had experienced the temptation to sunder it) in his *Aspects de l'Église*, no. 18 in the series Unam Sanctam (1949); the lectures were actually given in 1942–1943. See especially the third lecture, "L'Église corps du Christ".

[109] See Acts 20:28: "Take heed to yourselves, and to the whole flock, wherein the Holy Ghost hath placed you bishops, to rule the Church of God which he hath purchased with his own blood"; 1 Th 5:12; St. Augustine, *Sermo* 23, no. 2, where the words *plebs* and *praepositi* are used (PL 38, 574); St. Bonaventure, *In Hexam.*, 22, no. 9: "Praesidentes et subditi, docentes et discipuli, regulantes et regulati."

[110] Origen, *Contra Celsum*, bk. 7, chap. 4 (PG 11, 1426); St. John Chrysostom, *In I Cor.*, hom. 35 (PG 61, 300); Theodoret, *In I Cor.* (PG 82, 342); Synesius, *Epist.* 54 and 67 (PG 66, 1382 and 1431).

Ecclesiae"[111] and in consequence the indivisible unity of all those who are parts of this body. At our present level of thought there is, moreover, no question of two sections or groups. The thing in question is the Church herself, and her mysterious reality always transcends all those who belong to her and gather to her from all over the earth.[112] She is actualized and localized in their groupings, but she is neither divided nor multiplied by them, for she is always more than they are in their empirical reality. In her unity she is more than "the whole collection of pastors and flock";[113] without subsisting in the manner of a Platonic "idea", she is for all that more than a mere aggregate. The divine call that summons her into reality and the divine Principle that animates her make her always anterior and superior to anything that can be enumerated and distinguished in her; you can say that she was born of the Apostles, yet they themselves were first conceived by her.[114] And it is this Church in her entirety who is, in her unicity and her unity, indissolubly a hierarchical society and a community of grace, under two different aspects respectively.

* * *

The first of these two characters comes to her from God alone. For this reason she possesses it fully from the first instant of her existence and always hands it on whole, whatever the value

[111] Pius XII, allocution to the Sacred College, December. 24, 1945.

[112] See Is 60:1–6: "Lift up thy eyes round about and see: all these are gathered together, they are come to thee. Thy sons shall come from afar and thy daughters shall rise up at thy side"; Leo XIII, encyclical *Sapientiae christianae.*

[113] Or again, the sum total of the "body of pastors who teach" and the "body of peoples who receive the teaching", to use the expressions employed by Fénelon in his *Traité de l'autorité du souverain Pontife.* Fénelon was, of course, perfectly well aware that the Church is "the mystical body of Jesus Christ" (*Traité du ministère des pasteurs*, chap. 11).

[114] St. Jerome, *In Matt.*: "Sponsus Christus, sponsa Ecclesia est. De hoc sancto spiritualique connubio apostoli sunt procreati" (PL 26, 57a); Berengard, *Expositio super septem visiones libri Apocalypsis*, 6, 1: "Primogeniti gregis sunt Apostoli; quos primos genuit Ecclesia, et ex quibus Ecclesia nata est" (PL 17, 813a).

(humanly speaking) or the moral situation of the "instruments" God uses within her framework: "For when that is given which is of God, it is given as holy, even by one of unholy conscience." [115]

In this sense, she is entirely holy and unfailing. The Bride of Christ cannot be degraded; pure and uncorrupted, she knows one dwelling alone and keeps in chastity and modesty the sanctity of one hearth.[116] Her doctrine remains perpetually pure and the spring of her sacraments perpetually fresh. At the other end of the scale, the second character, which is the end and fruit of the first, is a treasure each man can lose; a Christian must simply hope, in all humility, for the single divine gift of final perseverance. Throughout the whole body of the Church, this treasure is always a variable quantity. The effects of grace vary in intensity from age to age and soul to soul, and we can never judge of them with certainty. Sanctity sometimes flowers more profusely and sometimes more intensely, sometimes in brilliance and sometimes in secret. We have no business to picture to ourselves, Donatist fashion, a group of the "perfect" or predestined saints.[117] In this world the Church is a mixed community and will stay like that to the very end—unthreshed corn, the ark with both clean and unclean animals,[118] a ship full

[115] St. Augustine, *Contra litteras Petiliani*, bk. 3, chap. 8, no. 9 (PL 43, 453); *De baptismo*, bk. 5, chap. 13, no. 15; St. Ambrose, *De mysteriis*, no. 27: "Non merita personarum consideres, sed officia sacerdotum."

[116] St. Cyprian, *De catholicae Ecclesiae unitate*, chap. 6 (vol. 1, pp. 214–15 in Hartel's edition; PL 4, 502–4). See also the fine distinctions made by St. Augustine in his *Contra litteras Petiliani*, bk. 3, chap. 37, no. 43 (PL 43, 470); Gregory of Elvira, *In Cantica*, hom. 1 (p. 246 in the Batiffol-Wilmart edition).

[117] Cf. St. Optatus of Milevis, *De schismate Donatistarum*, bk. 7 (pp. 158–82 in Ziwsa's edition).

[118] Origen, *In Ezechielem*, hom. 1, no. 11 (p. 335 in Baehrens' edition); *In Judic.*, hom. 8, no. 5 (ibid., p. 514); St. Cyprian, *Epist.* 54, no. 3 (p. 622 in Hartel's edition); St. Augustine, *In Psalm.* 47, no. 9 (PL 36, 539); *De fide et operibus*, chap. 5 (PL 40, 201); *De moribus Ecclesiae catholicae*, bk. 1, no. 76 (PL 32, 1342); *Sermo* 250, no. 2 (PL 38, 1164–65), etc.; St. Fulgentius of Ruspe, *De fide ad Petrum*, chap. 43 (PL 40, 777); St. Peter Damian, *Sermo* 37 (PL 144, 701–73); Ivo of Chartres, *Decretum*, pt. 1, chap. 43 (PL 161, 77), etc.; encyclical *Mystici*

of unruly passengers who always seem to be on the point of wrecking it. Whether in the eyes of God or of man, it is not righteousness which is the test of membership of the Mystical Body, that is, the Church. "Infidels" of good faith and good will, even Christian dissidents (whose situation is however quite different) are only "ordered" to her, "by a certain unconscious desire and aspiration",[119] and cannot be called her members in the full sense of this word, *reapse*.[120] Sinners, on the

---

corporis Christi; see Pius XI, encyclical *Mit Brennender Sorge*. On Song 4:7, the commentary by Ghisleri (already referred to above) explains that when the Bridegroom says to the Bride, "Thou art all fair, O my love, and there is not a spot in thee", these words are indeed addressed to the present Church, but that she is asserted to be "tota pulchra . . . non secundum vitae justitiam, sed secundum doctrinae veritatem"; or again, that the perfect beauty of the body of the Church is not something that she has in virtue of a perfected sanctity on the part of each one of her members, but rather on account of the harmonized variety of the groups that go to make her up—religious, doctors, virgins, prelates, and so on; finally, that the Church may be thought of as all fair in the best of her members and especially in the highest of them all, our Lady (*Commentarii in Canticum*, pp. 619–20). See also chapter 9, below.

[119] Encyclical *Mystici corporis Christi*. Nevertheless this does not mean that dissident Christians may not be truly incorporated in the Church, in a sense and to a degree that remains to be determined; for "there are degrees in incorporation in the Church." Cf. Benedict XIV, brief *Singulari nobis* (1749): "Eum qui baptismum ab haeretico suscepit, illius vi, Ecclesiae catholicae esse membrum tenemus"—and the commentary on this by Fr. Louis Richard, P.S.S., NRT (1952), pp. 485–92, under the title "Une Thèse fondamentale de l'oecuménisme: le baptême, incorporation visible à l'Église."

[120] Encyclical *Mystici corporis Christi*. It will be noted, moreover, that this phrase makes mention only of those who have themselves separated from the Church or have been individually cut off from her—"a corporis compage semetipsos misere separaverunt". For a fuller exegesis of this text and others closely connected with it, cf. A. Chavasse, "Ordonnés au corps mystique", NRT (1948), pp. 690–702; Liégé, RSPT (1948), pp. 351–58; C. Feckes, *Die Kirche als Herrenleib* (1949), pp. 59–60. See also D. M. Nothomb, P.B., "L'Église Corps mystique du Christ", IK (1952), p. 242, n. 4: "The word *reapse* is to be found nine times in the encyclical *Mystici corporis Christi*. On two occasions it clearly implies a note of perfection and plenitude which explicitly leaves place for a mode of realization which is incomplete but not, for all that, illusory. The encyclical *Mediator Dei* (1947) . . . employs the term *reapse* fourteen times, and

contrary, continue to be truly part of her, provided they have
not denied her;[121] indeed, as we well know, they are a vast
majority. Although they do not live according to the Gospel
they do still believe in the Gospel, through the Church, and
although this bond is not enough to *constitute* the Church, it is
enough, even when stretched to its utmost, to keep them her
members—though they may be "infirm", "arid", "putrid", or
even "dead" members.[122] The Church extends to them a patient
toleration.[123] Even the best of her children are themselves never
any more than in the way of sanctification, and their sanctity is

here it almost always implies a distinction from a mode of realization which is
either spiritual or incomplete, but not merely imaginary and not without value."

[121] Encyclical *Mystici corporis Christi*; cf. the condemnations of John Hus,
Quesnel, and the Synod of Pistoia (Cavallera, *Thesaurus*, pp. 233–34, 236); St.
Robert Bellarmine, *De Ecclesiae natura et proprietatibus* (*Opera omnia*, ed. J. Fèvre
[1870], vol. 2).

[122] St. Thomas Aquinas, ST III, q. 18, a. 3 ad 2: "Qui vero his subduntur
peccatis, non sunt membra Christi actualiter sed potentialiter; nisi forte
imperfecte, per fidem informem, quae unit Christo secundum quid, ut scilicet
per Christum homo consequatur vitam gratiae. Fides enim sine operibus
mortua est, ut dicitur Jac. ii. 20. Percipiunt tamen tales a Christo quemdam
actum vitae, qui est credere; sicut si membrum mortificatum moveatur
aliqualiter ab homine." It will be noted that the encyclical speaks of members
"of the Church", while St. Thomas here speaks of members "of Christ", which
is enough to explain the diversity of the shades of meaning as between one text
and the other. However, see *In III Sent.*, d. 13, q. 2, a. 2, sol. 2: "[Fideles
peccatores] non possunt dici membra [corporis Ecclesiae] proprie, nisi sicut
membrum mortuum, scilicet aequivoce"; and ad 2: "Ea quae sunt membra
aequivoce, id est secundum similitudinem tantum et situm." The divergence
between the present teaching of the Magisterium and that of St. Thomas on the
subject of the Church has been exaggerated; only a kind of thinking narrowly
and superficially limited to the conceptual plane, and taking no account of the
differences of circumstance, could regard these differences as fundamental.
Different viewpoints and different habits of thought naturally give rise to
different ways of phrasing things without for all that calling in question the
fundamental agreement of the doctrines concerned. See also J. de Guibert, S.J.,
De Christi Ecclesia, 2d ed., pp. 136, 139–40.

[123] St. Augustine, *De vera religione*, chap. 6, no. 10; *De fide et operibus*, chap. 27,
no. 49 (pp. 38 and 460, respectively, in Pegon's edition); St. Isidore of Seville,
Sententiae, bk. 1, chap. 16, no. 3: "Sancta Ecclesia catholica, sicut male viventes

always liable to shipwreck; all alike have to flee from the evil of the times to the mercy of God.[124] Thus it is that the Church which we are must say daily, as with one voice and without exception: "And forgive us our trespasses",[125] as the *Roman Catechism*, following the Council of Trent,[126] reminds us.[127] Every day she must call upon the power and the pity of Christ,[128] for each day in this world is a day of purification for her,[129] and each day she must wash her robe in the blood of the Lamb, "till she is purified in the fire of heaven and consummated in God".[130] When, therefore, the early Christian era took over a biblical and Pauline phrase and spoke of "the Church of the saints",[131] it did not create the presumptuous conception of a Church which, whether big or small, contained only the pure,[132] any more

---

in se patienter tolerat, ita male credentes a se repellit" (PL 83, 571b). See also Hugh of Saint-Victor, *In I Cor.*, q. 115: "Videtur quod [aliqui] sint de corpore Christi, et sint ejus membra, sed iidem, cum sint mali, sunt membra diaboli. Solutio: Non dicit Apostolus quod omnes habentes dona Spiritus sancti in unitate corporis consistant; vel Ecclesia large accipitur, scilicet multitudo omnium sacramentis Ecclesiae participantium; in quibus sunt quaedam putrida membra, et grana multa cum paleis, quae dicuntur esse in corpore, sed non de tempore" (PL 175, 534d).

[124] St. Augustine, *Sermo* 73, no. 4 (PL 38, 472).

[125] *Roman Catechism*, pt. 1, chap. 10, nos. 10–11.

[126] Session 6, chap. 11.

[127] St. Augustine, *De continentia*, chap. 11, no. 25: "Peccata, pro quibus quotidiana vox totius Ecclesiae est: *Dimitte nobis debita nostra*" (p. 170 in de Saint-Martin's edition); *De civitate Dei*, bk. 19, chap. 27 (PL 41, 657); St. Bede the Venerable, *In Cantica*, bk. 3: "Cum omnis Ecclesia veraciter confiteatur se peccato carere non posse" (PL 91, 1129d). Cf. the prayer "Deus, qui Ecclesiam tuam annua quadragesimali observatione purificas".

[128] Roman Missal, Prayer for the Fifteenth Sunday after Pentecost: "Ecclesiam tuam, Domine, miseratio continuata mundet et muniat".

[129] Pseudo-Anselm, *Homilia* 6 (PL 158, 621–22).

[130] Olier, *Grand' messe de paroisse*, p. 314.

[131] 1 Cor 14:33; Ps 88:5; Sir 44; Dan 7:18, etc. See also the Epistle of Barnabas, 6:16, St. Ignatius of Antioch, *Smyrn.*, 1, 2 (p. 156 in Camelot's edition).

[132] This misinterpretation has been made, notably in the case of Origen, where it has marred the interpretation of the whole of his ecclesiology. The Novatians, certainly, wanted to recognize only a "Church of the pure".

than it lost sight of the conditions of her this-worldly existence when it spoke of the "heavenly Church".[133] There was no implication of a distinction between a spiritual assembly, of whatever kind, and the hierarchical Church; on the contrary, the latter was called "the true Church", that is to say, the Church of the New Covenant, both ideal and concrete.[134] In using the phrase, Christians meant that all those who have entered the Church have been consecrated to God;[135] they gave witness of their belief in the fruits of baptism and their convic-tion that the whole of the Christian life, which consists in being "saints by [God's] call",[136] ought to be an unfolding of the logic of baptism. Like St. Paul, they proclaimed that being a Christian implies an obligation to sanctity,[137] and this meant neither lack of human experience on their part nor a contempt for the assembly of the faithful by and large, such as was indeed to be found among the sectarians with whom they were in conflict.[138] Notwithstanding those phrases which are intended to emphasize the contradiction between profession of Chris-tianity and a state of sin,[139] they were well aware that at one and the same time the Church is without sin in herself and never

[133] Dom Olivier Rousseau pointed this out in VS (April 1952), p. 380: "It is a mistake, I think, to criticize Origen for having applied the idea of motherhood sometimes to the heavenly Jerusalem and sometimes to the Church on earth, as if this were an inconsistency due to an imperfect ecclesiology."

[134] Origen, In Cant., bk. 1 (p. 90 in Baehrens' edition); De orat., chap. 20, no. 1. See also L. Cerfaux in Ephem. theol. Lovanienses (1939), pp. 148–49.

[135] See Ex 8:2; Lk 2:23.

[136] Rom 1:7. Fr. Huby, relating this text to Ex 12:16 and Lev 23:2–3, in which the "holy gathering" is being discussed, notes that "in the Old Testament the accent is principally on ἁγία, while in St. Paul it is on κλητός" (Saint Paul: Épître aux Romains, p. 50).

[137] Eph 5:3; Rom 16:2, etc. See above, p. 105, n. 86, and Bonsirven, Théologie du Nouveau Testament, pp. 343–44; St. Ignatius of Antioch, Magn., 4.

[138] Neither did it, of course, imply any dream of an invisible Church, as we find later on in the Confession of Augsburg, a. 7: "Est autem Ecclesia con-gregatio sanctorum."

[139] Thus St. Jerome, In Ephes.: "Qui ergo peccator est, et aliqua sorde maculatus, de Ecclesia Christi non potest appellari" (PL 26, 531c).

without sin in her members,[140] and they echoed St. Ambrose's "The Church is wounded not in herself but in us", though they also added, like him: "Let us have a care, lest our sin should become the Church's wound",[141] and in so doing made it clear that "the-Church-in-our-persons" is still the Church. Like the whole of the Christian reality, of which she is the summing-up, the *Ecclesia sanctorum* was in their eyes, when taken in the full sense of the words, something essentially eschatological. They were, of course, very far from regarding her as something that was merely "to come". After all, the eschatological is not something simply absent from the present, any more than what is transcendent is exterior to everyday reality; on the contrary, it is the foundation of the present and the term of its movement—it is the marrow of the present, as it were, and exercises over it a hidden power. But although they saw clearly that the Church was not just something that was to come, they also grasped the fact that her perfection is something proper to the hereafter. The Church of the saints is, in this world, an anticipation,[142] and would be an

---

[140] I have borrowed this way of stating the antithesis from Journet, *The Church of the Word Incarnate* (1955), 1:98.

[141] St. Ambrose, *De virginitate*, chap. 8, no. 48 (PL 16, 278d). Compare Origen, *In Jesu nave*, hom. 5, no. 6: "Per unum membrum macula in omne corpus diffunditur" (p. 320 in Baehrens' edition), etc.; Bossuet, *Élévations sur les Mystères*, 18th week, 18th meditation: by our sins "the whole face of the Church seems infected" (in Lachat's edition of the complete works [1862], 7:319).

[142] It was only later that certain distinctions were to be made, which were not, however, divisions: thus St. Bernard, *Sermo de aquaeductu*, no. 2: "Merito proinde canit Ecclesia, non illa quidem Ecclesia sanctorum quae in excelsis et in splendore est, sed quae interim peregrinatur in terris" (PL 183, 439a–b). Denis the Carthusian, again, puts the same thing somewhat differently, drawing on other authors: "Totum a suis partibus denominationem sortitur, imo denominationes diversas et quasi contrarias, sicut haec ipsa Ecclesia dicitur et lesancta et deformata, virgo et meretrix, secundum expositores nonnullos super illud Isaiae: *Quomodo facta est meretrix urbs fidelis?* Quoniam quidem in Ecclesia Deo pura mente adhaerent, plures vero mente, imo et corpore fornicantur ab eo" (*In Cantica*, a. 18; in *Opera omnia* [1898], 7:5, 406; see also above, p. 112, n. 118).

illusion if she were not a "hope"—"the substance of things hoped for".[143]

Thus we clarify and deepen the vision hinted at in the preceding chapter—that of a Church which goes beyond the limits of time to assume the dimensions of eternity itself. Yet if it is true that, as I said above, everything in her in the nature of a means is not meant to survive the end that such means procure, it is also true that this end is nothing other than herself—indeed, the fullness of the Church, her full consummation. Just as St. Ignatius of Antioch cried out that he would not be a man truly and fully until he had reached the dwelling of the unclouded light,[144] so the Church knows that she will not have realized the perfection of her being until the consummation of the paschal mystery.[145] And if perhaps we hesitate to concede as much, or think of her eternity as carrying on into the hereafter the characteristics of her temporal structure, this is only because we do not yet see her from a viewpoint wide-embracing enough. We are thinking of the Church only as the Church

[143] Heb 11:1. The reader will have realized already, from what has gone before, that the doctrine treated of in these last two paragraphs should not be exaggerated into the view that the essential bond of the Church is faith alone, as distinguished from charity. Msgr. Journet justly observes, in *L'Église du Verbe incarné*, 2:xxiv: "To want to define the unifying form of the Church as from below—that is to say, from sinners—is an error. Sinners and just are not members of the Church *ex aequo*. Sinful Christians could not manifest in their uniting the unity of the Church; a Church composed exclusively of sinners and without charity is an idea contrary to the Gospel and impossible from the Christian point of view, but a Church composed entirely of the just is not impossible and will in fact be the Church of heaven." See also Karl Rahner, RSR (1950), pp. 446–47; and Billot, *Tractatus de Ecclesia Christi*, 1:179: "consequitur ut necessaria proprietas sanctitas etiam membrorum." The opposite tendency is to be found in D. Palmieri, *Tractatus de Romano Pontifice*, 3d ed. (1902), pp. 51–52: Christ could not but will that the Church should contain "sanctos aliquos", but that is not part of her intrinsic constitution.

[144] *Ad Romanos*, 6, 2.

[145] See F. X. Durrwell, *La Résurrection de Jésus, mystère de salut* (1950), pp. 304–17.

Militant, not as the perfect and glorious Bride who no longer has "spot or wrinkle" [146] in any sense, gathered closely round her Bridegroom as a pure "assembly of the saints" and, in him, a transparent "communion of saints". [147]

It is this twofold aspect of the one Church in her present state that is, precisely, called up by the Pauline doctrine of the "body of Christ". Of course, none of the other expressions made use of in Scripture should be deliberately set aside. Indeed, none of them can be neglected with impunity, for all have their own proper significance, which is, moreover, willed by God.

---

[146] Eph 5:25–27: "Christ loved also the church and delivered himself up for it: That he might sanctify it, cleansing it by the laver of water in the word of life: that he might present it to himself, a glorious church, not having spot or wrinkle, or any such thing; but that it should be holy and without blemish"; St. Thomas, *in loc.*, lect. 8: "Effectus autem sanctificationis [Ecclesiae] est mundatio ejus a maculis peccatorum. . . . Finis autem sanctificationis est puritas Ecclesiae. . . . Et haec omnia intelligi possunt de exhibitione quae erit in futuro per gloriam. Si autem de exhibitione per fidem . . ."; and again, ST III, q. 8, a. 3 ad 2: "Esse Ecclesiam gloriosam, non habentem maculam neque rugam, est ultimus finis ad quem perducimur per passionem Christi. Unde hoc erit in statu patriae, non autem in statu viae: in quo si dixerimus quia peccatum non habemus, nosmetipsos seducimus, ut dicitur I Jo. i, 8." See also St. Jerome, *In Jer.* (PL 24, 887d); St. Augustine, *De doctrina christiana*, bk. 3, chap. 34, no. 49 (PL 34, 85); *De perfectione justitiae*, chap. 15, no. 35 (PL 44, 310); *De continentia*, chap. 11, no. 25 (pp. 170–72 in Saint-Martin's edition); *De haeres.*, 88 (PL 42, 48); *De gestis Pelag.*, chap. 12, no. 27 (PL 44, 336); *Retract.*, bk. 2, chap. 18: "Everywhere where I have recalled in these books [on the subject of baptism] that the Church has neither spot nor wrinkle, this must not be taken in the sense that she is already thus, but rather, that she is in preparation to become thus when she appears in glory. Now, in fact, because of the ignorance and feebleness of her members, she may as a whole say every day 'Forgive us our trespasses.'" See also St. Bede the Venerable: "Nunc tota virtutis nisu conatur, ut sit tota pulchra, et macula in ea non sit ulla" (PL 91, 1137); Torquemada, *Summa de Ecclesia*, bk. 1, chap. 5. See also St. Gregory the Great, *Moralia in Job*, bk. 2, chap. 34, no. 55 (PL 75, 583a); St. Bernard, *De festo omnium sanctorum*, s. 3 (PL, 183, 468–71); H. Pinard de la Boullaye, S.J, *Jésus vivant dans l'Église* (1937), pp. 250–51. Other texts are cited in Journet, 2:1115–29.

[147] Compare, above, p. 105, n. 86, and pp. 115–16, n. 136; and Nautin, pp. 54–66.

Although they do not cohere organically into a logical whole, they complete, correct, and balance one another; and thus they all join together to give us, not an exhaustive idea of the Church—which could not be—but a knowledge that is adapted to our condition. If we are to understand how to interpret them, "what elements to retain, and how they are to be extended, then we must acquaint ourselves with the living commentary on them given by the Church herself; it is she whom we must take as our guide."[148] And it is just that expression, the "body of Christ", which the Church points to as of special value—in close connection, of course, with the image of the Bride. You do not have to look far to see why. No one who reads St. Paul's Epistles can miss the fact that by this metaphorical expression he means a certain organism he thinks of as real—very much so—and whose members are at one and the same time diverse and united. This body is a visible society, with its own proper structure, in which there is a certain division of labor. Its members have functions of teaching and governing (for example) or of working miracles and discerning spirits; and this is a twofold differentiation into the "hierarchic" and "charismatic".[149] Yet at the same time it is a community that has a mysterious inner life, for all the diversities and oppositions that go to make it up are also resolved in it, and in the diversity of their functions all, being "made to drink of one Spirit", are one in Christ.[150] This has been described as the unified assembly of these functions "presented as the harmonized epiphany of one single Spirit"; as far as the Church is concerned, it does not denote merely one aspect of things, still less a reality "which can be set up in opposition to what we call today the hierarchy", but is "the revelation of her reality at depth".[151]

[148] De Montcheuil, *Aspects de l'Église*, pp. 20–21.

[149] The encyclical *Mystici corporis Christi* alludes to this distinction.

[150] 1 Cor 12:4–30.

[151] Louis Bouyer, "Où en est la théologie du corps mystique", RSR (1948), pp. 328–29, a study written in reaction against Wikenhauser's unilateral exegesis in *Die Kirche als der mystische Leib Christi nach dem Apostel Paulus* (1937).

The Pauline metaphor thus gives condensed expression to a twofold meaning, and in consequence it is possible to link up with it the two complementary teachings that are to be found not only in the writings of St. Paul but also in the Gospels and throughout the New Testament. It is, so to speak, the *stretto* where all the biblical themes on the subject of the Church interweave.[152] The Body of Christ is the house built by God upon the rock of the faith of Peter; in it every man finds his home and his work.[153] But it is also the vine in which one and the same sap runs alike through stem and branches.[154] Viewed from one standpoint, it is "the unity of a totality",[155] or all the Christians who go to make it up, "being assimilated to Christ, are the same One";[156] unlike the principalities and powers that Christ treads under foot in defeat, "the Church and he make only one", and the supremacy he exercises over her is one of sanctification and love.[157] Christ "upholds the Church and lives in the Church"; the Head "is of one nature with his Members, to which he communicates power, movement, and energy"[158]—so much so that the two names "Church" and "Christ" would seem to be interchangeable, as we can see as early as St. Paul.[159] That is where the expression "the Mystical

[152] See Louis Bouyer, "Jérusalem, la sainte Cité", VS (April 1952), p. 376.

[153] Mt 16:18–19; Eph 2:20–22; see also 1 Tim 3:15. For an exegesis of the conciliar definition, see A. Chavasse, "La Véritable Conception de l'infaillibilité papale d'après le concile du Vatican", in *Église et unité*, pp. 57–91.

[154] Jn 15:1–7.

[155] Dom Jacques Dupont, O.S.B., *Gnosis: La Connaissance religieuse dans les Épîtres de saint Paul* (1949), p. 426. There is a particular insistence on the unity of the body and the Spirit who animates it in Eph 2:16 and 18; 4:4.

[156] L. Cerfaux, *Théologie de l'Église*, p. 255. See also Godescalc, *De praedestinatione*: "Non modo caput Ecclesiae Christus, verum etiam ipsa Ecclesia tanquam sui capitis corpus et membra cum capite suo dicatur et sit Christus, ut ait apostolus" (p. 219 in Lambot's edition of 1945).

[157] P. Benoit, RB (1937), pp. 514–18.

[158] Louis Chardon, O.P., *La Croix de Jésus*, ed. F. Florand, p. 37.

[159] 1 Cor 12:12: "For as the body is one and hath many members; and all the members of the body, whereas they are many, yet are one body; so also is Christ." See also St. John Chrysostom, *In I Cor.*: "In place of Christ he puts the

Christ" finds its basis, and St. Augustine can say, in one of the nutshell paradoxes he loved so dearly: "Christ preaches through Christ."[160] But, considered from another viewpoint, this same body has a Head distinct from it, ruling it, directing its growth without growing itself, an organ of command; so much so that the link between body and Head seems predominantly one of subordination.[161] The Church is not subjected but she does submit. Christ leads and governs and, without any intermission in his own mysterious direction of her, has her led and governed visibly "by him who holds his place on earth; for since his glorious ascension into heaven she rests not only on him but also on Peter as upon a foundation visible to all."[162]

Church. . . . He names Christ instead of the Church, thus designating the body of Christ" (PG 61, 249–53); Acts 22:7–8.

[160] *Sermo* 35, no. 1 (PL 39, 1563); cf. *In Psalm.* 74, no. 4 (PL 36, 948–49). The phrase is quoted in *Mystici corporis Christi*; cf. Passaglia, *De Ecclesia Christi*, 1:35: "Quamdam propre idiomatum communicationem inter Ecclesiae corpus Christumque caput existere; adeo ut qui Ecclesiam audit, Christum audiat, et qui Ecclesiam divexat, Christum persequatur"; Lk 10:16; Acts 9:4.

[161] Eph 1:22–23: "and hath made him head over all the Church, which is his body"; J. Dupont, *Gnosis*, p. 448: "With Paul, the head is always that which commands"; F. Prat, *La Théologie de saint Paul*, 4th ed. (1913), 2:413; Dom Bernard Botte, O.S.B., *Recherches de théologie ancienne et médiévale* (1939), 11:182: "When a Greek or a Roman wishes to speak of someone in command he describes him as one who goes before—ἄρχων, *dux*. The Semite describes him as the 'head'." For the many shades of meaning, which it is impossible to discuss here in detail, see P. Benoit, O.P., "L'Horizon paulinien de l'Épître aux Ephésiens", RB (1937), pp. 359–61, 515, 523–24; J. Bonsirven, *Théologie du Nouveau Testament*, pp. 346–47.

[162] *Mystici corporis Christi*; see also the bull *Unam Sanctam*: "The one and only Church has only one body, having not two heads [i.e., two chiefs], which would be a monstrous thing, but one single head, that is, Christ, and Peter, Christ's vicar"; St. Thomas Aquinas, *Contra errores Graecorum* (15:256, in the Parma edition). In the same way, there are not two foundations for the Church, but one—see 1 Cor 3:11; St. Leo the Great, *Sermo* 83, chap. 1: "Tu es Petrus, id est, cum ego sim inviolabilis petra, ego lapis angularis qui facio utraque unum, ego fundamentum praeter quod nemo potest aliud ponere, tamen tu quoque petra es, quia mea virtute solidaris, ut quae mihi potestate sunt propria, sint tibi

But St. Paul's thought does more than merely cover the two aspects, already experienced by us, of the Church in her this-worldly state of *corpus mixtum*;[163] it covers also her state of becoming and her state of consummation. Under both aspects it is still the same body which St. Paul holds up to our contemplation and our participation. He shows us this body which is the Church, which lives and develops in this world and has a history to be followed, in the process of building itself up and growing until the day when it has reached full stature. That day will not break, as others have done, over this world; it will carry us outside history altogether. And in it the Church will be "a perfect man", the perfected body of all the saints together; all one, and now one in perfection, in the same Christ.[164] St. Cyril of Alexandria,[165] coming at the same thing from the opposite direction, speaks of the "body which is prepared" for us, like St. John talking of the New Jerusalem coming down from heaven in the glory of God, in Revelation.[166] And yet it is always the same body, just as there is only one Jerusalem, one Holy City, to hear the prophecy: "Arise, be enlightened, O Jerusalem: for thy light is come, and the

---

mecum participatione communia" (PL 54, 430a); and *Epist.* 10, chap. 1: "Hunc in consortium individuae unitatis assumptum, id quod ipse erat voluit nominari, dicendo: *Tu es Petrus*" (PL 54, 629a); and again, *Sermo* 3, chap. 3 (146b–c). See also the First Vatican Council, constitution *De Ecclesia Christi*, opening, and, below, chapter 7.

[163] The phrase is that of Pope Callistus, quoted by St. Hippolytus (*Elenchos*, bk. 9, chap. 12); it is found also in St. Augustine. It may be understood not only in terms of the admixture of sin, but also as referring to the complexity of the Church in her earthly condition.

[164] Eph 4:11–16.

[165] *In Joannem*, 11, 5 (PG 73, 324): *"Manda, Deus, virtuti tuae: confirma hoc, Deus, quod perfecisti in nobis.* You may see there clearly how by the loving kindness of God the Father, his power has become incarnate—that is to say, his Son—'confirming this', that is to say, the body which is prepared for us" (trans. T. de Regnon, *Études sur la sainte Trinité*, 3d series, 1:530).

[166] Rev 21:10–11; see also E. B. Allo, *L'Apocalypse* (1933), pp. 339–43: "A synthetic view of the Church, in time and eternity".

glory of the Lord is risen upon thee . . . and his glory shall be seen upon thee." [167]

To sum up: even though we may not find in the Epistles of St. Paul alone—any more than in any other sacred author taken in isolation—a completed doctrine of the Church, at any rate the Pauline concept of the "body of Christ", as it emerges from the succession of texts involved, seems the best fitted for integrating all the elements of that doctrine. If it does not constitute a definition properly so called,[168] it does at least provide a "particularly valuable analogical image to lead us toward a proper intellectual grasp of the Church's nature".[169] It can be applied to the Church under each of her aspects, this-worldly or other-worldly, institutional or mystical, and serves to show their deep-rooted unity. There is perfect equivalence between the *Ecclesia universalis* and the *corpus universorum*.[170] Today the adjective "mystical" is usually added to "body of Christ". This does of course serve to emphasize that it is truly the whole Church, indivisibly, which is a mystery. And although it is not in itself Pauline, it does sum up in a most satisfactory manner the thought of St. Paul, who related the Church and the "mystery" so closely as to come near to making the one the content of the other.[171] Thus we may

---

[167] Is 60:1–2; see also Gal 4:26: "But that Jerusalem which is above is free; which is our mother"—compare Heb 12:22; St. Jerome, *In Zachariam*: "Nos autem caelestem Jerusalem interpretamur Ecclesiam, quae in carne ambulans non vivit secundum carnem, cujus municipatus in Deo est" (PL 25, 1529d). On the subject of the heavenly Jerusalem in the New Testament and early Christian literature in general, see K. L. Schmidt, "Jerusalem als Urbild und Abbild", EJ 18 (1950): 207–48.

[168] L. Cerfaux, *Théologie de l'Église*, pp. 283–86; Valentin Morel, O.F.M.Cap., "Le Corps mystique du Christ et l'Église catholique romaine", NRT (1948), pp. 718–19, where he is criticizing certain expressions used by Fr. S. Tromp, S.J.; Dom C. Lialine, O.S.B., IK (1947), p. 53.

[169] Louis Bouyer, "Où en est la théologie du Corps mystique?", p. 313.

[170] St. Gregory the Great, *Moralia in Job*, bk. 34, chap. 4, no. 8 (PL 76, 722); Pseudo-Gregory, *In septem psalmos paenitentiae*, 5 (PL 79, 602), etc.

[171] Col 1:24–29; Rom 11:25. This is noted by d'Herbigny, among others (*Theologia de Ecclesia*, 1:97–98). See also H. Dieckmann, *De Ecclesia* (1925), 1:329;

say, borrowing the very words of the encyclical *Mystici corporis Christi*: "To describe this Church of Christ—which is the holy, catholic, apostolic, Roman Church—there is no name more noble, none more excellent, none more divine, than 'the Mystical Body of Jesus Christ'!"[172]

P. Demann, O.P., "Quel est le mystère d'Israël?", CS (1952), pp. 11–15, etc.; F. Prat, *La Théologie de saint Paul*, 2:412: "From the Pauline point of view, the mystical body of Christ is the most precise and complete notion of the Church"; L. Cerfaux, *Théologie de l'Église*, pp. 304–5: "Later the expression 'mystical body' was to be employed, and well employed, to describe this body."

[172] *Mystici corporis Christi*. See also, previously, Pius XI in the encyclicals *Mortalium animos* (1928), *Caritate Christi* (1932), and *Ad catholici sacerdotii* (1935): "Hanc non modo in unum Jesu Christi corpus potestatem assecutus est sacerdos, sed in mysticum etiam ejus corpus, quod est Ecclesia, excelsam amplissimamque auctoritatem" (AAS [1936], p. 12). On the thought of St. Thomas Aquinas, which sets up a close relationship between the interior of the Church and her hierarchical organization, see Y. Congar, *Esquisses*, p. 80; "Structure du sacerdoce chrétien", MD 27 (1951).

IV

The Heart of the Church

W E must now turn our attention to these two facts: the link-up made by St. Paul between the doctrine of the Church and that of the Eucharist, and the addition, at a relatively late date, of the word "mystical" to the Pauline expression "body of Christ". The two are closely connected, and an examination of them will bring us to the very heart of the mystery of the Church.

In Christian antiquity we do often come across a "spiritual body" or "great body" of Christ; or again a "complete body", a "universal" or "common" body, a "true and perfect" body, of which Christ is the "mystical head" and Christians the "mystical members". We come across the assembly of the blessed as in a "mystical Church", or again the "mystery of the body of Christ", or the "mystical union" of the faithful within the Body of Christ. Yet nonetheless it is only toward the midpoint of the Middle Ages—in the second half of the twelfth century—that this body of Christ which is the Church begins itself to be qualified by the adjective "mystical". Previously, this description was confined to the Eucharist.[1] But from that point onward it was to be the Church that was so called and thus distinguished from both the Eucharist and Christ in his earthly life or his heavenly glory.

Normally we do not try to confine the epithet to a sharp-edged meaning. It seems sufficient to note that in this usage "mystical" is placed in opposition to "natural"; the "mystical

---

[1] There are one or two among modern writers who have drawn attention to this—Franzelin, *De Eucharistia*, 2d ed. (1873), p. 146, following Hardouin, *De sacramento altaris* (1689), p. 133. See my *Corpus mysticum*, 2d ed. (1949).

body" is a supernatural organism that should be thought of in the image of a natural body, but by the same token contrasted with it. In its own mode of generalization the explanation is an accurate one; it is obvious and has the easily seen advantage of getting us down to bedrock, to the analogy of the human body that St. Paul put to good use and developed in the First Epistle to the Corinthians and the Epistle to the Romans. St. Thomas, following St. Paul, is very fond of recalling it—for example: "The whole Church is one single mystical body, in the likeness of man's natural body, having, like him, various members with various functions"—or again, "Christ is called the Head of the Church in the likeness of a natural head"; and then, elsewhere, he goes on to show the essential differences implied in the analogy.[2] The encyclical *Mystici corporis* follows exactly the same lines.[3]

But St. Paul did not stop there. No more did St. Thomas,[4] nor any of the authoritative spokesmen for the Church's Tradition; the encyclical *Mystici corporis*, following the encyclical *Satis*

---

[2] ST III, q. 8, a. 1: "Tota Ecclesia dicitur unum corpus mysticum per similitudinem ad naturale corpus hominis, quod secundum diversa membra habet diversos actus, ut Apostolus docet"; and ad 2: "In metaphoricis locutionibus non oportet attendi similitudines quantum ad omnia"; a. 3: "Haec est differentia inter corpus hominis naturale et corpus Ecclesiae mysticum"; *In III Sent.*, d. 13, q. 2, a. 1: "Christus dicitur caput Ecclesiae per similitudinem capitis naturalis." See also ST II-II, q. 183, a. 2 ad 3, etc. When the attempt is sometimes made to find over-close and over-material correspondences between the various parts of the human body and the diverse realities that the Church integrates, this is, of course, the result of forgetfulness of the second point noted by St. Thomas here. See below, p. 128, n. 7.

[3] Similarly, the *Codex Juris canonici* says (can. 100): "Catholica Ecclesia et Apostolica Sedes moralis personae rationem habent ex ipsa ordinatione divina."

[4] Leaving aside all mention of other texts (particularly those relating the Church to the Eucharist—see below), the mention of the Holy Spirit as the soul of the mystical body emphasizes his realism. "Sicut videmus quod in uno homino est una anima et unum corpus, et tamen sunt diversa membra ipsius, ita Ecclesia catholica est unum corpus, et tamen diversa membra, anima autem quae hoc corpus vivificat, est Spiritus sanctus" (*Expositio in symbolum*, a. 10); "Corpus Ecclesiae mysticum . . . totius autem hujus multitudinis Christus est caput" (ST III, q. 8, a. 4); also q. 68, a. 9 ad 2; *In III Sent.*, d. 13, q. 2, a. 2, sol. 2, etc.

cognitum of Leo XIII,[5] takes care to give a warning against those who are tempted to do so. A precision is made: the Church is not to be called "merely a body, but the body of Jesus Christ", and again a little further on: "Comparing now the mystical body with a moral body, we must notice also between these a difference which is by no means slight but, on the contrary, of the very highest importance."[6]

If, then, it is inappropriate to read into the Pauline analogy an allegory properly so called,[7] it is even less appropriate to interpret it as a mere comparison. Because St. Paul makes use of a metaphor, it does not follow that he has in mind a more or less "metaphorical" entity. But this misinterpretation has been made. To some minds the natural body seems to be the solid reality, and in consequence a mystical body can hardly be more substantial than a shadow, as far as they are concerned. Since the first is physical, the second can, for them, be no more than "moral"; since the first is real and true, the second can only be a body "mystically"—that is, to all intents and purposes, only in a manner of speaking—by comparison, say, or symbolically. For those who think in this way, the Mystical Body cannot be a body in the "proper" sense. Thus there has been a tendency to speak only of the "mystical body *of the Church*", or of the Church as forming "*a* mystical body".[8] There is of course

[5] "In the holy Epistles the Church is so often called 'a body' and also 'the body of Christ'. The Church is a body; she is visible to the eye; because she is the body of Christ, she is a living body, full of sap."

[6] See Dom Burkhard Neunheuser, O.S.B., "Die Lehre vom Geist Christi nach der Enzyklika *Mystici corporis*", in *Liturgie und Mönchtum* 4 (1949): 60–62.

[7] In passages like that in which Torquemada (*Summa de Ecclesia*, bk. 1, chap. 44, pp. 50–53) compares the Church member for member with the Bride of the Canticle, we need not see a "theory" in the modern sense of that word; these allegorical workouts are an aid to the contemplation of a mystery, and according to the view of the ancients they contain a certain element of "play", the *overall* intention of which is what we have to bear in mind.

[8] See Jacques Almain, *De potestate ecclesiastica et laïca contra Ockham*, chap. 5: "The Church is a mystical body whose head is the Pope" (quoted by Fénelon, *De l'autorité du souverain Pontife*, chap. 32; p. 151 in L. F. Guérin's edition of 1854).

nothing intrinsically wrong with these expressions. But though they are correct enough, they are also inadequate—and all the more so today when the very phrase "mystical body" has been appropriated so freely by the philosophers. If their use became exclusive, they would become seriously erroneous,[9] for they would no longer bring us the realization that those who form this "body of the Church" are really the "members of Christ". And if this happened, there would no longer really be any question of the Body of *Christ*, his "living Body",[10] which is animated by his Spirit as our own bodies of flesh are animated by our souls.[11] There would no longer be any question of that Body which is really Christ.[12] Instead of being the

[9] Of course, with many writers the question is one of a deficient vocabulary and an impoverished doctrine rather than of any formal error. Nominalism and the state of mind common during the "century of enlightenment" were among the principal causes of this.

[10] Gregory of Elvira, *Tractatus* 7: "Cum Deo credunt et templum ipsius efficiuntur, tunc membra Christi et corpus Ecclesiae nuncupantur" (p. 85 in the Batiffol-Wilmart edition); *Secunda Clementis*, chap. 2: "I think you are aware that the Church is the living body of Christ." When St. Clement of Alexandria (*Stromata*, bk. 7, chap. 14; 3:62, in Staehlin's edition) and others spoke of the "spiritual body" that is the Church, they were speaking also of a body living by the Spirit.

[11] F. Prat, *La Théologie de saint Paul*, 4th ed. (1913), 2:413: "What essentially distinguishes the mystical body from the moral entities mistakenly dignified with the name of body is that it is endowed with life and that its life comes to it from within." On this role of the Holy Spirit, see the forceful words of St. Augustine—among others—in *Sermo* 267, no. 4 (PL 38, 1231); *Sermo* 268, no. 2 (PL 38, 1234); or again, St. Basil the Great, *On the Holy Spirit*, no. 61 (PG 32, 181); St. Fulgentius of Ruspe, *Contra Fabianum*, frag. 29: "Hoc unum corpus Ecclesiae, unus Spiritus vivificat" (PL 65, 795); Hugh of Saint-Victor, *De sacramentis*, bk. 2. pt. 2, chap. 2: "Ecclesia sancta corpus Christi, uno Spiritu vivificata. . . . Omnes corpus propter Spiritum unum" (PL 176, 416b–c). Many other texts are collected in S. Tromp, S.J., "De Spiritu Sancto anima corporis mystici selecta e Patribus graecis et latinis", *Textus et documenta* (Rome, 1932), nos. 5 and 7.

[12] On the realism of the Pauline phrase, in which the "body" is equivalent to the "person" itself, see L. Malevez, S.J., "L'Église corps du Christ", RSR (1944); P. Benoit, O.P., "Le Corps du Christ dans saint Paul", RB (1938), pp. 115–19; Werner Goossens, *L'Église corps du Christ d'après saint Paul* (1949), p. 52, n.: "With St. Paul 'body' always means the whole man."

manifestation of the one Spirit,[13] the unity of the faith would be no more than a union, and the loss of the Church's internal integrative element would also be the loss of her own individuated being. She would no longer be "a true, entirely real living body with its own organs", a living "image of the Savior"[14] just as really one as his own individual body, though in another mode; she would no longer constitute "the Mystery of Christ" in its fullness, as the Fathers put it.[15] She would appear, more or less, to be just a "moral" body, or a "political body pure and simple", in which the members had only an "external connection"[16] with their head. And thus she would be a body only in the sense in which other social groups can be said to be such—groups that are not living organisms in the true sense of the term, any more than "moral persons" are really persons. The rich and lofty conception of the mystical body of Christ provided by the traditional faith would evaporate into "an ordinary imaginary personification",[17] and although one could certainly go on believing in a divine *origin* of the Church within such a framework, all the realism and the specifying quality of the Christian mystery would fade away.[18]

There have of course been times and places where this expression "mystical body" was indeed understood realistically, as

[13] St. Hilary of Poitiers, *In Psalm.* 65, v. 20: "Sermo itaque coeptus ex uno refertur ad plures. . . . Est namque unus Spiritus et una credentium fides" (p. 261 in Zingerle's edition); Pseudo-Gregory, *In septem psalmos paenitentiae*, 5 (PL 79, 602).

[14] Fénelon, *Traité du ministre des pasteurs*, chap. 2, in *Oeuvres* (Paris ed.), 1:154–55.

[15] St. Cyril of Alexandria, *De adoratione* (PG 68, 237).

[16] Chardon, *La Croix de Jésus*, p. 37, criticizing the extrinsic conception. The reaction had begun as early as with Cajetan when he wrote "with his usual penetration" (Journet, *L'Église du Verbe Incarné*, 2:594) that the mystical body is not "sicut unum corpus politicum" but "quemadmodum unum corpus naturale" (*De fide et operibus*, chap. 9).

[17] Scheeben, *Dogmatik*, bk. 5, no. 1612.

[18] The encyclical *Satis cognitum* has a reference and, as it were, an implicit answer to this minimizing way of looking at the matter in its rather curious sentence: "The Body of Christ, a mystical body, doubtless, but living nonetheless."

a real supernatural organism. But there has also been a tendency—as we have noted—to detach the mystical body, more or less, from the Church. To some, the qualifying of St. Paul's noun with this adjective seemed to encourage an overdevelopment of the "mystical" aspect of the Body of Christ—that is, as equated with "invisible", "interior", "spiritual", and "hidden"; so much so that it has been questioned whether sometimes "it has not come about that the adjective has swamped the noun".[19]

In order to steer safely between these two dangers (neither of which is in the least imaginary), it has been justly said that "mystical" means more than "moral" and that it implies an element of obscurity—of mystery, in fact—which its doctrinal interpretation should take into account.[20] Yet at the same time it has also been pointed out that this word is not, for all that, to be in any way taken as synonymous with "invisible", but that it refers rather to the sensible sign of a reality that is divine and hidden, pointing in no uncertain fashion to that Church which is, according to St. Paul, "the body of Christ". All this is well said. But to stop there would mean that no positive explanation had as yet been produced, and in consequence it is worthwhile to make matters more clear-cut yet, if we really want to give a truly concrete sense to the expression "mystical body", to get at the full range of its doctrinal riches and see how, in the words of *Mystici corporis*, it "blossoms like a flower from numerous passages of the Sacred Scriptures and the writings of the Fathers".

In point of fact, history provides us with the required elucidation and enables us to set aside both series of misinterpreta-

[19] Louis Bouyer, "Où en est la théologie du corps mystique?", RSR (1948).

[20] Franzelin, *Theses de Ecclesia Christi*, p. 310: "Ista igitur unio intima, realis, secundum quid physica, Christi capitis cum Ecclesia corpore suo, sane est in mysterio credenda per fidem, et recte dicitur mystica, ac propterea Ecclesia corpus Christi mysticum"; see also de Guibert, *De Christi Ecclesia*. In his *De Ecclesia Christi* (vol. 1), shortly after referring to the Church as a "mystical body", Passaglia added: "The true nature of the Church is entirely misunderstood by those who, like Kant, hold her to be no more than a society in which men unite themselves to practice virtue and profess religion."

tions—those that make "mystical" synonymous with "moral" or with "mysterious" in some vague sense, and those that tend to separate the *mystical* body from the *visible* Church. And in addition to doing this, it provides us with doctrinal material of primary importance.

St. Paul, as it happens, formulates in theory what emerges clearly from primitive Christian practice, and he does so by uniting in one the eucharistic mystery and that of the Christian community: "Is not the bread we break a participation in Christ's body? The one bread makes us one body, though we are many in number; the same bread is shared by all."[21] All the voices of Tradition vie with one another in commentary on this text, and the first theologians to speak of the Church as the *mystical* body of Christ are aiming at giving an exact commentary upon it. And they speak of it in a eucharistic context. By "the mystical body" they mean neither an invisible body nor a ghostly image of a real one; they mean the *corpus in mysterio*, the body mystically signified and realized by the Eucharist—in other words, the unity of the Christian community that is made real by the "holy mysteries" in an effective symbol (in the strict sense of the word "effective"). To read them is to prove the point. In different terms, it is "the union, indissolubly both spiritual and corporate, of the Church's members with Christ present in the sacrament".[22] Thus, the Mystical Body is the Body par excellence, that with the greatest degree of reality and truth; it is the definitive Body, and in relation to it the individual body of Christ himself may be called a figurative body, without any detraction from its reality.[23] In Scholastic terms, it

[21] 1 Cor 10:16–17 (Knox version).

[22] Cf. Gregory of Bergamo, *Tractatus*, chap. 18: "Istud unum corpus quod nos multi, sancto vivificante Spiritu, sumus, per hoc sacramentum, mystice designari, patenter his verbis expressit Apostolus" (p. 74 in Hurter's edition); chap. 19: "In eucharistia . . . corpus Christi, quod est Ecclesia, . . . mystice, vel sacramentaliter intimatur" (ibid., p. 80); Louis Bouyer, "Où en est la théologie du corps mystique?", p. 330.

[23] The teaching of Origen (richer from the viewpoint of ecclesiology than has often been thought) is already clear on this point: see *In Matt.*, bk. 11, no. 14

is of the same order as the *res* of a sacrament, *res sacramenti*; behind the *signum tantum*, or *sacramenti species*, and the *res-et-signum*, there lies the *res tantum*—that which is no longer the sign of anything else, since it is the final effect of the sacrament, *res ultima*.[24]

Thus everything points to a study of the relation between the Church and the Eucharist, which we may describe as standing as cause to each other. Each has been entrusted to the other, so to speak, by Christ; the Church produces the Eucharist, but the Eucharist also produces the Church. In the first instance the Church is involved in her active aspect (as described earlier)—in the exercise of her sanctifying power; in the second case she is involved in her passive aspect, as the Church of the sanctified. But in the last analysis it is the one Body which builds itself up through this mysterious interaction in and through the conditions of our present existence up to the day of its consummation.

* * *

The Church produces the Eucharist, and it was principally to that end that her priesthood was instituted—"Do this for a commemoration of me."[25] Every Christian is of course a priest, in a profound and primary sense of the term—though we must go on at once to explain it if very grave misunderstandings are to be avoided. Every Christian participates in the one and only sacrifice of Jesus Christ: "Just as we call Christians all those who have received the mystical unction in baptism, so also we should call priests all those who are members of the one Priest."[26] "All dignity is communal in the unity of the faith and

---

(p. 58 in Klostermann's edition); *In Joannem*, bk. 10, no. 35 (pp. 209–10 in Preuschen's edition), etc. See also my *Histoire et Esprit*, chap. 8, pp. 355–63.

[24] St. Thomas, *In IV Sent.*, d. 8, q. 2, a. 1; St. Bonaventure, *In IV Sent.*, d. 9, a. 2, q. 1 (Quaracchi ed., 4:208), etc.

[25] Lk 22:19; see also 1 Cor 11:25.

[26] St. Augustine, *De civitate Dei*, bk. 20, chap. 10 (PL 41, 676).

of baptism . . . the sign of the cross makes kings of all those who have been regenerated in Christ, and the unction of the Holy Spirit consecrates them all as priests";[27] Israel was "a kingdom of priests and a sacred nation".[28] The same holds true of the whole Church, for all Israel is summed up in Christ, and he is the sole true Priest, and all Christians are identified with him.[29] The "kingly priesthood" attributed to all of us by St. Peter[30] and St. John[31] is not a kind of metaphor, and we have even less right to call it a "priesthood, as it were": "We are rightly called priests because we are anointed with the oil of the Holy Spirit and the anointing of Christ."[32] It is a mystical[33] reality that cannot be surpassed or further deepened—in its own order—by any additional institution or consecration, any other priesthood. For this is what makes a Christ of the Christian, who is a member of the eternal King and Priest,[34] and if we want to

[27] St. Leo the Great, *Sermo* 4, chap. 1 (PL 54, 148); cf. 2 Cor 1:21; St. Thomas Aquinas, *in loc.*, lectio 5.

[28] Ex 19:6; see also Is 61:6; 2 Macc 2:17.

[29] Berengard, *In Apocalypsin*: "Sacerdotes Dei dicuntur, eo quod membra sint summi Sacerdotis" (PL 17, 810d; compare 767–68).

[30] 1 Pet 2:9; see also St. Leo the Great, *Sermo* 3, chap. 1 (PL 54, 145b); Pius XI, encyclical *Miserentissimus Redemptor* (May 8, 1928).

[31] Rev 1:6; 5:10; see also Rev 20:6. Cf. J. Lécuyer, "Le Sacerdoce royal des chrétiens selon saint Hilaire de Poitiers", in *L'Année théologique* (1949), pp. 302–25.

[32] St. Peter Damian, *Sermo* 46 (PL 144, 755b).

[33] St. Thomas Aquinas, *In IV Sent.*, d. 13, q. 1 ad 2: "Omnis bonus homo dicitur esse sacerdos mystice, quia scilicet mysticum sacrificium Deo offert seipsum, scilicet hostium viventem Deo (Rom. xii)."

[34] St. Isidore of Seville, *De ecclesiasticis officiis*, bk. 2, chap. 26, nos. 1–2: "On the orders of the Lord, Moses made up an ointment of chrism with which Aaron and his sons were anointed and signed with their holy priesthood. Then kings were consecrated with the same chrism; and for that reason they were called christs. But at that time, this anointing of kings and priests was figurative of Christ. After our Lord, true King and eternal Priest, had been sanctified by his heavenly Father with a mystical unguent, not only priest and kings but the whole Church was consecrated with the unction of holy chrism, inasmuch as all in her are members of the eternal King and Priest. Thus, because we are a royal and priestly race, we are anointed after baptism and take the name of

make good its claims to dignity we need do no more than recall the fact that our Lady was invested with it in an outstanding degree.[35] It is not a priesthood-on-the-cheap, a priesthood of inferior rank or a priesthood of the faithful *merely*; it is the priesthood of the whole Church. The Christian pride of the layman who has realized this fact may well often stand in need of enlightenment, but it can hardly need to be humbled.[36]

Christ" (PL 83, 823); Haymo, *In Apoc.*, bk. 1: "Quia enim caput fidelium rex est et sacerdos, congruenter et membra capitis, reges et sacerdotes vocantur" (PL 117, 946d).

[35] Gerson, *Tractatus nonus super Magnificat*, in *Opera Omnia*, ed. Ellies du Pin, 4:397b; Maurice de la Taille, *Mysterium Fidei*, p. 649: "Praedicata est a rectoribus populi christiani beata Maria *Virgo sacerdos*, quatenus prae reliquis christianis obtinuit *sacerdotium regale*, quod totius Ecclesiae est commune. Totum enim Corpus Sacerdotis factum est sacerdotale; sed eminentius pars nobliior, propius conjuncta capiti et ceteris membris praesidens"; René Laurentin, "Essai sur une maladie théologique: Marie et le sacerdoce", NRT (1947), pp. 271–83: "My conclusion is that we must dissociate the doctrine of the 'priesthood of the Virgin' from the title 'Virgin Priest', which has always done it such ill service" (p. 283). The same view is put forward in an unpublished thesis, *Sacerdoce de Marie: Étude d'une idée* (Paris, 1952): Mary possesses "by personal right as Mother of the Christ-God that universal priesthood which other Christians possess in a collective mode"; see also *Marie: L'Église et le sacerdoce* (1952), pp. 115–16, 375–82, 554–57. It will be noted that in the Sulpician hymn (1708: Office of the Presentation), the title *Virgo sacerdos* is recalled simply in order to exhort priests to break away from false joys in order to follow Mary in the way of personal sacrifice:

> Quid nos illaqueant improba gaudia?
> Cur nos jam pigeat vincula rumpere?
> Dux est Virgo sacerdos:
> Fas sit quo properat sequi.

There is a similar idea in the letter of Pius IX to Msgr. Van den Berghe (August 25, 1873), quoted in *Marie et le sacerdoce*, 3d ed. (1875), p. vi: "Adeo arcte se junxit divini Filii sui sacrificio, ut Virgo sacerdos appellata fuerit ab Ecclesiae Patribus . . . piis fidelibus et maxime clero veluti exemplar prae caeteris imitandum, et potissimum uti divini sacrificii sociam."

[36] Tertullian, *De monogamia*, chap. 7 (1:722, in Oehler's edition). On this priesthood of the ordinary Christian, see L. Cerfaux, "Regale sacerdotium", RSPT (1939), and *Théologie de l'Église suivant saint Paul*, pp. 111–18; P. Dabin, S.J., *Le Sacerdoce royal des fidèles dans les Livres saints* (1941), and *Le Sacerdoce royal des fidèles dans la tradition ancienne et moderne*, in the series Museum Lessianum (1950).

It is simply that a priesthood of this kind is entirely spiritual: "Each one of us is anointed unto priesthood, but it is a spiritual priesthood."[37] If we are to speak accurately, we must recognize that this term was not, to begin with, chosen to distinguish between the offering a Christian can make of himself and the ritual sacrifice of the Eucharist; it described the worship of the New Covenant by contrast with the "corporeal worship" that was the characteristic of the old; and when St. Thomas says that "the Church's sacrifice is spiritual", he means that in contrast to the sacrifice of the Law of Moses it "contains in itself a spiritual grace"—for it is not only a symbol of the "mystery of Christ" but also renews and applies it.[38] But the distinction of a twofold priesthood is for all that nonetheless explicit from the start. In addition to the priesthood that operates in the cultus, there is a priesthood that offers to God "the unspotted sacrifices of piety on the altar of the heart"[39] and brings it about that every Christian "carries his holocaust within him and himself applies the flame to it":

> Do you not know that a priesthood was given to you too, that is, to the whole Church of God, the whole nation of believers? It binds you to offer God a sacrifice of praise, a sacrifice of prayer, compassion, modest chastity, justice, and sanctity. . . . Each one of us should deck his head with the priestly insignia, that is to say, deck his spirit with the discipline of wisdom. . . . Each one of us should go in with the incense beyond the veil, and himself set fire to his holocaust on the altar, so that he may be consumed perpetually. If I give up all that I possess, if I carry my cross and follow after Christ, I have offered up a holocaust on the altar of God. If I give my body to be burned with the fire of charity and obtain the glory of martyrdom, I have offered

[37] St. Ambrose, *De sacramentis*, bk. 4, no. 3.

[38] ST I-II, q. 102, a. 4.

[39] St. Augustine, *De civitate Dei*, bk. 10, chap. 3 (PL 41, 280); bk. 20, chap. 10 (676); 1 Pet 2:5: "a holy priesthood, to offer up spiritual sacrifices, acceptable to God by Jesus Christ". See also Rom 12:1–2; St. Bonaventure, *De sancto Laurentio sermo I*: "Altare divinum est cor humanum."

myself as a holocaust on the altar of God. If I love my brothers
so as to give my life for them; if I fight for justice and truth to
the death; if I mortify my body by abstaining from all carnal
desire; if the world is crucified to me and I to the world—I have
offered a holocaust on the altar of God and I am the priest of my
own sacrifice.[40]

This does not, of course, mean that the thing is something
entirely individual; it cannot be come by or exercised save in
organic union with the community as a whole. And this in
turn does not mean that it is called a priesthood only meta-
phorically; the Christian community is really a "priestly
city",[41] and the Christian people, as a whole—a real Israel
among the nations—really plays a priestly role in relation to
the whole world[42] as it celebrates its "spiritual worship".[43] Each
one of its members is called upon to play his part in that
mediatory function which Clement of Alexandria rightly saw
as the particular function of the "gnostic"—that is, the perfect
believer who is the "living image of the Lord".[44] It is carried
out in the "true Temple", the "New Holy of Holies", which is
the body of the risen Son of God.[45] But this priesthood of the
Christian people is not concerned with the liturgical life of the
Church, and it has no direct connection with the production
of the Eucharist. Within the "holy nation", and for the purpose of making it holy, certain men are therefore "set aside" by

[40] Origen, *In Leviticum*, hom. 9, nos. 1, 2, 8, 9 (pp. 418–21, 432–36 in
Baehrens' edition). Fr. J. M. d'Ambrières reminds us of this text in his *Le
Sacerdoce du peuple chrétien* (1952), pp. 69–70.

[41] See St. Thomas Aquinas, ST III, q. 35, a. 7: "Jerusalem elegit ut esset
civitas simul regalis et sacerdotalis."

[42] St. Clement of Rome, *Corinthians*, chaps. 59–60; Aristides, *Apologia*, chap.
16; St. Hippolytus, *In Daniel*, 3, 24; Origen, *Contra Celsum*, bk. 8, 73–75, etc.
See also H. I. Marrou's commentary on the *Epistle to Diognetus* in *Sources
chrétiennes* no. 33 (1952), pp. 146–76.

[43] Rom 12:1; see also Phil 3:3, 2:17, 4:18.

[44] *Stromata*, bk. 7, chaps. 7, 9, and 13; see the commentary by Joseph Moingt
in his "La Gnose de Clément d'Alexandrie . . .", RSR 38 (1951): 107–10.

[45] St. Hippolytus, *In Daniel*, 1, 17; 4, 32.

a new consecration that is of a different order. They receive the imposition of hands, which has been handed down uninterruptedly from the first Apostles of our Lord,[46] and hear in their turn the words that those Apostles heard: "Do this for a commemoration of me." It is the "hierarchic"[47] Church that produces the Eucharist.

The priesthood of the bishop and his attendant clergy, who form with him the *ordo sacerdotalis* or *ordo ecclesiasticus*,[48] is thus not, properly speaking, a higher dignity in the order of the Christian's participation in the grace of Christ. It is not (if the expression may be excused) a sort of super-baptism that brings into being a class of super-Christians, though its recipient receives graces because of it and is by that very fact called, on new grounds, to the perfection of the Christian vocation:[49] "*Imitamini quod tractatis.*" Christianity has in its membership no discriminations of the type postulated by the gnostic or Manichean sects; for us there is no question of "psychics" and "spirituals" divided into two classes, or of "hearers" and "elect", "believers" and "perfected". Christians, throughout

---

[46] 1 Tim 4:14; 2 Tim 1:6. See also the constitution *Sacramentum ordinis* of Pius XII (November 30, 1947).

[47] If we are to understand the original force and grasp the original overtones of this term, we should take note of its original usage: see Pseudo-Dionysius, *Celestial Hierarchy*, chap. 3.

[48] Tertullian, *De idololatria*, chap. 7 (PL 1, 669a); *De exhortatione castitatis*, chap. 7 (PL 2, 922a); Origen, *In I Reg.*, hom. 1, no. 7 (p. 13 in Baehrens' edition); *In Ezechielem*, hom. 9, no. 2 (ibid., p. 409).

[49] 1 Tim 4:12–13; Titus 2:14; 1 Pet 5:3; Roman Pontifical, ritual for the ordination of priests: "Agnoscite quod agitis, imitamini quod tractatis: quatenus mortis dominicae mysterium celebrantes, mortificare membra vestra a vitiis et concupiscentiis omnibus procuretis"; St. John Chrysostom, *Dialogue on the Priesthood*, bks. 3 and 6; St. Thomas Aquinas, ST II-II, q. 184, a. 8; *Codex juris canonici*, vol. 2, tit. 3 ("De obligationibus clericorum"), can. 124: "Clerici debent sanctiorem prae laïcis vitam interiorem et exteriorem ducere eisque virtute et recte factis in exemplum excellere"; Pius XI, *Ad sacerdotiis fastigium*; Pius XII, *Menti nostrae*. See also C. Spicq, *Spiritualité sacerdotale d'après saint Paul* (1949); St. Catherine of Siena, *Dialogue*, 2, chap. 4; St. John Éudes, *Mémorial de la vie ecclésiastique*, in *Oeuvres* (1906), vol. 3; Olier, *Traité des saints ordres*, pt. 3, etc.

the diversity of their responsibilities and the duties of their state, are all ruled in their following of Christ by one and the same spiritual law,[50] participate in the same life, rejoice in the same grace and the same sacraments, and all this with a view to the same end: "All have the same grandeur and the same nobility, conferred by the same precious blood of Christ."[51] All are equally of the same brotherhood,[52] for "there is no respect of persons with God."[53] Similarly, there are no more distinctions like those which held good under the old dispensation. Then the priests alone had the sacred vestments that had to be worn for the ceremonial; but all the baptized have put on Christ and, more than that, have received the anointing formerly kept for the High Priest alone.[54] Then, it was he alone who could go into the Holy of Holies, and that once a year only; now, faith gives us all free entry through the blood of our Lord.[55] Then, Moses climbed Sinai in total solitude; now, all the faithful of Christ have access to the "mountain of Sion";[56] then, only Aaron's descendants laid hands on the sacred offerings, but now "the one and only priestly body of the Church is fed on the one and only Bread."[57] It is not only in virtue of their relation of subordination with regard to this second priesthood—as some theologians have thought—that the faithful can be called priests themselves; to argue thus is to argue against the most solidly

[50] St. Augustine, *Sermo* 96, no. 9 (PL 38, 588).

[51] Pius XI, encyclical *Arcanum*; see also Pius XII, encyclical *Mediator Dei* (November 20, 1947): "Si omnia, Mystici Corporis membra eadem participant bona et ad eadem dirigantur proposita, non omnia, tamen eadem fruuntur facultate, neque omnia possunt eosdem elicere actus" (AAS [1947], p. 538).

[52] See Mt 23:8; *Acta et decreta concilii Vaticani* (*Collectio Lacensis*, vol. 7, col. 777): "Postulata episcoporum Neapolitanorum".

[53] Rom 2:11. See also Tertullian, *Liber de exhortatione castitatis*, chap. 7 (PL 2, 971).

[54] Ex 30:23–33; Joel 3:1–2; Acts 2:17; Gal 3:27; 2 Cor 1:21.

[55] Heb 9:7–8, 10:19–22.

[56] Heb 12:18–24.

[57] Paul Dabin, S.J., *Sacerdoce royal*, pp. 468–69, with the references given there.

founded of traditions and even the very history of the language of Christianity.[58]

We are concerned here not with a superior rank of the "interior priesthood"—for that is common to all and cannot be surpassed in rank—but an "exterior priesthood" that is reserved for some only;[59] a charge entrusted to some only with a view to the "exterior sacrifice"[60]—*"Onus Diaconii, Onus Presbyterii, Onus Episcopatus".*[61] It is a "particular priesthood" within the "general priesthood",[62] designed to cover a particular function or "special service", as St. Leo the Great puts it.[63] That is what is meant by saying it is a "ministerial priesthood".[64]

Yet that expression would have been badly misunderstood if we were to make the opposite error of concluding from it that the priesthood is a sort of emanation from the community of

[58] Cf. Laurentin, *Marie, l'Église et le sacerdoce,* p. 646. The assertion, originally made by Palmieri (*Tractatus de Romano Pontifice,* 3d ed. [1902], p. 69), was quoted with approval by Msgr. Groeber in his 1943 memorandum to the bishops of Germany (no.13).

[59] The terminology is that of the *Roman Catechism,* pt. 2, chap. 7.

[60] François Tolet, S.J., *Commentaire de l'Épître aux Romains,* Rom 20:1, annotatio 15 (Lyons, 1603), pp. 502–3.

[61] Roman Pontifical; and also "summi sacerdotii ministerium".

[62] Phillips, *Du droit ecclésiastique,* 1:189–95.

[63] St. Leo the Great, *Sermo* 4, chap. 1: "Omnes enim in Christo regeneratos crucis signum efficit reges, sancti vero Spiritus unctio consecrat sacerdotes, et praeter istam specialem nostri ministerii servitutem, universi spirituales et rationabiles christiani agnoscant se regii generis et sacerdotalis officii esse consortes" (PL 54, 149a); *Sermo* 48, chap. 1: "Sacramentorum ministros" (298b).

[64] Votive Mass of Christ our High Priest, prayer: "Deus, qui ad majestatis tuae gloriam et generis humani salutem, Unigenitum tuum summum atque aeternum constituisti Sacerdotem, praesta, ut quos *ministros* et mysteriorum suorum dispensatores elegit, in accepto *ministerio* adimplendo fideles inveniantur" (my italics); Acts 1:17 and 25: "ministerium, διαχονία". See also Msgr. Berteaud, *Oeuvres pastorales,* 2:20: "There are no privileged persons in the Church; but there is an order, for the good of all". St. Peter Damian, *Epist.,* bk. 8, ep. 1, writes: "Constat ergo quemlibet christianum esse per gratiam Christi sacerdotem", which did not, however, prevent him from adding, "Ego autem, cui per sacerdotalis ordinis gradum injunctum est praedicationis officium" (PL 144, 461 and 464; cf. the somewhat overcautious note of the editor in col. 464).

the faithful; for it is a power received from Christ. "Jesus Christ alone can do in the priest what the priest does every day in the Church";[65] the faithful cannot confer or delegate a power that is not theirs. The priest who consecrates and offers the sacrifice is not just the representative or the spokesman of those who assist at the celebration of the mystery and participate in it to a certain degree. He does fulfill that office in certain actions, "even in liturgical actions, for the liturgy includes a whole section of worship that raises men toward God; but in the strictly sacramental actions of the liturgy, and especially in the consecration of the eucharistic offerings, the priest celebrates primarily the cultus of the Lord and is primarily the minister and sacramental representative of Christ; he celebrates, says theology, *in persona Christi*."[66] Ordinary prayer, whether of petition or offering, is said in the name of all, and then the priest stands before God as the *orator fidelium*, to quote a phrase of de Lugo's.[67] As its name shows, the Collect at the beginning of the Mass is the priest's summing up of the people's prayer—a fact that is also witnessed to by the plural *quaesumus* and expressions such as *Ecclesia tua* and *populus tuus* and *familia tua*, as also by the final "Amen" said by the server.[68] Similarly, in the Secret the celebrant presents himself before God "at the head of his people, in their name and with their offering", which is why he says at the beginning: *Orate, fratres*."[69] For the Mass is not only

[65] Olier, *Traité des saints ordres*, bk. 3, chap. 2.

[66] Y. Congar, "Structure du sacerdoce chrétien", MD 27 (1951): 75, also pp. 79, 81; and "Les Fidèles et l'offrande de l'eucharistie", LV 71:55–72.

[67] *De sacramento eucharistiae*, disp. 19, sec. 9, no. 127.

[68] See J. A. Jungmann's *Missarum solemnia* (French trans. [1952]: 2:14, 120, 145); St. Augustine, *Sermo* 272 (PL 38, 1247).

[69] Amalric, *De ecclesiasticis officiis*, bk. 3, chap. 19: "Precatur ut orent pro illo, quatenus dignus sit universae plebis oblationem offerre Domino" (PL 105, 1132); Rémi of Auxerre, *De divinis officiis*: "Fideliter considerandum est, quod tota Ecclesia Deo offerat illud sacrificium laudis" (PL 101, 1258); St. Peter Damian, *Liber qui appellatur Dominus vobiscum*, chap. 8 (PL 145, 237–38); Jungmann, *Missarum solemnia*, 2:361–65; Secret for the Seventh Sunday after Pentecost: "quod singuli obtulerunt". See also Pius XII, encyclical *Mediator Dei* (AAS [1947], 554–56).

"a deed of God", but also in part "an activity of man, who sets out with his earthly offering, at the call of God, toward a meeting with his Creator".[70] But the offering would be no more than an ineffectual "wish",[71] and the meeting would never take place, without the sacred action that is in no way the product of the community but implies, rather, the power of Christ and applies his merits.[72] At Mass the celebrant speaks in the name of the whole Christian community, which gives us the necessary grounds for saying that the Mass is "the one and only sacrifice of the Head and his members".[73] "We all offer together with the priest; we agree with all that he does and all that he says",[74] but at the essential moment he acts by the power of Christ,[75] or rather—to use the compact formulas of St. Thomas—he prays and offers *in persona omnium* but consecrates *in persona Christi.*[76]

[70] Jungmann, *Missarum solemnia*, 2:382.

[71] See Innocent III, *De sacro altaris mysterio*, bk. 3, chap. 6: "Non solum offerunt sacerdotes, sed et universi fideles; nam quod specialiter adimpletur ministerio sacerdotum, hoc universaliter agitur voto fidelium" (PL 217, 845).

[72] St. Thomas Aquinas, ST III, q. 64, a. 1 ad 2, concerning the sacraments in general; see also *In IV Sent.*, d. 19, q. 1, a. 2, sol. 2 ad 4. Dom Odo Casel writes: "Indeed, it is the whole *Ecclesia*, the holy assembly, which—according to the Council of Trent's expression—is the subject of the divine liturgy, when it is said that Christ transmitted his priesthood 'to his beloved Spouse, the Church, so that by the ministry of priests she may accomplish the mystical immolation' (sess. 22, chap. 1). And in the edifice of the Church, each member of this mystical body really collaborates in the cultus of the whole, each one in his degree. . . . It is indeed the *whole* Church, and not the clergy alone, which should take part *actively* in the liturgy, though always in accordance with *her* sacred order, and to the degree and in the measure laid down" (French trans., *Le Mystère du culte dans le christianisme* [1946], p. 96).

[73] Cf. Eugène Masure, *Le Sacrifice du Corps mystique* (1950), pp. 191–200.

[74] Bossuet, *Méditations sur l'Évangile*, day 63: "We come to that special benediction by which this body and blood are consecrated: listen, believe, consent. Offer with the priest, say Amen to his invocation and his prayer."

[75] Guy de Broglie, S.J., "La Messe: Oblation collective de la communauté chrétienne", GR 30 (1949): 561.

[76] St. Thomas Aquinas, ST III, q. 80, a. 12 ad 3: "Sacerdos in persona omnium sanguinem offert"; q. 82, a. 2 ad 2: "Sacerdos non consecrat nisi in persona Christi"; a. 1: "Hoc sacramentum . . . non conficitur nisi in persona Christi"; q. 83, a. 1 ad 3. See also Bourgoing's preface to the works of Bérulle:

Let it be said once more, therefore, that the institution of the priesthood and the sacrament of Orders do not create, within the Church, two degrees of membership of Christ and two different species of Christians, as it were. This is a fundamental truth of the faith. The priest is not, in virtue of his priestly ordination, more of a Christian than the ordinary believer; the Order he has received is for the sake of the Eucharist, but the Eucharist is for the sake of everyone. All are called, as from this present world, to the same divine life; and that is what makes all one in the same essential dignity, the "Christian dignity" that is a wonderful renewal of the dignity of man and was so magnificently celebrated by Pope St. Leo.[77] Everyone has it, whatever may be the particular function as signed to him in the great body of the Church. Yet from this last viewpoint there is, for all that, an indissoluble difference of situation and power between priests and laity, pastors and faithful. Thus, although personal sanctity cannot be determined socially or detected according to any rule (any such claim would be intolerable and tend to a warping of sanctity itself), the priestly character should always be greatly honored, even if it is not actually accompanied by the priestly responsibilities. Those who are invested with it, whatever the human circumstances of their appointing, participate in the Church's mission to engender and maintain the divine life in us, and this by a delegation from God himself. Christ, the true and only Priest, has chosen them as the instruments through which he is to act upon us,[78] and to this end has passed on to them something of what he received from his Father.[79] Through them alone are perpetuated in

"By the priestly consecration we are clothed with the very person of Jesus Christ; we speak, act, and consecrate as if we were Christ himself; and there takes place a sort of wonderful assumption of our person by the person of Jesus Christ, so that this great work of the Holy Eucharist may be realized and his body and blood produced on the altar."

[77] *De nativitate Domini, sermo* 4, chap. 1 (PL 54, 148b).

[78] St. Thomas Aquinas, *Summa contra gentiles*, bk. 4, chap. 76, also chap. 74; ST II-II, q. 184, a. 6 and 8. The vocation of the priest includes an interior element: "Superno quodam instinctu vocati", says the encyclical *Mediator Dei*.

[79] Mt 28:18–20; Jn 20:21–23; and see Mt 11:27.

this world "according to the order of the divine Redeemer, the functions of Christ the Teacher, King, and Priest".[80]

* * *

The Catholic hierarchy, or priestly order, thus exercises a threefold power, which corresponds to its threefold role of government, teaching, and sanctification; a power of jurisdiction, *magisterium*, and order[81] or, as Nicholas of Cusa puts it, *ordo, praesidentia, et cathedra*.[82] Each of these three ministries is equally of the essence of the Catholic hierarchy; or rather, they are three elements of one ministry that is itself unique and

[80] Encyclical *Mystici corporis Christi*; see also 2 Sam 7; Ps 110; Dt 18. Batiffol, in his *L'Église naissante et le catholicisme*, pp. vi–vii, writes: "The visible Church is not a society whose members are equal among themselves and have the same rights; she is a society in which there is perpetuated a divinely instituted power with which certain persons are invested so that they may sanctify, teach, and govern the others; the bishops, who are the successors of the Apostles, thus have, not an office or ministry devolved upon them by the faithful, but a *potestas* of divine right. That is the principle of the hierarchy."

[81] Encyclical *Mediator Dei*: "Jurisdictio, magisterium, potestas sacerdotalis." On this threefold role, see Yves de Montcheuil, *Aspects de l'Église*, chap. 7, pp. 80–95. Sometimes the distinction is in terms of two powers only—order and jurisdiction; in this case, government and magisterium fall under the heading of the second; thus Franzelin, *Theses de Ecclesia*, p. 46, and Journet, *The Church of the Word Incarnate*, vol. 1, passim. Other writers speak of the "sacramental power" and the "pastoral power"; yet others distinguish between the "priestly function" and the "governmental function", or the "priesthood" and "mission" (this last being twofold—to preach the Gospel and rule the Church). See Torquemada, *Summa de Ecclesia*, bk. 1, chap. 93: "Potestas spiritualis Ecclesiae duplex est, quaedam scilicet ordinis sive sacramentalis, et quaedam jurisdictionalis" (p. 104). This division into two powers is more synthetic in character and older in date. A résumé of views and discussions on this subject can be found in J. Bellamy, *La Théologie catholique au XIXe siècle* (1904), pp. 231–33. Billot (*Tractatus de Ecclesia Christi*, pp. 328–38) gives an exposé of the two kinds of division and comes down in favor of the threefold one, as does J. de Guibert (*De Christi Ecclesia*, pp. 161–67).

[82] *De Concordantia catholica*, preface, in *Opera omnia*, ed. G. Kallen (1939), 14:6; chap. 6: "Sacerdotio convenit virtus regitiva, vivificativa et illuminativa" (p. 56); also chap. 8 (p. 62).

indivisible and whose principle stands out as clearly as may be, from the founding of the Church onward.[83] For all three derive from the one single mission that Christ received from his Father and in virtue of which he was at one and the same time Teacher, Sanctifier, and King—a mission, moreover, that he passed on to his Church in a dependent mode, without dividing it up.[84] If, however, we do wish to establish a grading of the three ministries and discover which should be thought of as both the origin and final flowering of the other two, a first pointer is undoubtedly to be found in the very words "priesthood" and "hierarchy", which are at present used to indicate them all as a whole.[85] There is a parallel in the name "Sovereign Pontiff", which is the most commonly used title of him who is the Vicar of Christ[86] par excellence in this world. For these

[83] St. Clement of Rome, *Corinthians*, chap. 40: "Summo quippe sacerdoti sua munia tributa sunt, et sacerdotibus locus proprius assignatus est; et levitis sua ministeria incumbunt; homo laïcus praeceptis laïcis constringitur", etc.

[84] St. Augustine (quoting St. Cyprian), *De baptismo*, bk. 4, chap. 1, no. 1: "Haec est quae tenet et possidet omnem sui sponsi et Domini potestatem" (PL 43, 155); Dom Gréa, *De l'Église*, pp. 96–99.

[85] In the terminology of Pseudo-Dionysius, the bishop is the "hierarch", that is to say, first and foremost he who puts us into relationship with the sacred powers in the symbolic actions of the cultus and the administration of the sacraments (*Ecclesiastical Hierarchy*, chap. 3, etc.).

[86] See Heb 5:1. In virtue of this fact, it is all the more remarkable that this title is—as is well known—not scriptural but borrowed from the titular terminology of ancient Rome, and that on the other hand the Pope is not more of a "pontiff" than the other bishops are. As to priesthood and episcopate, he is on the same level as they (he himself addresses them as his "brothers"), though all of them receive their jurisdiction from him. See the *Codex juris canonici*, can. 108, no. 3; the hierarchy comprises "in virtue of divine institution, bishops, priests, and ministers, in the line of order, and in the line of jurisdiction, a supreme pontificate and a subordinate episcopate". See St. Bernard, *De consideratione*, bk. 4, chap. 7, no. 23 (PL 182, 788a), and also: Dom Gréa, *De l'Église*, pp. 136–37; Msgr. Van Roey, *L'Épiscopat et la Papauté au point de vue théologique*, Report at the Malines Conference, May 1925, quoted in Bivort de la Saudée, *Anglicans et Catholiques*, 2:155–66). St. Leo the Great describes the episcopate as "fastigium sacerdotii" (letter of October 10, 443; p. 402 in Jaffe's edition). St. Jerome, as is well known, wrote in his Epistle 146, no. 1: "Ubicumque fuerit

terms are not, in their origin, connected with any mission of teaching or ruling but with the carrying out of a sacred function. We may then agree with the Abbé René Laurentin when he says that "the liturgical dimension of the priesthood is its most properly and specifically priestly dimension" and that it is upon it that Scripture "centers the concept of the priesthood".[87]

Everything in the Church is organized with a view to the "new creature".[88] Everything done within her is done with a view to our sanctification, which is also—according to Christ's words—our "being made perfect in one";[89] it is to that end that the hierarchy governs and teaches. "For Jesus Christ sacrificed himself for the salvation of mankind, and it was for that that he brought us all his teachings and precepts; and what he orders the Church to seek in the truth of doctrine is the making holy and saving of men."[90] Recognition of authority in the Church is the first and indispensable condition without which we cannot have any part in her vitalizing work; but it is only a condition. A unity realized at that level alone could be nothing more

---

episcopus, sive Romae, sive Eugubii . . . , ejusdem meriti ejusdemque est et sacerdotii" (3:310–11, in Hilberg's edition); but he also wrote, in his *Dialogus contra Luciferianos* (no. 9): "Ecclesiae salus in summi sacerdotis dignitate pendet, cui si non exsors quaedam et ab omnibus eminens detur potestas, tot in Ecclesia efficientur schismata, quot sacerdotes" (PL 23, 165a); in that instance we are concerned only with the bishop in his own particular Church, but extension may be made to the universal Church, as in the encyclical *Satis cognitum*; see St. Jerome himself, *Adversus Jovinianum*, bk. 1, chap. 26: "Super Petrum fundatur Ecclesia. . . . Propterea inter duodecim unus eligitur, ut, capite constituto, schismatis tollatur occasio" (PL 23, 247).

[87] *Marie, l'Église et le sacerdoce*, pp. 11–12.

[88] 2 Cor 5:17.

[89] Jn 17:17–23: "Sanctify them in truth. . . . For them do I sanctify myself, that they also may be sanctified in truth . . . that they may be one, as we also are one . . . that they may be made perfect in one."

[90] Leo XIII, encyclical *Satis cognitum*. See also Damien Van den Eynde, *Les Normes de l'enseignement chrétien*, p. 180: "Without identifying the two, Irenaeus intimately associates the Church's sanctifying mission with her doctrinal mission."

than an external bond such as exists in human societies; and the Church was not created simply to duplicate, or substitute for, the powers of this world. Pastors receive "the spirit of government" first conferred on Christ[91] by his Father, with a view to an end that is at a higher level than that of mere ruling and concerns us more intimately. The very bread of the word of God, which is broken and distributed without pause by those who are its witnesses and ministers,[92] is not enough, on its own, to vitalize the soul; we have to drink from the wellspring of the sacraments, which has been handed into the keeping of the sanctifying Church.[93] And we must all be molten in that crucible of unity that is the Eucharist, the sacrament of sacraments "the noblest of all", which "consummates" them all and to which they are all "ordered".[94] When we get down to bedrock, "there is contained the whole mystery of our salvation", as St. Thomas says.[95]

To hold in their own hands the Eucharist—that is the supreme prerogative of those who form the hierarchy in the

---

[91] St. Hippolytus, *Apostolic Tradition*, no. 3.

[92] St. Cyril of Alexandria, letter on the Council of Nicaea (PG 77, 293), etc. See also Lk 1:2; First Vatican Council (DR, no. 1793).

[93] The man of faith is born of the preaching of the Gospel (1 Cor 4:15), but the obtaining of salvation demands that baptism should follow faith (Mk 16:16).

[94] St. Thomas Aquinas, ST III, q. 65, a. 3: "Omnia alia sacramenta ordinari videntur ad eucharistiam sicut ad finem." Also: "Sacramentum baptismi ordinatur ad eucharistiae receptionem" (a. 4 ad 3); "Id quod est commune omnibus sacramentis, attribuitur autonomastice huic, propter ejus excellentiam" (q. 73, a. 2, 3, and 4: see also q. 82, a. 2); *Summa contra gentiles*, bk. 4, chap. 74: "Inter sacramenta autem nobilissimum et consummativum aliorum est eucharistiae sacramentum"; chap. 61. Compare: *Suppl.*, q. 37, a. 2: "Ordinis sacramentum ad sacramentum eucharistiae ordinatur, quod est sacramentum sacramentorum"; Zigliara, *Propaedeutica ad sacram theologiam*, 4th ed. (1897), p. 362; Nicholas Cabasilas, *De vita in Christo*, bk. 4 (PG 150, 604).

[95] ST III, q. 83, a. 4: "In hoc sacramento totum mysterium nostrae salutis comprehenditur"; q. 79, c. 3; q. 80, a. 11. See also Louis Bouyer, "Que signifie la confirmation?", *Paroisse et liturgie* (1951), p. 6: "The Church in early days had an awareness that we have lost (but which we can regain) of the unity that joins all the sacraments in one single reality, the heart of which is the Eucharist."

Church and are "the ministers of Christ and the dispensers of the mysteries of God".[96] The hierarchy's "most priestly action",[97] and the supreme exercise of its power, lies in consecrating Christ's body and thus perpetuating the work of the Redemption[98]—in offering the "sacrifice of praise", which is the only one pleasing to God. In a broad sense, the whole Christian people is associated with that power at that point, and that is the meaning of St. Leo's words that the anointing of the Sovereign Pontiff "reaches to the very extremities of the whole body of the Church".[99] That exercise of the hierarchical power, in the name of Christ,[100] is one which constitutes the hierarchy's "primary and most august function".[101] So, if we are to understand the role of the hierarchy—which is to understand

[96] 1 Cor 4:1; see also 2 Cor 5:18–20.

[97] Secret for the ninth Sunday after Pentecost: "Concede nobis, quaesumus, Domine, haec divina frequentare mysteria, quia quoties hujus hostiae commemoratio celebratur, opus nostrae redemptionis exercetur" (this prayer is quoted in *Mediator Dei*).

[98] See Dom Anscar Vonier, O.S.B., *The Spirit and the Bride*, chap. 20, "In sinu Ecclesiae"; encyclical *Mediator Dei*.

[99] *Sermo* 4, chap. 1 (PL 54, 149); see also *Sermo* 21, chap. 3 (PL 54, 193). The life of the Church, writes Fr. Congar, "is obedient to two inseparable principles, the principle of hierarchy and that of community. According to Catholic tradition, ecclesiastical acts are carried out at one and the same time by one only—from the standpoint of power and validity—but by all, or by several, from the standpoint of concrete exercise. The hierarchy, which suffices for the valid carrying out of everything, continually conjoins itself with the cooperation and consent of the body of the faithful or the clergy" ("Bulletin de théologie dogmatique", RSPT [1951], p. 632). The very words of the Mass are eloquent on this point. See Henri Chirat, *L'Assemblée chrétienne de l'âge apostolique* (1949), pp. 274–77, on the role of the laity in the liturgical and sacramental life of the Church; also Pier Giovanni Caron, *I Poteri Giuridici del Laicato nella Chiesa primitiva* (Milan, 1948).

[100] Council of Trent, sess. 22, chap. 2; St. Thomas Aquinas, *Summa contra gentiles*, bk. 4, chap. 77; St. John Chrysostom, *In Matt.*, hom. 81, chap. 5, etc.

[101] Gréa, *De l'Église*, p. 283; Pius XI, *Ad catholici sacerdotii* (December 20, 1935): "Ex quo inenarrabilis perspicuo apparet catholici sacerdotii excelsitas, qui in idem Jesu Christi corpus potestate praeditus, in suis illud prodigaliter praesens facit" (AAS [1936], p. 12).

the Church—we must consider the hierarchy via the action by which this function is carried out.

We are all on our way toward the sanctuary of heaven and the liturgy of eternity. As from our present condition, the People of God is a "community of worship";[102] the very word "Church" means an assembly, as we have seen. This great assembly never ceases to be united, really united; but in accordance with the law of her sacramental essence, the invisible unity must be visibly signified and visibly brought about. And thus it can be said that her continuing existence does nonetheless have certain focal moments of intensity; and in point of fact she is never worthier of her own name than when the People of God gathers round its Shepherd for the eucharistic ceremony. Though only one cell of the whole body is actually present, the whole body is there virtually. The Church is in many places, yet there are not several Churches;[103] the Church is entire in each one of her parts: "One in many, mysteriously total in each."[104] Each bishop constitutes the unity of his flock, "the people adhering to its priest, cohering with the heavenly sacraments".[105] But each bishop is himself "in peace and in communion" with all his brother bishops, who offer

[102] C. Spicq, O.P., *L'Épître aux Hébreux* (1952), pp. 280–83; see also Théophane Chary, O.F.M., *Le Culte dans la littérature prophétique exilienne et post-exilienne* (unpublished thesis, Lyons Faculty of Theology, 1952).

[103] For the various shades of meaning in the vocabulary of St. Paul, the reader should consult the analysis in Cerfaux, *Théologie de l'Église*, pp. 78–88, 143–57; P. Benoit, RB (1937), pp. 356–57; see also J. Huby, *Saint Paul, Première Épître aux Corinthiens*, pp. 31–32, 216, 364; and see above, chapter 3.

[104] St. Peter Damian, *Super Dominus vobiscum*, chap. 5; and in chap. 6: "In omnibus una et in singulis tota", "est tota in toto, et tota in qualibet parte", etc. (PL 145, 235–36); St. Hilary of Poitiers, *Tractatus in Psalm.* 14, no. 3: "Etsi in orbe Ecclesia una sit, tamen unaquaeque urbs ecclesiam suam obtinet; et una in omnibus est, cum tamen plures sint, quia una habetur in pluribus" (p. 86 in Zingerle's edition).

[105] The first phrase is that of St. Ignatius of Antioch; the second, that of St. Cyprian (*De unitate Ecclesiae*, chap. 6; 1:215, in Hartel's edition). The two are logically connected. See also St. Ignatius, *Trall.*, 3, 1; *Smyrn.*, 8, 1; *Magn.*, 7, 1, and J. Colson, *L'Évêque dans les communautés primitives*, in the series Unam Sanctam, no. 21 (1951).

the same and unique sacrifice in other places and make mention of him in their prayer as he makes mention of all of them in his.[106] He and they together form one episcopate only[107] and are all alike "at peace and in communion" with the Bishop of Rome, who is Peter's successor and the visible bond of unity; and through them, all the faithful are united. They pray to God, "the Master of peace and concord",[108] for his holy and catholic Church; asking him to give her peace, protection, unity, and government over the whole face of the world.[109] Such is the opening of the Canon of the Mass, the introduction to the sacred moment in which the Church makes ready to realize the Eucharist.

What happens in that solemn gathering at the heart of each diocese happens also, with the same fullness and the same effects, in the humblest village Mass or the quiet Mass of the monk in his "desert"; the scale and the setting are of little importance. Each priest participates in the bishop's[110] consecrating power; he has received a communication of the same "spirit", and wherever he officiates he always forms part of

[106] Speaking of those who separate themselves from communion with the Church by refusal to obey the Apostolic See, Hormisdas declares: "eorum nomina inter sacra non recitanda esse mysteria" (April 2, 517; quoted in Cavallera, *Thesaurus doctrinae Catholicae*, p. 212).

[107] St. Cyprian, *De unitate Ecclesiae*, chap. 5: "Episcopatus unus est, cujus a singulis in solidum pars tenetur; Ecclesia una est, quae in multitudinem latius incremento fecunditatis extenditur" (1:214, in Hartel's edition); St. Cyril of Alexandria (PG 77, 293); St. Celestine (PL 50, 505–11); see also Hubert du Manoir de Juaye, S.J., *Dogme et spiritualité chez saint Cyrille d'Alexandrie* (1944), pp. 343–45.

[108] St. Cyprian, *De oratione dominica*, chap. 8: "Pacis doctor atque unitatis magister . . . Deus pacis et concordiae magister, qui docuit unitatem" (PL 4, 521).

[109] "Te igitur, clementissime Pater, . . . quae tibi offerimus pro Ecclesia tua sancta catholica, quam pacificare, custodire, adunare et regere digneris, toto orbe terrarum; una cum famulo tuo Papa nostro N., et Antistite nostro N., et omnibus orthodoxis atque catholicae et apostolicae fidei cultoribus." See Pseudo-Isidore, *Expositio in missam*, no. 17 (PL 83, 1147–48).

[110] St. Thomas Aquinas, *In IV Sent.*, d. 13, q. 1, a. 1, s. 12 ad 2: "Sacerdos participat ab episcopo potestatem consecrandi."

its "precious spiritual crown"[111]—and everything else follows. Just as there is only one faith and only one baptism, so there is only one altar in the Church.[112] It does not matter whether there is a large visible gathering there, or whether there is one diminutive server ringing the bell all to himself; it is always "the sacrifice of the community".[113] The great assembly is operative everywhere; the bonds of unity weave together. In each place the whole Church is present for the offering of the sacrifice.

* * *

But if the sacrifice is accepted by God and the Church's prayer listened to, this is because the Eucharist, in its turn, *realizes the Church*, in the strict sense of the words. The Eucharist is the sacrament "by which the Church is now united",[114] as St. Augustine puts it; it completes the work that baptism began. "From the side of Christ as he lay upon the cross there flowed the sacraments whereby the Church is built."[115] We have

[111] St. Ignatius of Antioch, *Magn.*, 13. On the relation of the episcopate to the presbyterate within the unity of the priesthood, see Ephrem Boularand, "La Consécration épiscopale est-elle sacramentelle?", BLE (1953), pp. 3–36; Joseph Lecuyer, "Épiscopat et presbytérat dans les écrits d'Hippolyte de Rome", RSR (1953), pp. 30–50.

[112] Florus of Lyons, *Expositio missae* (p. 43 in Duc's edition). Rémi of Auxerre, *Enarratio in Osee*, chap. 8: "Altare sanctae Ecclesiae unum est, licet per diversa orbis terrarum loca multa construantur altaria, sicut una fides, unum et baptisma secundum Pauli apostoli dogma" (PL 117, 63c); compare St. Ignatius, *Magn.*, 7: "One single prayer, one single supplication, one single spirit, one single hope in charity and irreproachable joy. Run together, all of you, to be reunited in one single temple of God, as round one altar, in the one Jesus Christ. . . ."

[113] Theodore of Mopsuestia, *Sixteenth Catechetical Homily* (p. 531 in the Tonneau-Devreesse edition).

[114] *Contra Faustum*, bk. 12, chap. 20 (PL 42, 265).

[115] This formula occurs frequently. It is the traditional interpretation of Jn 19:34; compare St. Augustine, *De civitate Dei*, bk. 22, chap. 17 (PL 41, 779); St. Thomas Aquinas, ST III, q. 64, a. 2 ad 3: "Per sacramenta, quae de latere Christi pendentis in cruce fluxerunt, dicitur esse fabricata Ecclesia Christi."

already been "baptized [in one Spirit] into one body";[116] now, in each one of its members—ourselves—this body receives the same food and drink for the feeding of its life and the perfecting of its unity—"We are made perfect in the body"[117]—for there is only "one sole Eucharist".[118] And thus the *social* body of the Church, the *corpus christianorum*, united round its visible pastors for the Lord's Supper, really does become the *Mystical Body of Christ*;[119] it is really Christ who assimilates it to himself, so that the Church is then truly the "Corpus Christi *effecta*".[120] Christ comes among his own, makes himself their Food; each one of them, thus united to him, is by the same token united to all those who, like Christ himself, receive Christ. The Head makes the unity of the Body, and that is

[116] 1 Cor 12:13. See also St. Thomas Aquinas, ST III, q. 39, a. 6 ad 4; Theodore of Mopsuestia, *Fifteenth Catechetical Homily*, no. 40 (p. 523 in the Tonneau-Devreesse edition).

[117] St. Thomas Aquinas, ST III, q. 73, a. 3: "Ex hoc ipso quod pueri baptizantur, ordinantur ad eucharistiam . . . et recipiunt rem ejus. . . . Res hujus sacramenti est unitas mystici corporis, sine qua non potest esse salus." See also Dom Hugo Lang, O.S.B., "Die Bedeutung der heiligen Sakramente für das *Corpus Christi Mysticum*", *Liturgie und Mönchtum* 4 (Maria-Laach, 1949): 46–59.

[118] St. Augustine, *In Psalm.* 39, no. 12 (PL 36, 442); St. Ignatius of Antioch, *Philad.*, chap. 4.

[119] 1 Cor 11:20. This is what Dom Gréa means when he says (*De l'Église*, p. 283) that the "eucharistic communion" is the "substantial foundation" of the ecclesiastical communion. See also St. Julian of Toledo: "Per escam et sanguinem dominici corporis fraternitas cuncta copuletur" (Mozarabic Prayer, PL 96, 759b); St. Augustine, *Sermo Denis* 3, no. 3: "Ne dissolvamini, manducate vinculum vestrum" (PL 46, 828).

[120] The texts are given in *Corpus mysticum*, 2d ed., pp. 103, 197–202. See St. Thomas Aquinas, ST III, q. 73, a. 3: "Res tantum hujus sacramenti est unitas corporis mystici, id est Ecclesiae, quam hoc sacramentum significat et causat": Franzelin, *Theses de Ecclesia Christi*, p. 317: "Postremo sacramentaliter Ecclesia non solum significatur sed efficitur corpus mysticum, unum in se et intime unitum cum Christo capite per unionem eucharisticham . . ."; Dom A. Stolz, O.S.B., *De Ecclesia*, p. 12: "[Ecclesia] formaliter et essentialiter constituitur per caenam eucharisticam"; Cardinal Maglione, letter to M. Eugène Duthoit, in *Semaine sociale de Bordeaux* [1939], pp. 7–8; Pius XII, allocution of May 1942.

how it is that the *mysterium fidei* is also the *mysterium Ecclesiae*, par excellence.[121]

Within the last few years there have been many who have restored to its rightful place of honor the symbolism of the eucharistic species and recalled for us the wonderful formulas of the liturgy and the patristic texts in commentary upon them, setting out for us afresh the theological doctrine of the final fruit of the sacrifice and the sacrament. So there is no need to spend time here[122] in covering the same ground again. "Our Lord's aim in multiplying his body" is to make "but one Church of all the world; of all men, but one worshipper; of all their voices, but one praise; of all their hearts, but one Victim in himself".[123] These words of Olier well convey—in the vocabulary proper to the "French School" of the seventeenth century—the traditional teaching received from St. Paul and frequently recalled by the ecclesiastical Magisterium. The Eucharist is the effective sign of the spiritual sacrifice offered to God by the whole Christ; "for the sacrifice of Christians is such that all, in the fullness of their numbers, are one single body in Christ." [124] The Church thus really makes herself by the celebration of the mystery; the holy and sanctifying Church builds up the Church of the saints. The mystery of communication is rounded out in a mystery of communion—such is the meaning of the ancient and ever-fresh word "communion", which is currently used to describe

[121] St. Albert the Great, *Liber de sacramento eucharistiae*, d. 6, tract. 2, chap. 1, no. 15; see Dom Hild, O.S.B., on the liturgical mystery in St. Albert the Great, in the Dom Odo Casel memorial volume (1951), pp. 260–73.

[122] See my *Catholicism*, pp. 88–111. Some new texts concerning the Eucharist as "sacramentum corporis mystici" have been published by Fr. Damian Van den Eynde, in his *Les Définitions des sacraments pendant la première période de la théologie scolastique* (1950), pp. 144, 148, 158–59, 171; see also Garnier of Rochefort, *Sermo* 18 (PL 205, 687b). There is a good doctrinal summary in Dom Gaspar Lefèbvre's *Le Christ vie de l'Église* (1949), chap. 9.

[123] Olier, *Grand' messe de paroisse* (1687), pp. 379–80.

[124] Gloss on 1 Cor 11:3 (PL 114, 510d); see also Pius XII, allocution of May 1942.

the sacrament.[125] The Church of this world is embodied in the Church of heaven,[126] and the ministerial hierarchy, thus preparing that kingdom of priests which Christ wishes to make of us all to the glory of his Father,[127] is, in the exercise of its most sacred function, thus entirely at the service of the hierarchy of sanctity.

"O sign of unity, O bond of charity."[128] There is indeed something exalting in a mystery of this kind for him who receives it in a spirit of faith and tries hard to carry it on into his personal life and awareness—or rather, to carry it out there. Hence the lyricism with which someone like St. Augustine, for example, speaks of it. Yet we should not let ourselves be mistaken as to its nature. As Simone Weil puts it, "Undoubtedly there is a real intoxication in being a member of the Mystical Body of Christ. But today a great many other mystical bodies, which have not Christ for their head, produce an intoxication in their members that to my way of thinking is of the same order."[129] Those lines may serve as a warning for us in their very lack of understanding of the *mystery of faith*. In the present welcome efforts to bring about a celebration of the liturgy that is more "communal" and more alive, nothing would be more

[125] The texts are given in *Corpus mysticum*, pp. 27–34; see also Harphius, *Theologica mystica* (1611), bk. 1, chap. 19: the Eucharist is the sign of ecclesiastical unity, "cui per hoc sacramentum homines congregantur: et secundum hoc vocatur communio" (p. 53; see also chap. 20, pp. 59–60); *Roman Catechism*, pt. 2, chap. 4, no. 52; pt. 1, chap. 9, no. 25.

[126] This is the way in which the prayer *Supplices* of the Canon of the Mass has sometimes been interpreted: see Garnier of Rochefort, *Sermo* 26: "Orat enim sacerdos, ut per virtutem sacramenti tota simul Ecclesia militans et triumphans in unum corpus Christi uniatur, id est, ut Ecclesia militans, quae in praesenti sacramento figuratur, et quasi in inferiori altari offertur, in sublime altare, quod est Ecclesiae triumphans, perferatur, et Capiti suo, Christo scilicet cujus est corpus uniatur" (PL 205, 746).

[127] Rev 1:6.

[128] St. Augustine, *In Joannem*, tract. 26, no. 13 (PL 35, 1613); Leo XIII, encyclical *Mirae caritatis* (May 28, 1902).

[129] Simone Weil, *Waiting for God*, trans. Emma Craufurd (1951; reprint, New York: Harper & Row, 1973), p. 81.

regrettable than a preoccupation with the success achieved by
some secular festivals by the combined resources of technical
skill and the appeal to man at his lower level. To reflect for a
moment on the way in which Christ makes real the unity
between us is to see at once that it is not by way of anything
resembling mass hysteria, or any sort of occult magic. The
faithful do not gather for the commemoration of Christ as an
assembly of initiates come to partake of a secret that is to set
them apart from the common herd. They are not a mob from
which a common personality is to be conjured up by the inten-
sifying of its latent properties, resources, values, and predi-
lections (not to mention its powers of self-deception and even
its potentialities of the diabolical kind). The Catholic liturgy is
luminous in its very mysteries, balanced and reposeful in its
very magnificence; everything in it is ordered, and even that
which calls most strongly to our being at the level of the senses
comes by its meaning only through faith. Its fruit is joy but the
lesson it teaches is one of austerity; the sacrifice that is its center
is "a symbol and representation of the Passion of the Lord",[130]
and sacrament of his sacrifice, and the memorial of his death.
Through the communion that is its consummation it feeds us
on his Cross, and it would be of no value if it did not bring
about interior sacrifice in all those who take part in it. The
"unanimous life of the Church" is not a natural growth; it is
lived through faith; our unity is the fruit of Calvary, and results
from the Mass' application to us of the merits of the Passion,
with a view to our final redemption.

"As often as the commemoration of the host is celebrated,
the work of our redemption is in operation."[131] That is the

---

[130] St. Thomas Aquinas, ST III, q. 83, a. 2 ad 2; and c.: "In celebratione hujus
mysterii attenditur repraesentatio dominicae passionis et participatio fructus
ejus." St. Augustine, *In Psalm.* 100: "De cruce Domini pascimur, qui corpus
ipsius manducamus" (PL 37, 1290); Preface of the Blessed Sacrament according
to the Use of Lyons: "Nos unam secum hostiam effectos ad sacrum invitat
convivium."

[131] See above, p. 148, n. 96.

liturgy's own definition of the meaning of the liturgical action. We get our share in the gift of unity by linking ourselves, in the depth of the soul, with this work of redemption; by freely welcoming into ourselves the "remission of sins" that is the first-fruit of the shedding of Christ's blood, and thus dying to ourselves and renouncing the evil that disintegrates us. Without these wholly interior realities there would be nothing more than a caricature of the sacred community. We must, then, never forget that the eucharistic mystery is a continual reference—and more than a reference—to the mystery of the Cross: "You shall announce the death of the Lord, until he come."[132]

The Church, like the Eucharist, is a mystery of unity—the same mystery, and one with inexhaustible riches. Both are the Body of Christ—the same Body. If we are to be faithful to the teaching of Scripture, as Tradition interprets it, and wish not to lose anything of its essential riches, we must be careful not to make the smallest break between the Mystical Body and the Eucharist. It is even more important that we should not see the ecclesial symbolism of the Eucharist as a mere "secondary sense", or, as Cardinal du Perron put it, "a moral and accessory meaning", an "oblique and collateral doctrine", a "harmonic". We should not see in the patristic explanations of it nothing more than "moral" discourses fit merely to edify the piety of the hearers once "instructed in the substance of the faith".[133] The two mysteries must be understood by one another and their point of unity grasped at depth.

It would therefore be wrong to do no more than talk of a "physical" body of Christ present in the Eucharist and then of another body that is "mystical", merely linking the two more or less closely. "That is certainly not how St. Paul saw it. For him, there is only one body of Christ—Christ's resurrected humanity. But the Church, which exists only by participation in this humanity of Christ, the 'life-giving Spirit', who is offered to

---

[132] I Cor 11:26; see also Mt 26:28; St. Ambrose, *De sacramentis*, bk. 4, nos. 24 and 20; Gerhoh of Reichersberg, *Liber contra duas haereses* (PL 194, 1179–80).

[133] The texts are given in *Corpus mysticum*, 2d ed., pp. 285–87.

her in the Eucharist, is herself simply the 'fullness of him who fulfills himself wholly in all things'." [134] Thus it was "at the Last Supper that the formula 'body of Christ' received the stamp that gave the expression its character". [135] According to St. Paul there is a "mystical identification" between Christ and his Church, and the reality of the eucharistic presence is a guarantee for us of the "mystical" reality of the Church. Similarly, the latter, witnessed to everywhere in Christian belief, is also in turn a witness to the former; for the Church could not be built up and her members could not be gathered together in an organism that was *really one and really alive* by means of a rite that contained only in a symbolic fashion him whose body she was to be and who alone could be her living unity. [136] In any case,

[134] Bouyer, *Vie monastique*, pp. 148–49; *La Bible et l'Évangile* (1951), pp. 81–82, 90; *L'Incarnation et l'Église: Corps du Christ dans la théologie de saint Athanase* (1943), p. 99. Compare F. Kattenbusch, "Der Quellort der Kirchenidee", in *Festgabe für Adolf Harnack* (1921), pp. 143–72. This teaching of St. Paul's gives us the necessary clue for understanding the words of St. Augustine that have often been interpreted as a denial of the eucharistic presence, or as at least raising a difficulty concerning it. The truth of the matter is, on the contrary, that they are a compressed expression of the mystery in its fullness. See, for example, sermons 243 and 272 (PL 38, 1116 and 1246): "It is your very own mystery which is laid upon the Lord's table; it is your mystery which you receive; you reply 'Amen' to the affirmation of what you are yourself." I have dealt with this problem in greater fullness in chapters 1 and 8 of *Corpus mysticum*.

[135] L. Cerfaux, *Théologie de l'Église*, pp. 201–15. A similar exegesis of St. Paul's thought is given by P. Samain in his "Eucharistie et corps mystique dans saint Paul", *Revue diocésaine de Tournai*.

[136] St. Jerome, *Adversus Jovinianum*, bk. 2, chap. 29: "Vis scire quomodo cum Christo unum corpus efficiamur? Doceat te ipse, qui condidit: Qui comedit meam carnem, etc." (PL 23, 326). Eucharistic realism and ecclesial realism are the guarantee one of the other. Today it is above all our faith in the Real Presence, made precise and explicit as a consequence of centuries of controversy and analysis, which leads us to faith in the ecclesial body; the mystery of the Church, effectively signified as it is by the mystery of the altar, should have the same kind of nature and the same kind of depth. With the early Fathers and particularly among the school of St. Augustine, the approach was often the inverse of this; emphasis was on the effect rather than the cause. They went straight to the *virtus unitatis* of the sacrament. Yet the ecclesial realism to which they bear us witness everywhere in the most explicit fashion is also the

the eucharistic liturgy follows St. Paul's line of thought: "that we may be numbered among his members, in whose body and blood we communicate".[137] Let us listen for a moment to Theodore of Mopsuestia, in his second homily on the Mass, where he is giving a commentary simultaneously on the liturgical text and on the teaching of the First Epistle to the Corinthians: "When we are all fed on the same body of our Lord, we become the one and only body of Christ", he says. St. Leo, with his usual forcefulness and profundity, says the same, and in his words we can hear the voice of all the great Catholic Doctors: "The participation of the body and blood of Christ effects nothing short of this, that we pass over unto that which we receive."[138] The head and the members make one single body; the Bridegroom and the Bride are "one flesh". There are not two Christs, one personal and the other "mystical". And there is certainly no confusion of Head with members; Christians are not the "physical" (or eucharistic) body of Christ, and the Bride is not the Bridegroom. All the distinctions are there, but they do not add up to discontinuity; the Church is not just a body, but *the* Body of Christ;[139] man must not separate what

---

guarantee of their eucharistic realism, should this ever be in question, for the cause must be adequate to the effect. This argument was already brought out by the authors of *Perpétuité de la foi de l'Église catholique sur l'Eucharistie*, comp. J. Migne (Paris, 1841–1848), 2:427.

[137] Postcommunion for Saturday after the third Sunday of Lent (Gelasian and Gregorian Sacramentaries); see also the *Liber mozar. sacram.*, col. 630: "Definieras unam tibi de gentibus congregandam Ecclesiam copulare. Cujus copulationis mysterium in hoc sacramentum corporis et sanguinis tui vera exhibitione complesti."

[138] *Sixteenth Catechetical Homily*, no. 24; see also *Sermo* 63, chap. 7 (PL 54, 357c); *Epist.* 59, chap. 2 (PL 54, 868); St. Cyril of Alexandria, *In Joannem* (PG 74, 341–44 and 557–60).

[139] L. Cerfaux, *Théologie de l'Église*, p. 211, analyzing 1 Cor 12:27; also p. 212: "This body of Christ with which the mystical identification is made is nothing other, be it repeated, than the real personal body that lived, died, is glorified and with which the bread is identified in the Eucharist"; St. Augustine, *Sermo* 137, no. 1: "Cum ergo sit ille caput Ecclesiae, et sit corpus ejus Ecclesia, totus Christus et caput et corpus est" (PL 38, 754); *Sermo* 144, no. 5 (790).

God has united—therefore "let him not separate the Church from the Lord." [140]

It is the same with the Eucharist as it is with the spiritual sense of Scripture, which does not eliminate the literal sense or add something else to it but rather rounds it out and gives it its fullness, revealing its depths and bringing out its objective extension. Through this "spiritual breaking" the "mystery of the Bread" is opened up, and we come to understand its ecclesial sense.[141] As Alger of Liège says, summarizing the belief of the centuries: "Christ is not brought to be where the totality is not brought to be."[142] Pope Pelagius before him had said the same thing in slightly different terms: "Those who do not wish to be in unity cannot have the sacrifice, since they do not have the Spirit that dwells in the body of Christ";[143] St. Gregory the Great, again, says: "The true sacrifice of the Redeemer is offered up in the one Catholic Church",[144] and the old homelist who drew his inspiration for his celebration of Easter from Origen adds: "The Victim is not taken outside the holy House."[145] These statements and many others like them[146] do not mean that

---

[140] Origen, *In Matt.*, 14, 17 (p. 326 in Klostermann's edition).

[141] See the texts given in *Corpus mysticum*, pp. 82–83.

[142] *De sacramentis corporis et sanguinis Domini*, bk. 3, chap. 12 (PL 180, 847); Gerhoh of Reichersberg, *Liber contra duas haereses*, chap. 6 (PL 194, 1183–84); see "La 'res sacramenti' chez Gerhoh de Reichersberg", in *Mélanges L. Vaganay* (Lyons, 1948), pp. 35–42; St. Ignatius of Antioch, *Smyrn.*, chap. 8, no. 1 (p. 163 in Camelot's edition).

[143] Pelagius I, *Epist. Viatori et Pancratio*: "Semetipsos segregantes, Spiritum non habent (*Jud.*, 19). Quibus omnibus illud efficitur, ut quia in unitate non sunt, ut quia in parte esse voluerunt, ut quia Spiritum non habent corporis Christi, sacrificium habere non possint" (PL 69, 412); "In una domo comedetur, nec efferetur de carnibus ejus foras": St. Isidore of Seville, *Quaestiones in Exodum*, chap. 15 (PL 83, 295a–b); St. Martin of Leon, *Sermo* 4 (PL 208, 264b–c).

[144] *Moralia in Job*, bk. 35, chap. 8, no. 13 (PL 76, 756c). This is the traditional interpretation of the law laid down in Exodus.

[145] *Easter Homilies*, 1, no. 15: in *Sources chrétiennes*, no. 36 (1953), p. 68.

[146] St. Albert the Great, *Liber de sacramento eucharistiae*, d. 3, tract. 3, chap. 2, no. 4: "Extra Ecclesiam non est Deus in sacramentis": St. Augustine, *Sermo* 71, chap. 19, no. 32 (PL 38, 463).

there can be no valid consecration under schism; the problem they envisage is not that of an objective presence but that of a spiritual fruit.[147] But they do mean that the eucharistic mystery necessarily extends into that of the Church and that the mystery of the Church is indispensable to the fulfilling of the eucharistic mystery: "What the schismatic produces is not the body of Christ. . . . An altar cut off from unity cannot bring together the reality of the body of Christ."[148] "The mystery of Jesus Christ is accomplished when all his members are united to offer themselves to him and with him."[149] For "it is in the Eucharist that the mysterious essence of the Church receives a perfect expression",[150] and likewise it is in the Church's catholic unity that the hidden significance of the Eucharist produces the fruit of effective results: "For the virtue that is there understood is unity, that, built into his Body, made members of him, we may be what we receive."[151] If the Church is thus the fullness of Christ, Christ in his Eucharist is truly the heart of the Church.[152]

---

[147] St. Thomas Aquinas, ST III, q. 82, a. 7, explaining St. Augustine; ibid., ad 1: "Extra Ecclesiam non potest esse spirituale sacrificium, quod est verum veritate fructus, licet non sit verum veritate sacramenti."

[148] Pelagius I, *Epist. Viatori et Pancratio*. See also M. de La Taille, *Mysterium fide*, 3d ed., 406–8.

[149] Bossuet, *Explication de quelques difficultés sur les prières de la messe*; St. Augustine, *Sermo* 272: "Qui accipit mysterium unitatis et non tenet vinculum pacis, non mysterium accipit pro se, sed testimonium contra se" (PL 38, 1248).

[150] See Dom Augustin Kerkvoorde, O.S.B., summarizing Scheeben, in *Le Mystère de l'Église et de ses sacrements*, in the series Una Sanctam, no. 15 (1946), pp. 81–86.

[151] St. Augustine, *Sermo* 57, no. 7 (PL 38, 389).

[152] Olier, *Grand' messe de paroisse*, p. 61: "In the heart of the Church, that is to say, in Jesus Christ in the Most Holy Sacrament: that is the true heart and the true source of life in the Church"; Nicholas Cabasilas, *Explanation of the Liturgy*, chap. 38: "The Church is signified in the holy mysteries, not as in symbols, but as the members are signified in the heart"; Franzelin, *Theses de Ecclesia Christi*, p. 313: "Ex his omnibus intelligimus, quomodo Ecclesia ab hoc sacrificio et sacramento eucharistico velut a corde et centro vitae participet in seipsa conjunctionem ac compenetrationem humani et divini."

V

THE CHURCH IN THE WORLD

A GAIN, paradox; the mystical Bride, the Church with the hidden heart, is also a being very much visible among the beings of this world. The fact may be misunderstood but it can hardly be missed. Like all human institutions, the Church has her exterior façade, her temporal aspect, often ponderous enough—chancelleries, code of law, courts. There is certainly nothing "nebulous and disembodied" about her—far from it. She is no "misty entity"; the fact that she is a mystery lived by faith does not make her any the less a reality of this world; she walks it in broad daylight, making her presence known to all and claiming her rights. She is everywhere interwoven with the social fabric, as one of the determinants of its texture. She describes herself as a "perfect society"[1] and in a sense duplicates civil society, yet by that very fact she restrains civil society within certain limits—or at any rate attempts to do so. There is—disastrously—a rivalry between the two and a more or less unceasing struggle, each complaining of the encroachments of the other: "Nothing is more unstable and precarious than their equilibrium."[2] Even when men seek agreement from both

---

[1] Pius IX, allocution *Maxima quidem* (June 9, 1862), and *Syllabus Errorum*, prop. 19: "Ecclesia non est vera perfectaque societas plene libera, nec pollet suis propriis et constantibus juribus sibi a divino suo fundatore collatis; sed civilis potestatis est definire quae sint Ecclesia jura ac limites, intra quos eadem jure exercere quaerat"; Leo XIII, encyclical *Immortale Dei* (November 1, 1885): "Societas est genere et jure perfecta, cum adjumenta ad incolumitatem actionemque suam necessaria . . . omnia in se et per se ipsa possideat"; "Intelligi debet Ecclesiam societatem esse, non minus quam ipsam civitatem, genere et jure perfectam"; encyclical *Satis cognitum*, etc.

[2] Joseph Lecler, *L'Église et la souveraineté de l'État* (1946), p. 23; St. Augustine, *De civitate Dei*, bk. 19, 117 (PL 51, 645–46).

sides, it is rare for the two bodies of legislation involved to harmonize completely; conflict has scarcely been resolved when it breaks out again, sometimes masked and sometimes violent, sometimes petty and sometimes tragic.

Twenty centuries of history bear witness to the fact that balance between the two is almost impossible to come by. Sometimes the State becomes the persecutor, and sometimes churchmen usurp the rights of the State. Every form of separation and union of the two has its own dangers, and the symbioses of the greatest perfection are by that very fact the more dangerous, for here the best runs easily into the worst, and when it does it is not always clear which power has become the slave of the other—whether it is the Church that is domineering over "the world", or the world that is taking possession of the Church. We escape a tearing apart of the two only by confusion of them, and the denunciation of that confusion is itself the breeding ground of fresh mutual opposition. Here the most satisfactory situations are situations of perpetual "reciprocal embarrassment".[3] Human existence is everywhere complicated by all this, if not agonized by it; the believer and the citizen seem divided one against the other within the same individual.

In view of all this we may ask ourselves—as many statesmen and philosophers have done—whether everything would not be simpler without this source of embarrassment, the Church —more orderly, more reasonable? Such a dualism was un-

---

[3] *Paul Claudel interroge le Cantique des cantiques* (1948), p. 90; see Joseph Hours, "La Démocratie chrétienne et l'État", TH (October 1952), p. 78: "Ever since Christianity came to make distinction between the spiritual and temporal powers, formerly mixed up together, the relation between the two has been difficult to establish, bad often, acceptable sometimes, and perfect never. Two primrose paths tempt the representatives of the two powers: the one submits the Church to the State to the point of making her a government ministry; the other submits the State to the Church, to the point of placing in the hands of the priesthood the unified power made up out of the two. Between these two dangers, the Scylla and Charybdis of politics, humanity seeks its path as history progresses toward its goal."

known to the ancient world; there, even when the priest was distinct from the head of the family, the military leader, or the magistrate, each man's religion was that of his polity. When new cults arose, civil society granted them recognized status only by absorbing them, and they lent themselves to this reasonable solution. However different their forms of government, Greeks and Jews alike knew nothing of this running sore which the institution of the Catholic Church has set up in states and consciences; the trouble dates from the proclaiming of the Gospel, for it was the Gospel that first distinguished what we today call the temporal and the spiritual. It was the Gospel that made two things of Church and State, with neither their boundaries nor their interests coinciding. It was the Gospel that, "separating the theological system from the political system, made the State no longer one and caused the internal divisions that have continually disturbed the Christian peoples". From it has resulted, in practice, "a perpetual conflict of jurisdiction that has made any kind of good *polity* impossible, and we have never been able to succeed in knowing whom, master or priest, we ought to obey." The Church gives men "two laws, two leaders, two motherlands; she subjects them to contradictory duties and prevents them from being men of religion and citizens at one and the same time." One remedy alone will prove effective; a return to the ancient system—"reunion of the two heads of the eagle" and "a reduction of all to political unity, without which neither State nor government will ever be well constituted".

The voice is, of course, the eloquent one of Rousseau,[4] and it acts as a sounding board for heaven knows how many others. He summarizes a long doctrinal tradition[5] that can be heard as early as in the cry of Benzo of Alba, turning on Gregory VII and

[4] *Contrat social*, bk. 4, chap. 8.

[5] Cf. P. M. Masson, *La Religion de Jean-Jacques Rousseau*, vol. 2, chap. 5, pp. 178–204. Rousseau makes an explicit reference to Hobbes: "The philosopher Hobbes is the only one who has reached a clear view of both the evil and its remedy."

twisting Christ's words: "Ye cannot serve two masters!"[6] And there is scarcely a day that does not bring some fresh echo of the tradition. The supporters and the adversaries of the State join forces in a common complaint; Proudhon, for example, regretted that Christianity, which had been able to "restore to the world a spiritual element that it had lost", had not had more skill in uniting Church and State. He criticized the Gospel for having destroyed the "communal conscience" in those countries that adopted its law and replaced it with "disturbance, rebellion, and regicide"—a condition of violence that the revolution would put an end to by "bringing the Church back into the State".[7] Other thinkers deplored equally "the troublesome split that developed in the Christian era between the religious and civil orders"—and (to quote one of them) "the mutual opposition of Christianity and citizenship". Recently M. Merleau-Ponty wrote: "The Church's roots are not in the society of men; she crystallizes at the edge of the State. . . . For a second time men are alienated by a second burdensome supervision."[8] Surely the first alienation—obviously inevitable—was enough; why another? Why should we postulate the principle of all these unresolvable conflicts? Why should not one of these powers absorb the other[9]—either a Church shaped to the measure of citizenship or a State responsible for the whole of man? Wouldn't everything be simpler so?

It is not only the theorists of the State who advocate this kind of thing. Theologians and canonists, going beyond the great Augustinian dream of spiritual unity and peace in justice, which lay at the origins of Christianity—or, rather, going in another direction—have sometimes reasoned in the same way. They have been irritated by the same complications and carried

[6] *Liber ad Heinricum*, 4 (MGH, *Scriptores*, 11:634).

[7] Proudhon, *La Fédération et l'unité en Italie* (1862), p. 97; *De la Justice dans la Révolution et dans l'Église*, new ed., bk. 4, pp. 400–409.

[8] *Sens et non-sens* (1948), p. 362.

[9] See M. Cayla, *Pape et empereur* (1861): "It is time to make short work of the difficulty by discarding the old prejudice of the distinction of the powers."

away by the same ideal of oversimplification. For there are two ways of reuniting the eagle's two heads, as Rousseau put it—ways that are contraries but lead to a similar result. Why should there be two heads in society—why indeed two "perfect societies" at all? Surely two heads and one body add up to a monster? But as soon as the society concerned is the Church, the Mystical Body, it would seem to follow that the Pope, whose titles are of a more sacred kind than those of the secular ruler, should concentrate in his person all power by having at his disposal at one and the same time both the "two swords".

We can without difficulty concede the point that whichever side the absorption were effected from, everything would become infinitely simpler and much more practicable—in theory, at any rate. The only question is whether this simplicity is desirable, and whether so easy a life is really an ideal.

The coming of human dominion has already made things extremely complicated on this planet. From the moment of the first glimmer of intelligence and the first prick of the moral law there have been problems, conflicts, scruples, and inhibitions without number, complication and disorder without end. Everything was very much simpler in a world that was as yet ruled by the innocent darkness of instinct—and much easier; everything moved much more directly to its end—if end is the right word. There is no limit to the trouble continually produced by the human privilege of reflection; scarcely has it been exercised when it gives rise to "more disorder in one single consciousness than would be needed to tear the universe apart".[10] Rousseau was certainly tempted by the idea of a return to a paradise conceived as existing before all the dissociative processes discussed above, and a nostalgia of the same kind still infects the psychic subsoil of our nature, from which it may blossom in subtle temptation. Yet in that crude form at least the thing can hardly claim us as its victims—and even less so, in the

[10] Pierre Emmanuel, *Babel* (1952), p. 185; see also p. 171: Man in the raw is "a savage entanglement of contradictions".

form of a return to the other side of the Gospel, supposing that this were in any way possible.

It is not a question of asking ourselves what would be the simplest state of affairs, for simplicity, as such, is neither an ideal nor a criterion. The condition of simplicity, which pulls at us so irresistibly, is to be found in our end, not in our beginning; it is not a basic datum but a reward—integration, not mutilation. To desire a given condition of simplicity at whatever price is to ride roughshod over ourselves, for we do not have that simplicity in us. Let us consider for a moment what we do have; then, without shutting our eyes to the inevitable complications that arise from the Church's instituting, we can see in her, as she is in the world, a wonderful sign of the divine wisdom.[11]

* * *

Man's nature is twofold—he is animal and spirit. He lives on this earth and is committed to a temporal destiny; yet there is in him something that goes beyond any terrestrial horizon and seeks the atmosphere of eternity as its natural climate—which fact already shows us the conflict that is located in man and is enough to undermine the principle of state religion. That religion "is founded upon error", as Rousseau had to recognize at the very moment when he wished to inspire in us a nostalgia for it. Whatever its particular details may be, it makes an absolute of human society and the earthly order—*the* absolute, in fact. And so the only way of justifying it that Rousseau could see was to transform it into a mere convention. The articles of the profession of faith imposed by the ruler are to be accepted, "not exactly as dogmas of religion, but as sentiments of social conscience, without which it is impossible to be either a good citizen or a faithful subject".[12] This is to change an error into a

[11] Rousseau says again (*Contrat social*, bk. 4, chap. 8): "All institutions which place man in contradiction with himself are valueless." That is certainly true. But to begin by taking note of the dualities and oppositions that are present in man, and take them into account, is not to put man in a state of self-contradiction but—on the contrary—to strive to give him harmony and unity.

[12] Ibid.

lie, and without any diminution of its exorbitant claims—for the State will be able to banish those who reject these articles of faith and put to death those who retract assent to them.

The duality set up by the Gospel will obtain to an even greater degree if it is true that God has intervened in history, our own history; if he wished to provide not only secretly for the good of each individual but publicly—socially, as it were— for the good of the whole human race;[13] if the Christian mystery is founded on real facts, and the whole divine revelation has taken a historical form, so that we cannot recognize it save through the succession of an authentic witness, and so that it reaches us through a Tradition. Christ's Resurrection created a new world; it marked the beginning of a fresh age and set up on earth a type of existence that is absolutely novel—"Behold all things are made new."[14] It inaugurated "the eighth day".[15] Yet for all that it neither transformed the social nature of man nor cancelled out the temporal conditions of his existence. The eternal Easter has already begun, yet "all things continue as they were from the beginning of the creation."[16] For the time being, the new world fits into the old one; the eighth day exists only in the seven others, and from now onward man will, in this life, form part of two cities, whose content will be these two worlds respectively. He will not stop being a member of an earthly city, because he will not stop being a man, and of the earth; but he

[13] St. Augustine, *De vera religione*, chap. 25, no. 46: "Quoniam divina Providentia non solum singulis hominibus quasi privatim, sed universo generi humano tanquam publice consuluit, quid cum singulis agatur, Deus qui agit atque ipsi cum quibus agitur sciunt; quid autem agatur cum genere humano, per historiam commendari voluit et per prophetiam" (PL 34, 142).

[14] 2 Cor 5:17.

[15] Epistle of Barnabas, 15:8–9; St. Justin, *Apologia* 1, chap. 67, no. 7 (p. 144 in Pautigny's edition); *Dialogue with Trypho*, chaps. 24, 1; 41, 4; 138, 1–2; St. Clement of Alexandria, *Stomata*, bk. 5, 106 and bk. 6, 57; St. Gregory Nazianzen, *Discourse* 44, *For the New Sabbath*, chap. 5 (PG 36, 612–13). On the octagonal baptisteries, see Doelger, "Das Oktagon und die Symbolik der Achtzal", *Antik. und Christentum*, 4, 3, pp. 153–87. See also my *Affrontements mystiques*, p. 92.

[16] See 2 Pet 3:4.

will not be bound to the earthly city any more by the same exclusive ties as before, for he will have been given entry to a new city in which his new existence is to unfold. This new city, the sheltering womb and matrix of the new world, is the Church—the new universe[17] already active at the very heart of our earthly and mortal existence; it is through her that God re-creates and re-forms the human race.[18] The earthly Church is already "that Jerusalem, which is above . . . our mother"; St. Paul tells us that she is free and makes us free with that liberty which Christ has won for us.[19]

It can, of course, be maintained that by the mere fact of revealing to man that he was made for a higher world—an earth "in which justice dwelleth" [20]—Christ placed in him a prin-ciple of spiritual liberty that was the outcome of an interior need stronger than any tyrant.[21] Simply by having said "My kingdom is not of this world" and "Render . . . to Caesar the things that are Caesar's, and to God the things that are God's",[22] he definitively founded the "spiritual kingdom" that sits in judgment upon, and renders relative, all the kingdoms of this world. So that in this matter one may invoke him without recognizing the authority of his Church—a position main-tained by many of the supporters of a "pure Gospel"—which is

[17] See St. Gregory of Nyssa, *In Cantica canticorum*, hom. 13 (PG 44, 1049–52): "The foundation of the Church is the creation of a new universe. In her, according to the words of Isaiah, new heavens and a new earth are created; in her is formed another man, in the image of him who created him."

[18] St. Augustine, *Epist.* 118, chap. 5, no. 33: "Totum culmen auctoritatis lumenque rationis in illo uno salutari nomine atque in una ejus Ecclesia recreando et reformando humani generi constitutum est" (PL 33, 448).

[19] Gal 4:26 and 5:1; see Vatican Council I, constitution *De Ecclesia*, prologue: Christ founded his Church "to make the salutary work of Redemption per-petually durable".

[20] 2 Pet 3:13: "But we look for a new heaven and a new earth according to his promises, in which justice dwelleth."

[21] Gregory of Elvira, *Tractatus* 18: "Qui semel in Christo manumissus est, tyrannicam non patitur servitutem" (p. 197 in the Batiffol-Wilmart edi-tion).

[22] Mt 22:21; Jn 18:36; see also Lk 12:14; Mt 22:24–27.

not the full Gospel. Such was the view that Rousseau wanted to defend against the theorists of despotism. He was not able to make up his mind to twist Christianity out of shape so far as to make it play the part of ancient paganism, as far as the State was concerned; and so, without much care for coherence, he added to the "religion of the citizen" a "religion of man", "unique, eternal, and unchangeable in every country", "without temples, altars, or rites, restricted to the purely interior worship of the supreme God and the eternal demands of morality". But a deism of this type, even supposing it could invoke the authority of Christ, would furnish no solution to the problem posed for us so bluntly, in either of its alternative forms.

Such a system of worship would in fact set up again—insofar as it could be made effective—that very dualism which it was supposed to do away with and, in consequence, all the conflicts that arise therefrom. It would rob the State of the loyalty of the citizen and break up "social unity", at any rate in that form which, so it is claimed, it would assure. In virtue of its spirit of universal charity, it is "contrary to the particularized social spirit", which is of necessity that of all "civil and political societies";[23] it would even be sufficient, as St. Augustine remarks, to make religion "accused of being the State's enemy".[24] And anyhow, does anyone really think it would be practicable for men as a whole? From time to time someone would stand up

---

[23] Rousseau, letters to Usteri of April 30 and July 18, 1763; see the notes regarding *Émile* in *Fragments inédits*, ed. Jansen (1882), p. 20.

[24] St. Augustine, *Epist.* 138, chap. 2, no. 10: "Cum vero legitur, praecipiente auctoritate divina, non reddendum malum pro malo . . . accusatur religio, tanquam inimica reipublicae" (PL 33, 529). In this letter Augustine is replying to the objections of the pagan Volusianus, which had been passed on to him by Marcellinus (*Epist.* 136). See also Joseph Vialatoux, *La Cité de Hobbes: Théorie de l'état totalitaire* (1935), p. 167: "To proclaim a kingdom of God is to let loose—apparently—a new war in the heart of the citizen. For will not the coming of this kingdom make us the subjects of two masters? And shall we not, in consequence, run the risk of finding ourselves divided between two laws—that of the State and that of God? This problem was bound to disturb, at the very least, the author of *Leviathan*."

and speak for conscience, proclaiming that "we ought to obey God rather than men",[25] but his voice would soon be silenced and all would return to order, so-called. The champions of the "pure Gospel" would take refuge in some celestial daydream that would be totally ineffective against tyranny[26] and would lead men to say—to quote Rousseau once more—that "true Christians are made to be slaves"—if indeed the silencing was not even more thoroughgoing, so that even this dream itself disappeared. Interior freedom would have had its day, for the majority at all events, and there would no longer be a "spiritual kingdom".

Noting that Christian states made more than one attempt to reestablish the system of the ancient world, Rousseau expresses his regret at their failure. "The spirit of Christianity always won", he says. "The sacred cultus always either stayed or became once more independent of the sovereign, and without any necessary connection with the body of the State."[27] One wonders whether he would have said the same today, and what he would think of our recent "secular religions". The totalitarian mentality—for which, perhaps, as a forerunner, he must bear some of the responsibility—has surely registered success and developed threats that would give him occasion to think

---

[25] Acts 5:29.

[26] See Vialatoux, *La Cité de Hobbes*, p. 168 (commenting on Hobbes): "What king would be stupid enough to inflict the punishment of death on a subject because he learned that all the man was doing was waiting for another king at the end of this world? It suffices earthly kings to have absolute rule in their respective polities."

[27] A similar nostalgia can be found in Auguste Comte (*Cours de philosophie positive*, lesson 60): "Antiquity alone has been able to offer, up to now, a complete political system comprising a whole homogeneity." The distinction between spiritual and temporal in Comte is quite different from that which the Church professes; see my *The Drama of Atheistic Humanism*, English trans. (San Francisco, 1995), pp. 193–95. We may apply here what Erick Weil wrote concerning the politics of Rousseau in general: Rousseau wished to be "faithful to antiquity", but knew that his theories were "unrealizable"; he was too late—"the rot had made such progress that no power in the world could stop it" ("Jean-Jacques Rousseau et la politique", *Critique*, no. 56, pp. 17 and 21).

again. He himself said that although "national religions are useful to the State as parts of its constitution", they are none-theless "harmful to mankind".[28] In point of fact Christianity changed profoundly the conditions of man's government, by changing the nature and the form of worship;[29] but there has been a swing of the pendulum in the opposite direction. "The movement that drives on earthly societies to be 'as gods' has today reached its zenith",[30] by commandeering and falsifying more than one of the Christian values; it too, in its own turn and in its own way, has "brought the City of God down out of heaven to earth and out of eternity into time", once more proclaiming—in practice, at least—that all men belong to this city as parts, and that the parts count for nothing save in relation to the whole.[31] And by so doing it has set up the State in its old claims to be the supreme end for all and to make itself—in the persons of those who embody its power—an object of adoration. Christians who stick to their faith have once more become "unbelievers" and "enemies of the human race",[32] as they were in the eyes of ancient paganism; they are accused of being "destroyers of solidarity". Confronted with these successes and threats and claims, the Christian cannot but find a tremendous reserve of power in the well-known axiom: "God loves nothing better than the freedom of his Church." Even with all her ponderous earthly equipment, the Catholic Church is seen, with ever-increasing clarity, to be the one effective guarantee of spiritual liberty.

Even here and now she is a power for liberation, in an initial sense at the wholly human level, and as regards the whole mass of men. She does not stop short at exhorting them to a higher life;

[28] Rousseau, *Letters écrites de la montagne*, 3:130.

[29] See Fustel de Coulanges, *La Cité antique*, bk. 5, chap. 3.

[30] Robert Rouquette, S.J., "L'Église derrière le rideau de fer", *Études* (April 1952), pp. 3–4.

[31] Étienne Gilson, *Les Métamorphoses de la Cité de Dieu*, p. 106, on the subject of Roger Bacon's vision of a Christian republic. Cf. Aristotle, *Politics*, bk. 8, chap. 1.

[32] See the *Martyrdom of Polycarp*, 3, 12, and the *Epistle to Diognetus*, 5, 2.

she provides them with an environment that brings it to them and an atmosphere that strengthens them in it.[33] The all-too-numerous facts that can be cited against this do no more than prove that men are men, that even in the Church minds can often remain part secular, and that abuses can creep in anywhere. As Renan said: "There is no immaculate history"[34]—a statement banal enough but particularly painful in this case; *optimi corruptio pessima*. But facts of this kind should not be allowed to hide from us something equally, and fundamentally, evident; that the effective distinction of the two powers, which is an indispensable condition of spiritual life, is tied up with the existence of a supranational and universal Church, "a divine institution embracing all nations and transcending them"[35]—and that the only Church of that kind in the world and the world's history is the Church founded by Christ. Hence the outcry against a religion "which sets itself up above society", which is "a plague destructive of the social order", and from which "the earth must be delivered".[36] As Cardinal Manning pointed out in his *Caesarism and Ultramontanism*, it does not matter whether Caesarism be manifested in a person, a senate, or the masses (we might add today, or by a single party)—it always means tyranny on the political level and persecution on the spiritual level, and can never mean anything else. The Church always was and always will be the source of human liberty and the mother of freedom. Liberty of thought and of the individual, liberty of conscience in the family and the

[33] See Leo XIII, encyclical *Immortale Dei*: "Everything which is of use in protecting the people against the license of princes who do not have its good at heart, everything which checks the unjust encroachments of the State against the community or the family, everything which is concerned with honor and the human personality and safeguards for it equal rights for all—where all this is concerned, the Catholic Church has either taken the initiative or extended its patronage or its protection, as the monuments of past ages witness."

[34] *Le Judaïsme comme race et comme religion* (1883).

[35] Pius XI, encyclical *Ubi arcano* (December 23, 1922).

[36] Dupuis, *Abrégé de l'origine de tous les cultes* (1836), p. 490: "Blind obedience to a hostile leader, even if he does bear the name of Head of the Church, is a crime of *lèse-nation*."

State—these always stem from the limitation of the temporal power.[37]

Every country of our history-worn Europe has proved by experience that "the impediments placed in the way of the regular exercise of pontifical jurisdiction"—which is the sign and condition of Catholic unity—"did not profit the exercise of episcopal jurisdiction in any way, but rather the civil power", and that power's efforts at constraint upon conscience. It was the development of the Roman power that, with the growth of the Church, defended the bishops and, with them, the faithful. Without the support of their communion with Rome, Christian communities crumble away and are easily subjugated. Since it is no longer faced by a strong and organized spiritual power —strong preeminently in the deep-rooted and enthusiastic assent of the Catholic conscience—the State makes itself master of the whole of man, and there is no longer any barrier left to the extremes of absolutism.[38]

From time to time there have arisen *spirituali* who have become disturbed at the power of the Church, and whom the Church has had to disown (I do not, of course, mean the saints, who are continually recalling her to the Gospel virtues). These men, who have often been moved by noble ideals and have also believed themselves to be serving the cause of the pure Gospel, have challenged the Church's right to the very conditions of her effective presence in this world. Some of them have in fact played, on occasion, a genuinely prophetic role, despite their exaggerations, and both "true and false reform" are to be found entangled in the movements they

[37] Henry Edward Cardinal Manning, *Caesarism and Ultramontanism* (1874). See Bautain, *La Religion et la liberté* (1865): "The setting up of the Church is the very realizing of freedom in the world"; also pp. 20–21: "By maintaining spiritual authority intact in this world the Church has maintained human dignity." Cf. H. Rahner, *Abendländische Kirchenfreiheit* (1943).

[38] See the Abbé H. Hemmer, *Rapports des papes et des évêques* (Malines Conference), quoted in Bivort de la Saudée, *Anglicans et Catholiques*, pp. 199, 204, 207; I. Döllinger, *Die Kirche und die Kirchen*, in particular the chapter on the Churches and civil liberty.

headed. In practice, their concern was often with real and serious abuses, which either an inner complicity or ingrained habit prevented those around them from seeing—worldly display, excessive money-mindedness, interference in purely secular matters, political Machiavellianism, the use of spiritual means for entirely this-worldly ends, and so on. The arguments used against them were often weak enough, sometimes plainly false;[39] sometimes they were the victims of men not worth their little fingers. But for all that their intransigence was, in principle, nonetheless blind.[40] By a logical train of reasoning whose full implications they did not see, but which were to show themselves very clearly as from the advent of Lutheranism, they eagerly invoked the support of princes and sought refuge with them when things became difficult. When they demanded that the Roman Pontiff "should restrict himself to his spiritual mission", which "consists solely in preaching and absolving", and that he should "leave the emperor to be emperor, without hindrance", they were making use of equivocal formulae that they endowed with a sense illegitimately restrictive.[41] Even while they believed themselves to be working in the service of Christian perfection, they were in

[39] See, for example, the curious *Dialogus contra fraticellos S. Jacobi de Marchia*, published by Baluze in his *Miscellanea* (1761), 2:595–605, or the sermon of John XXII that seeks to prove by means of the text "whatsoever you shall bind upon earth" that Christ has placed all power and all earthly possession in the hands of Peter's successor.

[40] See the condemnations of the Vaudois by Innocent III in 1208, that of the Spirituals by John XXII (1317, 1322), and the twenty-sixth proposition of the *Syllabus errorum* of Pius IX.

[41] The formulas are those of Luther in his *An den christlichen Adel* (1520). We all know their consequences. On the divine right of states sanctioned—for practical purposes—by Lutheranism, see, for example, the theologian Brenz, as quoted and summarized by Lucien Bernarcki in *La Doctrine de l'Église chez le cardinal Hosius* (1936), pp. 181–92. On the struggle of Ubertino of Casale with John XXII and his relationship with Louis of Bavaria, see Frédégaud Callaey, O.F.M.Cap., *Idéalisme spirituel au XIVe siècle: Étude sur Ubertin de Casale* (1911), pp. 236–51. For the "spiritual" movement in the Middle Ages, the reader should consult the study by Fr. Chenu, LV (June 1954).

reality serving the cause of those who were its enemies. They recruited as auxiliaries to their forces imperialist and royalist jurists who, in many instances, were trying to bring down the spiritual power embodied by the Church so as to establish the divine right of kings. They stood as a justification for men who were continually drawing on ancient law for weapons against the papacy, and by the same token assembling an arsenal for use against the freedom of the peoples.

There are grounds for fearing that today, within a very different social and political context, certain utopias of a similar kind are being sketched out. There is a danger that an exaggerated or misdirected critique of what is freely labelled "Constantinian Christianity" (the exaggeration in question should certainly be described, rather, as "Theodosian") may tend to restrict, and restrict dangerously, the Church's sphere of action. It is to be feared that among those who advocate a "return to the spiritual" there are some who, led astray by a dangerous ambiguity, really have in view not so much purity of the apostolate as an obscuring of Christianity and its own very spirit by the gods of the age; and that, in aiming at the liberation of a Gospel that they believe to be in captivity, some well-intentioned Christians are doing little more than striking a compromise—without wishing to do so—with the forces that wish to suppress it by either suppressing or subjugating the Church. Thus, although their point of departure is a real desire to break with real abuses, rejecting alliances that are unjustifiable and disentangling the faith in all its austere transcendence, they would in fact compromise that very achievement at which they have aimed. They would, in practice, hinder the spreading of that "testament of freedom" which has been handed on to us from the first Apostles of Christ[42] (though admittedly under ever-imperfect conditions), and their labors would enslave the homeland of freedom. They would be helping to banish from the earth "that spiritual freedom, the taste for which was given

---

[42] St. Irenaeus, *Adversus haereses*, bk. 3, chap. 12, no. 14, and chap. 15, no. 3.

to the world by the words of Christ",[43] and which the world will lose even its very taste for insofar as it rejects Christ. Which would indeed be the occasion to cry once again with St. Paul: "O senseless Galatians, who hath bewitched you? . . . By the freedom wherewith Christ has made us free, stand fast and be not held again under the yoke of bondage."[44]

* * *

But the Church does not assure man of his liberty alone; her task is more positive than that. She is also the herald and architect of unity.

Another statement that Rousseau was compelled to make— the fact is, of course, only too clear in itself—was that State religion, even when it lays claim to the whole of man, cannot unite all men: "to each State its own religion". Thus he depicts each people as "in a natural condition of war with all the others"—or at any rate leaves them thus. They can hope to escape internal division only at the cost of divisions that are at once less curable and more dangerous. There is a fight to the death between them, and if at the end there are only two left, the rupture is nonetheless deadly for that. Dreams of universality[45] always crystallize as against another people, race, or system—provided, of course, that they do not remain simply in the category of pleasant daydreams. When "the longing for the

[43] M. Paris, *Prière*.

[44] Gal 3:1 and 4:31—5:1.

[45] Stoicism was not a dream of this kind, as has sometimes been said. It did not really anticipate the Christian faith even in idea alone. See Étienne Gilson, *Les Métamorphoses*, pp. 6–7: "The Stoic wise man is a 'cosmopolitan', but in the first place the universe is a whole very much greater than any society would be, even if it stretched to the limits of the earth, and in the second place no one can be a citizen of it in the true sense, because the cosmos is not a society. To take one's place in a universal physical order whose laws one accepts and with which one wishes to be in union may be an act of wisdom, but it is not an act of citizenship. The Stoics do not seem to have conceived the ideal of a universal society co-extensive with our planet and capable of uniting the whole of mankind."

ultimate union" eventually comes to light, it is conceived by each in the form of the wish that "he himself, or his family, or his own country, shall have universal dominion", as Guillaume Postel naïvely put it.[46]

It seems a depressing outlook for a humanity whose unalterable longing is perpetually powerless. "For millennia a powerful instinct has driven it through an apparent chaos of social dispersion and encounter, catastrophe and adventure, construction and disintegration, toward a 'life in common' that translates into external terms something of the unity it experiences obscurely within itself. But, as we see only too clearly, humanity can never get to the end of all the forces of opposition that are everywhere at work and that humanity itself perpetually generates and revitalizes. Societies expand without ceasing to be closed; they interpenetrate only to clash with greater violence, and beneath their own internal cohesion there persists the mutual hostility of souls." It is an opposition of Jew and Gentile, which is the symbol of all oppositions. Yet a Redeemer has come, who has made out of these two opposed bodies one single thing—his Church,[47] which is the house visibly built by him on the Rock of Peter and within which he undertakes the work of reuniting for common worship of the one God "the children of God that were dispersed".[48] It is "the City that is one in fellowship",[49] as the psalm says so magnificently; there is to be heard the great voice that proclaims to all people that they are the children of the same Father.[50] The Spirit of the

[46] *La Vierge vénitienne*, trans. Henri Morard (1928), p. 51.

[47] Eph 2:14–15; Col 1:20–27. In the Pauline idea of "mystery" there is thus identity between the Redemption and the building up of the Church. An individualist Christianity is thus not only seriously incomplete; it is something unthinkable.

[48] Rom 3:29; 1 Tim 2:5–6; Jn 11:15–16, 17:2.

[49] Ps 121:3 (Knox version); see J. Bonduelle, O.P., "Une Ville 'où se resserre l'unité' ", VS (April 1952); St. Hilary of Poitiers, *In Psalm.* 121, no. 5 (PL 9, 663a).

[50] See *Prima Clementis* 160, 4; St. Clement of Alexandria, *Stromata*, bk. 7, chap. 17, no. 107, etc.

Lord dwells there, and in that Spirit we at last find that internal principle of unity which the world pursues in vain;[51] a principle which is also that of freedom, since it brings it about that each man who has overcome himself enters spontaneously into the life-rhythm of all. Thus drawn together and reconciled, "signed with one Spirit",[52] we are no longer without "hope . . . and without God in this world", but "by him we have access both in one Spirit to the Father." [53] Here we have again the unique and harmonious body in which we become "members one of another" [54] and in which each member concurs in the good of the others;[55] it is the Heavenly Jerusalem in our midst. This is our Mother who, in making us free, makes us all "one in Jesus Christ":[56]

> Glorious things are said of thee:
>> O city of God!
> I will be mindful of Rahab and of Babylon
>> among my worshippers,
> Behold the foreigners, and Tyre, and the people
>> of the Ethiopians:
> There was their birthplace!
> All shall say to Sion, My Mother: this man and that
>> is born in her,
> And the Highest himself hath founded her!

[51] Dom Anscar Vonier, O.S.B., in his *The People of God* (French trans., *Le Peuple de Dieu*, p. 180); see also Leo XIII, encyclical *Divinum illud* (1897).

[52] Nicetas of Remesiana, *Explanatio symboli*, no. 10 (PL 54, 871b).

[53] Eph 2:12–22.

[54] Rom 12:5.

[55] Eph 4:4; 1 Cor 12:4–13; Eph 2:18: "For by him we have access both in one Spirit to the Father"; see also the Nicaeo-Constantinopolitan Creed: "Spiritum sanctum Dominum et vivificantem"; St. Augustine, *De civitate Dei*: "Spiritus sanctus est Patris et Filii amor et connexio; ad ipsum pertinet societas qua efficimur unum."

[56] Gal 3:28. It is not, of course, by mere chance but rather in virtue of a deep-reaching logic that this Epistle to the Galatians is at one and the same time the charter of both Gospel freedom and Gospel unity.

The Lord shall tell in his writings of peoples
    and of princes,
Of them that have been born in her.[57]

God gathers all men into the city he has founded, like a
scribe entering one by one on the municipal register the names
of those who have been granted citizenship. And all men are
reborn in it in order to become fellow citizens. "There, the
courtesan becomes a virgin and the Ethiopian white"; those
who camped under the tents of Cedar are now at home in the
light-filled palaces of the "true Solomon".[58] We read this
prophecy at the feast of the Epiphany, and those elements in it
which are already realized are our promise for the future.

It is true that we are as yet well out in our balance sheet.
The Church applies to herself the psalmist's prophecy, but
from the human standpoint the claim is a crazy one. Celsus
said so centuries ago, and in his voice we can hear that of the
"realist" through the ages: "The Christians say that they want
to establish unity in the world; but anyone who gets that idea
into his head gives proof thereby of his lack of knowledge of
the world." Does the experience of the centuries not show
that the thing is a fantasy? "Just as souls are allotted to men at
birth, so special spiritual natures are allotted to peoples."[59] But
"our faith is a victory", and what is impossible to men is possible with God. It is, of course, true that on earth the thing is
no more than an anticipation, despite all its visible results—
for the political realizations of a *respublica Christiana* are
another matter altogether. In practice, the Church can, at
best, do no more than pacify and moderate; she can reduce the

<hr />

[57] Ps 86:3–6; see St. Bruno of Segni, *in loc.*: "Mater Sion, dicit homo. Ac si
dicat: Haec est mater et revera mater, quae pietatis sinum omnibus aperit, nullis
materna viscera claudit, omnes suscipit, omnes ex affectu fovit et nutrit" (PL
164, 1033d).

[58] St. Gregory of Nyssa, *In Cantica*, hom. 2 (PG 44, 792b–d); St. Augustine,
In Psalm. 86 (PL 37, 1100–1105).

[59] Symmachus, *Supplication to the Emperors Theodosius and Valentinian II*, no. 8.

effectiveness of the principle of our conflicts, but she cannot get rid of it. The "one accord" of the Acts scarcely lasted a day.[60] The secular world goes on its way; every day its subjections weigh us down and its conflicts tear us apart—"We are in Christ—and also in this age."[61] The "perfect man" is not something realized, but an ideal at horizon distance;[62] we are saved "by hope" and we still have to "wait".[63] But that does not mean that the principle of salvation is not already in us and active. The man who has faith does not have to wait in order to enact within himself the twofold embryonic experience of freedom and unity; and this is never more so than when all the appearances seem to the contrary. The mystery of the Church is never lived more intensely than it is then. For the same thing holds good of the Church in her members as of the Church in her Head; she can redeem with him only as she was redeemed by him—on the Cross.

A subtle snare—that of "pure inwardness"—awaits the man whose ambition is to "liberate" her. What goes to make up the world is considered by him a fatal illusion or a degradation of being; it is seen only as "the place where the deadly cycle runs its course"[64]—the deadly cycle of evil or non-being. The universal fact of mysticism bears witness to the powerful pull of that program which consists in turning away from this world, leaving it to its own vanity, breaking free from human solidarity and making a solitary escape into the spirit. One wonders how many have lost their souls in the belief of finding them thus—in introversion, a return to the "primordial state", the exploration of the self, the search for the center where man becomes one with the one and

---

[60] Acts 2:46, 4:24, 5:12, 8:6, 15:25; see also Rom 15:6; 1 Cor 1:10, 12:13.

[61] St. Augustine, *In Joannem*, tract. 81, no. 4: "Sumus in Christo. . . . Sumus adhuc in hoc saeculo" (PL 35, 1842).

[62] Eph 4:13: "until we all meet into the unity of faith and of the knowledge of the Son of God, unto a perfect man."

[63] Rom 8:24–25.

[64] Plato, *Theaetetus*, 176a.

only Essence.[65] Even within Christianity itself the man who is concerned with "the interior life" may experience a temptation of this sort, under forms that are (to some extent, at any rate) less misleading.[66] But the Church provides a way out of the trap. She, too, calls us to "interiority"; through all her Doctors and masters of the spiritual life she emphasizes again and again that our souls are made in the image of God, that the loftiness and grandeur of their being lies in their capacity for God,[67] and that entering into her is "entering into the truth of God".[68] Again, she teaches (with the necessary explanations) "that the heart's treasure and the treasure of the heavens are one and the same, and that the same opening reveals both".[69] She has a place for methodical training in the spiritual life, and commends such a training, since she does not believe that in this sphere all technique is incompatible with the sovereign primacy of grace—indeed, she is much more concerned, in this matter, about standards of judgment apt to put up with mediocrity and encourage illuminism.[70]

[65] See René Guénon, *Aperçus sur l'initiation* (1946), p. 219: "The passing over from the 'exterior' to the 'interior' is a passing over from multiplicity to unity, from the circumference to the center, to the unique point from which it is possible to the human being, once restored to the prerogatives of his 'primordial state', to raise himself up to states higher yet, and by the realization of his total essence to be at last, effectively and actually, what he is potentially from all eternity."

[66] See St. Augustine, *Sermo* 37, no. 6: "Invenis alium dicentem tibi: 'Sufficit mihi in conscientia Deum colere, Deum adorare; quid mihi opus est aut in ecclesiam ire, aut visibiliter misceri Christianis?' Lineam vult habere, sine tunica lanae" (PL 38, 224).

[67] St. Bernard: "Celsa creatura in capacitate Majestatis" (there are, of course, innumerable similar texts).

[68] St. Bonaventure, *Itinerarium mentis in Deum*, chap. 1: "Oportet etiam nos intrare ad mentem nostram, quae est imago Dei aeviterna et spiritualis, et intra nos; et hoc est ingredi in veritatem Dei."

[69] St. Isaac of Nineveh, quoted by Nicephorus the Hermit, *Tractatus de sobrietate et cordis custodia* (PL 147); see E. Kadloubovsky and G. E. H. Palmer, *Writings from the Philokalia on the Prayer of the Heart* (1951), p. 30.

[70] Cf. H. de B., *La Prière du Coeur* (1953), pp. 27–29.

But all the same, she still protects us from deceptive short cuts. Being, as she is, a body that is at one and the same time mystical and visible, she frees us, by the very fact of her existence, from the illusions of a spiritual vocation conceived as solitary and disembodied. Instead of initiating us into some way of interiorization or handing on to us some secret of mental concentration, she invites us to say in act as well as in words: "Thy Kingdom come; thy will be done." And she reminds us ceaselessly of the demands of our social vocation and the reality of our earthly condition. In so doing she recalls us to worship of the true God; the man who separates himself from the community of brotherhood turns imperceptibly from God to worship himself.

"Universal salvation, just like individual salvation, is accomplished, and can only be accomplished, in concrete time and through history."[71] In the Church everything rams home this law to the individual Christian; everything summons him to the thought of eternity—but also firmly sets on one side the temptation to "leap clear of time" and disposes him to take seriously both existence and the drama that plays itself out therein. In the Church, everything reminds him of his neighbor; even when he abandons this world, in virtue of a special vocation, of which he is never the sole judge, this should be only in order to serve it, for if, in the external sense, he cuts himself off from other men, this is only so as to be united to them. Even the barest-stripped varieties of prayer are still brotherly prayer, and at his own post the solitary is always at work on the common task. "The highest of divine favors do not break his partnership in the sufferings and victories of the Church militant",[72] and he

---

[71] H. C. Puech, distinguishing the Christian idea of salvation from that of the ancient myths, in the report of the International Congress on the History of Religions (Amsterdam, 1951), p. 49.

[72] Joseph Maréchal, S.J., *Études sur la psychologie des mystiques* (1937), 2:15, on the perfect mystic, who is, "by virtue of that very fact, the perfect Christian". Hugh of Saint-Victor, *De amore sponsi ad sponsam*: "Quanto magis mundum

never wishes to "save himself alone",[73] for he knows that Christ wills to "lead us to life together".[74] The Christian life, whatever its external form, is always directed to "the building up of the body of Christ"[75]—beyond all the distinctions (often superficial enough) between active and contemplative life and in spite of all specialization. A Christian never stops being a member of this body, and that is why his spiritual life, instead of evaporating in an illusory "contemplation", is unfolded in a time that is moving toward its consummation; it is implanted in human history, but implanted without being engulfed. For it is harvested in eternity. "One generation passeth away and another generation cometh";[76] but in the Church of Christ "the generation of generations" continually grows, for its perpetual stabilization is in God.[77] Thus, history does not resolve itself into "the continuous and painful creation of an ultimate caste of inheritors"[78] that is itself marked down for death. Time is not purely destructive; in proportion as decaying elements crumble away there emerges what is destined to life. And already here in our present condition—even humanly speaking—the Church

---

fugiendo Deo appropinquare incipimus, tanto magis in unum congregamur" (PL 176, 994a).

[73] See St. Augustine, *Sermo* 17, no. 2 (PL 38, 125); St. Teresa of Avila, *Book of the Foundations*, chap. 1.

[74] Rule of St. Benedict, chap. 72.

[75] See Eph 2:22; 1 Cor 3:9; 2 Cor 6:16; Mt 16:18. We have watered down all these expressions that signify the building-up of the Church of God. In point of fact we are not concerned here with an individual and moral "edification"—a stimulation of Christian awareness by means described as "edifying"—but rather with a real construction of the great social and spiritual body that is the Church, by the union of all the faithful animated by the Spirit of Christ. See E. Boismard, O.P., RB (1949), pp. 465–66, following a dissertation by K. L. Schmidt.

[76] Qo 1:4.

[77] St. Augustine, *In Psalm.* 101, nos. 10–14; see also Étienne Gilson, *Philosophie et incarnation selon saint Augustine* (Montreal, 1945), pp. 47–49.

[78] Henri Chambre, "Signification philosophique et théologique du marxisme", *Chronique sociale de France* (1952), p. 358.

guarantees that communion between us which our modern civilizations know nothing of,[79] and which was in any case never anything but transitory. "The Bride of Christ never ceases to be aware of that total humanity whose destiny she carries in her womb."[80]

Such is her twofold gift. She is the ark of salvation, which rescues us from the flood of a world that perishes;[81] but at the same time she is also the storehouse of human hope;[82] *mundus reconciliatus Ecclesia*. "The Church is the world, reconciled."[83]

* * *

The Church is in the world, and by the effect of her presence alone she communicates to it an unrest that cannot be soothed away. She is a perpetual witness of the Christ who came "to shake human life to its foundations", as Guardini puts it,[84] and it is a fact that she appears in the world as a "great ferment of discord".[85] God says to her, as he did to one of his Prophets: "Lo, I have set thee this day over the nations, and over king-doms, to root up and to pull down, and to waste and to destroy"

[79] See André Malraux, *La Monnaie de l'Absolu* (1950), p. 50; also p. 51: "A civilization of man alone will not last for very long." Man without God is always man alone. Our age, substituting as it has the historical for the eternal, has by the same token substituted succession for communion.

[80] *Paul Claudel interroge le Cantique des cantiques*, p. 63. See also Eph 1:10: the Church "recapitulates" all things in Christ.

[81] Gregory of Elvira, *Tractatus* 12 (p. 139 in the Battifol-Wilmart edition).

[82] This was something very firmly grasped by St. Ignatius Loyola, not as a theoretician, but as a mystic and man of the Church. The point has been well emphasized by Fr. Hugo Rahner, S.J., in his little book *The Spirituality of St. Ignatius Loyola: An Account of Its Historical Development*, trans. Francis John Smith (Chicago, 1953). See Paschal Rapine, commenting on St. Augustine's *In Joannem*, tract. 32: "so that in order to be a truly spiritual man it is necessary to be a good ecclesiastic" (*Christianisme fervent*, 1:12).

[83] St. Augustine, *Sermo* 16, no. 8 (PL 38, 588); see Pseudo-Chrysostom, *Opus imperfectum in Mattheum*, hom. 23 (PG 56, 755).

[84] Romano Guardini, *L'Essence du christianisme*, trans. P. Lorson (1950), p. 34.

[85] Paul Claudel, *Sous le signe du dragon* (1948), p. 118. See also his preface to Jacques Rivière's *À la Trace de Dieu*, pp. 17–21.

as well as "to build and to plant",[86] and after all, Scripture, which proclaims the fact throughout, is itself wholly "the book of the battles of the Lord".[87] There is no disguising this point; it is essential. We must not forget that the Church is "militant". She is "the army of Christ",[88] the "levy of the living God";[89] "the levy of the great King", in which we were enrolled at baptism and confirmation.[90] She will not let us overlook the fact that there is no "participation [of] justice with injustice . . . or . . . fellowship [of] light with darkness [or] concord [of] Christ with Belial", and that "to recognize the one God is to declare total war on all the others." [91]

> The Incarnate Word is our King; now, he came into this world to give battle to the devil, and all the saints who lived before his coming are, as it were, soldiers who form the advance guard of the royal army; those who have come since then, and are to come, up to the end of the world, are the soldiers who march behind their King. The King himself takes his place at the center of his army, and he advances surrounded by the defensive wall which his troops form around him. And although all

[86] Jer 1:10. Cf. the cry of the prophet in 15:10: "Woe is me, my mother! Why hast thou borne me, a man of strife, a man of contention to all the earth?"; and Origen, *In Josue*, hom. 13, no. 3 (p. 373 in Baehrens' edition).

[87] Rupert of Deutz, *De victoria Verbi Dei*, bk. 2, chap. 18: "Ergo liber bellorum Domini universa Scriptura est"; "Quid enim aliud continetur vel agitur in Scripturis sanctis, nisi bellum et certamina Verbi Dei ad destructionem peccati et mortis?" (PL 169, 1257d and 1258a); Gerhoh of Reichersberg (PL 194, 997b); Origen, *In Judic.*, hom. 6, no. 2 (p. 500 in Baehrens' edition).

[88] St. John Chrysostom, *Dialogue on the Priesthood*, bk. 6.

[89] Tertullian, *Ad martyres*, chap. 3: "Vocati sumus ad militiam Dei vivi, jam tunc in sacramenti verba respondimus" (PL 1, 624a); St. Ambrose, *De sacramentis*, 2, 4: "Unctus es quasi athleta Christi."

[90] St. Cyril of Jerusalem, *Fourth Catechesis*, chap. 3 (PG 33, 428b); see A. M. Roguet, "Caractère baptismal et incorporation à l'Église", MD 32 (1952): 77: "It is baptism which has made us soldiers of Christ. . . . Confirmation makes of us prophets and witnesses, even martyrs", but "we may make a connection between martyrdom and fighting."

[91] 2 Cor 6:14–16; Origen, *De oratione*, second petition of the *Pater*; *In Exod.*, hom. 8, no. 4.

sorts of different arms can be seen in so great a multitude—for the sacraments and observances of the ancient peoples are not the same as those of the new—still, all are fighting for the same King and, under the same standard, pursue the same enemy and are crowned in the same victory.[92]

The thing is not, of course, to be taken in an external sense, as if it were a matter of one human power ranged against others. Neither the Church's weapons nor her objectives will be those of this world: "For though we walk in the flesh, we do not war according to the flesh." [93] The war she conducts under the standard of the Cross and in the pattern of the great struggles of the Redemption and in continuity with it is a spiritual conflict. She is in action against "the rulers of the world of this darkness, against the spirits of wickedness in the high places",[94] and each one of us has constantly to be winning his own inner freedom, in conflict with hostile powers. The enemy has to be pursued and wiped out in the heart of each soldier,[95] for "we do not come to Christ by way of repose and delight, but through all kinds of tribulations and temptations." [96] There are two "agonies", which stand over against each other in all those who want to follow Christ: the Christian agony and the agony of this world, the agony that redeems and the agony that breaks down, the agony of the Cross and the agony of sin.[97] The line that

[92] Hugh of Saint-Victor, *De sacramentis christianae fidei*, prologue, chap. 2 (PL 176, 183b–c); see Origen, *In Judic.*, hom. 9, no. 2 (p. 520 in Baehrens' edition); St. Cyprian, *Ad martyres et conf.*, bk. 2, epist. 6; St. Augustine, *De diversis quaestionibus* 83, q. 61, no. 2; Cassian, *Collatio* 5, chaps. 14 and 24, no. 1; *Collatio* 20, chap. 8, nos. 10–11; St. Ignatius Loyola, *Spiritual Exercises*, meditations on the Kingdom and the Two Standards; *Histoire et Esprit* (1950), pp. 185–92 and 212–14.

[93] 2 Cor 10:3.

[94] Eph 6:12.

[95] Origen, *In Josue*, hom. 1, no. 7 (p. 295 in Baehrens' edition); hom. 5, no. 2 (ibid., p. 316); hom. 13, no. 1 (ibid., p. 371).

[96] Origen, *In Cantica*, bk. 3 (p. 222 in Baehrens' edition).

[97] Cassian, *Institutiones* 5, 13; *Collationes* 5, 14 and 24; 13, 18; 20, 8. Hans Urs von Balthasar, *Der Christ und die Angst* (Einsiedeln, 1951).

divides the two opposed camps is an invisible one that runs through our consciences. But, inevitably, the conflict breaks out exteriorly too—"The Church is unceasingly torn by internal as well as by exterior conflict";[98] the "mystery of iniquity" is at work without as well as within.[99] The great struggle that had its prelude in heaven is fought out among men through the whole of time.[100] People do not like their apathy thus disturbed, and they are afraid of too lofty a vocation; the bonds of flesh and blood take some breaking. The world views as an insult and a provocation anything that does not conform to its own ideas; feeling itself threatened by the least of the Church's spiritual conquests, it is never without reaction to them.

The Church in the world is thus the Church amid conflict, prefigured by the warrior Israel led by Yahweh to the conquest of its inheritance. Her God is the God of peace, and she herself is "a blessed vision of peace";[101] she desires as her members men who are gentle and peaceful, she preaches him who has made "peace through the blood of his cross",[102] and when her message is listened to she always exercises a pacifying influence. But she has to begin by tearing us away from the false peace which was that of the world before Christ and in which we are always trying to take refuge again. For "the preparation of the Gospel of peace" the Church must equip us all with "the armor of God", as St. Paul points out.[103] We are in slavery; she is to deliver us, and deliverance does not come about without conflict. It is only at her border that God has given her peace.[104]

[98] Primasus of Adrumetum, *In Apocalypsim*, bk. 1 (PL 68, 810–11).

[99] 2 Th 2:7.

[100] Rev 11:7, 12:7.

[101] Hymn for the Dedication of a Church: "Caelestis urbs, Hierusalem, Beata pacis visio."

[102] Col 1:20.

[103] Eph 6:11–17; see also 1 Th 5:8–9.

[104] Ps 147:14; see St. Cyril of Jerusalem, *Eighteenth Catechesis*, chap. 17 (PG 33, 1049a); Vladimir Soloviev, *Trois Entretiens*, trans. E. Tavernier (1916), p. 124: "In the spiritual warfare as in political conflict, the only good peace is that which is concluded when the end of the war concerned is achieved."

So, before she can be the festive Jerusalem, which celebrates its Lord in a peace finally achieved, she has to pass through the status of Jacob, whose name signifies struggle and toil.[105] Before she can be crowned on high, she must clash with the powers of this world; and she will never be in triumph and glory in it,[106] whatever the illusions periodically recurring in some of her children. The misbehavior of those who call themselves such is a perpetual bitterness to her—even more than persecution, schism, and heresy.[107] She goes on her way in

[105] See Adam Scotus, *Sermo 8 in adventu Domini, De triplici sanctae Ecclesiae statu*: "Quae itaque Sion est in conversione, Jacob in tribulatione, jam est Jerusalem in pacis possessione" (PL 198, 144a). This sermon reveals one of the temptations of the Middle Ages. After the period of struggle, that of the persecutions, the conversion of the world having taken place under Constantine and after, the time of peace had at last come: "Quid jam superest, nisi ut dum ei pacis tranquillitas indulta est, a nomine quod est Jacob, in quo laboriosa ejus expressa est lucta, ad nomen illius pacis insigne prae se ferens conscendat, quod est Jerusalem?" However, after having enumerated in the same strain three successive states of the Church, the preacher goes on, by a sort of afterthought, to add the fourth: "Ecce quadripartitum sanctae Ecclesiae insigne, quia primo spiritualibus videns oculis Redemptorem et redemptionem suam surgit et ad Deum suum se convertit. Secundo adversarios lucrando ad fidem salubriter eos supplantat. Tertio a laboriosa lucta jam libera effecta et pace reddita, vineam plantat in montibus, dum sacram exponit Scripturam in verbis sublimibus. Quarto exsultat in die Domini, dum in claritate laetatur beatae ac beatificantis visionis" (cols. 144–45). We may well think fortunate (or perhaps simply lacking in awareness?) these men who thought that henceforth they would have nothing else to do, while they awaited the day of vision face to face, but give themselves over peacefully in the serene heights of the soul to the contemplation of the Holy Scriptures.

[106] There is the hint of an illusion in Haymo's reflections as he comments on the Song of Songs: "Subjectis principibus catholicae fidei, Ecclesia, quae antea premebatur, coronatur, et gloriatur in Christo, sicut factum est tempore Constantini, quando illo converso mirabiliter glorificata est Ecclesia" (PL 117, 320a). But compare *In Apoc.*: "et haec pugna perseverat usque ad finem saeculi" (col. 1085b–c). See also St. Gregory the Great, *In Ezech.*: "Ab Abel sanguine passio jam caepit Ecclesia" (PL 76, 966).

[107] St. Bernard, *In Cantica*, sermo 32, no. 19; Hildebert, *Sermo 98, De pace in Ecclesiam sub summo pontifice in persecutione constanter servanda*: "Nec solam ab extraneis patitur Ecclesia, sed etiam a domesticis et fratribus suis, et pejora sunt bella intestina . . . quam forensica" (PL 171, 795b–c).

suffering and reproach, and adversity does not crush her any more than prosperity—always precarious—satisfies her; she steels herself in advance against vainglory by the process of self-humiliation, and her reaction to misfortune is one of hope.[108] But she does not in any way come to terms with the enemy, for she cannot be unfaithful to him who said: "I came not to send peace, but the sword"—the sword of the Christian proclamation, the "effectual [word] . . . more piercing than any two-edged sword":[109] she cannot be unfaithful to the Christ who said "a man's own enemies shall be they of his own household",[110] the Christ who was a sign contradicted[111] from the beginning to the end of his earthly existence.

Of course, the Church seeks for understanding and unity, "accord and harmony", as "the most effective means of moving toward the good of the human race",[112] and she is prepared to obtain that unity by every concession that would not be a betrayal. She loves order, submission, and respect; often, indeed, she is accused of loving them too much. In this mixed-up world, she respects even the *pax Babylonica*, which she has need of in her pilgrimage if she is to lead her children to the heavenly peace,[113] for she knows that "there is no power but from God" and that such power is "God's minister to thee for

---

[108] St. Gregory the Great, *Moralia in Job*, bk. 19, chap. 19, no. 45: "Scit sancta Ecclesia in passionibus crescere, atque inter opprobria honorabilem vitam tenere. Scit nec de adversis dejici, nec de prosperis gloriari. Novit contra prospera mentem suam in dejectione sternere, novit contra adversa animam ad spem superni culminis exaltare" (PL 76, 164c).

[109] Heb 4:12; St. Hilary of Poitiers, *In Matthaeum*, chap. 10, no. 22: "Ubique odia, ubique bella, et gladius Domini inter patrem et filium, et inter filiam matremque desaeviens. . . . Dei igitur verbum nuncupatum meminerimus in gladio: qui gladius missus in terram est, id est, praedicatio ejus hominum cordibus infusa" (PL 9, 975b); Origen, *In Jesu nave*, hom. 12, no. 1; hom. 14, no. 1.

[110] Mt 10:34–39.

[111] Lk 2:34; 12:51–53; see Col 1:20.

[112] Leo XIII, encyclical *Arcanum* (February 10, 1880).

[113] St. Augustine, *De civitate Dei*, bk. 19, chaps. 17 and 26 (PL 41, 645–46 and 656): "Legibus terrenae civitatis . . . obtemperare non dubitat" (col. 645).

good".[114] She prays for those who wield it, reminding them all of "the true and substantial greatness", even the "superhuman dignity" of their authority, and wishes them to be obeyed in conscience.[115] She herself submits to the law of the earthly city;[116] like her Master, she always says "Render to Caesar the things that are Caesar's", preaching perfect loyalty even toward powers that persecute.[117] "Secular experience, a keen sense of individual and social psychology, and above all the demands of her spiritual end"[118] habitually inspire in her an attitude so moderate that many people find it disconcerting. They are sometimes tempted to find her too accommodating, and it is not uncommon for her to find herself obliged to cool down a zeal that is too belligerent. But for all this she never forgets to add "—and to God the things that are God's"; in doing which she has no aim other than "giving witness to the truth", as she has an imperious duty to do. Yet that is enough to make her accused, from the opposite direction, of "playing politics" and abusing religion, as Jesus was accused of doing before Pilate.[119] And all this sets the dividing sword in each individual heart and each level of society.

That excellent Pope Gelasius, by nature a most peaceable man, wished to make clear the respective attributes of the "royal power" and the "sacred authority of the Pontiffs". For, he said, it was important that "the spiritual power should keep its distance from the entanglements of this world and that,

[114] Rom 13:1–4; Eph 5 and 6; 1 Pet 2:13 and 18.

[115] 1 Tim 2:2; Leo XIII, encyclical *Diuturum illud* (June 29, 1881); Benedict XV, encyclical *Ad beatissimi* (November 1, 1914).

[116] St. Augustine, *De civitate Dei*, bk. 19, chap. 17 (PL 41, 645); St. Clement of Rome, *Ad Cor.*, 61 (p. 127 in Hemmer's edition); Tertullian, *Apol.*, chaps. 30–33 (pp. 92–96 in Waltzing's edition).

[117] See St. Cyprian, *Epist.* 81 (the last before his arrest and martyrdom): "Quietem et tranquillitatem tenete" (p. 842 in Hartel's edition).

[118] André Latreille (with André Siegfried), *Les Forces religieuses et la vie politique* (1951), p. 70, etc.

[119] Jn 18:28–40; see Pius XI, Discourse before the Sacred College, Christmas 1937.

fighting for God, it should not become involved in secular matters; while in its turn the secular power should take care not to take over the direction of divine matters. Thus, with both powers remaining dutifully in their places, both would handle competently the things that fell within their sphere."[120] His pronouncements are valuable for the light they shed on the true nature of the Church's rule and the Kingdom she wishes to set up:

> Non eripit mortalia
> Qui regna det caelestia.[121]

But it is hardly necessary to point out that reality only very rarely corresponds to his idyllic ideal and also that such an ideal should not lead us to the conclusion that the realm of God and that of Caesar are two domains that are at once analogous yet mutually extrinsic. When the Church fights in the service of God, she cannot avoid all the traps laid for her by the world. "The affairs of God" are not specialized affairs

[120] Gelasius, *De anathematis vinculo* (c. A.D. 495): "Christus, memor fragilitatis humanae, quod suorum saluti congrueret dispensatione magnifica temperans, sic actionibus propriis dignitatibusque distinctis officia potestatis utriusque discrevit, suos volens medicinali humilitate salvari, non humana superbia rursus intercipi; ut et christiani imperatores pro aeterna vita pontificibus in digerent, et pontifices pro temporalium cursu rerum imperialibus dispositionibus uterentur, quatenus spiritualis actio a carnalibus distaret incursibus; et ideo, *militans Deo, minime se negotiis saecularibus implicaret* [2 Tim 2:4]; ac vicissim non ille rebus divinis praesidere videretur, qui esset negotiis saecularibus implicatus; ut et modestia utriusque ordinis curaretur, ne extolleretur utroque suffultus, et competens qualitatibus actionum specialiter professio aptaretur" (PL 59, 108–9).

[121] Roman Breviary, Hymn for the Epiphany; see St. Augustine, *In Joannem*, tract. 51, no. 13, quoted by Pius XI in his letter of June 10, 1924, to Msgr. Audolent: if Christ is King, "this is not in order to levy taxes or raise troops or fight visible enemies; he is King of Israel for the ruling of souls, preparing eternal blessings, and leading those who believe, hope, and love"; Pius XI, encyclical *Quas primas* (December 11, 1925): the kingship of Christ is "wholly spiritual". Some Ultramontanes, at the beginning of the seventeenth century, would have made a correction to the first of these two verses—"Jure eripit mortalia"; see Jansenius, Letter 6 (September 13, 1617), quoted in Jean Orcibal, *Correspondance de Jansénius* (1947), p. 21.

that contain no element likely to set up disturbance in the affairs of this world, and it would be a perversion of the Gospel maxim if we were to invoke it to "justify a state of affairs in which everything is given to Caesar and nothing to God".[122] St. John Chrysostom was already putting people on guard against complacent interpretations of this kind. "When you hear the phrase 'render unto Caesar the things that are Caesar's', you must understand it of the things that are not opposed to the service of God; for the things that were opposed to it would be not so much a tribute paid to Caesar as a tribute paid to Satan."[123] Without in the very least usurping the role of the temporal sovereign, Pope Gelasius showed himself quite capable of reminding the emperor Anastasius that the sovereign is not "above the Church", like St. Ambrose in the case of Theodosius, or the aged Hosius in the case of Constantine. And in so doing he was making an authoritative appeal to the imperial conscience.[124]

The ideal described by Gelasius and so courageously defended by him was to be given the Church's definitive approval in modern times by Leo XIII in his encyclical *Immortale Dei.* "God", he said, "has divided the government of the human race

[122] Vladimir Soloviev, in the introduction to *La Russie et l'Église universelle* (1889). On these grounds an attempt has been made to "confirm the pagan character of our social and political life", whence the stumbling block of a society "which professes Christianity as its religion and remains pagan, not only in its life but also as to *the laws* governing that life".

[123] *In Matt.*, hom. 70, no. 2 (PG 57, 656).

[124] Gelasius, letter to the emperor Anastasius (A.D. 494): "Proinde, sicut non leve discrimen incumbit pontificibus, siluisse pro divinitatis cultu, quod congruit; ita his (quod absit) non mediocre periculum est, qui, cum parare debeant, despiciunt. Et si cunctis generaliter sacerdotibus recte divina tractantibus, fidelium convenit corda submitti, quanto potius sedis illius praesuli consensus est adhibendus, quem cunctis sacerdotibus et divinitas summa voluit praeeminere, et subsequens Ecclesiae generalis jugiter pietas celebravit?" (PL 59, 42). Cf. chap. 54 of St. Athanasius' *History of the Arians*; St. Gregory Nazianzen, *Orat.* 17, *Ad Theodosium*: "Te quoque, imperator, imperio meo et throno lex christiana subjicit. Imperium enim et nos episcopi gerimus; adde etiam praestantius et perfectus."

between two powers. Each of them is supreme in its own field; each is enclosed within the limits perfectly determined and traced out in conformity with its nature and end, and each thus has a sphere in which its own rights and proper activity find exercise."[125] God wishes there to be established between them "the bond of a close concord", stemming from "a reciprocal interplay of rights and duties".[126] This is the perfect blueprint, and it should be the starting point of all practice. But in the same encyclical Leo XIII himself recalls—as did Pope Gelasius—that "in human affairs, all that is sacred, on whatever account—all that concerns the salvation of souls and the worship of God, whether of its own nature or because it should be considered such in virtue of the cause with which it is bound up—all this comes under the jurisdiction of the Church's power and the Church's judgment." [127] This is, of course, no more than the

[125] Encyclical of November 1, 1885.

[126] Leo XIII, encyclicals *Praeclara gratulationis* and *Nobilissima Gallorum gens*; St. Augustine, *De civitate Dei*, bk. 19, chap. 17: "ut . . . servetur . . . inter civitatem utramque concordia" (PL 41, 645).

[127] "Quidquid igitur est in rebus humanis quoquo modo sacrum, quidquid ad salutem animarum cultumve Dei, pertinet, sive tale illud sit natura sua, sive rursus tale intelligatur propter causam ad quam refertur, id est omne in potestate arbitrioque Ecclesiae." Pius XI spoke similarly in the encyclical *Quadrigesimo anno*: "However, on no account can the Church abandon the responsibility entrusted to her by God, and which lays down for her a law of intervention, not indeed in the technical sphere—where she lacks the appropriate means and competence—but in all that concerns the moral law." I cannot see why the political sphere should constitute an exception here, as some have claimed it should. For the law is the same for all manifestations of human activity, public and private alike; it is the general law that holds good concerning the relations of nature and grace. Since grace is not something cut off from nature and since the spiritual is everywhere involved with the temporal, the Church has, in a most eminent sense, authority over all things "by concomitance and repercussion", without having to step outside her own role in order to get it. If this were not so we should have to concede that, practically speaking, she has authority over nothing and is perpetually reduced to speaking in terms of the abstract only. In the same way, she cannot limit herself to outlining principles in the sphere of the absolute, without ever pointing to the applications of them; she cannot simply proclaim her teaching and law *au-dessus*

Gospel requires. But insofar as she persists in reminding the world of the fact, the Church can never count on peace.

There are more than enough gruesome facts to demonstrate the point. This demand of the Gospel has been answered, within living experience, both as to its moderation and as to its unyieldingness, by a whole line of martyrs and confessors and in every variety of tragic circumstance. Some of the greatest among our bishops have made the claim—more than one in our own day and destined to honorable memory because of it. We may recall the distant example of Waso of Liège, in 1044, who, in order to show the depth of his loyalty in the temporal order, declared: "Even if the emperor were to have my right eye torn out, I would not, for that, stop using my left eye for his honor and in his service", but who also said, to his master Henry III: "To the Sovereign Pontiff we owe obedience and to you, O King, faithfulness; it is to you that we give account of our secular administration, but to him, of all that concerns the divine office."[128] And we can well imagine that by this last phrase he did not mean some trifling matter of liturgical regulations. He is one of those churchmen who have preserved justice and spiritual freedom by the very process of maintaining God's rights through the Catholic faith. Waso of Liège did no more than apply the principle that had made so many martyrs in the first centuries of the Church's existence. When he came before his emperor he found himself in the situation of the baptized subjects of the emperor Julian:

> Julian was an infidel emperor—apostate, wicked and idolatrous. There were Christian soldiers in the service of this infidel emperor. But whenever the cause of Christ was in question, they recognized no leader other than him whom they had in

de la mêlée. She should be able to make a decision when she judges that the situation demands it—that is to say, to approve or condemn, hic et nunc, the concrete realities, writings, activities, institutions, and so on with which that teaching and that law find themselves involved.

[128] Gesta episcoporum Leodiensium, 2:58, 60; quoted by A. Fliche in La Réforme grégorienne (1924), 1:114, 124.

heaven. When Julian wanted to make them sacrifice to idols, they put God first. But when he said to them, "Go and fight the enemy", they obeyed him at once. They made a distinction between the realm of eternity and that of time; but they were not subject to a temporal master any the less because of the eternal sphere.[129]

Allowing for the difference of period and circumstance, we can surely recognize exactly the same attitude in another churchman, the Chinese priest Tong Che-Tche. Consider, for example, these excerpts from the speech, since become famous, which he made at Chungking on June 2, 1951, before the civil and religious authorities:

Today, a movement which has grown up outside the Catholic hierarchy is urging us on to attack him who represents the Pope, who represents Jesus Christ. . . . Gentlemen: I have only one soul and I cannot divide it up; but I have a body which can be divided up. It seems to me that the best thing to do is to offer my whole soul to God and the holy Church, and my body to my country. . . . Since I cannot remedy [the conflict in which Church and State are opposed], there is nothing I can do better than offer my soul to one side and my body to the other, in sacrifice, in the hope of promoting understanding between them. . . . I am a Chinese Catholic. I love my country; I also love my Church. I dissociate myself from everything that is opposed to the laws of my country, just as I dissociate myself from everything that is opposed to the laws of my Church, and above all things I dissociate myself from everything that can sow discord. But if the Church and the Government cannot come to an agreement, sooner or later every Chinese Catholic will have nothing left to do but die. Then why should one not offer one's body at once to hasten the mutual understanding of the parties concerned?[130]

---

[129] St. Augustine, *In Psalm.* 124, no. 7 (PL 37,1653–54); see St. Justin, *Apol.* 1, chap. 17 (PG 6, 353). We may also recall, among many others, the example of St. Thomas More; see his writings during his imprisonment.

[130] This speech has been published in its entirety in *Études*, 271:3–9, and *Église vivante* 3 (1951): 303–9: "Fr. Tong's action woke the sorely beset Christian

These are not the words of a rebel or a sower of strife. Like the feudal bishop of the eleventh century—and, to be sure, the Christian defenders of Rome—the twentieth-century Chinese patriot is not merely loyal and duly submissive; he has a burning love for his people and a total devotion to them, and his Catholic loyalty casts no slur upon them. But once more the *hubris* of the temporal power, which wants to make good its grasp on the whole of the individual man, leaves no end possible other than martyrdom.

If, instead of thinking of the two powers in question as abstract essences, we think of them under the aspect of concrete reality—"existentially", as they say these days—we shall perhaps come to see that the State always tends to overstep the domain it has inherited, as if under some fatal gravitational pull. "Without the moderating influence of the spiritual sovereignty, it moves as if by instinct toward the most burdensome form of pagan absolutism." [131] And we can understand how conflicts incessantly flare up again, despite the efforts of so many men of good will. In the State there is always an obscure will to power, more or less conscious and more or less active—an irrational force of expansion that will not endure any obstacle and is impatient of all limitations. Even if it does adapt itself to a compromise for a time, it does not subscribe to the principal restrictive of its power, which was formulated by St. Ambrose in the words: "Those things that are divine are not subject to the

---

body to life. On June 10 the Vicar Capitulary, who had previously given way, made from his pulpit . . . a public retractation the terms of which were the equivalent of a solemn profession of faith. This was a real thunderbolt and aroused joy and enthusiasm throughout the whole of the diocese. . . . The Vicar Capitulary was the first to be arrested. Fr. Tong suffered the same fate on July 2; next day he was glimpsed, bound, and surrounded by police; then, he disappeared. When his speech-*cum*-testament was read and the news of all this got about, a wave of pride, courage, and strength swept across the whole Church in China" (Tch'ang djen Tsuain, "Fidelité de l'Église de Chine", p. 309).

[131] J. Lecler, *L'Église et la souveraineté de l'état* (1946), p. 37.

imperial power."[132] It will not willingly admit that there is—to quote Origen—"within the heart of every society another kind of homeland, which is founded by the Word of God."[133] Any kind of "double membership" is suspect to it and held to be something not far off treason. And this is why, even when the ecclesiastical power renounces (as it has) certain claims or certain forms of supremacy whose origins are adequately explained by history alone (and even, in a considerable measure, justified by history), clashes still occur, from the very nature of things. The Church may declare henceforward a thing of the past some whole former order which was "a consequence of public law then in force" and was exercised "by the consent of the Christian powers".[134] She may discourage the excesses of certain theologians who are belligerent or simply out of date; she may refuse all varieties of "temporal jurisdiction" or "civil" jurisdiction, whether ordinary or extraordinary, whether "for the good of the faith as a whole" or "by reason of default". But one thing she cannot do, and that is renounce her commission to give authoritative direction to the conscience by reminding

[132] See Latreille, *Les Forces religeuses*, p. 40: "All power tends to absolutism, as if by some law of gravity; and this absolutism seeks to lead it to include in itself not only temporal authority but also spiritual authority; such was the caesarism of the monarchs of yesterday and such—with an even greater threat to inner freedom—is the totalitarianism of contemporary dictators." See also Pius IX, allocution *Maxima quidem* and *Syllabus*, no. 39.

[133] Origen, *Contra Celsum*, bk. 8, chap. 75 (p. 292 in Koetschau's edition). Celsus was already criticizing Christians for a "secession inward", which made them "ingrates". Both suspicion and persecution cannot help but accentuate a similar duality.

[134] Pius IX, declaration of July 20, 1871, in *Civiltà cattolica*, 8th series, 3:485. A similar declaration was made by Pius XII in his discourse to the members of the tribunal of the Rota, October 6, 1946, in *Documentation catholique* (1946), col. 1187. Cf. Gosselin, "Recherches historiques sur le droit public au moyen âge relativement à la déposition des princes temporels" (in Fénelon, *Oeuvres* [1843], vol. 1). There is thus no occasion to criticize the Church for having "usurped the right of princes" in the past (cf. prop. 2 of the *Syllabus*). Ever since the encyclical *Immortale Dei*, all attempts to revive the theory of the so-called "direct power", or even that of the "indirect power" in its original meaning, have been doomed to failure.

everyone, on every possible occasion, of the universal kingship of Christ. As has been well said, Christianity is universal not only in the sense that all men have their Savior in Jesus Christ, but also in the sense that the whole man finds his salvation in him. But all the destinies of Christianity are in the hands of the Church; and the Church is thus also Catholic in the sense that nothing human can be outside her concern. While we should certainly reject, as unworthy of her, that kind of intervention which puts her more or less on the same footing as the powers of this world, there cannot be any question of limiting her competence to certain spheres of activity that are materially determined. Her power is spiritual in its object, as in its nature and its end; but it extends nonetheless for that to all that is human, for it extends to all that is spiritual in every human affair in which it is engaged.[135] In accordance with the wish Fénelon expressed so boldly,[136] the Church has unequivocally rejected the last remains of a situation that was created by history and is not in any way of her essence. "She claims for the servants of the Gospel and the faithful of Christ nothing other than common rights like security and freedom."[137] Even where Christian nations are concerned, she does not make use of any kind of

[135] Pius XI, encyclical *Quas primas*; see my article "Le Pouvoir de l'Église en matière temporelle", RSR (1932), pp. 329–54; Yves de Montcheuil, *L'Église et le monde actuel* (1945); Joseph Lecler, *L'Église et la souveraineté de l'état* (1946). Gerson writes: "All men, princes or others, are subject to the Pope insofar as they may wish to abuse their power in opposition to divine and natural law" (*Sermo de pace et unione graecorum*, consideratio 5).

[136] In the *Appendix* discovered and published by Ernest Jovy in his *Fénelon inédit d'après les documents de Pistoia* (Vitry-le-François, 1917). Clement XI read this memorandum and signified his approval. Cf. Jean Orcibal, "Fénelon et la cour romaine", in *Mélanges d'archéologie et d'histoire* (1940), pp. 280–81. Fénelon, in his Latin dissertation on the authority of the Sovereign Pontiff, had already given a clear exposition and justification of the essentials of the doctrine that was to prevail.

[137] Pius XI, encyclical *Rerum Ecclesiae*. The same expression is to be found in Pius XI's letter to the bishops and prefects apostolic of China, June 15, 1926, and in his message to China of August 1, 1928 (*Documentation catholique*, October 10, 1928).

temporal sovereignty or political *altum dominium*; so that today there is no longer any occasion to mistake her for a this-worldly power. To all those who have the eyes to see she appears in the noble simplicity of her spiritual authority. But that is quite enough to perpetuate the conflict.

* * *

If we consider not only the State but, through it, all the earthly powers the Church is commissioned to bend by her witness to the law of God, then the struggle will seem yet more inevitable and more merciless. "Before the preaching of the Word of God, all was peace; as long as the sound of the trumpet had not rung out, there was no conflict; but ever since, the Kingdom of God suffers violence."[138] The great city pictured for us by St. Leo, at the moment when Peter and Paul entered it, as "a forest full of roaring beasts" and "an ocean with depths full of whirlpools", exists always and everywhere, in every party and every heart. It is the city built by Cain with strokes of evildoing, as St. Jerome put it, and it will not be brought down as long as time subsists.[139] It is Babylon the proud, fighting Christ for power. It is the spiritual Sodom, and it is the spiritual Egypt, which swallows up the bodies of the murdered saints, while its inhabitants "rejoice over them and make merry: and shall send gifts to one another, because these . . . prophets tormented them that dwelt upon the earth".[140] In a nutshell, it is the world, in its evil sense—the world that seeps up through a thousand and one sources within the very center of the islands that have been won from its muddy morass. The finest "Christian social order" imaginable will not get rid of it;[141] the more she spreads, the more the Church finds

---

[138] Origen, *In Josue*, hom. 12, no. 1; hom. 14, no. 1.

[139] *Epist.* 46 (1:336, in Hilberg's edition).

[140] Rev 17:5, 11:8–10.

[141] See my *Paradoxes in Faith*, chaps. 6, 8, and 11. The "best of worlds" will not be the Kingdom of God; it could be a world of "dead souls". A social paradise can be a hell from the spiritual point of view. On the two senses of the word "world" in the Scriptures, see St. Augustine, *Sermo* 96, nos. 4–9 (PL 38,

it within her, ever more subtly dangerous than before. "For in the same house, in the same town, and in the same community, citizens of Jerusalem and Babylon are mingled together."[142] More: the fight goes on within each individual one of her members, and will do so till the end of time. The Church is well aware of the fact; though she is never discouraged, she is also no utopian. The Reign of Christ, which she continually promotes and prays for, will, she knows, never be established on earth, where disturbance, error, and perversity will always appear to compromise her work. The serene clarity of her faith does not stop her speaking of the apparent "blind advance of things", and she is a perpetual witness of the defeat of the good. She sees all about her the resurgence of idolatries and her own children at one another's throats.[143]

We experience individually what the Church experiences; her dangers are ours, and her battles are ours too. If the Church were, in each one of us, more faithful to her mission, she would doubtless often be the more loved, as her Master was loved. She would be more readily listened to; certainly she would—again, like him—be more misconceived and more persecuted:[144] "I have given them thy word, and the world hath hated them."[145]

586–88); Didymus the Blind, *In Epist. Judae* 5, 19 (pp. 79–81 in Zoepel's edition).

[142] St. Caesarius of Arles, *Expositio in Apoc.* (*Opera Omnia*, ed. G. Morin, [1942], 2:261); see Origen, *In Jer.*, hom. lat. 3, no. 2 (p. 309 in Klostermann's edition), etc. There is a misinterpretation of St. Augustine and St. Thomas in G. Mensching, *Sociologie religieuse*, French trans. (1951), pp. 256–57. See also A. Lauras and H. Rondet, "Le Thème des deux cités dans l'oeuvre de saint Augustin", in *Études augustiennes* (1953), in the series Théologie.

[143] See my *Catholicism*, pp. 272–74. As early as during the first century of monasticism, St. John Chrysostom wrote that "the song of the chaste spouses of Christ is already scandalously broken in upon by a thousand interruptions, which bring with them a thousand other voices" (*Dialogue on the Priesthood*, bk. 3).

[144] See St. Thomas, *In Joannem*, 15, 18: "Et ideo secundum Augustinum non debent se membra supra verticem extollere, nec recursare se in corpore esse, nolendo mundi odium sustinere cum capite."

[145] Jn 17:14; cf. 15:10–21.

Since the depths of men's hearts would thus be laid bare in an even broader daylight than now, there would be even greater scandal, and from that scandal there would come a new impetus to Christianity, for "it is a proof of power when it [Christianity] is hated by the world." [146] The "decline in anticlericalism" upon which we are in the habit of congratulating ourselves is thus not, necessarily, always a good sign. Certainly, it may derive from a change in the objective situation or a real bettering of things on both sides of the quarrel. But it may also be a sign that although those by whom the Church is known still present to the world things of real value, they have nonetheless adapted themselves to it—to its ideas, its conventions, and its ways. In consequence, they will be less of an embarrassment. The Gospel warns us that the salt can lose its savor. And if we—that is, most of us—live more or less in peace in the midst of the world, it is, perhaps, because we are lukewarm.

---

[146] St. Ignatius of Antioch, *Ad Romanos*, 3, 3.

VI

THE SACRAMENT OF CHRIST

THE Church is a mystery; that is to say that she is also a sacrament.[1] She is "the total *locus* of the Christian sacraments", and she is herself the great sacrament that contains and vitalizes all the others.[2] In this world she is the sacrament of Christ, as Christ himself, in his humanity, is for us the sacrament of God.[3]

That which is sacramental—"the sensible bond between two worlds"[4]—has a twofold characteristic. Since, on the one hand, it is the sign of something else, it must be passed through, and this not in part but wholly. Signs are not things to be stopped at, for they are, in themselves, valueless; by definition a sign is something translucent, which dissolves from before the face of what it manifests—like words, which would be nothing if they did not lead straight on to ideas. Under this aspect it is not something intermediate but something mediatory; it does not isolate, one from another, the two terms it is meant to link. It does not put a distance between them; on the contrary, it unites them by making present that which it evokes.

---

[1] Cf. Dom J. Gribomont, O.S.B., "Du Sacrement de l'Église et de ses réalisations imparfaites", IK 22 (1949): 345–67; J. Pinsk, "Die sakramentale Welt", in *Ecclesia orans* (1938); S. Tyszkiewicz, S.J., *Sainteté de l'Église*, pp. 188–92.

[2] Council of Florence, *Decretum pro Jacobitis*, 1441–42: "Tantumque valere ecclesiastici corporis unitatem, ut solum in ea manentibus ad salutem ecclesiastica sacramenta proficiant." See also Fr. Tonneau, O.P., in VI 6 (1937): 330.

[3] See the Ambrosian missal, Preface for the first Sunday in Advent: "manifestans plebi tuae Unigeniti tui sacramentum"; St. Augustine, *Epist.* 187, no. 34: "Non est enim aliud Dei mysterium, nisi Christus" (PL 38, 845).

[4] Joseph de Maistre, "Lettre à une dame russe", in *Oeuvres*, 8:74.

On the other hand, sacramental reality is not just any sign, which is provisional and can be changed at will. It is essentially related to our present condition, which is not one embodied in the epoch of figures pure and simple, nor yet one that includes the full possession of the "truth".[5] The second aspect of its twofold characteristic, which is not to be dissociated from the first, thus consists in this: that it can never be discarded as something that has outlived its usefulness. We never come to the end of passing through this translucent medium, which we must, nevertheless, always pass through and that completely. It is always through it that we reach what it signifies; it can never be superseded, and its bounds cannot be broken.

In Christ also we find this twofold characteristic. "If you had known me, you would without doubt have known my Father also. . . . Philip, he that seeth me seeth the Father also."[6] Nobody, even at the highest peak of the spiritual life, will attain a knowledge of the Father that will dispense him, from that point onward, from going through him who will, always and for all, be "the Way" and "the Image of the invisible God".[7] And the same holds good for the Church. Her whole end is to show us Christ, lead us to him, and communicate his grace to us; to put it in a nutshell, she exists solely to put us into relation with him. She alone can do that, and it is a task she never completes; there will never come a moment, either in the life of the individual or in the life of the race, in which her role ought to come to an end or even could come to an end. If the world lost the Church, it would lose the Redemption too.

The New Testament, which founded the Church by giving her the inheritance of Israel, is also the "last Testament". The Church is not like the Law—a "pedagogue", necessary to the growing young but rightly dispensed with by maturity. "The divine education" entrusted to her with reference to us is

---

[5] On the substantial meaning of the word when used in this way, see my *Corpus mysticum*, chap. 9; also *Histoire et Ésprit*, pp. 217–30.

[6] Jn 14:7–9.

[7] Col 1:15; Jn 14:6.

something with the duration of time itself, and in it we already have, not a heralding or a preparation more or less remote, but "the whole coming of the Son of Man".[8] And she is constantly present in the dialogue of the soul with its Lord. She intervenes actively at every phase of it, but without any inhibiting effect on its intimacy, which, on the contrary, she guarantees. A man who believes himself to be a prophet or rich in spiritual gifts must remind himself that before all else he is bound to submit to the commandments of his Lord as they are declared to him by that Lord's Church—otherwise he will prophesy in vain and all his gifts will merely lead him to his own destruction.[9] One who gives way to the temptations of a false spiritualization and wants to shake off the Church as a burdensome yoke or set her aside as a cumbersome intermediary will soon find himself embracing the void or end up by worshipping false gods. If a man begins by using her as his support and then comes to believe that he can go beyond her, he will be nothing more than a mystic run off the rails. Those who anticipate a future "setting-up of the Heavenly Jerusalem", which will inaugurate "a new period of history" on earth and finally assure "the complete triumph of the spiritual", may imagine that they are prophesying a return of the human race into paradise lost;[10] but in reality, the thing is no more than a diseased and pride-ridden dream. It was thus that the heretical Tertullian said: "Hardness of heart reigned until Christ, and the weakness of the flesh endures till the Paraclete",[11] or again: "The Law and the Prophets taught the world's childhood; its youth was brought to flower by the Gospel; now, through the Paraclete, it reaches maturity."[12] The proclamations of a Third

[8] Origen, *In Matt. series*, 47: "In qua totus est adventus Filii hominis" (p. 98 in Klostermann's edition).

[9] 1 Cor 14:37–38: "If any seems to be a prophet or spiritual, let him know the things that I write to you, that they are the commandments of the Lord. But if any man know not, he shall not be known."

[10] René Guénon, *Autorité spirituelle et pouvoir temporel* (1930), pp. 151–52.

[11] *De monogamia*, chap. 14.

[12] *De velandis virginibus*, chap. 1.

THE SACRAMENT OF CHRIST 205

Age, an age of "contemplatives" succeeding the age of "Doctors", or a Church of John to follow that of Peter,[13] or a future Kingdom of the Spirit following the actual Kingdom of Christ and the discipline of his Church—these have all generated disastrous schisms. They may, certainly, give, from time to time, a new attractiveness to the original Montanism, which they transform into a sort of philosophy of history, according to the tastes of the age;[14] they may well sometimes make their appearance entangled with thinking of a high order; but they are nonetheless for all that mere Utopias, and of a dangerous variety too.[15]

Lessing cried: "It will come, certainly it will come, the age of perfection! It will come—the time of the New Gospel, the Eternal Gospel, which is promised to men in the very books of the New Covenant!"[16] This lyrical outburst is the expression of nothing other than a very commonplace theory of Progress; and it proclaimed nothing other than an age of rationalism—which in point of fact came all right, and which we are in a position to judge for ourselves. . . . But the words of Joachim of Flora, or those of his more daring disciples, are always finding new lips to repeat them and new hearers to be thrilled by them. It is not long since they were heard from Nicholas Berdiaev, in the service of an ideal very different from that of Lessing. Here, they prophesied a new revelation that was to be "definitive", a new "epoch of the Spirit", a "Church of the Holy Spirit" in which would be read the "eternal Gospel", a "religion of greater man"

[13] See Joachim of Flora, *The Ten-Stringed Psaltery* (p. 156 in the translation of Emmanuel Aegerter), and again: "Just as the veil of Moses was drawn aside by Christ, so that of Paul will be drawn aside by the Holy Spirit" (p. 157)—to all of which St. Bonaventure replied in his *In Hexaemeron*, collatio 16: "Post novum Testamentum non erit aliud" (Quaracchi edition, 5:403).

[14] This point was made with regard to Joachim of Flora by Eugène Anitchkof in his *Joachim de Flore et les milieux courtois* (1931), p. 169.

[15] It was perhaps a certain tendency to justify the Church too much on natural grounds and to forget the role the Holy Spirit normally plays in her that made Joseph de Maistre somewhat indulgent to the *illuminati* by way of compensation. See the eleventh conversation of the *Soirées de Saint-Pétersbourg*.

[16] Lessing, *Der Erziehen des Menschengeschlechts*.

corresponding to "a new structure of human consciousness" at last "freed from the encrustations that immobilized it" and "set free from the slavery of objectification".[17]

It is possible that in these "intuitions"—as in those of Joachim of Flora himself—we should allow for a certain awkwardness of expression. Perhaps the "new aeon" glimpsed after our "old, agonizing epoch" is to open out before us only at the end of the present world, for we are also told that there will then be set up "new relations between man and the cosmos" and that "messianic expectations cannot be realized within history, only outside history".[18] And last, it may be the case, either where Berdiaev is concerned or at any rate with certain others, that prophetic proclamation is scarcely more than a stylistic device necessary for conveying the necessity of a perpetual recourse to the Spirit if we are to prevent ourselves from becoming bogged down in objective existence. But in any case it must be said quite clearly, and in opposition to the illusions conjured up by promises of this kind, that the prophetic epoch is past. Today we have reality in our signs, and this state of affairs cannot be superseded as long as this world lasts. Insofar as we misinterpret this situation, we shall lapse from our condition of hope into mythology.

From the moment when Christ was glorified, the Spirit was given to us, and it was this gift of the Spirit on the day of Pentecost that completed the constituting of the Church.[19]

---

[17] *Dialectique existentielle du divin et de l'humain* (1947), pp. 225 and 228–44.

[18] Joachim of Flora, *The Ten-Stringed Psaltery* (pp. 65, 221, 226–27 in the translation of Aegerter).

[19] 1 Th 4:8; 1 Cor 2:12; Jn 7:39: "Now this he said of the Spirit which they should receive who believed in him; for as yet the Spirit was not given, because Jesus was not glorified." See also Joachim of Flora, *Super quattuor evangelia*: "Etsi secundum litteram completa est post resurrectionem Domini promissio illa Filii de donatione Spiritus sancti, secundum tamen illam plenitudinem quam ostensurus est cum fuerit a rebelli quoque Judaeorum populo converso ad Dominum per Eliam et ejus socios glorificatus, etiam nunc dicere possumus: Spiritus non erat datus, quia Jesus nondum erat glorificatus" (ed. Buonaiuti [Rome, 1930], p. 24).

Thus the age of the Spirit is in no sense something still to come; it coincides exactly with the age of Christ:[20] "The communicating of Christ—that is, the Holy Spirit."[21] The Spirit teaches us "all truth" but neither speaks of himself nor seeks his own glory, any more than Christ, the Father's Envoy, sought his own glory.[22] Faithful to the mission he received from him in whose name he was sent to us, he makes us understand his message—"brings it to mind"—but adds nothing to it. He comes, as it were, to put the seal on his teaching;[23] he opens our awareness to his Gospel but does not transform it. He spoke often before the coming of Christ, but that was solely to proclaim Christ's coming—"who spake by the Prophets". And he has continued to speak since Christ returned to the Father, but only to bear him witness, as Christ bore witness to the Father;[24] it is all for the proclaiming of Christ's unique lordship and never in order to substitute himself for Christ. In a word, the Spirit is "the Spirit of Jesus".[25]

---

[20] Rom 8:9–10: "if the Spirit of God dwells in you. Now if any man have not the Spirit of Christ, he is none of his. And if Christ is in you. . . ." See also Gal 4:6; Didymus the Blind, *On the Holy Spirit* (as translated by St. Jerome): "Idem autem Spiritus Dei et Spiritus Christi est, deducens et copulans eum qui in se habuerit Domino Jesu Christo" (PG 39, 1068); St. Hilary of Poitiers, *De Trinitate*, bk. 8, chap. 27.

[21] St. Irenaeus, *Adversus haereses*, bk. 3, chap. 24, no. 1.

[22] Jn 12:49–50; see also Saint-Jure, *L'Homme spirituel*, pt. 1, chap. 1; Jules Monchanin, "Théologie et mystique du Saint-Esprit", DV, no. 23, p. 76: "A mystique of the Holy Spirit is not a mystique of the Holy Spirit alone, but the mystique of Christ par excellence and the mystique of the Father too; it is a perpetual invitation to pass through appearances, to pass through the Scriptures and dogma and the liturgy—which it maintains and perfects by interiorizing them—to contemplate without end the *prosodos* and *exodos* of a deified creation, and—with an even greater love—the going-out and returning-again of the Trinity."

[23] "Quodammodo obsignaturus" (Leo XIII, encyclical *Divinum illud*).

[24] Jn 14:26, 15:26, 16:13–14; see also 7:39, 20:22; St. Epiphanius of Salamis, *Adversus omnes haereses*, 7, on the Montanists, who claim: "Paracletum plura in Montano dixisse, quam Christum in evangelium protulisse."

[25] 1 Cor 12:3; and see St. Basil, *Treatise on the Holy Spirit*, chap. 18; Acts 16:7.

There is no other Spirit than this Spirit of Jesus, and the Spirit of Jesus is the Soul that animates his body, the Church.[26] Just as the letter of the Law drew together the first People of God, so the Spirit forms the new People of God.[27] Today we are "in the Spirit" as we are "in Christ", and we may say, with St. Paul, that we have been baptized in one single Spirit to form one single body, or, as St. Basil comments, in one single body to form one single Spirit.[28] The Church is "the society of the Spirit".[29] And it is in the Church that the Spirit glorifies Jesus, just as it is in her, the "House of Christ", that he is given to us[30] in a "final and eternal alliance".[31] It is a bad business when an attempt is made to separate the Church from the Gospel; a bad business when people want to get rid of the spiritual leaven that she mixes into the meal of humanity,[32] and when anyone tries to "extinguish the Spirit"[33] in the Church. But it is an equally bad business when anyone claims to set the Spirit's flame free by rejecting the Church.[34]

---

[26] St. Augustine, *Sermo* 268, no. 2: "Quod est spiritus noster, id est anima nostra, ad membra nostra, hoc est Spiritus sanctus ad membra Christi, ad corpus Christi, quod est Ecclesia" (PL 38, 1232); *Sermo* 267, no. 4 (col. 1231); also Rom 8:9; 2 Cor 3:17; Gal 4:6; and chapter 4, above.

[27] 2 Cor 3:6–11; Phil 3:3; and also 1 Cor 12:13; Eph 4:4, etc.

[28] St. Basil, *On the Holy Spirit*, chap. 26, no. 61, commenting on 1 Cor 12:18 (PG 32, 181b); see also the remarks of S. Tromp, S.J., in his *De Spiritu Sancto anima corporis mystici*, 1:34.

[29] "Societas Spiritus"—St. Augustine, *Sermo* 71, chap. 19, no. 32 (PL 38, 462); and chap. 23, no. 37: "congregatur in Spiritu sancto" (col. 466).

[30] Pseudo-Bede, *In Joannem* (PL 92, 862a–b); St. Augustine, *De Trinitate*, bk. 15, chap. 19, no. 34.

[31] St. Justin, *Dialogue*, chap. 11, no. 2.

[32] See Origen, *Scholia in Lucam*, 13, 21: "Accipi potest mulier pro Ecclesia, fermentum pro Spiritu sancto" (PG 24, 565).

[33] 1 Th 5:19. Or to prevent the perpetual rejuvenation of the deposit entrusted to the Church and the actual vessel that contains it (see St. Irenaeus, *Adv. haeres.* 3, 24, 1).

[34] Or to prophesy another Gospel beyond that of Christ, which is preached by the Church; see Joachim of Flora's *Liber introductorius in expositionem in Apocalypsin*, chap. 5: "The first of the three ages of the world unrolled under the

The Church is the sacrament of Christ. This means, to put it another way, that there is between her and him a certain relation of mystical identity. Here again we encounter the Pauline metaphors and the rest of the biblical images, which the Christian tradition has continually explored. One and the same intuition of faith is expressed throughout. Head and members make one single body, one single Christ;[35] the Bridegroom and the Bride are one flesh. Although he is the Head of his Church, Christ does not rule her from without; there is, certainly, subjection and dependence between her and him, but at the same time she is his fulfillment and "fullness".[36] She is the tabernacle of his presence,[37] the building of which he is both Architect and Cornerstone. She is the temple in which he teaches and into which he draws with him the whole Divinity.[38] She is the ship and he the pilot,[39] she the deep ark and he the central mast, assuring the communication of all those on board with the heavens above them.[40] She is paradise and he its tree and well of

---

reign of the Law; the second was initiated by the Gospel and lasts up till the present; the third will begin toward the end of this century; indeed, we can already see it opening, in a complete spiritual liberation. . . . This age of spiritual understanding, which is about to open continuously before us, will be under the reign of the Holy Spirit. . . . The angel held an eternal Gospel; and what do we find in this Gospel? Everything that goes beyond the Gospel of Christ" (trans. Aegerter, 2:90–118).

[35] St. Augustine, *In Psalm.* 54, no. 3: "Caput et membra, unus Christus" (PL 36, 629); St. Thomas, ST III, q. 48, a. 1: "Caput et membra, quasi una persona mystica"; see also q. 49, a. 1; q. 19, a. 4; *De veritate*, q. 29, a. 7 ad 2.

[36] Eph 1:23; also Joseph Huby, *St. Paul: Épîtres de la captivité*, pp. 167–71.

[37] Berengard, *In Apocalypsin* (PL 17, 884b–c, 937b); see also Ex 25:8.

[38] Origen, *In Lucam*, hom. 18 and 20 (pp. 123–24 and 132 in Rauer's edition); St. Augustine, *Enchiridion*, chap. 56 (PL 40, 259).

[39] St. Hippolytus, *De antichristo*, chap. 59.

[40] Hugh of Saint-Victor, *De arca Noe moralia*, bk. 2, chap. 7: "Columna in medio arcae erecta . . . ipsa est lignum vitae quod plantatum est in medio paradisi id est Dominus Jesus Christus in medio Ecclesiae suae, quasi praemium laboris" (PL 176, 640). Here we may recognize the symbol of the Cosmic Tree, of which I have made a study in my *Aspects of Buddhism*, trans. G. Lamb (London, 1953), chap. 2.

life;[41] she is the star and he the light that illuminates our night.[42] He who is not, in one way or another, a member of the body does not receive the influx from the Head; he who does not cling to the one Bride is not loved by the Bridegroom. If we profane the tabernacle, we are deprived of the sacred presence, and if we leave the temple, we can no longer hear the Word. If we refuse to enter the holy house or take refuge in the ark, we cannot find him who is center and crown of both. If we are contemptuous of paradise, we are neither fed nor given drink. And if we persuade ourselves that we can do without this received light, we remain perpetually plunged in the night of ignorance . . .

Practically speaking, for each one of us Christ is thus his Church. We may think of her particularly under the aspect of the hierarchy, remembering Christ's words: "He that heareth you heareth me: and he that despiseth you despiseth me";[43] or again, we may think of the Church as the whole body, the whole assembly at the heart of which he is and manifests himself, and in the heart of which the praise of God rises continuously in his name.[44] But in either case the same thing holds good. Joan of Arc's words to her judges convey at one and the same time the depths of the *mystique* of belief and the practical good sense of the believer: "It seems to me that it is all one,

[41] St. Irenaeus, *Adversus haereses*, bk. 5, chap. 20, no. 2 (PL 7, 1178a); Tertullian, *Adversus Marcionem*, bk. 2, chap. 4: "translatus in paradisum—jam tunc de mundo in Ecclesiam" (p. 338 in Kroymann's edition); Berengard, *In Apoc.* (PL 17, 778d); Hugh of Saint-Victor, *De arca Noë morali*, bk. 2, chap. 9: "Dominus Jesus Christus in medio Ecclesiae suae quasi lignum vitae in medio paradisi plantatus est, de cujus fructu quisque digne manducate meruerit, vivet in aeternum" (PL 176, 643); Richard of Saint-Victor, *Allegoriae*, bk. 1, chap. 6: "Fons qui est in paradiso, Christum significat. Quatuor flumina fontis, quatuor sunt Evangelia Christi" (PL 175, 638–39); etc. See also 4 Esdras 103, 52, on Jerusalem: "Vobis apertus est paradisus, plantata est arbor vitae . . . , aedificata est civitas."

[42] Origen, *First Homily on Genesis*, no. 5, etc.

[43] Lk 10:16; Mt 10:40.

[44] Ps 34:18, 25:12, 67:27.

Christ and the Church, and that we ought not to make any difficulty of it." These words of a simple believer are also a summing-up of the faith of the Church's Doctors.[45]

Whatever the difficulties we encounter and the disturbances that threaten to throw us off our balance, we should always keep a firm hold on that equivalence. Like Ulysses bound to the mast in self-defense—in spite of himself— against the voices of the Sirens, we should, if need be, hold on, without eyes or ears for anything else, to the saving truth formulated for us by St. Irenaeus: "Where the Church is, there is the Spirit of God, and where the Spirit of God is, there is the Church and all grace, and the Spirit is Truth; to sever ourselves from the Church is to reject the Spirit"—and in virtue of that "to shut ourselves out of life".[46] We should always share the belief of St. John that it is impossible to understand the Spirit without listening to what he says to the Church.[47] We should remember that there is no substantial hope of unity outside that institution which received the promises of unity. We should hold as an absolute principle that there can never be a valid reason for separating ourselves from her.[48] We

---

[45] St. Augustine, *De doctrina christiana*, bk. 3, chap. 31, no. 44: "Christi et Ecclesiae, unam personam nobis intimari" (PL 34, 82); St. Gregory the Great, *Moralia in Job*, preface, chap. 14: "Redemptor noster unam se personam cum sancta Ecclesia, quam assumpsit, exhibuit." All of which does not cancel out the subordination of the Church to Christ, but rather assumes it. In fact, St. Gregory adds: "De ipso enim dicitur: Qui est caput omnium nostrum, et de Ecclesia ejus scriptum est: Corpus Christi quod est Ecclesia"; see also bk. 35, chap. 14, no. 24: "Christus et Ecclesia, id est caput et corpus, una persona est" (PL 76, 762c).

[46] *Adversus haereses*, bk. 3, chap. 24, no. 1. That is why the Church is "arrha incorruptelae, et confirmatio fidei nostrae, et scala ascensionis ad Deum" (ibid.).

[47] See Rev 2:7, etc.; St. Bernard, *In vigilia nativitatis Domini*, sermo 3, no. 1: "Ecclesia, quae secum habet consilium et spiritum Sponsi et Dei sui" (PL 183, 94d).

[48] St. Augustine, *Contra epistulam Parmeniani*, bk. 3, chap. 5, no. 28: "Nulla est igitur securitas unitatis, nisi ex promissis Dei Ecclesiae declarata. . . . Inconcussum igitur firmumque teneamus, nullos bonos ab ea se posse dividere" (PL 43, 104–5).

should try to understand the traditional axiom formulated by
Origen—"No one is saved outside the Church"[49]—both in its
magnificent breadth and in all its exacting rigorousness, as far
as we are concerned. We must grasp the breadth because, as
St. Augustine explained, "in the ineffable prescience of God,
many who appear to be outside are within"; they are of the
Church at least "by wish or desire", while "many who seem to
be within are without", and "the Lord knows his own" everywhere.[50] But we must also grasp the rigorousness, for he who
"cuts himself off from the Catholic communion" and "goes
out of the House" of salvation "makes himself responsible for
his own death".[51] So that we must never give any place to the
disastrous idea of "breaking the bond of peace by a sacrilegious
usurpation".[52] And it is no use flattering ourselves that we can
still remain "in the society of Christ" although we have put
ourselves outside the Church. As St. Augustine puts it, "to
live by the Spirit of Christ, one must remain in his body";[53]

---

[49] *In Jesu nave*, hom. 3, no. 5 (pp. 306–7 in Baehrens' edition).

[50] *De baptismo*, bk. 5, chap. 27, no. 38 (PL 43, 195–96); see also chap. 16, nos.
20–21; chap. 21, no. 29 (cols. 186–87, 191); *De ordine*, bk. 2, chap. 10, no. 29 (PL
32, 1008): "Illud divinum auxilium . . . certius quam nonnulli opinantur,
officium clementiae suae per universos populos agit."

[51] *De baptismo*, bk. 5, chap. 19, no. 25, and chap. 4 (PL 43, 189 and 179);
Origen, *First Homily on Genesis*: "Si quis forte exierit mortis suae ipse fit reus";
St. Hilary of Poitiers, *De mysteriis*, chap. 9; *Paschal Homilies* 1, no. 13; Lactantius,
Divin. institut., bk. 4, chap. 30 (PL 6, 542–43); St. Fulgentius of Ruspe, *De
remissione peccatorum*, bk. 1, chap. 19 (PL 65, 543); St. Gregory the Great, *Moralia
in Job*, bk. 14, no. 5 (PL 75, 1043). On the views of St. Cyprian, see G. Kopf,
" 'Hors de l'Église point de salut': Origines d'une formule equivoque", in
Cahiers universitaires catholiques (1953), pp. 302–10.

[52] St. Augustine, *De baptismo*, bk. 2, chap. 6, no. 7: "Vos ergo quare separa-
tione sacrilega pacis vinculum dirupistis?" (PL 43, 130).

[53] Quoted by Cardinal Feltin in his pastoral letter for Lent in 1951, *Le Sens de
l'Église*; see also *Epist.* 185, chap. 11, no. 50: "Proinde Ecclesia catholica sola est
corpus Christi. . . . Extra hoc corpus neminem vivificat Spiritus sanctus. . . .
Non habent itaque Spiritum sanctum, qui sunt extra Ecclesiam" (PL 33, 815);
In Joannem, tract. 27, no. 11 (PL 35, 1621); *De consensu evangelistarum*, bk. 3, no.
72: "Ne quisquam se Christum agnovisse arbitretur, si ejus corporis particeps

and again: "[It is] in proportion as one loves the Church of Christ that one has within the Holy Spirit."[54]

It is possible that there may be many things in the human context of the Church that deceive us. And it is also possible that we may be profoundly misunderstood within her, without the things being our fault; we may even have to undergo persecution within the very heart of the Church—that has happened—though we should be wary of presumption in interpreting our own case thus. In such a situation patience and loving silence will be of more value than all else; there is nothing to be feared in the judgment of those who do not see the heart,[55] and we can comfort ourselves with the thought that the Church never gives Christ to us better than on these occasions when she offers us the chance of sharing in the likeness of his Passion. We shall continue to serve by our witness the faith she will continue to preach. The trial may be all the heavier if it comes not from personal ill-will but from a situation that may appear to be impossible of solution; for in such a case wholehearted forgiveness and forgetfulness of self are not enough to carry one through. However, we should be glad before "the Father who seeth in secret" for participating thus in that *veritatis unitas* which we ask for all on Good Friday. And we ought certainly to be glad if we are, in this way, able to buy at the cost of spiritual suffering that very personal experience which will lend power to our words when it becomes our responsibility to help steady some fellow Catholic whose faith has been shaken—as did St. John Chrysostom when he said: "Do not separate yourself from the Church! No power is as powerful as she. The Church is your hope; the Church is your salvation; the Church is your refuge. She is higher than

---

non est, id est, Ecclesiae!" (PL 34, 1206); St. Gregory the Great, *In septem psalmos paenitentiae*, bk. 5 (PL 77, 602).

[54] St. Augustine, *In Joannem*, tract. 32, no. 8: "Quantum quisque amat Ecclesiam Christi, tantum habet Spiritum sanctum" (PL 35, 1646).

[55] St. Robert Bellarmine, *De romano Pontifice*, bk. 1, 4, chap. 20.

heaven and bigger than earth. She never ages, and her vitality is eternal." [56]

* * *

The Church—the whole Church, the only Church, the Church of today and yesterday and tomorrow—is the sacrament of Christ; strictly speaking, she is nothing other than that, or at any rate the rest is a superabundance. Yet there are many, who do not by any means wish to be her adversaries, who misconceive her nature, seeing only her human greatness. Without considering themselves obliged to modify their opinions according to her teaching or to enter into her spirit, they show her "every variety of respect" and sometimes even go so far as to feel for her a sort of "filial affection".[57] Some of them are particularly struck by the power of order and conservation she stands for; they admire her long enduring, her wonderful stability amid the storms of the age, the prudence of her government, the principle of authority that she maintains, the social cohesion that she guarantees, and the reconstruction she gives us hope of. For them she is, even more than the announcer and guardian of the Gospel, the awe-inspiring inheritor of the Greek and Roman worlds. For some, she is simply anti-this or anti-that; others see in her a great force of dynamism and progress, which jolts the nations out of their inertia, fills the hearts of a chosen few with the passion for justice, and imparts to the whole of history an impulse that cannot be checked. The humanists may praise her for having, during the Dark Ages, preserved ancient culture in her monasteries and perpetuated in our midst the miracle of Mediterranean civilization; they are grateful to her for her encouragement of the arts and have a connoisseur's appreciation of the beauties of her liturgy, although as a rule they know only of its Latin form, or at

---

[56] Homily, *De capto Eutropio*, chap. 6 (PG 52, 402); quoted in the encyclical *Satis cognitum*.

[57] See Alexis de Tocqueville, letter to Arthur de Gobineau, January 14, 1857, in *Correspondance*, 2d ed. (1909), p. 306.

any rate restrict their serious attention to that form alone. There are very intelligent men, much aware of the problems of their day, who feel confidence in her as the only spiritual force capable of mastering those problems and, in the long run, resolving them. Praise is freely given in many quarters to her civilizing influence, her moral discipline, the magnificent panorama of her educational and charitable work, and the care she bestows on each of the phases of human life.

Catholics are by no means unmoved by all this admiration, praise, and hope. Despite the limitations of them, the view they give is nearly always accurate and penetrating in some respect at least. There can never be enough said about the profound humanity of the Church, particularly in our own day, when the noble word "humanism" has been more and more monopolized by the enemies of God, and that with the consent of Christians themselves.[58] But as soon as essentials are misconceived, the wrong turning is not very distant. We no longer understand the Church at all if we see in her only her human merits, or if we see her as merely a means—however noble—to a temporal end; or if, while remaining believers in some vague sense, we do not primarily find in her a mystery of faith. Under such circumstances the very things admired in her are denatured, and her praises are mere vanity—if indeed they do not become blasphemies.

[58] Among many other similar statements on the part of the hierarchy, see Leo XIII, encyclical *Militantis Ecclesiae* (August 1, 1897), à propos the tercentenary of St. Peter Canisius: "Re ipsa ostendere, fidem divinam non modo a cultu humanitatis nullatenus abhorrere, sed ejus esse veluti culmen atque fastigium . . . naturam non hostem, sed comitem esse atque administram religionis." Msgr. Charles Moeller has justly observed: "Far from seeing in the humanistic approach of the Jesuits a concession to sick modern minds, and viewing Jansenism as the abiding Christian attitude, we should, on the contrary, maintain that the former is one of the most fertile adaptations the Church has ever made in the whole course of her history" (*Humanisme et sainteté* [1946], p. 217). See also Fr. Charmot, *L'Humanisme et l'humain* (1934); Fr. de Dainville, *Les Jésuites et l'éducation de la société française: La Naissance de l'humanisme moderne* (1940), vol. 1; Henri Bernard, *Matthieu Ricci et la société chinoise de son temps*, and the special issue of *Social Order* (St. Louis, May–June 1953), "Christian Humanism".

Often, for example, she is seen as a sort of museum piece slowly emptying of life, so that all admiration for her is directed to her past. Or again, she sometimes becomes the battlefield of opposing forces, fought for by this party against that; each wants to claim as its own the right to deploy her moral forces against the other. Each party calls on her to declare herself a supporter of the cause for which it has proclaimed a crusade—this group enlists her in the service of "reaction", that in the service of "revolution".[59] As soon as one party seems to have succeeded in gaining control, the opposition turns from her, and the former's reasons for prizing her become so many reasons for the latter's running her down and bringing charges against her. Thus, from time to time, paradoxical situations arise; some people would have us believe that they support the Church although they do not believe in her divine mission, while others start to doubt her because she does not follow them in the path of their dreams. On occasion she may seem to have let herself be compromised, for the Holy Spirit who presides over her does not give infallible clear-sightedness or energy to all those who are her representatives or claim her support, and he does not guarantee them against *faux pas*. There may be not only politicians but churchmen too who try to make the Bride of Christ the instrument of maneuverings at the purely human level.[60] But the Church is aware of what she is and faithful to what she believes, and it is

---

[59] Cf. the observations of Fr. Philippe Laurent, "Le Complexe social en France", *Études* (October 1951), pp. 19–25: "Le Social et le Religieux".

[60] His Holiness Pope Pius XII, Christmas message, 1951: "The divine Redeemer founded the Church with a view to passing on through her to humanity his truth and grace until the end of time. The Church is his mystical body. She is wholly of Christ, and Christ is wholly of God. Politicians (and sometimes even churchmen) who want to make the Bride of Christ their ally or the tool of their national or international political groupings, strike at the very essence of the Church and damage her own life; in a word, they degrade her to that very level on which the struggles of temporal interests are fought out. That remains true, even where ends and interests are involved which are legitimate in themselves."

not long before she asserts her independence—upon which, resentment wells up on every side. Some reproach her bitterly with leaving her traditional defenders in the lurch in order to fall in with the fashions of the time, and the more full of praise they were before, the more bitter and violent they are then. They get to the pitch when they are ready to view her as a power "foreign to the West and outside our classical civilization";[61] while at the same time others—equally wide of the mark—write her off as obviously spent, stupid, and ineffective and consign her to the past for good.

Thus initial misunderstandings bear their fruit. Even among so-called staunch Catholics and even when it is the faith itself that is in question, there are, unfortunately, few who really take their decisions with reference to their faith—that is, for reasons that are of the faith; in view of which it is scarcely surprising that "men of the world"—particularly, perhaps, the best among them—are always, sooner or later, scandalized by the Church —that is, if they *are* just "men of the world" and no more. It does not matter whether they want to change her or to keep her as she is; they will always be impatient at what they consider her timidity and her lukewarmness, though beneath the surface she is, of course, much more "involved" and far more ardent than they. In fact, the Church does not belong to any party; she is the Church of God. Although she is a witness among men to divine things, she already dwells in eternity.

When the spirit of faith flags within, the contempt of the man outside finds encouragement, and the stratagems and calculations of human wisdom give rise to antagonisms without number. Each man cites one of the "outside" doctrines or parties in order to secure a triumph for his own ideas over those of another—who is, in fact, his brother. When this happens, the quarrels of the Church's own children do not merely weaken the Church; they disfigure her in the eyes of the

[61] See Pierre Lafue, "L'Église et la civilisation", *Mercure de France* (December 15, 1927), p. 525.

world: "The sensual man perceiveth not these things that are of the spirit of God." [62] For my own part I will go so far as to say that if the Church were not what she claims to be—if she did not, essentially, live by faith in Jesus Christ, the faith proclaimed by Peter on the road to Caesarea,[63] I should not wait for her to deceive me at the human level before I separated from her. For in that case not all her benefits on the human level, nor all her splendor, nor all the riches of her history, nor all her promise for the future would be able to make up for the dreadful void at the heart of her. The hypothesis is of course not merely false but impossible; yet were things so, all those good things would be the garish trappings of an imposture, and the hope planted by her in our hearts would be a deception, and we should be "of all men most miserable".[64] If Christ is not her wealth, the Church is certainly destitute;[65] if the Spirit of Christ does not flourish in her, she is certainly sterile.[66] If Christ is not her Architect, and his Spirit is not the mortar that binds together the living stones of which she is built, then her building is indeed fallen into ruin.[67] If she does not reflect the unique beauty of the face of Christ,[68] the

[62] 1 Cor 2:14.

[63] See St. Leo the Great, *Epist.* 28, chap. 5: "Catholica Ecclesia hac fide vivit, hac proficit" (PL 54, 777a); St. Ambrose, *Epist.* 21, no. 24: "Ecclesiam congregavit . . . fides Dei" (PL 16, 1057), etc.; also Leo XIII, encyclical *Tametsi futura* (November 1, 1900): "Tueri in terris atque amplificare imperium Filii Dei . . . munus est Ecclesiae."

[64] See 1 Cor 15:14–19. Newman said in 1831, with that somber pungency that sometimes marked the first part of his career: "Much more unworthy has been the practice of boasting of the admission of infidels concerning the beauty or utility of the Christian system, as if it were a great thing for a divine gift to obtain praise for human excellence from proud or immoral men" (*Fifteen Sermons Preached before the University of Oxford between A.D. 1826 and 1834* [London, 1900], p. 71).

[65] *Epistle to Diognetus*, chap. 6, no. 2.

[66] See St. Hippolytus, quoted by Nautin, p. 46.

[67] Origen, *In Gen.*, hom. 2, no. 4; *In Lev.*, hom. 7, no. 2 (pp. 379–80 in Baehrens' edition).

[68] St. Ambrose, *In Psalm.* 48, no. 11 (p. 367 in Petschenig's edition).

Church is without beauty, as she is if she is not the tree whose root is the Passion of Christ.[69] The knowledge on which she prides herself is false, and the wisdom that is her ornament is false, if both are not summed up in Christ;[70] if her light is not "light illuminated", coming wholly from Christ,[71] she certainly has us captive in the shadow of death. All her teaching is a lie if she does not announce the Truth which is Christ;[72] all her glory is vanity if she does not find it in the humility of Christ.[73] Her very name is something foreign to us if it does not at once call to mind the one Name given to men for their salvation.[74] If she is not the sacrament, the effective sign, of Christ, then she is nothing.

* * *

The Church's unique mission is that of making Christ present to men. She is to announce him, show him, and give him, to all; the rest, I repeat, is a superabundance. We know that she cannot fail in this mission; she is, and always will be truly, the Church of Christ—"I am with you all days, even unto the consummation of the world."[75] But she should also be in her members what she is in herself; she should be *through* us what she is *for* us. Christ

[69] St. Augustine, *Sermo* 44, no. 2: "Unde haec tanta pulchritudo [Ecclesiae]? De nescio qua radice surrexit, et ista pulchritudo in magna gloria est. Quaeramus radicem. Consputus est, humiliatus est, flagellatus est, crucifixus est, vulneratus est, contemptus est; ecce hic species est; sed in Ecclesia gloria radicis pollet. Ergo ipsum describit sponsum illum contemptum, inhonoratum, abjectum: sed modo videre habetis arborem, quae surrexit de ista radice et implevit orbem terrarum. *Radix in terra sitienti*" (PL 38, 259).

[70] See St. Augustine, *De Trinitate*, bk. 13, chap. 19, no. 24 (PL 42, 1034), etc.

[71] Origen, *In Gen.*, hom. 1, nos. 5–7.

[72] St. Irenaeus, *Adversus haereses*, bk. 3, chap. 5, no. 1: "Apostoli autem, discipuli Veritatis existentes extra omne mendacium sunt. . . . Veritas ergo Dominus noster existens."

[73] St. Leo the Great, *Sermo* 25, chap. 5: "Agnoscat igitur catholica fides in humilitate Domini gloriam suam et de salutis suae sacramentis gaudeat Ecclesia, quae est corpus Christi" (PL 54, 211b).

[74] Acts 4:12.

[75] Mt 28:20.

should continue to be proclaimed through us and to appear through us. That is something more than an obligation; we may go so far as to say that it is an organic necessity. The question is, do the facts always answer to it? Does the Church truly announce Christ through our ministry?

The question is certainly one that should be asked. The problem it raises is more than one of the moral order or one of individual conduct. It is a cue not so much for exhortation as for reflection. The problem is not one of stirring up or redirecting a zeal that is always flagging[76] but of protecting that zeal against perpetually recurrent dangers; and if this is to be done we must periodically fix our eyes on the essential in its divine simplicity, without getting any false ideas about the inevitable complexities of action.

The Acts of the Apostles, which tell us the story of the first period of the Church, also show us, from start to finish, this proclaiming of Christ. They open with the words of the risen Christ to his disciples—"But you shall receive the power of the Holy Spirit coming upon you, and you shall be witnesses unto me in Jerusalem, and in all Judea and Samaria, and even to the uttermost part of the earth."[77] And they close with the description of Paul "preaching the kingdom of God and teaching the things which concern the Lord Jesus Christ".[78] Every day, in Jerusalem, the Twelve went to the Temple or to some particular house, "teaching and preaching Christ without ceasing".[79] When they were hunted out of the holy city, the first Christians

---

[76] However, it is worthwhile listening to what Rémi of Auxerre has to say to preachers in the course of his commentary on Malachi, and which holds good for all times: "Quando praedicator, qui spiritualem panem, id est doctrinam populis dividere deberet, blanditur potentibus et divitibus hujus saeculi, eaque loquitur quae illis placeant . . . panem utique doctrinae polluit, et ipsi Domino contumeliam facit, dum mensam Scripturarum divinarum saeculari doctrinae, quae est mensa idolorum, putat esse similem" (PL 117, 281b).

[77] Acts 1:8.

[78] Acts 28:31; see also Rom 1:1, etc.

[79] Acts 5:42.

at once, in their dispersal, spread abroad "the word";[80] when the deacon Philip, going down from Jerusalem to Gaza, meets on his way a man of good will who is reading the Prophet Isaiah without being able to understand what he reads, he sets to work to explain matters by proclaiming Christ.[81] Again, the men of Cyprus and Cyrene who come to Antioch have no business more urgent than proclaiming the Lord Jesus;[82] at Thessalonica, Paul and Silas act in exactly the same way, as soon as they have entered the Synagogue.[83] Paul writes to the Corinthians: "For we preach . . . Jesus Christ our Lord: and ourselves your servant through Jesus."[84] The whole of the newborn Church acted and spoke "in the name of Jesus Christ";[85] she is always doing what the angels did by night over Bethlehem—bringing "to all the people" tidings of great joy; for, she says, a Savior is born to you, and he is Christ the Lord.[86]

We may have as much zeal as these first proclaimers of Christ, and we may indeed be better than they at stirring people up—we may have better technical resources. But has our message retained the purity of theirs? Is our bearing witness always as much "conformed to the Gospel of Christ"?[87] A zeal that is certainly active and sincere may not always be equally enlightened or freed from human ways of looking at things; and the faith that is its origin may not always be sufficiently purified. But let us suppose that all our technology is, nevertheless,

[80] Acts 8:4: "They therefore that were dispersed went about preaching the word of God."

[81] Acts 8:35.

[82] Acts 11:20.

[83] Acts 17:1–3.

[84] 2 Cor 4:5; see also Col 1:25: Paul became "a minister" to "fulfill the word of God"; Eph 6:18–20: "[Pray] for me that I may open my mouth with confidence, to make known the mystery of the Gospel, for which I am an ambassador in chains: so that therein I may be bold to speak according as I ought."

[85] Acts, *passim*. See André Rétif, *Foi au Christ et mission* (1953), pp. 84–110.

[86] Luke 2:10.

[87] See the *Martyrdom of Polycarp*, 19, 1.

necessary; we may still well ask ourselves whether it may not, through a proliferation that will eventually get out of control, end up by weaving a web in which our very zeal may be trapped.

It is perfectly true that apologetic makes its demands; that Catholicism has interests to be looked after, that the mass of the faithful have to be organized and protected, that there is every kind of project to be set on foot and kept going, and that each individual one answers a different need. There are techniques to be Christianized—and thus, first, to be learned. There are endless difficulties to be overcome, endless explorations to be made, endless fights to be won, innumerable organizations to be run. Every kind of problem, both theoretical and practical, thrusts itself on our attention—in law, science and politics, economics and finance. All sorts of specialized jobs call for their respective skills and the necessary devotion, either of the spectacular or the hidden kind. Every variety of activity unfolds and extends its ramifications in the service of other activities, which are in themselves no more than links in the chain. Account has to be taken of differences in mentality—slowness here, prejudice there; now one has to handle carefully tender susceptibilities or interests that may well be quite legitimate, now again one has to embark patiently on long programs of spadework; there must be no rushing matters and no quenching of the smoldering wick. Neither due publicity nor propaganda must be neglected. Perhaps it will be necessary to make protective arrangements; certainly it will be necessary to find a proper place in social, national, and international life, to maintain contacts at the official level, and so on. All this is "for the Gospel's sake",[88] certainly; in the last analysis, it is all for the sake of the Kingdom of God, yet often enough in ways that are indirect, to say the least. It is all directed toward the same end; but often enough the nature of the means has little enough in common with that of the end, wholly admirable as the latter

[88] 1 Cor 9:23.

may be. Nevertheless, all these things are perhaps necessary, implied in the logic of the human condition; they cannot be evaded, for such an evasion would be one of the forms of that "pure-Gospel" Christianity which is in fact never wholly faithful to the Gospel and could even be a sort of desertion. So we must be on our guard against a facile "superiority" and keep things in proportion; the laws of common sense and the concrete demands of charity must not be lost sight of. We should accept and give a warm welcome to everything a given situation may suggest to the ingenuity of the enthusiastic and be open to all forms of action that will make sure that the Church can make her presence felt everywhere. Yet when all this has been granted, a question still remains, in the long run; does the essential message manage to get through by way of a network so complex? There is a law, of universal application, that if you overstep the bounds of moderation you defeat your own intentions; and it may be asked whether we do not encounter here an instance of it. Does preparation for the apostolate, organization of the apostolate, the auxiliary service of the apostolate, and all the rest of it always leave us the time and the availability that are necessary to an apostle? Is there not a risk of confining ourselves within a closed circle? May we not sometimes end up by cutting ourselves off from those we are trying to make contact with, or by lessening within ourselves—even falsifying—the very spirit we wish to maintain? In a word: Is the Gospel always proclaimed enough?

To put the matter in a slightly more subtle fashion: it can happen that, through lack of skill, we make the Church herself into a sort of dead end. In her, as we know, the encounter of the soul with Christ takes place;[89] that is a fact of experience as well as a teaching of the faith. Hence, we preach the Church; which is as it should be. We explain the irreplaceable role she plays and establish her authority; the more she seems to us to be misconceived, the more we exert ourselves in praise of her. There is

[89] St. Gregory the Great: "Nuptiarum domum, id est sanctam Ecclesiam."

nothing biased in this; we are, in principle, overwhelmingly justified. Yet this insistent preaching is capable of working against what we wish for. Sometimes it takes on an apologetic tone, almost a note of self-assertion or special pleading, which is, to a certain extent, the symptom of a hidden weakness. If we thus speak of the Church and the Church alone, we are not in fact showing her in her reality—her sacramental reality. Without intending to, we let our vision of the Church stop short at the Church, and thus, as far as those are concerned who are not already living her mystery, she becomes, as it were, opaque, losing the luster of her mystical transparency; from which comes the commonly experienced feeling that churchmen are making a gospel out of themselves. In consequence, we encounter a certain holding back, withdrawal, and even distrust, which are accentuated the more we multiply our appeals for trust, submission, and filial self-abandonment. As Karl Barth has pointed out in his *Dogmatics in Outline*, if the Church has no end other than service of herself, she carries upon her the stigmata of death;[90] and every Catholic will agree with him. But do we always manage to avoid giving an impression of that kind?

Perhaps we may go even farther. We have to take into account the hostility of our age and get down deep into the currents that pull it into its position, if we are not going to swim with them without realizing it. And one of the most powerful among these currents of thought is that of immanentism, which attacks the realities of the faith not so much by a frontal denial as by an interior undermining. It claims to deepen them and to discover the real meaning of them by a process of interiorization; its guiding principles are those of a sacramentalism turned inside out. In its essentials this system of thought stems equally from Hegel and Comte, and it is at present widespread. According to it, God is not "dead"; he is assimilated. He becomes the symbol of man, as man has become the truth of God. Thus the Church becomes that great

---

[90] Karl Barth, *Esquisse d'un dogmatique*, French trans., p. 144.

being whose cult prepares peoples formerly monotheistic for the cult of the one and only true Supreme Being; she is the sacrament of Humanity, over an indispensable transition period. And thus is made manifest what Comte called "our growing tendency toward a real homogeneity between worshippers and the beings that are worshipped". According to this interpretation—which at the same time claims to be a philosophy of history—the growing interest of Catholicism in the dogma of the Church marks (after the interest in Christology and its pendant Mariology)[91] a new stage in the opening perspective of faith in God. It is one step farther in the long process of immanentizing, which is finally to "lead to the complete elimination of the fictitious being".[92] Thus man will acquire the disposition to enter into himself and prepare for his apotheosis, and thus, perhaps, "finally the religion of God made man will end up, by an inevitable dialectic, in an anthropology." By ripening the dogma of the Incarnation to its fruition in the dogma of the Church, Catholicism will give it its final stage of development and itself contribute to the liquidation of all theology; for it will lead us to an eventual realization that religion was "the fantastic realization of the human essence" and that it should be treated "as the symbolic expression of the social and human drama" that is alone real.[93]

[91] For "the apotheosis of humanity would not be complete if the Feminine did not have her part in it" (Louis Ménard, *Rêveries d'un païen mystique*, p. 516).

[92] Auguste Comte, *Système de politique positive*, 2:108; 3:455; cf. p. 433, on the subject of medieval Catholicism. There are similar ideas in Proudhon; see my *Proudhon et le christianisme* (1945), pp. 245–61.

[93] I have borrowed these expressions from M. Maurice Merleau-Ponty, who is himself quoting and justifying Marx, in his *Sens et non-sens*, pp. 151 and 258. To declare a dialectic "inevitable" because it follows the implication of its own tendency and its own negation is neither to provide an argument nor even to show that one has understood the teaching under discussion. Nevertheless, the author is careful to recognize that the Incarnation is an "ambiguous message" (p. 357); he deplores the fact that it is not "followed out in all its consequences" in Christianity. "The religion of the Father remains. . . . God is not with us in his entirety" (p. 361).

It is of course nonsense that an evolutionary system of this type should claim to reveal to us the inner depths of our own beliefs. Yet we should not be too quick to cry out in protest, as if there were never any danger of anything like that in ourselves. There are quite a few things of a kind to give the lie to any pretension of that sort; perhaps a certain almost exclusive emphasis on the Church's capacity to bring about social order and temporal well-being, or certain cloudy ideas concerning the "mystical body", or a kind of confused mysticism dazzled by the idea of a Body without the Head;[94] perhaps some wild idea secretly cherished "of a continuity without any radical cleavage between Creator and creature, and Savior and redeemed".[95] We may suspect that it was perhaps a deviation of this kind that was so vehemently denounced by the fifteenth-century theologian Torquemada when he criticized the members of the Council of Basel for having genuflected when they sang the article in the Credo that concerns the Church.[96] At any rate, we should not think that in order to avoid the danger it is always enough to cultivate the habit of putting forward the affirmations of the faith word for word unchanged; a shift in the center of interest can sometimes be the symptom of a doctrinal debilitation and hollowness more serious than far more obvious errors, which may be no more than innocent mistakes of vocabulary. No sincere Christian will go so far as to profess a "sociological pantheism"; but that is not to say that everyone will always, both in his emotional reactions and his practical conduct, be effectively strengthened in advance against the present tendency to absorb God into the human community.[97] There is no call to exagger-

[94] See the error condemned in the encyclical *Mystici corporis*: "To confuse into one single physical person the divine Redeemer and the members of the Church."

[95] See Louis Bouyer, "Où en est la théologie du corps mystique?", RSR (1948), p. 314.

[96] Torquemada, *Summa de Ecclesia*, bk. 1, chap. 20, p. 23; see also above, p. 41, nn. 95–96.

[97] This tendency has been noted by Edmond Ortigues, S.M., in *Cahiers universitaires catholiques* (December 1950), p. 142.

ate the danger, but it is as well to be on guard against it. So we must be careful always to manifest the Church and, first of all, always to understand her, in her total truth. We must make it our constant preoccupation, through her and in her, to listen to him whom she proclaims and to rise toward him for whom, solely, she exists.

Each one of us is a member of the unique body, and each one of us, in his own small way, "is" the Church.[98] The Church is meant to proclaim the Gospel through each one of us and to announce it to "every creature".[99] She is meant to make its light enlighten the eyes of every man who comes into this world, like the candlestick, which is, simply, a flame-bearer.[100] In each one of us she is meant to efface herself before her Lord, to be no more than a finger that points toward him,[101] a voice that transmits his. Each of us, in his own way and his own degree, is meant to be a "servant of the Word".[102] The priest's words before he reads the Gospel at Mass—"The Lord be in my heart and on my lips, so that I may worthily proclaim his Holy Gospel"[103]—should not be merely a ritual formula. If that desire does not inspire both our preaching and our church work at all times, we deserve the verdict wrongly passed by the Israelites whom Jeremiah denounced: "The prophets have spoken in the wind, and there was no word of God in them."[104]

[98] St. Augustine, *Sermo* 138, no. 10: "Amate hanc Ecclesiam, estote in tali Ecclesia, estote talis Ecclesia!" (PL 38, 769).

[99] See Mk 16:15.

[100] Absalom, *Sermo* 30, *In Matt.* 5: "Per lucernam lumen evangelicae praedicationis, per candelabrum Ecclesia designatur. . . . Candelabrum [enim] ex se non lucet, sed lucernam sibi superimpositam portat" (PL 211, 177–78).

[101] See St. Ambrose, *In Lucam*, bk. 5, chap. 97: "Fides quoque digito Ecclesiae reperitur" (PL 15, 1162c).

[102] See Acts 4:4.

[103] "Dominus sit in corde meo et in labiis meis, ut digne et competentur annuntiem Evangelium suum!"

[104] Jer 5:13; see also A. Brien, "Pedagogie", NRT (1952), p. 566: "Our words should be at once humble and powerful, always animated by the sense of the presence of God."

And if we are to announce the Gospel "worthily and in a seemly manner", the one thing above all others we must bear in mind is that we are unworthy of it and do not understand it—that the Gospel always condemns us.[105]

* * *

The Gospel is not announced by word only. It is announced—and to an even greater extent—by living. It is by living by Christ's Spirit that the Church manifests him and spreads his name abroad like a perfume.[106] The Christians described for us in the Acts were not, as a whole, apostles, in the many strict senses of the word. Yet all of them contributed to the spreading of the new "fire", to the degree in which they were truly of the Church, forming "one heart and one soul". And this "brotherly love"[107] has always been, from that time onward, the Church's best act of witness and her most powerful attraction. As St. Ignatius of Antioch was to say: "The Church is a choir; the bishop presides over the making of its music, which, like the music of the spheres, is silent neither by day nor by night." No doubt St. Ignatius here has in mind liturgical gatherings; yet from his viewpoint, those were themselves the symbol of another harmony, both more interior and on a far greater scale, "the harmony of universal charity, in which the singing is of Christ".[108] "The holy Church throughout all the world doth acknowledge thee."

Once heard, that harmony has an attractive power that is irresistible. The house of God is built up in song: *cantando*

---

[105] See Lanza del Vasto, *Commentaire de l'Évangile* (1951), p. 37: "Anyone who ventures to teach the Gospel runs the risk of seeing rise up against him the great and terrible truths which he himself has affirmed."

[106] See Song 1:2.

[107] 1 Th 4:9.

[108] *Ad Ephes.*, chap. 4, no. 1. Similarly, the word "unanimity" is frequent in St. Clement of Rome's Epistle to the Corinthians. On Christ as the "Music of the Father" and his song of the beatitudes, see the fine passage by Rupert of Deutz in his *In Matt.*, bk. 4 (PL 168, 1389).

aedificatur.[109] The "living stones" gather and crystallize into organic form through a mutual call to joy:

> Congaudentes jubilemus
> Harmoniae novum genus
>   Concordi melodia;
> Deponamus vetus onus,
> Dulcisque resultat sonus
>   Ex nostra concordia! [110]

And thus charity, breaking the bounds of the community, spreads outside, in a longing to "sing with all the earth".[111] It anticipates every appeal, is attentive to every kind of suffering, and stretches out its arms to those who "sit in the shadow of death" and who, roused by the music of its lyre, rise up and go to meet it—for Christ is, through his Church, the new Orpheus. When he pours out to his own the Easter joy that breaks out in a "new harmony",[112] he also gives them the wonderful power which brings it about that "all those who look at them want to sing";[113] when he tears them free from the decrepitude of evil or fear, he sets them singing that song which is perpetually new and tells the whole world how sweet his yoke is and how light his burden,[114] for their deeds set a serene light shining out over the darkness of the age and cover the barrenness of the wasteland with a life-bringing dew.[115] Or again, to borrow the words of St. Gregory of Nyssa: When the Christian community is faithful to him who gathers it together in order to dwell

---

[109] St. Augustine, *Sermo* 27, no. 1 (PL 38, 178). See the first response of the Roman office of the Dedication: "In dedicatione templi decantabat populus laudem, et in ore eorum, dulcis resonabat sonus."

[110] Sequence for the Dedication of Churches according to the Use of Saragossa (Misset and Weale, *Thesaurus hymnologicus*, 2:379).

[111] St. Augustine, *Sermo* 33, no. 5 (PL 38, 209).

[112] St. Clement of Alexandria, *Protreptica*, chap. 1.

[113] See Paul Claudel, *The Satin Slipper*, day 3.

[114] St. Augustine, *Sermo* 9, chap. 7, no. 8 (PL 38, 81–82).

[115] St. Paulinus of Nola, *Epist.* 23, nos. 33–34 (PL 61, 278–79).

in its midst, each man can see the beauty of the Bridegroom through the Bride, and thus all can marvel at what no creature can fathom. For as St. John says, no man has seen God or can see him; yet, as St. Paul adds, he has made out of the Church his body, built up in love. He puts a reflection of his own beauty on the face of the Church; and thus those who love the Bridegroom rise, through her, to the invisible God. Just as the eye, which cannot bear to look directly into the sun, sees it reflected in the mirror of water, so also, in looking at the face of the Church, the eyes of the soul contemplate the Sun of Righteousness as if in a flawless mirror.[116]

There lies the great power in the Church's witness;[117] that is her triumph, a triumph we are always too inclined to think of in secular terms.[118] It is a triumph won in the Spirit, when the Church is carried along by his breath and the glory that streams from her when she appears as "the woman clothed with the sun".[119]

Unfortunately, this triumph is never complete. The glory is not always in full blaze—very much the contrary; those who see us from outside do not have to shut their eyes in order not always to see the beauty of the divine countenance, which we so busily disfigure,[120] or not to find within view that "land burning with love" which every Christian community ought to be.[121] Bossuet put the matter vigorously enough:

[116] St. Gregory of Nyssa, *In Cantica canticorum*, hom. 8 (PG 44, 949a–b); cf. hom. 13 (cols. 1049–52).

[117] Acts 4:33; see also Paul Doncoeur, S.J., *La Sainte Vierge dans notre vie d'hommes* (1940): "Is it possible to imagine a world in which the priest would not be a witness of Jesus Christ?"

[118] See St. Augustine, *De perfectione justitiae*, chap. 15, no. 35: "Non dicendum est Ecclesiam esse gloriosam quia reges ei serviunt: ubi est periculosior majorque tentatio" (PL 44, 310).

[119] Rev 12:1.

[120] See Origen, *In Cantica*, bk. 3 (p. 232 in Baehrens' edition).

[121] See Pascal, *Pensées*, no. 772 (Brunschvicq edition): "*Effundam spiritum meum*. All peoples were in infidelity and concupiscence, all the world was burning with charity."

O damnable faithlessness of those who glory in the name of Christian! Christians bring about their own destruction; the whole Church is bloody with the murder of her children by her children; and as if so many wars and such slaughter were not enough to satisfy our pitiless inhumanity, we rend each other in the same cities, the same houses, under the same roofs, with irreconcilable enmity. We perpetually ask for peace, and we make war on ourselves. . . . We have so forgotten the Gospel, which is a discipline of peace! . . . By means of our dissensions we set up to reign over us the devil, who is the author of discord, and hunt out the Spirit of peace, that is, the Spirit of God. If indeed, O my Savior, you wished that the holy union of the faithful should be the mark of your coming, what do all Christians now do but proclaim from the housetops that your Father never sent you, that the Gospel is a fantasy, and that your mysteries are so many fables? [122]

There is, I am afraid, all too much excuse for the Gentiles if they do not always hear the joyful song of the "new man", which should be that of all those whom the maternal Church has regenerated and united in Christ,[123] and do not sense in our hearts that "exultant peace" which the resurrected Christ brings with him,[124] or find among us "that Muse of joy which dwells in the tent of the just",[125] or see "the springtime of the soul, the springtime of the Spirit"[126] blossoming wherever the name "Catholic" is held in honor, and the world flowering once more as if it were a second paradise.[127] And they have all

[122] Bossuet, *Sur le mystére de la Sainte Trinité* (1655; in *Oeuvres oratoires*, ed. Lebarq [1914], 2:64–65).

[123] See St. Augustine, *De cantico novo, sermo ad catechumenos*, chap. 1, no. 1 (PL 40, 678–79); St. Ambrose, *De sacramentis*, bk. 2, no. 7: "Deposuisti peccatorum senectutem, sumpsisti gratiae juventutem"; *Paschal Homilies* 1, no. 20: "the newness that is in Christ".

[124] Col 3:15; see Acts 8:8.

[125] St. Hilary of Poitiers, *In Psalm.* 149, no. 2 (p. 867 in Zingerle's edition).

[126] St. Gregory Nazianzen, *Discourse* 44, *in fine* (PG 35, 620d).

[127] See Rupert of Deutz, *In cantica*, bks. 1 and 4: "reflorescere mundum Ecclesiis"; "novum fluere paradisum, id est novam propagari Ecclesiam de multitudine gentium" (PL 168, 862c and 901d).

too much excuse if, when they look at our lives, they are unable to understand how Catholic obedience is the foundation of that higher freedom which alone can bring about unity. They can scarcely be blamed for not suspecting that the Church really perpetuates on earth the work of the Son of God, who came into the world to deliver the human race from the demons who oppressed it,[128] if we do not ourselves actively show them, through the "new ways of the Gospel",[129] that for us the "old slavery" is passed and all things made new. They can scarcely be blamed for not believing that the risen Christ lives forever in his Church if we do not prove to them that he really is our Passover and that he has effectively rid us of the old leaven and continues to feed us "with the unleavened bread of sincerity and truth".[130] They can scarcely be blamed if they do not see in the Christian community the bearer of a message of salvation when they see it behaving just like any other party, sect, or clique and if its lack of sensitivity or internal divisions present them with the horrifying spectacle of a Catholicism without any heart. They can hardly be blamed if they are not drawn to men who claim to have a part in the Holy Spirit but seem to be forever occupied in crucifying afresh the God whom they claim to worship.[131] It will not matter what we *say*; they will still be sceptical and seem to us a living pronouncement of the words: "Neither have you heard his voice at any time, nor seen his shape. And you have not his word abiding in you."[132] They can scarcely be expected to believe in the Bridegroom if, through our lives, the Bride seems to be barren.

In this way, and through our fault, the Church finds herself forced onto the defensive. Because of us, men of good will who

---

[128] See St. Albert the Great, *Sermo* 10, *In dominica infra nativitatem Domini*: "ut ingressus in mundum, genus humanum ab oppressione daemonum liberaret" (*Opera* [1651], 13:26).

[129] Theodore of Mopsuestia, *Sixth Catechetical Homily*, no. 12 (ed. Tonneau and Devreesse, pp. 153–55).

[130] 1 Cor 5:7–8.

[131] Heb 6:4–6.

[132] Jn 5:37–38.

are, without knowing it, in search of Christ, are in a position where they might well make their own the words of the Song of Songs: "I will rise and will go about the city. In the streets and the broad ways I will seek him whom my soul loveth. I sought him, and found him not."[133] Moreover, movements of an anarchic type grow up around the Church, and even within her; every age produces new examples. Such, for example, was the upsurge of mysticism toward the end of the eighteenth century in reaction against the dried-up and superficial rationalism of the preceding generation. And instead of drawing men to the faith of the great Christian community, as often as not all it did was to lose them to some illuminist sect or other. In this unfortunate period there were only too many symptoms likely to persuade people that priests had "lost the word of power" and no longer had any knowledge of the "mysteries of the Kingdom of God",[134] as Claude de Saint-Martin put it. There was the even more tragic spectacle of little groups that, gripped by some fever of the spirit, separated from the Church, reviling her as wholly "of the flesh",[135] despairing of ever receiving from her the bread for which they hungered, and accusing her of having

[133] Song 3:1–2.

[134] St. Martin of Leon, *Ecce Homo*; Joseph de Maistre, *Quatre chapitres sur la Russie*, chap. 4 (in *Oeuvres*, 8:329). In some unpublished notes, de Maistre speaks of religious minds who, "not being content with what they see, look for something more substantial and form an attachment to mystical ideas" (quoted by E. Dermenghem in his *Joseph de Maistre: Mystique*, 2d ed. [1946], p. 71). He regarded this as a normal occurrence in "Protestant Europe"; the abnormal aspect of the thing is that such an attitude should be able to arise within Catholicism.

[135] See John XXII, condemning the Fraticelli in 1318: "Duas fingit ecclesias, unam carnalem, divitiis pressam, . . . sceleribus maculatam, cui Romanum praesulem aliosque inferiores praelatos dominari asserunt; aliam spiritualem, . . . in qua ipsi soli eorumque complices continentur." Such a condemnation would perhaps not have been necessary if, during the century that had just passed, there had been many in the Church who had been possessed of the generous and truly evangelical clear-mindedness of a man like Pope Innocent III; see Fr. Chenu, "L'Expérience des spirituels du XIIIe siècle", LV (June 1953), pp. 75–94.

forgotten her Savior. And at the origin of their secession there was very probably not only a great deal of zeal but much uprightness of heart, much good will, much love for Christ and his Gospel—as well as much illusion and much childishness. They had plenty of scope for the denouncing of abuses, apathy, inconsistency, and scandals among us;[136] in a field so big there is always a rich harvest to be gathered, even during the finest periods.[137] But against all this, what they failed to see was that with all their fervor and all their criticisms, they were still parasites, only existing through the great Church and continuing to live (and not for long at that) on the capital that she had saved for them, already lost to the great common work and the great witnessing. Yet our own fidelity ought not to make us pharisaical. We have to admit that aberrations of this sort can be compensatory phenomena; they are perhaps, in their way, the signs of our own apathy.[138] And in the ordinary way events are not long in making plain the errors involved. Yet we should be wrong if we took this as the occasion to become yet more stubbornly entrenched in the fortress of our own clear conscience, when in point of fact we should be applying to ourselves, to some extent at any rate, Christ's words: "Woe to him by whom offenses come." [139] It is indeed woe to any man who drives out his brother.

[136] See Fénelon, *Lettres sur l'Église*, 7: "It is true that you may see among us many Doctors empty of God and full of themselves, and much ignorance and even superstition among the people; but the true Church is not exempt from scandals. The bad seed must be left to grow with the good, lest a rash reform uproot the good seed with the bad and destroy instead of reform."

[137] St. Augustine, *Epist.* 268, no. 7: "Non moveberis scandalis, quae abundabunt usque in finem" (PL 33, 952).

[138] See the pastoral letter of Cardinal Feltin on unity in the Church, Lent 1952: "There would not be, doubtless, so much sympathy toward certain currents, communities, sects, and secret societies—which are today on the increase—if former children of the Church did not have recourse to them to find—vainly, moreover—what they have not been able to find directly in their brothers in Christ."

[139] When a man falls away, he may perhaps drag others down with him in his fall, and then we quickly cry out about the scandal he has caused. But how are

But all these deviations are powerless against the Church herself. Men may be lacking in the Holy Spirit, but the Holy Spirit will never be lacking to the Church. In virtue of her witness and sovereign powers, she will always be the Sacrament of Christ and make him really and truly present to us.[140] She will always reflect his glory, through the best of her children.[141] Even when she shows signs of weariness, germination is in progress toward a new spring, and in spite of all the obstacles we heap up, the saints will spring up once more.

---

we to be sure that he has not himself been scandalized first, and that in the true sense of the word? Perhaps we have ourselves—in some way we fail to see—been the occasion of his disaster. See H. C. Chéry, O.P., "Les Sectes bibliques", LV 6 (1952): 107: "The very success of the sects ought to urge us to an examination of conscience."

[140] See Moehler's letter to the Countess Stolberg (1834).

[141] See 2 Cor 3:7–18.

VII

ECCLESIA MATER

THE story is told of a priest who, shortly after apostatizing, said to a visitor who was about to congratulate him: "From now onward I am no more than a philosopher—in other words, a man alone." It must have been a bitter reflection, but it was true. He had left the home outside which there will never be anything save exile and solitude. Many people are not aware of this truth because they live in the passing moment, alienated from themselves, "rooted in this world like seaweed on the rocks".[1] The preoccupations of daily life absorb them; "the golden mist of appearances"[2] forms a veil of illusion around them. Sometimes they look in a hundred and one different places for some substitute for the Church, as if to deceive their own longings. Yet the man who hears in the depths of his being the call that has stimulated his thirst for communion—indeed, the man who does no more than sense it—grasps that neither friendship nor love, let alone any of the social groupings that underlie his own life, can satisfy it. No more can the arts or philosophizing or independent spiritual exploration; for these are only symbols, the promise of something other than themselves, and, in the bargain, deceptive symbols whose promise is not fulfilled. Such bonds as these are either too abstract or too particularized, too superficial or too ephemeral; they are all the more powerless in proportion as they had the greater pull. There is nothing created by man and nothing on man's level that can wrench him free from his solitude; it grows deeper the more he discovers concerning himself; for it is nothing other

[1] Clement of Alexandria, *Protrepticos*, bk. 9, chap. 86, no. 2.
[2] Pierre van der Meer de Walcheren, *Journal d'un converti*, 3d ed. (1921), p. 4.

than the reverse side of the communion to which he is called and has both the breadth and depth of that communion.

God did not make us "to remain within the limits of na-ture"[3] or for the fulfilling of a solitary destiny;[4] on the contrary, he made us to be brought together into the heart of the life of the Trinity.[5] Christ offered himself in sacrifice so that we might be one in that unity of the divine Persons.[6] That is to be the "recapitulation", "regeneration", and "consummation" of all things, and anything outside that which exerts a pull over us is a thing of deception.[7] But there is a place where this gathering together of all things in the Trinity begins in this world; "a family of God",[8] a mysterious extension of the Trinity in time, which not only prepares us for this life of union and gives us a sure guarantee of it,[9] but also makes us participate in it already. The Church is the only completely "open" society, the only one that measures up to our deepest longings and in which we can finally find our whole shape. "The people united by the unity of the Father and the Son and the Holy Spirit":[10] that is the Church. She is "full of the Trinity".[11] The Father is in her "as the principle to which one is united, the Son as the medium in which one is united, the Holy Spirit as the knot by which all

---

[3] Bérulle, *Oeuvres de piété*, 143, 3.

[4] St. Paschasius Radbertus, *In Matt.*, preface: "Jam caelos uniti in Christi corpore penetrare speramus" (PL 120, 41d); see also J. Lebreton, "L'Église corps du Christ", RSR (1946), p. 248.

[5] St. Irenaeus, *Adversus haereses*, bk. 5, chap. 36, no. 3: "Etenim unus Filius, qui voluntatem Patris perficit; et unum genus humanum, in quo perficiuntur mysteria Dei . . . , ut primogenitus Verbum descendat in facturam . . . et capi-atur in ea, et factura iterum capiat Verbum et ascendat ad eum" (PG 7, 1224b).

[6] Jn 17:19–23.

[7] Jn 17:23; 1 Cor 15:28.

[8] Eph 2:19; 1 Tim 3:15; 1 Pet 4:17.

[9] Heb 3:5–6.

[10] St. Cyprian, *De oratione dominica*, chap. 23 (p. 285 in Hartel's edition); Origen, *In Cant.*, bk. 1 (p. 103 in Baehrens' edition); St. Hilary of Poitiers, *De Trinitate*, bk. 8, nos. 11 and 19 (PL 10, 243–44, 250), etc.

[11] Origen, *Selecta in Psalmos*, 23, 1 (PG 12, 1265): "He who is in the Church, which is full of the Holy Trinity, inhabits the universe."

things are united; and all is one". It is not only that we know this; we already have an anticipatory experience of it in the obscurity of faith. For us, according to the mode that suits our earthly condition, the Church is the very realization of that communion which is so much sought for. She guarantees not only our community of destiny but also our community of vocation; the bonds with which she seems to bind us have no other aim than freeing us, uniting us, and giving us room to breathe. She is the matrix that forms that "unity of the Spirit" which is no more than a mirage if there is not "unity of the body" as well.[12] She is the "perfect dove", like the Holy Spirit himself; in her unity we all become one, as the Father and Son are one.[13] Hence the fullness conveyed by the joyful words in which we bind ourselves to the gift we receive from heaven—"Amen to God".[14]

When we have entered the holy dwelling, whose dimensions are vaster than those of the universe, and have become members of the Mystical Body—

> we have at our disposal for loving, understanding, and serving God not only our own powers but everything from the Blessed Virgin in the summit of heaven down to the poor African leper who, bell in hand, whispers the responses of the Mass through a mouth half eaten away. The whole of creation, visible and invisible, all history, all the past, the present, and the future, all the treasure of the saints, multiplied by grace—all that is at our disposal as an extension of ourselves, a mighty instrument. All the saints and the angels belong to us. We can use the intelligence of St. Thomas, the right arm of St. Michael, the hearts of

[12] See Eph 4:3-4 and St. John Chrysostom's commentary thereon, hom. 9, no. 3 (PG 62, 72).

[13] St. Gregory of Nyssa, *In Cantica*, hom. 15 (PG 45, 1116-17); see my *Catholicism*, p. 396, as well as other excerpts cited there. See also Song 6:8.

[14] Bossuet, *Quatrième lettre à une demoiselle de Metz*, no. 7; see also Bl. Mary of the Incarnation, *Explication des mystères de foi*, 3d ed. (1878), p. 79: "The Holy Catholic Church. This article contains the grace of our vocation, for God has only called us in order to incorporate us into his Church and make us members of the mystical body of his Son."

Joan of Arc and Catherine of Siena, and all the hidden resources that have only to be touched to be set in action. Everything of the good, the great, and the beautiful from one end of the earth to the other—everything that *begets* sanctity (as a doctor says of a patient that he has *got* a fever)—it is as if all that were our work. The heroism of the missionary, the inspiration of the Doctors of the Church, the generosity of the martyrs, the genius of the artists, the burning prayer of the Poor Clares and Carmelites— it is as if all that were ourselves; it is ourselves. All that is one with us, from the North to the South, from the Alpha to the Omega, from the Orient to the Occident; we clothe ourselves in it, we set it in motion. All that is in the orchestral activity by which we are at one and the same time revealed and made as nothing. In the core of the vast gathering of Christianity there is to be found the equivalent of all that which, in the individual body, is entrusted to the choir of cells—nourishment, respiration, circulation, elimination, appetite. The Church transposes, and paints outside us on a vast scale, all that is in us almost without our knowing it. Our brief and blind impulses are wedded, taken up again, interpreted, developed, by vast stellar movements. Outside ourselves we can decipher at astronomic distances the text written on a microscopic scale in the farthest depths of the heart.[15]

Beyond all realization at the human level and in spite of the tearing apart that is the wages of sin and the way of redemption, the mystery of communion is in action. In her very visibility the Church is the vital nucleus around which gather, from age to age and in ways often hidden from us, all those who are to be saved. Those whom she has already united are truly the soul of the world, the soul of this great human body, as the second-century author of the *Epistle to Diognetus* put it.[16] There is an

[15] *Paul Claudel interroge le Cantique des cantiques.*

[16] Chap. 6, nos. 1, 2, 7, 10: "Christians are in the world what the soul is in the body. The soul is spread into all the members of the body as Christians are spread in the cities of the world. . . . Christians are as if held in the prison of the world; yet nonetheless it is they who bear up the world. . . . The post God has assigned to them is so noble that they are not allowed to desert it." The commentary given by H. I. Marrou on this passage in his translation (in the

amazing boldness in such an assertion; the Christian who made it was the voice of a tiny flock, wretched and persecuted, considered beneath contempt by the wise and the powerful of the world. It is true that this small group was growing rapidly; it gathered fresh members every day, and a shrewd observer might have foreseen even then that before long it would swamp the Empire. But this was not the foresight that gave to the writer of the epistle his sure and serene audacity. There was no question of any prophetic insight into any earthly future; it was purely a matter of faith and an awareness of speaking in the name of the Church of God. We may say that he spoke as an "ecclesiastic" in the true sense.

As far as our current speech is concerned, that term is much worn, not to say debased. It has become a professional title for entry in official registers, the appropriate label that goes with a particular dress. Even within the Church we scarcely ever use it save as a purely external descriptive term. One wonders who will give it back its breadth and dignity and make us aware once more of the associations it once called to mind. In the original sense of the term, the "ecclesiastic"—the *vir ecclesiasticus*—is a churchman, without any obligatory distinction into layman or

---

series *Sources chrétiennes*, no. 33 [1952], pp. 65–67) throws a clear light on "the cosmic role of the Christian" in the early apologetic tradition: "Here the point at issue is not that of Christians themselves—their fortunate destiny and their progress and their method of turning to account in the service of their transcendent interests their implanting in this wicked world; rather, it is a question of fruitfulness with regard to others, their fruitfulness for the world itself; and of the presence and action of Christians within the heart of that world itself. . . . Christians fulfill in the world a function analogous to that which, in current Hellenistic thought, had devolved onto the world soul. . . . [As Origen was to show], it is because the Church is the Mystical Body of Christ that we can accord her this role of world-soul which pagan thought had allotted to a divine power. . . . These Christians are, precisely, a handful of men who are unknown and despised and scattered abroad through an empire which responds to their appeal by hatred and persecution. That contrast, so proudly emphasized, suggests fruitful reflections to the mind of the modern reader." See also St. Irenaeus, *Adversus haereses*, bk. 3, chap. 24, no. 1: "The Church ought to 'ensoul' creation."

cleric. He is a man in the Church; better, a man of the Church, a man of the Christian community. If this sense of the word cannot be altogether salvaged from the past, the reality signified should at any rate remain. It is much to be hoped that a sense of it will revive among us.

* * *

"For myself," said Origen, "I desire to be truly ecclesiastic".[17] He thought—and rightly—that there was no other way of being a Christian in the full sense. And anyone who is possessed by a similar desire will not find it enough to be loyal and obedient, to perform exactly everything demanded by his profession of the Catholic faith. Such a man will have fallen in love with the beauty of the House of God; the Church will have stolen his heart. She is his spiritual native country, his "mother and his brethren", and nothing that concerns her will leave him indifferent or detached; he will root himself in her soil, form himself in her likeness, and make himself one with her experience. He will feel himself rich with her wealth;[18] he will be aware that through her and her alone he participates in the unshakeableness of God.[19] It will be from her that he learns how to live and die. Far from passing judgment on her, he will allow her to

[17] *In Lucam*, hom. 2 and 16 (pp. 14 and 109 in Rauer's edition); cf. the *Dialektos* (pp. 140 and 142 in Scherer's edition); St. Athanasius (see G. Müller, *Lexicon Athanasium*, 1, 452); St. Gregory of Nyssa, *Contra Eunomium*, bk. 2, no. 12 (PG 45, 544); St. Jerome, *passim*: Rémi of Auxerre (PL 117, 39a, 82b); see also St. Martin of Leon (PL 208, 30b–c), etc.

[18] Cf. Moehler, *Athanasius der Grosse*: "Athanasius clove to the Church as a tree cleaves to the soil"; and again: "Rooted in the Church with his whole being and through the whole of his past, he became her faithful image; her firmness, indeed her veritable immutability, thus became wholly the portion of Athanasius. This unity of existence with the Church had a further result: since he was wholly fed on her fruits and since his whole life was bound up with the Church and by her with Christ—or, by Christ with the Church—he felt himself blessed with these interior riches"; compare St. Augustine, *De baptismo*, bk. 5, chap. 17, no. 23 (PL 43, 188).

[19] St. Augustine, *In Psalm.* 121, no. 6: "Ipsius stabilitatis participat illa civitas cujus participatio est in idipsum" (PL 37, 1623).

judge him, and he will agree gladly to all the sacrifices demanded by her unity.

Being a man of the Church, he will love the Church's past. He will meditate over her history, holding her tradition in reverence and exploring deep into it. Granted, the last thing he will do will be to devote himself to a cult of nostalgia, either in order to escape into an antiquity he can reshape as he likes or in order to condemn the Church of his own day, as if she were already grown decrepit[20] and her Bridegroom had cast her off.[21] Any attitude of that kind will repel him, spontaneously. He may, certainly, take pleasure in going back in spirit to the age of the newborn Church,[22] when, as St. Irenaeus put it, the echo of the Apostles' preaching was still audible[23] and "Christ's blood was still warm [and] faith burned with a living flame in the heart of the believer." But for all that he will be sceptical

---

[20] See the ninety-fifth condemned proposition of Quesnel: "The truths [of the faith] have become, as it were, a foreign language to the majority of Christians, and the way in which they are preached is as it were an unknown language, so far removed is it from the simplicity of the Apostles and so far is it above the reach of the faithful. And it is not realized that this falling-off is one of the most obvious signs of the decrepitude of the Church and the anger of God against his children."

[21] See Saint-Cyran to St. Vincent de Paul: "Yes, I admit, God has granted me great enlightenment. He has given me to know that there is no longer any Church. . . . No, there is no Church any more: God has given me to know that there has not been any Church for five or six hundred years past. Before then, the Church was as a great river with its clear waters, but now what appears to us to be the Church is no more than mud. . . . It is true that Jesus Christ built the Church upon rock; but there is a time to build up and a time to tear down. She was his bride; but now she is an adulteress and a prostitute; that is why he has repudiated her, and he desires that another, who will be faithful, should be substituted for her" (in Abelly, quoted by Coste, *Monsieur Vincent*, 3:140–41); and see St. Vincent de Paul, *Correspondance*, ed. Coste (1923), 11:355. Texts and testimonies of like kind are in Jean Orcibal's *Jean Duvergier de Hauranne* (1947), pp. 602–4, but these are to some extent counterbalanced by others quoted on pp. 621–25.

[22] See Gilbert of Hoyland, *In Cantica*, s. 13, no. 12: "Contemplare adhuc initia lactentis Ecclesiae" (PL 184, 64b).

[23] *Adversus haereses*, bk. 3, chap. 3, no. 3 (PG 7, 849).

about those myths of the Golden Age which give such a stimulus to the natural inclination to exaggeration, righteous indignation, and facile anathematizing. In any case, he knows that Christ is always present, today as yesterday, and right up to the consummation of the world, to continue his life, not to start it again;[24] so that he will not be forever repeating "It was not so in the beginning". His questionings are not directed to a "dumb Church and dead Doctors", and he will have no "petrifaction" of Tradition, which is for him no more a thing of the past than of the present, but rather a great living and permanent force[25] that cannot be divided into bits. He will, of course, never take it into his head to appeal from the present teaching of the Magisterium to some past situation, doctrinal or institutional, or invoke such things in order to apply to that teaching an interpretation that would in fact be an evasion;[26] for he will

---

[24] De Caussade, *Abandonment to Divine Providence*; Bossuet, *Sixième avertissement aux Protestants*, no. 109: "The Church is always alive to explain herself."

[25] St. Irenaeus, *Adversus haereses*, bk. 1, chap. 10, no. 2: ἡ δύναμις τῆς παραδόσεως (PG 7, 552); St. Basil the Great, *De Spiritu Sancto*, chap. 29, no. 73: τό τῆς παραδόσεως ἰσχυρόν (PG 32, 204); cf. the Oratorian Morin, *Commentarius historicus de disciplina in administratione sacramenti paenitentiae* (1865), preface; St. Nicephorus of Constantinople, *Antirrheticus* 3 (Against the Emperor Leo the Armenian; PG 100, 638–91); M. J. Scheeben, *Dogmatique*, trans. Belet, 1:231.

[26] Saint Cyran says that we should never "talk of the things of God according to our own minds, but rather follow wholly in all matters the authority and tradition of the Church"; but he also adds: "The spirit of Jesus Christ cannot alter anything of his institutions or his commands, nor even anything of the orders of those whom he established after his Ascension by the Holy Spirit which holds his place in the Church" (*Pensées sur la sacerdoce*). Similarly Arnauld, having recalled the Church's early teaching and discipline, says: "It is impossible that she should not have the same sentiments today" (*De la fréquente communion*, in *Oeuvres*, 27:443; see also pp. 125–28). There is a criticism of this attitude in the work of D. Petau, S.J., *De la pénitence publique* (1644), and in F. Bonal, O.F.M., *Le Chrétien du temps*, pt. 3, chaps. 8–9, 2d ed. (1688), 2:100–120. The same tendency is condemned again in the encyclical *Humani generis* in the criticism of those who seek to "explain away the recent decrees and constitutions of the Magisterium by reference to the writings of the ancients"; cf. St. Prosper of Aquitaine, writing to St. Augustine on the subject of the Pelagians: "Obstinationem suam vetustate defendunt" (PL 33, 1003).

always accept the teaching of the Magisterium as the absolute norm.[27] For he believes both that God has revealed to us in his Son all that is to be revealed, once and for all, and that, none-theless, divine thought "adapts the understanding of the mys-tery of Christ at each epoch, in the Church and through the Church".[28] Thus he will grasp firmly the fact that although the Church does not, in the exercise of her Magisterium, propose to us anything newly invented, so also "the Church says noth-ing on her own account" and does not claim to be herself "the true source of revelation", as she is sometimes wrongly said to do and blamed for doing.[29] She only follows and declares the divine revelation "through the interior direction of the Holy Spirit, who is given her as her Teacher", and "those who are afraid that she may abuse her power in order to establish false-hood have no faith in him by whom she is ruled." [30] He will view Scripture, Tradition, and the Magisterium as the one and only threefold channel by which the Word of God reaches him; and he will see that, far from damaging one another or im-posing limitations on one another, these three things provide

[27] Pius XI, encyclical *Mortalium animos* (1928): "The Magisterium of the Church—which was set up in this world by divine wisdom in order to preserve perpetually intact and to hand on the deposit of revealed doctrine—is exercised each day by the Roman Pontiff and the bishops in communion with him. But he also has the duty—when there is question of putting up effective resistance to the errors and attacks of heretics or imprinting with greater clarity and precision on the minds of the faithful certain explanations of sacred doctrine—of proceeding to opportune definitions by means of decrees and solemn deci-sions. The employment of this extraordinary Magisterium does not introduce any invention and does not add any novelty to the sum of the truths that are at least implicitly contained in the deposit of revelation divinely handed on to the Church; but it declares truths which might perhaps appear obscure to some, or bids us to regard as of faith those that others would still submit to debate." See A. Vacant, *Le Magistère de l'Église et ses organes* (1887); J. Bellamy, *La Théologie catholique au XIXe siècle*, pp. 234–42; Scheeben, *Dogmatique*, 1:250–520.

[28] Jean Levie, S.J., "Exégèse critique et interprétation théologique", *Mé-langes Lebreton*, 1:252.

[29] See Karl Barth, *Dogmatique*, French trans. (1953), 1:33–34.

[30] Bossuet, *Exposition de la doctrine catholique*, chap. 19, in *Oeuvres complètes*, ed. Migne (1867), vol. 1, col. 1164.

mutual support, establishing order among themselves, confirming, elucidating, and exalting. He will see that their fates are bound up together and will recognize in them the "threefold cord" that cannot be broken.[31]

But he will not consider that his total loyalty to the Magisterium dispenses him from making and keeping an in-depth contact with the Church's Tradition, any more than it excuses him from the study of the Scriptures, which will always be the "soul of real theology". The Magisterium itself constantly encourages him to maintain such a contact, and in it he is looking for something other and something more than the results of scientific investigation. He knows that ecclesiastical culture in the true sense is never come by without a loving and disinterested knowledge of what may rightly be called the "classics" of his faith. What he will look for is not so much the company of "great intellects" as that of "truly spiritual men",[32] and so he will, as far as possible, get on to intimate terms with those who prayed to Christ and lived, worked, thought, and suffered for him in the Church before him; for such men are the fathers of his soul. By often keeping their company he will acquire

---

[31] Qo 4:12; St. Cyril of Jerusalem, *Fifth Catechesis*, chap. 12: κτῆσαι καί τήρησον μόνην τὴν ὑπὸ τῆς Εκκλησίας νυνί σοι παραδιδομένην τὴν ἐκ πάσης Γραφῆς ὠχυρωμένην (PG 33, 520b). As Moehler observed, "the Church, the Gospel and Tradition always stand or fall together." See St. Ambrose, *In Lucam*, bk. 6, no. 33: "Corpus ejus [Christi] traditiones sunt Scripturarum; corpus ejus Ecclesia est" (PL 15, 1677a). When one sees the unconscious ease with which it comes about that champions of "Scripture alone" put in its place a personal system and blind themselves to all the passages that contradict it, one is less inclined than ever to think that the authority of the universal Church, sparing us as it does the aberrations of our own minds, sets itself up in illicit rivalry with the Bible.

[32] See St. Augustine, when he opposes "pie doctos et vere spirituales viros" to "magna ingenia", in *Epist.* 118, chap. 5, no. 32 (PL 33, 448), and again when he refuses to have his attention distracted from his daily prayer by "*operosae disputationes*", even when these last become necessary for the defense of the truth, in *De dono perseverantiae*, chap. 7, no. 15, and chap. 25, no. 63 (PL 45, 1082 and 1131); see also *Contra Julianum opus imperfectum*, bk. 1, chap. 117: "Ecclesiam docuerunt, quod in Ecclesia didicerunt" (PL 44, 1125).

something at least of that Catholic ethos, lack of which neither knowledge of the scientific type nor orthodoxy itself can compensate for. Any man who does this will really understand, for example, the enthusiasm of Newman when, in his Anglican days, he discovered the true Church in "the Church of the Fathers" and, through a sort of Platonic reminiscence (or, rather, an illumination from the Holy Spirit), recognized in her his spiritual mother.[33]

Whether we like it or not, there are many non-essential things that change according to time and place.[34] But without blinding himself to the plain fact of this diversity, the man of the Church will make it his business to see also the continuity that exists at an even deeper level of reality. There will, of course, be no question of excluding from view anything the Church approves of, while on the other hand he will also have his personal preferences, being aware of affinities that God has doubtless not willed in vain and cultivating such. But for all that he will always give special attention to certain facts and periods of particular importance; the age of the first martyrs, the rise of monasticism, the main stages in the formation of dogma, the work of the great saints and Doctors, the great spiritual revivals, and so on. He will take into account the history of missionary expansion, in its main outlines at least, and he will not forget the ancient tradition of Eastern Christianity, the "basic stratum",[35] the massive main trunk from which we all spring. If he is himself a scholar, he will put to the best use he can the method

---

[33] J. H. Newman, *Apologia pro vita sua*, chap. 5: In the triumphant zeal of this Church of the Fathers for the mystery of faith "I recognized my spiritual Mother. 'Incessu patuit dea.' The self-conquest of her ascetics, the patience of her martyrs, the irresistible determination of her bishops, the joyous swing of her advance, both exalted and abashed me." See also his *Historical Sketches*, 2:219; *Mary, the Mother of Jesus* (New York: Catholic Book Exchange, 1894), pp. 32–33; Bossuet, *Défense de la tradition et des Saints Pères*, pt. 1, bk. 4, chap. 18; L. de Grandmaison, *Études* (1903), 3:476.

[34] See Newman, *Mary*, 28–29.

[35] Louis Bouyer, "Les Catholiques occidentaux et la liturgie byzantine", DV 21 (1952): 17.

of his own particular discipline, though he will never lose sight of the fact that Catholic tradition does not open the whole of its secret even to an exhaustive inquiry and that it becomes fully intelligible only to him who keeps in the line of its axis and studies it from the inside as one who lives by the faith of the Church.[36]

Since he is a man of the Church, he will not acquire a culture of this type just for interest's sake, taking pleasure in it "as one who tours the monuments of a great city".[37] On the contrary, he will be wholly at the service of the great community, sharing its happinesses and its trials and taking part in its battles.[38] He will always be on guard against allowing the upper hand, in himself, or about him, if he can help it, to a sensibility more alive to the causes of this world than to the cause of Christ. He will cultivate in himself and try to encourage in his fellows the sense of Catholic solidarity,[39] with a particular horror of anything that looks like esotericism. He will resist the pull of the world, and a sure instinct will lead him to recognize spiritual danger in good time.

He will not be an extremist, and he will be wary of excesses; still, he will be aware that in the sacraments of the Church he has received not a spirit of fear but one of power,[40] and in

[36] See Moehler, sketch for the preface to *Die Einheit in der Kirche*; this text, translated in G. Goyau's *Moehler*, pp. 20–21, is quoted by de Grandmaison in his "Jean-Adam Moehler et l'École catholique de Tubingue", RSR 9 (1919); see also my *Histoire et Esprit*, pp. 9–12.

[37] Clement of Alexandria, *Stromata*, bk. 1, chap. 1, no. 6, 3.

[38] See Champion de Pontallier's complaint in his *Le Trésor du chrétien* (1785), 1:129: "Whence comes it that the faithful, who were once soldiers, have now become idle spectators of the pitiless war that is daily waged against their Mother?" (quoted by B. Groethuysen, *Origines de l'esprit en France*, vol. 1: *L'Église et la bourgeoisie* [1927], p. 39).

[39] This is urged by Cardinal Feltin in his pastoral letter on unity in the Church, when (following Fr. Congar) he speaks of the "horizontal dimension" of this unity: "It is not enough to hold close to our Head, to the Head of the Church—that is, to Christ—as individuals; nor is it enough even to hold firm to his Body in general. We must do more; we must feel and wish ourselves *one* with other Catholics, our brethren."

[40] 2 Tim 1:7.

consequence he will have no hesitation in joining battle for the defense and the honor of his faith. Since he knows that it is possible to sin much by omission, he will speak and act boldly "in season and out of season", even at the risk of displeasing many people—even at the risk of being misunderstood by those whose agreement he values most highly.[41] He will, of course, carefully avoid all situations whose danger has been pointed out for him by competent authority. But he will also bear in mind the positive duties of which that authority reminds him—duties whose urgency he can see for himself but that he might be inclined to neglect in the light of a purely human prudence. He will always want to be ready to give any man a reason for the hope that is in him, as St. Peter urged in the early days,[42] and will be wary of making himself unable to do so by getting used to too narrow a world or by concern for his own peace. He will always make it his concern to think not only "with the Church" but "in the Church",[43] as St. Ignatius put it—which implies a deeper faith, a closer participation, and, ipso facto, a more spontaneous behavior—that of a real son, of someone who is at home. He will always let himself be enlightened, guided, and shaped, not by habit or convention, but by dogmatic truth; he may be as much aware as the next man, even more than the next man, of the "difficulties of religion"—as was Newman; but he will be no more capable than Newman of making a real connection between "apprehending those difficulties, however keenly . . . and on the other hand doubting the doctrines to which they are attached". He will be no more tempted than Newman was "to break in pieces the great legacy of thought thus committed to us for these latter days" by men like St. Irenaeus, St. Athanasius, St. Augustine, and St. Thomas;[44] rather,

[41] See 2 Tim 3:10–15 and 4:2–5.

[42] 1 Pet 3:15.

[43] Cf. Leturia, "Sentido Verdadero en la Iglesia Militante", GR (1942), pp. 137–68; and the text of the first of the rules for orthodoxy: "Ad certe et vere sentiendum in Ecclesia militanti, sicut tenemur, serventur regulae sequentes."

[44] Newman, *Apologia*, chap. 5.

he will make it his business to preserve it and draw attention to it. He will be anxious to show those who cling to it, with a care that is sometimes a cowardice, that this inheritance is even richer and more fruitful than they think. On the other hand, he will reject all modern self-sufficiency and any kind of doctrinal liberalism.

But in a true man of the Church the uncompromisingness of the faith and attachment to Tradition will not turn into hardness, contempt, or lack of feeling. They will not destroy his friendliness, nor will they shut him up in a stronghold of purely negative attitudes. He will take care to remember that in her members the Church should be nothing but a "yes", as she was in her Head, all refusal being nothing more than the other side of a positive affirmation. He will not give way to the spirit of compromise any more than she does, but like her he will always want to "leave open every door through which minds of different kinds may reach the same truth".[45] He will not want to "disquiet . . . them who are converted", any more than she does, and this much-to-be-desired moderation, identical with that of the Apostle James at the Council of Jerusalem, will seem to him not only more human and wiser, but also more respectful of the plan of God than can be the demands of a certain type of zealous Catholic.[46] Following her example, he will refuse to develop a craze over one single idea, like a common-or-garden fanatic,[47] since, like the Church, he believes "that there is no salvation save in balance",[48] as is indeed shown by the whole of dogma and confirmed by the whole history of heresy. He will be equally careful not to confuse orthodoxy or doctrinal firmness with narrow-mindedness or intellectual apathy, echoing

---

[45] These words of Étienne Gilson in praise of St. Thomas Aquinas (in *Jean Duns Scot: Introduction à ses positions fondamentales* [1952], p. 627) would serve equally well, in my opinion, to define the spirit of the Church herself; see also Clement of Alexandria, *Stromata*, bk. 1, chap. 5, 29.

[46] Acts 15:19.

[47] The expression used by Chesterton in *Orthodoxy*.

[48] St. Gregory Nazianzen, *Second Discourse*, chap. 34 (PG 35, 441b–c).

the words of St. Augustine: "A thing is not right just because it is hard";[49] and he will remember that one of his duties is to "elucidate for the men of his time the things necessary for salvation".[50] He will take great care that some generalized idea does not gradually come to take the place of the Person of Christ;[51] careful though he is concerning doctrinal purity and theological precision, he will be equally careful not to let the mystery of faith be degraded into an ideology; his total and unconditional faith will not come down to the level of a sort of ecclesial nationalism.[52] And when he pauses for self-examination, he will be very much on the lookout against the fatal mistake of those "theologians" who, having become "wise and prudent . . . , make the Gospel a scientific objective and flatter themselves to have a knowledge of it possessed of a greater perfection than that of the mass of the faithful", while all the time "it is often they themselves who have the least understanding of it in the sense that Christ had in mind." [53]

He will hold himself apart from all coteries and all intrigue,[54] maintaining a firm resistance against those passionate reactions from which theological circles are not always free, and his vigilance will not be a mere mania of suspicion. He will understand that the Catholic spirit, which is at the same time both rigorous and comprehensive, is a spirit that is "charitable rather than

[49] De civitate Dei, bk. 14, chap. 9, no. 6 (PL 41, 417). And the great bishop adds, "aut quia stupidum, ideo sanum." See also Pierre Charles, S.J., "L'Esprit catholique", NRT (1947), p. 228: "Catholic orthodoxy is infinitely larger than any system of human wisdom, because it respects the whole of God's handiwork."

[50] St. Ignatius Loyola, Rules for Thinking with the Church.

[51] Romano Guardini, L'Essence du catholicisme, trans. P. Lorson, pp. 88–89, and Fr. Perrin, in his introduction to Simon Weil's Waiting for God (p. 26 in the original French edition), have recently drawn attention to this issue.

[52] See the just observations of Jacques Maritain in his Religion and Culture (p. 65 in the original French edition).

[53] J. N. Grou, S.J., L'École de Jésus-Christ (1923), Lesson 51, "De qui l'Évangile est connu", pp. 285–86.

[54] "Sine ulla conventiculorum segregatione": St. Augustine, De vera religione, chap. 6, no. 11 (p. 40 in Pegon's edition).

quarrelsome",[55] in distinction from every kind of "spirit of faction" or mere sectarianism, whether the aim of it be to evade the authority of the Church or, on the contrary, to make a corner in it. For a man of this kind all praiseworthy initiative, every new enterprise that is duly approved, and every new center of spiritual vitality is an occasion for giving thanks. He will be no friend of the "itch for . . . controversy"[56] because he will be well aware that the devil (who has a whole art of sowing disorder) shows brilliant skill in disturbing the body of the Church under cover of speculative debate;[57] he will dread the false rigorism that hides the unity at depth which exists in spite of it and will not show himself hostile on principle to legitimate diversity. He will, on the contrary, consider it necessary— "provided that the unity of charity in the Catholic faith be preserved"—for we cannot wipe out "the diversity of human sensibility";[58] he will even regard it as beneficial, "so that the multiform wisdom of God may be made known through the Church".[59] The thing is surely witnessed to by the fact that

[55] Rapine, *Le Christianisme fervent*, 1:21; see also Bérulle, *Discours de controverse* (1609): "As the gall of the animals sacrificed was removed in the sacrifices of the old days which were offered for conjugal peace and concord, so also we should remove the bitterness and gall of contention from those labors which are dedicated and consecrated to the peace and concord of the Bride of God, that is, the Church" (quoted by Jean Dagens in *La Jeunesse de Bérulle* [1952], pp. 234–35).

[56] 1 Tim 6:4 (Knox version); Fénelon, *Lettres sur l'autorité de l'Église*, 7 (*Oeuvres*, Paris ed., 1:212); also St. Clement of Alexandria, *Stromata*, bk. 1, chap. 3, no. 1.

[57] St. Gregory Nazianzen, *Sixth Discourse*, chap. 13 (PG 35, 740a–b); see also Jean Plagnieux, *Saint Grégoire de Nazianze, théologien* (1952), p. 217.

[58] See St. Anselm, *Ad Waleranni querelas responsio*, chap. 1 (he is talking about rites): "Habemus enim a sanctis Patribus, quia si unitas servatur caritatis in fide catholica nihil officit consuetudo diversa. Si autem quaeritur unde istae natae sunt consuetudinem, varietates, nihil aliud intelligo, quam humanorum sensuum diversitates" (PL 158, 552c–d).

[59] Eph 3:10; see also Fr. Yves de Montcheuil's brilliant study, "L'Unité et la diversité dans l'Église", in Chaillet's *L'Église est une: Hommage à Moehler*; S. Tyszkiewicz, S.J., *Sainteté de l'Église*, pp. 130–49; and the letter of John Henry

already "the theology of St. Paul is not identical with that of St. John."[60] He will not transform these diversities—by means of a narrow and superficial logic—into oppositions and contradictions, but see them, rather, as finding completion and fusion in the "bond of love", "like the gradations of color on the throat of the turtle dove".[61] If he were to take it upon himself to reduce everything to uniformity, he would consider himself as marring the beauty of Christ's Bride.[62]

Even when it so happens that these diversities do become divergences, he will not start to worry as soon as the Church starts to feel them. He will not have to reflect for very long to see that they have always existed in the Church and always will; and that if they were ever to come to an end it would only be because her spiritual and intellectual life had come to an end.[63] Far from losing patience, he will try to keep the peace and, for his own part, make a real effort to do that hard thing—retain a mind bigger than its own ideas. He will cultivate "that sort of freedom through which we transcend what involves us most

---

Newman to W. G. Ward, February 18, 1866, in *The Letters and Diaries of John Henry Newman*, ed. Charles Stephen Dessain, vol. 22 (London: Thomas Nelson and Sons, 1972), p. 157 (quoted in Henri Bremond's *L'Inquiétude religieuse*, 1:251).

[60] H. Paissac, O.P., "Théologie, science de Dieu", LV 1 (1951): 54.

[61] Paul Claudel, *Un Poète regarde la croix*, and the letter to André Gide of March 3, 1908: "Those who are like Christ are alike among themselves with a magnificent diversity." Any *diatessaron* cannot help but impoverish and make banal the one and fourfold Gospel, despite the practical advantages of such an arrangement.

[62] See Torquemada, *Summa de Ecclesia*, bk. 1, chap. 10, p. 84: "Fuerunt autem haeretici quidam venustatis et pulchritudinis Ecclesiae adversarii." In spite of the word *haeretici*, Torquemada does not make any further explicit allusion to diversities of the theological order, which are, however, discussed by Moehler in his *Symbolique*, trans. F. Lachat (1836), 1:xlv–xlvii.

[63] See Newman's letter to Ward of February 18, 1866. He points out that this is a consequence of our militant state: "No human power can hinder it; nor, if it attempted it, could do more than make a solitude and call it peace. And, thus thinking that man cannot hinder it, however much he try, I have no great anxiety or trouble. Man cannot, and God will not."

remorselessly" and which is "a mysterious, winged, ironic way of transcending our differences".[64] And if he is not to despair of managing this even where minds seriously divided are concerned, he will—all the more so—be confident of doing it where his brothers in the faith are concerned. By that very fact he will be protected against the terrible self-sufficiency that might lead him to see himself as the incarnate norm of orthodoxy, for he will put "the indissoluble bond of Catholic peace"[65] above all things and will hold it a black mark against himself to tear the seamless robe even by the smallest "schism of charity".[66] Even when polemic cannot be avoided, he will see that it does not embitter him and that the actions of those whom St. Paul already described as "false brethren" will not provide him with an excuse for using weapons like theirs. For he will always remember that "the wisdom from above first indeed is chaste, then peaceable, modest, easy to be persuaded", that charity is "without dissimulation", and that "the

---

[64] Jacques Maritain, "Les Chemins de la Foi", in *Foi en Jésus-Christ et monde d'aujourd'hui* (1949), p. 29. See also Newman's portrait of the "narrow mind": Newman, "Wisdom as Contrasted with Faith and with Bigotry", in *Fifteen Sermons Preached before the University of Oxford* (London: Longmans, Green, 1892), pp. 305–11.

[65] St. Cyprian, *De catholicae Ecclesiae unitate*, chap. 14: "It is impossible for discord to have entry to the Kingdom of Heaven" (1:222, in Hartel's edition); St. Augustine, *De baptismo*, bk. 1, chap. 18, no. 28, commenting on Cyprian: "He was a son of the peace of the Church", and again (bk. 5, chap. 17, no. 23): "Nihil [erat] ei in Ecclesia carius unitate"; also chap. 27, no. 38 (PL 43, 187–88 and 195); St. Peter Canisius, *Confessions*, bk. 1, 1, p. 22, quoted by Fr. Broutin, *Le Mystère de l'Église*, no. 1.

[66] See Boniface VIII, bull *Unam Sanctam* (1302): "Caritatis Ecclesiae unitatem. Haec est tunica illa Domini inconsutilis [Jn 19:23]"; Adam Scotus, *Sermo* 40, chap. 8 (PL 198, 368b). There is all too much truth in Fr. Congar's remark in *Le Christ, Marie et l'Église*, p. 32: "It seems that the devil has breathed into modern man a spirit of schism, in the strictest sense of the word; for instead of making common ground over essentials while respecting differences, he seeks only to make distinction, to be in opposition as much as possible, and to turn into a reason for opposition the very thing which he could hold with others in a spirit of communion." Compare Eph 4:16; the Church builds herself up in charity.

fruit of justice is sown in peace." [67] His whole behavior will show that the spirit of power which he has received is also "a spirit . . . of love and of sobriety".[68] If only from experience, he will know well that there is no trusting in men, but the depressing proofs of this will not dim his joy as the years accumulate them; for God himself is the Maintainer of that joy, and the devotion he has sworn to the Church cannot but be purified by this particular experience.

Since he is a member of a body, he will be responsive to what affects the other members, whatever his own place and function may be. Anything that bears hard upon the body as a whole, or paralyzes it, or damages it affects him too, and he can no more be indifferent to it than he can be amused by it. Thus he suffers from the evils inside the Church, and he will want the Church, in all her members, to be ever purer and more closely united, more attentive to the demands of the soul, more active in witness, more passionate in the thirst for justice; in all things more spiritual and farther yet from all concession to the world and its falseness. He will want to see her always celebrating a pasch of "sincerity and truth" [69] in all her members. For him there will be, of course, no question of cherishing utopian dreams, and he will always direct his accusations against himself first and foremost; yet he will not resign himself to Christ's disciples' settling down in the all-too-human or stagnating outside the great currents of humanity. He will see the good, be glad of it, and set himself to making it visible to others, but without blinding himself to the faults and sufferings that some try to deny while others are scandalized by them; he will not consider that loyalty or simply experience of human nature obliges him to condone every abuse. And he will, moreover, be aware that the mere passing of time wears out many things, so that many innovations

---

[67] James 3:17–18; Rom 12:9; see also 1 Cor 14:33.

[68] 2 Tim 1:7. On the moderation of St. Leo the Great, see Hugo Rahner in Grillmeier and Bacht's *Das Konzil von Chalkedon: Geschichte und Gegenwart* (1951), vol. 1.

[69] 1 Cor 5:8.

are necessary if dangerous novelty is to be avoided, and that "a reforming impulse is natural to the Church." [70] Since he is not "obsessed with the past",[71] he will have no desire to run down in advance all desire for change, or experiment with a view to it, in those things that are of time; rather, he will make an effort at the discernment of spirits, searching with those who search. He will be wary of possible opposition to the work of God through a severity that is too quick off the mark or too unbending and take care not to bring to a halt some necessary advance because it has been marked by a false step or two; his instinct will always be to redirect an impulse rather than to repress it. But for all that, he will not evade his duty if circumstances call on him to intervene. He will only take care that he is not moved by some impulse other than that of faith. He will be aware—some times agonizingly aware—of the twofold nature of the responsibility he has assumed: "Being a minister of Christ and responsible for Christ's teaching, he will dread equally both betraying its integral truth by being too compliant, and compromising its divine authority by human systems; being a director of souls, he will dread equally both impoverishing in them the Christian faith by which they should live, and making that faith intolerable to them by demands that are unjustified." [72] Yet the very thing that gives rise to this kind of perplexity is also the thing that carries him through it.

A man of the Church will always remain open to hope; for him, the horizon is never closed. Like St. Paul, he will want to be full of rejoicing in his sufferings and will go so far as to believe himself called, in this manner—as all are called—to "fill

[70] Msgr. P. W. von Keppler, *Uber wahre und falsche Reform* (1930), p. 24; quoted by Karl Adam, *Le Vrai Visage du catholicisme*, trans. E. Ricard, p. 270.

[71] Yves de Montcheuil, *Vie chrétienne et action temporelle* (1943).

[72] Jules Lebreton, S.J., "Chronique de théologie", *Revue pratique d'apologétique* 3 (1907): 543; also 4:221: "Surely, when it is a question of two Christians sincerely discussing their faith, there can be nothing more between them than a passing misunderstanding born of the darkness of the human condition and due to be dispersed on the morrow by the light of God."

up those things that are wanting in the sufferings of Christ . . . for his body, which is the Church", knowing that in Christ he has "the hope of glory".[73] In common with the community of believers, he waits for the return of him whom he loves, and he does not lose sight of the fact that everything should, in the last analysis, be judged with reference to that end. But at the same time he is aware that this waiting is an active waiting and should not divert us from any of the things to be done in this world; that, on the contrary, it makes those things more urgent and demanding. His attitude is, in fact, an eschatological one—but it is the eschatology of St. Paul and not that of the *illuminati* of Thessalonica,[74] and it certainly does not imply (as some people appear to think) neglect of the duties of the present, lack of interest in this existence, or a putting of charity into cold storage until the end of the world.

He will welcome and make his own, as his deep intention, the concern for truth, authenticity, and "poverty of spirit", which are characteristic of an age "in which the great fear of a well-formed soul is of imposture, and this more in the sphere of the sacred than in any other".[75] As one who has had a way opened to the Heavenly Jerusalem, the "city of truth", where he has encountered the "God of truth", "the true God in whom there is no lie",[76] he will bear in mind that the Holy Spirit is the enemy of all that is not true,[77] and that Christ himself put good faith in the company of justice and mercy[78] as constituting together the three most important precepts; and he

[73] Col 1:24–27.

[74] 2 Th; see Georges Didier, "Eschatologie et engagement chrétien", NRT (1953), pp. 3–14.

[75] P. R. Régamey, O.P., "Architecture et exigences liturgiques", MD 29 (1952): 87.

[76] Zech 8:3: "Jerusalem . . . the city of truth"; Ps 30:6; *Martyrdom of Polycarp*, 14, 2; Rom 3:4: "But God is true"; Rev 15:3.

[77] Wis 1:5: "For the Holy Spirit of discipline will flee from the deceitful"; and see James 4:8.

[78] Mt 23:23; see also 12:36.

will shun the pious fraud in all its forms[79]—though he will also understand the value of silence. He will realize that there is a moment for everything; that the best of undertakings can be wrongly timed; and that in the final analysis it is not for him to pass judgment in the matter. Thus he will not be bewildered if he sometimes has to "sow in tears".[80] Even when what he does receives the utmost approval, he will want to remember always that just as he reaps what has been sown by others before him, so he must not count on gathering in even where he has sown. And last, he will hold out against the temptation offered by the oversimplified solution, which in some way compromises the fullness, balance, and depth of the Catholic heritage, even when it does not touch the faith directly.[81]

* * *

The man of the Church does not stop short at mere obedience; he loves obedience in itself and will never be satisfied with obeying "of necessity and without love".[82]

For the fact is that all action that deserves to be called "Christian" is necessarily deployed on a basis of passivity. The Spirit from whom it derives is a Spirit received from God. It is God himself, giving himself to us in the first place so that we may give ourselves to him; insofar as we welcome him into ourselves we are already not our own.[83] This law is verified in the order of faith more than anywhere else. The truth that God pours into our minds is not just any truth, made to our humble human

[79] One hears all too often reflections such as the following, which are not without factual foundation: "It is a fact that metaphysical certitude—their assurance of holding the essential truth—makes some of our priests none too scrupulous as far as relative truths are concerned" (François Mauriac, *La Pierre d'achoppement* [1951], p. 31).

[80] See Ps 125:5; and 118:165: "and to them there is no stumbling block."

[81] See the fine passage by Newman in the fifth chapter of his *Apologia*; and Jn 4:37–38.

[82] *The Imitation of Christ*, bk. 1, chap. 9.

[83] 1 Cor 6:19; see also St. Augustine, *De Trinitate*, bk. 12, chap. 3: "Subhaeremus" (PL 42, 999).

measure; the life he gives us to drink is not a natural life, which would find in us the wherewithal to maintain itself. This living truth and this true life find foothold in us only by dispossessing us of ourselves; if we are to live in them we must die to ourselves; and that dispossession and death are not only the initial conditions of our salvation, they are a permanent aspect of our life as renewed in God. And this essential condition is brought about, par excellence, by the effect of Catholic obedience. In that obedience there is nothing of this world and nothing servile; it submits our thoughts and desires, not to the caprices of men, but to "the obedience of Christ".[84] Fénelon says justly: "It is Catholicism alone that teaches, fundamentally, this evangelical poverty; it is within the bosom of the Church that we learn to die to ourselves in order to live in dependence."[85] An apprenticeship of this sort never comes to an end; it is hard on nature, and those very men who think themselves most enlightened are the ones who have most need of it (which is why it is particularly healthy for them), so that they may be stripped of their false wealth, "to humble their spirits under a visible authority".[86]

This is perhaps the most secret point in the mystery of faith, and that which is hardest of access to a mind that has not been converted by the Spirit of God. So that it is scarcely surprising that many men consider the exercise of authority in the

---

[84] 2 Cor 10:5; also Rom 1:5.

[85] Fénelon, *Entretien avec le chevalier de Ramsay*, in A. de Campigny et al., *Les Entretiens de Cambrai* (1929), p. 136: "Up to this point you have desired to possess the truth; now the truth must possess you, make you captive, and strip you of all the false wealth of the intellect"; *Lettres sur l'autorité de l'Église*, 1 (*Oeuvres*, 1:202); see also Pseudo-Augustine, *Sermo de obedientia*: "O sancta obedientia! Tu humilitatem nutris, tu patientiam probas, tu mansuetudinem examinas" (PL 40, 1249).

[86] Fénelon, *Lettres sur l'autorité*, 2 (*Oeuvres*, 1:202–3). However, Fénelon is showing only one of the two aspects of the truth when he adds: "The mysteries are proposed to us in order to subdue our reason and sacrifice it to the supreme reason of God." Quesnel wrote maliciously of him (May 12, 1704): "He is as outlandish about the authority of the Church as he is about the love of God."

Church[87] an intolerable tyranny. Moreover, whether the unbeliever condemns it or admires it, he cannot help but form a very misleading idea of it, for "if the Church were only a human society, even though the most venerable and experienced ever known", her demands would not be justified.[88] For his part, the Catholic knows that the Church commands only because she obeys God.[89] He wants to be a free man, but he is wary of being one of those men who make liberty "a cloak for malice". He knows, too, that obedience is the price of freedom, just as it is the condition of unity: "He who is not bound by this chain is a slave."[90] He will be careful to distinguish it from its counterfeits and caricatures—unfortunately all too freely current—and his aim will be to please, not men, but God.[91]

History and his own experience combine to show him both the desire for the knowledge of divine things, which stirs the

[87] Dom Anscar Vonier, *L'Esprit et l'Epouse*, trans. L. Lainé and D. B. Limal (Paris: Éditions du Cerf, 1947), p. 20. On the practice of obedience, the reader should consult the article by Fr. Mersch, "La Raison d'être de l'obéissance religieuse", NRT (1927), and Henri Mogenet, S.J., *La Vocation religieuse dans l'Église* (1952), pp. 101–8; the principles of this work hold good for all varieties of Catholic obedience.

[88] Yves de Montcheuil, *Mélanges théologiques*, pp. 121–22: "That is why those among the unbelievers who have exalted the conception of authority and discipline in the Church while reducing her to a merely human institution have been able to do so only by underestimating the value of the person; hence their doctrine of obedience, far from being in true conformity with the Catholic faith, is an immoral one."

[89] See St. Cyril of Alexandria, *Fragmenta in Cantica* (PG 69, 1292a); Rom 1:5; St. Peter Damian, *Sermo* 45 (PL 144, 743b).

[90] St. Augustine, *Sermo* 268, no. 2 (PL 38, 235); also St. Gregory the Great, *Moralia in Job*, bk. 35, chap. 14, no. 28: "Sola namque virtus est oboedientia quae virtutes caeteras menti inserit, insertasque custodit. . . . Tanto igitur quisque Deum citius placat, quanto ante ejus oculos, repressa arbitrii sui superbia, gladio praecepti se immolat. . . . Vir quippe obediens victorias loquitur, quia dum alienae voci humiliter subdimur, nosmetipsos in corde superamus" (PL 76, 765b and c); Carl Feckes, *Das Mysterium der heiligen Kirche*, p. 211.

[91] See Gal 1:10; St. Gregory the Great, *In Evangelia*, hom. 6, no. 2: "Et quid per arundinem, nisi carnalis animus designatur? Qui mox ut favore vel detractione tangitur, statim in partem quamlibet inclinatur?" (PL 76, 1096c).

human spirit, and the weakness which lays that spirit open to falling into every kind of error. In consequence, he appreciates the benefit of a divine Magisterium, to which he freely submits. He thanks God for having given him that Magisterium in the Church and experiences a foretaste of the peace of eternity in placing himself under the eternal law by the obedience of faith.[92] He will make the appropriate evaluation of the scope of each one of the acts of the hierarchy—numerous and varied as they are—without splitting them up one from another or setting them in mutual opposition; he will accept them all as obedience demands and understand them as obedience understands them, never adopting an argumentative attitude where obedience is concerned, as if there were some question of defending at all costs a threatened autonomy. He will not countenance any contest with those who represent God,[93] any more than he would with God himself.

Even in the grimmest cases—in such cases most of all, in fact—he will find a certain harmony of what seems to be imposed from outside and what is inspired from within; for the Spirit of God does not abandon him, any more than the Spirit of God ever abandons the Church as a whole, and what he does in the Church as a whole is also what he does in each Christian soul.[94] The baptismal instinct of the child responds with a leaping joy to the demands made upon it by its

[92] St. Augustine, *De civitate Dei*, bk. 19, chap. 14 (PL 41, 642); cf. Ps 118:45: "And I walked at large; because I have sought after thy commandments."

[93] See Massillon, *Sermon sur la Parole de Dieu*, in *Oeuvres*, ed. Lefèbvre (1838), 1:165; Fénelon, *Lettres sur l'autorité*, 1: "A man may reason with another man; but with God he can only pray, humble himself, listen, be silent, and follow blindly."

[94] On this principle, which we have already met with earlier on, which guarantees the life of the person by saving it from individualism and is equally important for ecclesiology and the spiritual life alike, see my *Histoire et Esprit*, chap. 4. See also Jean Mouroux, *L'Expérience chrétienne* (1953), p. 202: "In the end, because it is in the same Spirit on which authority and obedience are based, exteriority, as real as it may be, is rooted and ends in a more profound interiority, which is the very mystery of the Church."

Mother:[95] "Wherever the Spirit of the Lord is, there also is freedom." [96]

Even when doctrine is in no sense involved—in the day-to-day sphere of exterior activity, where the question is one of decisions whose object is in itself a matter for discussion—the man who has the real spirit of obedience will not spend any longer than he can help over considerations at the human level, which, however shrewd and sensible, cannot in the long run help but obscure the light of faith. Even though he can neither obscure them nor always hold all of them as of no account—a supernaturalized attitude is not something built up on the ruins of common sense—he will, for all that, rise above the contingencies that are in danger of coming between him and pure divine will. He will have confidence in his superiors and make it his business to see their point of view from the inside. Whether or not there be a bond of natural sympathy between him and them, he will owe them a sincere affection and try to make less onerous for them a responsibility from which his own soul benefits;[97] bearing in mind the axiom *discernere personam est tollere oboedientiam*,[98] he will see in them Christ himself. Granted, the aid given to the Church by the Holy Spirit is no guarantee that he will never have any orders to carry out save those arising from the wisest possible choices—the history of the Church is not that kind of idyll, and there would be something rather absurd about it if it were. Yet it does not matter whether the man who gives him a command in the name of God be right or wrong, obtuse or clearsighted, pure or mixed in his motives, determined (in his heart of hearts) to act justly, or not—as long as that man is invested with legitimate authority

[95] See H. Clerissac, O.P., *Le Mystère de l'Église* (1918), p. 121; St. Augustine, *In Epist. Joannis*, tract. 3, no. 13 (PL 35, 2004).

[96] 2 Cor 3:17; also Ps 118:45: "And I walked at large; because I have sought after thy commandments"; St. Augustine, *De Spiritu et littera*, chap. 16, no. 28 (PL 44, 218); St. Gregory the Great, *Moralia in Job*, bk. 35, chap. 14, no. 32: "Ipsa obedientia, non servili metu, sed caritatis affectu servanda est" (PL 76, 768a).

[97] See Heb 13:17.

[98] A. Gagliardi, *De plena cognitione instituti S. J.* (1841), p. 67.

and does not command him to do evil, he knows that it would always be wrong to disobey. And the man of the Church knows that though obedience "can never oblige us to do anything evil", it can "cause us to interrupt or omit the good we were doing or wanted to do".[99] That is something he knows in advance and with a conviction of faith that nothing can shake; and history confirms the fact with a whole series of examples both good and bad. Even if this truth is in certain cases a hard one, it is, as far as he is concerned, first and foremost a "wonderful truth".[100]

Certainly, as long as the order is not final, he will not abandon the responsibilities with which he has been invested by his office or circumstances. He will, if it should be necessary, do all that he can to enlighten authority; that is something which is not merely a right but also a duty, the discharge of which will sometimes oblige him to heroism. But the last word does not rest with him. The Church, who is his home, is a "house of

[99] St. Gregory the Great, *Moralia in Job*, bk. 35, chap. 14, no. 29: "Sciendum vero est, quod numquam per obedientiam malum fieri, aliquando autem debet per obedientiam bonum quod agitur, intermitti" (PL 76, 766b); Leo XIII, encyclical *Diuturnum illud*: "Whenever there were question of infringing either the natural law or the will of God both command and execution thereof would be equally criminal"; St. Ignatius Loyola, *Letter on Obedience*, no. 16 (he is quoting St. Bernard): "Ubi tamen Deo contraria non praecipuit homo."

[100] See the prayer by Newman: "Let me never for an instant forget that Thou hast established on earth a kingdom of Thy own, that the Church is Thy work, Thy establishment, Thy instrument; that we are under Thy rule, Thy laws and Thy eye—that when the Church speaks, Thou dost speak. Let not familiarity with this wonderful truth lead me to be insensible to it—let not the weakness of Thy human representatives lead me to forget that it is Thou who dost speak and act through them" (quoted from Louis Bouyer, *Newman: His Life and Spirituality* [New York: P. J. Kenedy & Sons, 1958], pp. 341–42). See also R. Grosche, *Pilgernde Kirche*, pp. 210–25, "Newman and die kirchliche Autorität"; St. Gregory the Great, *In Evangelia*, hom. 26, no. 6: "Sed utrum juste an injuste obliget pastor, pastoris tamen sententia gregi timenda est, ne is qui subest, et cum injuste forsitan ligatur, ipsam obligationem suae sententiae ex alia culpa mereatur. . . . Is autem qui sub manu pastoris est, ligari timeat vel injuste; nec pastoris sui judicium temere reprehendat, ne etsi injuste ligatus est, ex ipsa tumidae reprehensionis superbia, culpa quae non erat, fiat" (PL 76, 1201b); St. Thomas Aquinas, *Suppl.*, q. 21, a. 4.

obedience".[101] If then he finds himself prevented from realizing some apparent good, he will remember that even if his action be justified, it is not that action which matters. The work of redemption, to collaboration in which he has been called by God, is not subject to the same laws as human undertakings. And ultimately all he has to do is to take his place in the divine plan by which God leads him, through his representatives; thus, he cannot fail to have a share in "the infallible security of Providence".[102] In the last analysis no man can ever betray a cause or break faith with another man, himself, or God when he simply obeys. There will be no sophism, no appearance of good or persuasion of justification, that can cut off from the man of the Church the light of St. Paul's words when he proposes for our imitation Christ *factus obediens*. He can never forget that the salvation of mankind was accomplished by an act of total self-abandonment, that the Author of that salvation, "whereas he was indeed the Son of God, . . . learned obedience by the things which he suffered",[103] and that it is through him alone, with him alone, and in him alone that we can be "at one and the same time the saved and those who save".[104] The mere recalling of this fact carries more weight with him than any amount of theory and discussion; it will always be a safeguard against his reducing Christian obedience—which is conformity with the obedient Christ—to a virtue that is primarily of social

[101] Origen, *In Matt. series*, 77: "Oportebat autem haec in Bethania fieri, quae interpretatur domus obedientiae. . . . Domum autem obedientiae Ecclesiam intelligi oportere dubitat nemo." (The phrase was, of course, taken over by St. Ignatius in his *Letter on Obedience*.)

[102] François Charmot, S.J., *La Doctrine spirituelle des hommes d'action* (1938), p. 315: "I do not maintain that superiors are infallible—that is to say, that if we consider their views and their reasons we shall not be able to find error in them. What I do maintain is that Providence is infallible—as the [First] Vatican Council affirms—and that in conforming our conduct to its plans we do participate in that Wisdom, in practice."

[103] Heb 5:8, also 10:5–13; Phil 2:8; Preface for Feasts of the Holy Cross.

[104] Pius XII, encyclical *Mystici corporis*, following Clement of Alexandria, *Stromata*, bk. 7, chap. 2.

importance. For to see nothing more in it than that particular aspect—which is, of course, most certainly there—will be, in his eyes, a misunderstanding of its most valuable element.[105]

A true son of the Church will not, of course, be preoccupied to excess with these extreme cases (which must nonetheless be taken into account if the principle of Catholic obedience is to be isolated in its pure state). Even where he has a duty to act, and in consequence a duty to judge, he will on principle maintain a certain distrust with regard to his own judgment; he will take good care to have himself in hand, and if it so happens that he incurs disapproval, he will, far from becoming obstinate, if necessary accept the fact that he cannot clearly grasp the reasons for it. He will apply to himself on such occasions this homely truth—that even with the best of intentions we can still grossly deceive ourselves (or perhaps simply fail to take everything into account) and that it is a healthy thing to be warned of the fact. And, finally, he will under all circumstances be much aware that he cannot be an active member of this Body if he is not, first and foremost, a submissive member, quick and docile in response to the direction of the head. Even if he is submissive to all that is obligatory, he will not be content to carry on his work in the odd corners of his community, as it were. He will not grant himself the right to call himself a son of the Church unless he is, first of all and always, a child of the Church, and that in all sincerity.

Here we come again upon the fundamental distinction that was made earlier.[106] The Church is a community, but in order to be that community, she is first a hierarchy. The Church we call our Mother is not some ideal and unreal Church but this hierarchical Church herself; not the Church as we might dream

---

[105] It is for this reason that I consider inadequate Fr. Deman's explanation in his *Pour une vie spirituelle objective*. Everything not comprised under the term "object"—understood in Fr. Deman's sense—is not necessarily the pernicious and inconsistent "subjective" element that I deplore as much as he does; see Louis Lallemant, S.J., *La Doctrine spirituelle*, sixth principle, sec. 3, chap. 5 (pp. 400–403 in the new edition of 1908).

[106] In chapter 3, above.

her but the Church as she exists in fact, here and now. Thus the obedience which we pledge her in the persons of those who rule her cannot be anything else but a filial obedience. She has not brought us to birth only so as to abandon us and let us take our chance on our own; rather, she guards us and keeps us together in a maternal heart.[107] We continually live by her spirit, "as children in the womb of their mothers live on the substance of their mothers".[108] And every true Catholic will have a feeling of tender piety toward her. He will love to call her "Mother"—the title that sprang from the hearts of her first children, as the texts of Christian antiquity bear witness on so many occasions.[109] He will say with St. Cyprian[110] and St. Augustine:[111] "He who has not the Church for Mother cannot have God for Father."

When a Catholic wants to expound the claims the Church has on his obedience, he feels a certain embarrassment or, rather, a certain melancholy. It is not that her title-deeds are

[107] St. Cyprian, *De catholicae Ecclesiae unitate*, chap. 23: "ut consentientis populi corpus unum gremio suo gaudens Mater includat" (1:230, in Hartel's edition), and again: "Quicquid a matrice discesserit, seorsum vivere et spirare non poterit, substantiam salutis amittit" (ibid., p. 231); *Epist*. 40, no. 3 (ibid., p. 607). Some other texts are given in my *Catholicism*, pp. 53–54.

[108] Bérulle, *Discours de l'état et des grandeurs de Jésus*, 10.

[109] See Joseph Plumpe's excellent monograph *Mater Ecclesia: An Inquiry into the Concept of the Church as Mother in Early Christianity* (Washington, D.C., 1934), and Christine Mohrmann in *Vigilae christianae*, 2, 1.

[110] *De catholicae Ecclesiae unitate*, chap. 6 (p. 214 in Hartel's edition); *Epist*. 74, no. 7: "Ut habere quis possit Deum Patrem, habeat antea Ecclesiam matrem" (ibid., p. 804); *De lapsis*, chap. 9 (ibid., p. 243); Tertullian, *De oratione*, chap. 2 (PL 1, 1154).

[111] *In Psalm*. 88, *sermo* 2, no. 14: "Amemus Dominum Deum nostrum, amemus Ecclesiam ejus; illum sicut patrem, istam sicut matrem. . . . Tenete ergo, carissimi, tenete omnes unanimiter Deum patrem et matrem Ecclesiam" (PL 38, 1140–41); *Sermo de Alleluia*: "Neque potent quispiam habere Deum patrem, qui Ecclesiam contempserit matrem" (pp. 332–33 in Morin's edition); *Contra litteras Petiliani*, bk. 3, chap. 9, no. 10 (PL 43, 353); *Sermo* 216, no. 8: "Pater Deus est, mater Ecclesia" (PL 38, 1081); *De symbolo ad catechumenos* (PL 40, 668); *Epist*. 80, chap. 2 (PL 33, 188); *Epist*. 98, chap. 5 (PL 33, 362); etc. See also Origen, *In Levit*., hom. 2, no. 3 (p. 452 in Baehrens' edition).

inadequate. But when taken in the dryness of the mere letter, the claims do not do justice to something that is, as far as he is concerned, essential. He can comment on the illuminating complex of Scripture texts, point to the facts of history, develop the arguments that are suitable to the occasion. But when he has done all this, all he has done is to establish the fact that we ought to submit, as a matter of justice and our own good; he has not been able to convey the spontaneous leap of his own heart to obedience, nor the joy he feels in his submission.[112] He has established an obligation, but he has not communicated an enthusiasm. He may have justified the Church, but he has not been able to make her true character understood from within. If he is to do that, he must achieve much more. If he is to overcome the revulsion of the "natural man", he will have to turn his argument into a channel for the living witness of his own faith; he will have to show the splendor of the Catholic vision. The Church, who is the bringer of the good news and the bearer of life, must not be presented as a domineering power or a pitiless drawer-up of rules. He must not be content with giving a precise explanation of how the Church's authority is in principle neither arbitrary nor extrinsic;[113] he must go on to give some idea at least of how, through the exercising of that power, each one of the faithful is effectively sustained in his self-giving to Christ; how the fabric it weaves links each man effectively to his brethren; how all still hear today the voice of their Lord through the human voice that teaches and commands.[114] And finally he must explain—or, rather, communicate some sense of—the spiritual fruitfulness

---

[112] The point has been noted by Fr. Pierre Charles, "Vicarius Christi", NRT (1929), p. 450.

[113] In particular, the supreme decisions of the Magisterium interpret the tradition of the whole Church and assume the collaboration of the faithful themselves, as being a declaration of their faith. See, for example, J. V. Bainvel in his introduction to Bellamy's *Théologie catholique au XIXe siècle*, p. xiv.

[114] The Church, said Moehler, is "Jesus Christ renewing himself without ceasing" (*Symbolik*, chap. 5, no. 36).

of sacrifice. He must display some of the great miracles of Catholic sanctity—miracles that spring up under the shadow of obedience in the seedbed of humiliation.

* * *

The Roman Church is the object par excellence of accusations of tyranny; she is even sometimes—absurdly—put on a parallel with the various systems of political absolutism. And she is also the primary object of the objections of many Christians, who nevertheless recognize the necessity of a visible authority. Conversely, it is primarily of her that the Catholic thinks when he calls the Church his Mother. In common with tradition, he considers her as "root and Mother of the Catholic Church",[115] as "the Mother and mistress of all the Churches", as "Mother and mistress of all the faithful of Christ".[116] He considers her head as "the head of the episcopate" and "the father of the Christian people",[117] "the master of the whole household of Christ", as St. Ignatius Loyola puts it. For him, the See of Rome is the "Holy See", the "Apostolic See" par excellence.[118] He

[115] St. Cyprian, *Epist.* 48, chap. 3; cf. *Epist.* 59, chap. 14.

[116] Fourth Council of the Lateran, chap. 5; Eugenius of Carthage, in Victor of Vita's *Historia persecutionis africanae provinciae*, bk. 2, chap. 41 (p. 40 in Petschenig's edition); Paschasinus, at the Council of Chalcedon (Mansi, 6:580); Council of Sardica; Hadrian, Letter to the Patriarch Tarasius (Mansi, 12:1081); Innocent III: "totius christianitatis caput et magistra" (PL 214, 59a, 21d; 215, 710), etc.

[117] St. Augustine, *Epist.* 43, chap. 5, no. 16: "Patrem christianae plebis" (PL 33, 167); St. Leo the Great, *Sermo* 4, chap. 2: "Unus Petrus elegitur, qui . . . omnibus apostolis cunctisque Ecclesiae patribus praeponatur, ut, quamvis in populo Dei multi sacerdotes sint multique pastores, omnes tamen proprie regat Petrus, quos principaliter regit et Christus" (PL 54, 149–50); St. Paschasius Radbertus, *Expositio in Mattheum*, bk. 7, chap. 15: "In ipso [Petro] est forma omnium in quo unitas Ecclesiae commendatur" (PL 120, 528a); see also P. Batiffol, *Cathedra Petri* (1938), pp. 169–95, and 95–104: "Petrus initium episcopatus".

[118] For the history of this title, see Batiffol, *Cathedra*, pp. 151–68; St. Augustine, *Epist.* 43, chap. 3, no. 7: "Romanae Ecclesiae, in qua semper apostolicae cathedrae viguit principatus" (PL 33, 162).

knows that Peter was given the charge of not only the lambs but the sheep as well; that Christ himself prayed that the faith of Peter might not fail; and that he gave Peter the keys of the Kingdom of Heaven and the command to confirm his brethren.[119] He realizes that Peter personifies the whole Church[120] and that just as each bishop is the bridegroom of his own particular Church, so Peter, the Bishop of Rome, may be said to be the bridegroom of the Universal Church,[121] the whole of which has in him its visible foundation.[122] As against a frequently lodged objection (based on a misunderstanding), he will, of course, be equally clear that this visible foundation in no way prejudices that unique Foundation which is Christ, any more than the visible chief shepherd puts into eclipse the Good Shepherd,[123] since here there is no question of duplication, the

---

[119] Mt 16:18–19. For the exegesis of this text, see Léon Vaganay, "Pierre chef et docteur", in *Tu es Petrus* (1934), pp. 3–26; F. M. Braun, O.P., *Aspects nouveaux du problème de l'Église* (1942), pp. 81–98; J. C. Didier, "D'une interprétation récente de l'expression 'lier-délier' ", MSR (1952), pp. 55–62. With regard to the fundamental text in Matthew 16, it may be noted that while Loisy accepted its application to Peter as head of the Church but denied its historicity and authenticity (*Évangiles synoptiques*, pp. 7–8), today Herr Oscar Cullmann accepts the historicity of it but would restrict all legitimate application to Peter as a historical individual, i.e., to the exclusion of his successors: *Peter: Disciple, Apostle, Martyr* (London, 1953).

[120] St. Augustine, *Epist.* 53, chap. 1, no. 2: "[Petrus] cui totius Ecclesiae figuram gerenti Dominus ait: super hanc petram" (PL 33, 196); *In Joannem*, tract. 124, no. 5 (PL 35, 1973); *Sermo* 295, no. 2 (PL 38, 1349). On the significance of the Papacy in the Church, see G. Dejaifve, S.J., "Sobornost ou Papauté", NRT (1952).

[121] See Pius VI, *Caritas illa* (June 16, 1777).

[122] See the anti-Modernist oath of 1910: "Ecclesiam . . . super Petrum apostolicae hierarchiae principem . . . aedificatam"; Origen, *In Exod.*, hom. 5, no. 4: "magno illi Ecclesiae fundamento et petrae solidissimae"; *In Rom.*, bk. 5, no. 10 (PG 14, 1035); St. Augustine, *Epist.* 57, chap. 9, no. 21: "Petrus etiam, Apostolorum caput, caeli janitor, et Ecclesiae fundamentum" (PL 33, 145); these phrases are drawn from a text of Roman provenance sent to Augustine by the priest Casulanus, but Augustine does not query them when he quotes them: see *Liber mozarabicus sacramentorum*, ed. M. Férotin, col. 140.

[123] Jn 10:1–18, 21:15–19; St. Thomas Aquinas, *In Sent. IV*, d. 17, q. 3, a. 1, sol. 5: the *potestas excellentiae* pertains to Christ alone "qui est Ecclesiae

very name "Peter" having been chosen by Christ to express this identity of submission, which is in itself the fruit of faith.[124] Believing as he does that the Church has received the promise of perpetuity and victory over death, and holding that it was she who was in Christ's mind in that scene on the road to Caesarea, he will naturally grasp the consequence that as long as the Church goes on building herself up and subsisting in her visible state—that is to say, as long as this world lasts[125]—she cannot be without a visible foundation for her building. Peter was not given his office simply in order to relinquish it almost at once;

---

fundamentum"; see Berengard, *In Apoc.*: "Non enim aliud fundamentum est Petrus, et aliud Christus Jesus, quia Petrus membrum est Christi Jesu" (PL 17, 849c–d); 1 Cor 3:11; see also above, p. 122, n. 62.

[124] St. Augustine, *Sermo de amore Petri*: "In Petro Ecclesiam cognoscendam. Aedificavit enim Christus Ecclesiam non super hominem, sed super Petri confessionem. Quae est confessio Petri? *Tu es Christus Filius Dei vivi.* Ecce petra, ecce fundamentum, ecce ubi est Ecclesia aedificata, quam portae inferorum non vincunt. . . . Ergo iste discipulus a Petra Petrus, quomodo a Christo christianus est" (ed. C. Lambot in RBN 49 [1937]: 253); *Sermo* 76, no. 1 (PL 38, 479); see also *Retract.*, bk. 1, chap. 21, no. 1 (p. 400 in Bardy's edition), and the commentary thereon by Rozaven, *L'Église catholique justifiée*, pp. 161–62; Rupert of Deutz, *In Matthaeum*, bk. 3: "Super petram fidei, quam confessus est Petrus, Ecclesiam suam aedificat" (PL 168, 1385a); Gilbert Foliot, *Exposito in Cantica*, 3, 1: "Tu es Petrus, id est, in fide mei tanquam petra firmus; et sic Petrus a me tanquam petra nominatur. Et super hanc petram quam me esse intelligo et in te esse constituo, aedificabo Ecclesiam meam, id est, vires sum daturus Ecclesiae, et aedificabo tam firmiter, quod portae inferi non praevalebunt adversus eam" (PL 202, 1244d).

[125] Vatican Council, constitution *Pastor aeternus* (July 18, 1870); St. Leo the Great, *Sermo* 3, chap. 3: "Manet ergo dispositio veritatis, et beatus Petrus in accepta fortitudine petrae perseverans, suscepta Ecclesiae gubernacula non reliquit" (PL 54, 146b); chap. 2: "Soliditas illius fidei quae in apostolorum principe est laudata, perpetua est; et sicut permanet quod in Christo Petrus credidi, ita permanet quod in Petro Christus instituit" (PL 54, 145–46); St. Thomas Aquinas, *Summa contra gentiles*, bk. 4, chap. 74: "Tamdiu igitur oportet hanc potestatem perpetuari, quamdiu necesse est post mortem discipulorum Christi usque ad saeculi finem"; see also Godefridus de Sancto Victore, *Microcosmus*, chap. 103 (p. 115 in Delhaye's edition of 1951).

he was given it to hand on after him.[126] "In his successors—the bishops of the See of Rome, which was founded by him and consecrated by his blood—he lives, presides, and judges perpetually."[127]

Finally, the Catholic will not be content merely to grant and grasp that in the last analysis the Church is, so to speak, concentrated whole in Peter; the seeing of the fact will be an occasion of joy to him. He will not be worried by those who try to persuade him that he has "lost the sense of the totality of the Church" and that in submitting himself to the power of the pope he has resigned himself to a belief that is, as it were, merely belief at the word of command—as if "in Romanism properly understood" the whole doctrine and life of the Church resided only in the single person of its head.[128] For we do not deny the existence of a circle when we know that it must have a center; and it is no abolishment of the body when we say that it has a head. To superficial explanations of this kind, which are the result of what one might describe as an optical illusion, he will oppose the evidence of faith and reply, in the words of one of his bishops:

> When the pope makes an act of doctrinal authority, this is no exterior yoke imposed by a particular man on a religious society in the name of his own intelligence, even though it might be that of a genius. He is defining the faith of the Church. He is in no way subject to her consent; yet the truth he translates into our language and renders precise is the truth by which she lives; the belief whose meaning he confirms is our belief—he

[126] See Cerfaux, "Saint Pierre et sa succession", RSR (1953), pp. 188–202; G. Dejaifve, S.J., "M. Cullmann et la question de Pierre", NRT (1953), pp. 365–79: "the interpretation of the *logion* that attributes to Christ the will to build an enduring Church on a fragile foundation destined to disappear does scant justice either to the coherence of the image or the wisdom of its author."

[127] The Roman legate Philip, at the Council of Ephesus (Mansi, vol. 4, col. 1296).

[128] See A. S. Khomiakov, *L'Église latine et le Protestantisme au point de vue de l'Église d'orient* (1872), pp. 104, 142, 160, 301.

analyzes its content, counters its potential weakenings, and maintains its vigor. Thus, when we say to the Church, in the words which the Apostle used to Christ, who founded her: "To whom shall we go? Thou hast the words of eternal life", this is not in virtue of some fatigue of spirit, which seeks to place itself under an authority to escape the effort of thought and the labor of living; rather it is, as Newman put it, in virtue of a sense of coming to rest in the Catholic plenitude.[129]

He can also appeal in this matter to the declarations of the popes themselves, who, when they are preparing to define some point of the faith, far from considering themselves as having to "pronounce an oracle",[130] weigh up not only Scripture but "time-honored tradition, the perpetual belief of the body of the Church, and the agreement of the bishops and the faithful".[131] In this way the meaning of papal infallibility becomes clear—as well as the reason for it; it is an infallibility that is not something separate from that of the whole Church any more than it is derived from an infallibility of the bishops or other members; it is an infallibility that is in reality that of the Church herself, although, in the case of the man who gives it sovereign interpretation in order to bring all controversy to a close, it is personal and absolute.[132]

That is why, in short, the Catholic recognizes Peter as he who has charge of the universal Church, without any of the petty reservations of Gallicanism.[133] That is why he holds that he is—to

[129] Msgr. Blanchet, at the Institut Catholique inaugural Mass, November 1950.

[130] A. S. Khomiakov, *L'Église latine*, pp. 107–10.

[131] Pius IX, bull *Ineffabilis* (1854): "quam divina eloquia, veneranda traditio, perpetuus Ecclesiae sensus, singularis catholicorum Antistitum se fidelium conspiratio et insignia Praedecessorum Nostrorum acta, constitutiones mirifice illustrant atque declarant."

[132] Controversy has often misunderstood the phrase "Ex sese, non ex consensu Ecclesiae" used by Vatican Council I, as if it meant a separate infallibility.

[133] See St. Leo's phrases: "Totius Ecclesiae princeps", "curam Ecclesiae universalis habens", etc. Cf. P. Batiffol, *Le Siège apostolique* (1924), pp. 613–14.

quote the expression given authoritative status by the [First] Vatican Council—"the supreme judge of the faithful" and he who holds the fullness of power in the Church;[134] that is why he makes his own the words of St. Ambrose: "Where Peter is, there the Church is."[135] He will always see in Peter both the unshakeable rock upon which his own firmness is based[136] and "the center of Catholic truth and unity",[137] the one and only visible center of all the children of God.[138] In the authority of Peter he sees the support of his faith and the guarantee of his communion.[139] And thus his fidelity to the Christian faith finds concrete

[134] Constitution *Pastor aeternus*, chap. 3: "Judicem supremum fidelium . . . totam plenitudinem hujus supremae potestatis."

[135] *In Psalm.* 40, no. 30 (PL 14, 1082a). While others, whose view stops short at details on the human and earthly level, seem to be perpetually afraid of some campaign to dominate, such a man as this will have a spontaneous confidence in the explanation given by St. Ambrose in the name of the heads of the Church: "Nec quaedam nos angit de domestico studio et ambitione contentio, sed communio soluta et dissociata perturbat." There is a commentary on these words in Batiffol's *Cathedra Petri*, pp. 78–79.

[136] St. Leo the Great, *Epist.* 10, chap. 1: "Qui ausus fuisset a Petri soliditate recedere" (PL 55, 629a); *Sermo* 3, chap. 2 (PL 54, 145–46); *Sermo* 5, chap. 4 (PL 54, 155a); *Sermo* 51, chap. 1 (PL 54, 309b); Hormisdas, *Epist. inter ea* (A.D. 517): "Sedes apostolica . . . in qua est integra et verax christianae religionis et perfecta soliditas"; St. Gregory the Great, *Epist. ad Theodelindam* (A.D. 594): "In vera fide persistite et vitam vestram in petra Ecclesiae, id est in confessione beati Petri, solidate" (PL 77, 712–13).

[137] Pius IX, bull *Ineffabilis Deus*.

[138] See Fénelon, letter to Alamanni of July 15, 1710: "By the grace of God, I am bound to the Holy See by the most lively and tender affection. One cannot love religion without loving that Holy Mother who has given us birth in Jesus Christ and who still feeds us with the spirit of life. One cannot love unity save inasmuch as one desires that all Christians should be reunited in this one and only center of the children of God" (quoted in Guérin, pp. 394–95).

[139] It is worth reading Bossuet's extremely shrewd reflection in his *Exposition de la doctrine de l'Église catholique*, chap. 19, on the subject of dissidents: "Moreover, if our adversaries consult their conscience, they will find that the name of the Church has more authority over them than they dare to admit in controversy; and I do not believe that there is among them one single man of good sense who, if he saw himself to be alone in holding some particular view, would not be horrified at such singularity, however evident the point seemed to him

expression in his love for Peter,[140] to whom he is bound, despite all exterior vicissitudes, by every fiber of his soul.

* * *

That picture of the Catholic in whom the consciousness of churchmanship is lively is, of course, altogether too meager and abstract an affair, besides being—obviously—overidealized. Here, as in all things, there is normally a big gap between the most sincere faith and the most loving disposition, on the one hand, and effective practice, on the other; for man is always inconsequential. But the important thing to take note of is not the tribute we all pay, more or less heavily, to human weakness but, rather, the nature and scope of our desires. The mystery of the Church and the good things she brings are always beyond what we manage to live of them in actual practice. We never draw upon more than a meager part of the wealth that our Mother has at her disposal. Yet every Catholic who is not an ingrate will have in his heart that hymn of gratitude which has been given words by a great contemporary poet: *"Louée soit à jamais cette grande Mère majestueuse, aux genoux de qui j'ai tout appris!"* [141]

Yes, may she be praised, this great Mother, at whose knees we have in fact learned everything and continue, every day, to learn everything!

It is she who daily teaches us the law of Christ, giving us his Gospel and helping us to understand its meaning. It is hard to imagine where the Gospel would be or what state it

---

in itself; so true is it that in these matters men have need to be supported in their attitudes by the authority of some society which thinks the same as they. That is why God, who has made us, and who knows what is fitting for us, willed, for our own good, that all particular matters should be subject to the authority of his Church, which is without doubt the best established of all authorities" (ed. Migne, vol. 1, col. 1165).

[140] Cf. the wonderful *Spiritual Testament* of Cardinal Faulhaber, reprinted in *Documentation catholique* (October 19, 1952), cols. 1505–10.

[141] Paul Claudel, "Ma Conversion", in *Contacts et circonstances*; also in *Pages de prose*, chosen and presented by André Blanchet, p. 279. "Praised be forever that great and majestic Mother at whose knees I have learned everything!"

would have reached us in if, *per impossibile*, it had not been composed, preserved, and commented on within the great Catholic community [142]—hard to picture the deformation and mutilation it would have suffered both as to text and as to interpretation. . . . But there is, after all, no need to have resource to these hypotheses; history speaks forcefully enough. There is no counting the number of aberrations that have been based upon an appeal to the Gospel, or the number of those who have, in consequence of them, lapsed into "atheistic and impious doctrines or stupid and ridiculous beliefs". Origen had already noticed this, and that great biblical thinker did not hesitate to point a warning finger at "the temptation hidden in the reading of the sacred books",[143] when they are not read *in the Church*. And our own day adds its own lessons to those of the past. "The meaning of the written mystery can belong only to the social unity that carries within itself the revelation of that mystery";[144] and although we may say, with St. Francis de Sales, that "Scripture is entirely adequate to teach us all things", in a certain sense, we should also add, as he did, that "it is in us that there lies the inadequacy since, without Tradition and the Magisterium of the Church, we should not be able to determine the meaning that it ought to have." [145] Thus, when we consult Tradition and listen to the Magisterium, "it is not that we prefer the Church to the Scriptures but, rather, the explanation of the Scriptures given by the whole Church to our own explanation." [146] We believe that the Word of God is

[142] See Jacques Guillet, S.J., "La Naissance de l'Évangile dans l'Église", LV (October 1952).

[143] *De oratione*, chap. 29, no. 10; St. Irenaeus, *Adversus haereses*, bk. 4, chap. 26, no. 5 (he is talking about bishops): "Scripturas sine periculo nobis exponunt" (PG 7, 1056a–b); and chap. 33, no. 8: among the bishops is to be found "sine fictione Scripturarum tractatio . . . secundum Scripturas expositio legitima, et diligens, et sine periculo, et sine blasphemia" (1077b–c).

[144] See Khomiakov, *L'Église latine*, p. 279.

[145] Letter to a Jesuit Father, August 17, 1609 (*Oeuvres*, 14:191).

[146] Fénelon, *De l'Éducation des filles*, chap. 7; also *Deuxième Lettre sur l'autorité de l'Église*: "A visible authority [is necessary] which speaks and decides, so that all minds may be submitted, united, and fixed in one and the same

"addressed *to the Church*",[147] and that is precisely why we listen to it and read it *in the Church*. We do not, however, praise the Church—as has been done on several occasions—for having surrounded the Gospel with a protective covering so as to render it "inoffensive", or for having purged it of its "impure miasmas". For praise of that kind would be the worst of blasphemies. The Church has neither glossed over the paradoxes of the Gospel nor changed its vividness nor sentimentalized its power[148] nor betrayed its spirit. The Church is always the paradise in the midst of which the Gospel wells up like a spring[149] and spreads out into four rivers to make the whole earth fruitful. Thanks to the Church, the Gospel is proposed to all, both the great and the small of the world, from generation to generation, and if it does not produce in us its fruition of life, the fault is ours.

---

explanation of the Holy Scriptures", and: "It is necessary that there should be an authority which lives, speaks, decides, and explains the sacred text" (*Oeuvres*, 1:223–24); Moehler, *Die Einheit in der Kirche*, appendix 7; see also Luther, *Appellatio Fr. Martini Luther* (to Frederick of Saxony against Leo X, November 17, 1520): "quod sacram Scripturam sibi subjiciat [Papa]" (*Opera Omnia* [1600], 2:258).

[147] See Karl Barth, *Dogmatique*, French trans., 1:251.

[148] Harnack himself had to recognize the fact, in the very course of a lecture in which his anti-Catholic prejudice comes out, *Das Wesen des Christentums*: "In the Church the temporal has not diminished the power of the Gospel; in spite of the weight which threatens to crush it, it continually frees and renews itself. It works as a leaven" (*L'Essence du christianisme*, French trans., p. 317). Compare St. Irenaeus' phrase, "potestatem Evangelii" (*Adversus haereses*, bk. 3, preface).

[149] See chapter 9, below; also St. Irenaeus, *Adversus haereses*, bk. 5, chap. 20, no. 2 (PG 7, 1178a–b); St. Cyprian, *Epist.* 73, chap. 10 (p. 785 in Hartel's edition); St. Paulinus of Nola, *Epist.* 32, no. 10 (PL 61, 336):

> Petram superstat ipsa Petra Ecclesiae,
> De qua sonori quatuor fontes meant
> Evangelistae viva Christi flumina.

See also the descriptions by Lucien de Bruyne of the early baptisteries of Naples, Milan, and Oued Ramel (Tunisia), in his "La Décoration des baptistères paléochrétiens", in *Miscellanea liturgica in honorem L. Cuniberti Mohlberg* (1948), 1:200–204; St. Peter Damian, *Sermo* 14 (PL 144, 572c).

May this great Mother be praised, too, for the divine mystery that she communicates to us through the twofold and ever-open door of her doctrine and her liturgy! May she be praised for the centers of religious life that she brings into being and protects and whose fervor she keeps aflame! May she be praised for the interior universe that she discovers to us, in the exploration of which she gives us her hand as guide![150] May she be praised for the desire and the hope that she sustains in us![151] May she be praised, too, for unmasking and dispersing the illusions that deceive us, so that our adoration may be pure! May this great Mother be praised!

This chaste Mother pours into us and sustains a faith that is always whole and that neither human decadence nor spiritual lassitude can touch, however deep they may go. This fruitful Mother continually presents us with new brothers; this universal Mother cares equally for all, little and great alike—the ignorant and the wise, the ordinary parishioner and the picked body of consecrated souls. This venerable Mother makes sure for us the inheritance of the ages and brings forth for us from her treasure things new and old. This patient Mother is always making a fresh start, untiringly, in her slow work of education and gathering together again, one by one, the threads of unity that her children are always tearing apart. This careful Mother protects us against the enemy who prowls around us seeking his prey; this loving Mother does not hold us back for herself but urges us on to the encounter with God, who is all love. Whatever the shadows the Adversary casts, this clear-sighted

[150] See de Walcheren, *Journal d'un converti*, p. 240: "I—being still outside the Church, in a state of expectancy—sense in advance, and with an ever-increasing joy, an infinite world into which the spirit may go exploring and in which the soul may find God—*abyssus abyssum invocat*—and in comparison with which the visible world must be a negligible thing, almost nonexistent. What a magnificent, unimaginable universe must be hidden within the Church!" A presentiment, of course, not to be proved false.

[151] See Rev 22:17 and 20: "And the Spirit and the bride say: Come. . . . Surely I come quickly: Amen. Come, Lord Jesus!" It is through her that we remain "immovable from the hope of the Gospel" (Col 1:23).

Mother cannot help but recognize one day for her own the children whom she has borne, and she will have the power to rejoice in their love while they in their turn will find security in her arms. This zealous Mother sets in the hearts of her best children a zeal that carries them all over the world as the messengers of Christ; this wise Mother steers us clear of sectarian excesses and the deceptive enthusiasm that is always followed by revulsion; she teaches us to love all that is good, all that is true, all that is just, and to reject nothing that has not been tested.[152] This sorrowful Mother with the sword-pierced heart relives from age to age the Passion of her Bridegroom;[153] this strong Mother exhorts us to fight and bear witness to Christ;[154] and she does not hesitate to make us pass through death—from the first death, which is baptism, onward—in order to bear us into a higher life. For all these benefits we owe her our praise; but we owe it to her above all for those deaths she brings us—the deaths that man himself is incapable of and without which he would be condemned to stay himself indefinitely, going round and round in the miserable circle of his own finitude.

Praised may you be, Mother of love at its most lovely, of healthy fear, of divine knowledge, and holy hope! Without you our thoughts are diffuse and hazy; you gather them together into a strong body.[155] You scatter the darkness in which men

[152] See 1 Th 5:21; 1 Jn 4:1; etc.

[153] See Lk 2:35; St. Augustine, *Sermo* 62, chap. 3, no. 5: "Quod tunc corpus ipsius in turba patiebatur, hoc patitur Ecclesia ipsius" (PL 38, 416); Ambrose Autpert, *Sermo in purificatione B. M.*, no. 53: "Ipsam beatam Virginem, cujus animam gladius transfodisse perhibetur, typum Ecclesiae praetendisse reperimus"; also Charles Journet, *Les Sept Paroles du Christ en croix* (1952), p. 530.

[154] St. Augustine, *Sermo* 301, no. 1, on the mother of the Maccabees: "Una mulier, una mater, quomodo nobis ante oculos posuit unam matrem sanctam Ecclesiam, ubique exhortantem filios suos pro illius nomine mori, de quo eos concepit et peperit?" (PL 38, 1380).

[155] St. Gregory the Great, *Moralia in Job*, bk. 2, chap. 52, no. 82: "Exhortatione sanctae Ecclesiae cunctae in auditorum mentibus diffusae cogitationes ligantur" (p. 240 in de Gaudemaris' edition).

either slumber or despair or—pitifully—"shape as they please their fantasies of the infinite".[156] Without discouraging us from any task, you protect us from deceptive myths; you spare us from the aberrations and the aversions of all churches made by the hand of man. You save us from destruction in the presence of our God! Living Ark, Gate of the East! Unflawed mirror of the activity of the Most High! You who are the beloved of the Lord of the Universe, initiated into his secrets, and who teach us what pleases him! You whose supernatural splendor never fades, even in the darkest hours![157] It is thanks to you that our darkness is bathed in light! You through whom the priest goes up every day to the altar of God, who gives joy to his youth! The Glory of Libanus is in you,[158] under the obscurity of your earthly covering. Each day you give us him who is the Way and the Truth. Through you we have hope of life in him.[159] The memory of you is sweeter than honey, and he who hears you shall never be put to confusion.[160] Holy Mother, unique Mother, immaculate Mother! O great Mother! Holy Church, true Eve, sole true Mother of all the living![161]

---

[156] Renan, discourse given at Quimper, August 17, 1885.

[157] See Wis 7:26, 8:4, 9:9 and 18, 6:12; also 8:10–11: "For her light cannot be put out. Now all good things come to me together with her."

[158] Is 60:13; cf. 45:14.

[159] St. Irenaeus, *Adversus haereses*, bk. 3, chap. 4, no. 1: "Haec est Vitae introitus" (PG 7, 855b).

[160] See Sir 24:17–21; Judith 13:25.

[161] Tertullian, *De anima*, chap. 43: "Vera mater viventium . . . Ecclesia" (p. 372 in the Reifferscheid-Wissowa edition); *Adversus Marcionem*, bk. 2, chap. 4 (p. 338 in Kroymann's edition); St. Ambrose, *In Lucam*, bk. 2, chap. 86: "Haec est Eva mater omnium viventium. . . . Mater ergo viventium Ecclesia est" (PL 15, 1585a), etc. On the motherly care of the Church, see St. Augustine, *De moribus Ecclesiae catholicae*, bk. 1, chap. 30 (PL 32, 1336); *De nuptiis*, bk. 2, chap. 4, no. 12: "Nam in hoc, quod appellata est vita materque viventium, magnum est Ecclesiae sacramentum" (PL 44, 443); *De Genesi contra Manichaeos*, bk. 2, chap. 24, no. 37 (PL 34, 216), etc.; Ambrosian Rite, Preface for the Dedication of a Church (ed. Paredi [1937], p. 201); Guerricus, *In Assumpt.*, sec. 1, no. 2 (PL 185, 188b–c).

VIII

OUR TEMPTATIONS
CONCERNING THE CHURCH

L OVE should, of course, be our only response to our Mother
 the Church; yet in fact there are many temptations that
trouble us with regard to her. Some are clear enough, and
violent; others are less clear, and all the more insidious. There
are some that are perennial and some that are peculiar to our
time, and they are all too varied—even to the point of mutual
opposition—for any one of us ever to think himself sheltered
from the threat they constitute.

There will always be men who identify their cause with
that of the Church so totally that they end by equating the
Church's cause with their own, and this in all good faith. It does
not occur to them that if they are to be truly faithful servants
they may have to mortify much in themselves; in their desire to
serve the Church, they press the Church into their own service.
It is a "dialectical transition", inside-out from *pro* to *contra*, as
easy as unobtrusive. For them the Church is a certain order of
things which is familiar to them and by which they live; a certain state of civilization, a certain number of principles, a certain complex of values, which the Church's influence has more
or less Christianized but which remain nonetheless largely human. And anything that disturbs this order or threatens this
equilibrium, anything that upsets them or merely startles them,
seems to them to be a crime against a divine institution.

Where there is question of confusion of this sort, it is not
always a matter of those crude forms of "clericalism" that esti-
mate the amount of honor paid to God by the privileges accorded to his ministers or measure the progress of divine rule
over souls and the social reign of Christ by the influence, either

279

hidden or open, of the clergy on the course of secular affairs. Here the whole order of thinking may well be on the loftiest plane—as when Bossuet, toward the end of his life, adjusted the whole Catholic order in accordance with a Louis-Quatorze pattern of things and was unable to see anything but a threat to religion in the mixed forces that began to disintegrate that particular synthesis, which was, of course, a brilliant one but was also matter for questioning in some aspects, at least—a thing contingent, and by essence perishable. Against those forces he made his stand, and that with every ounce of his strength.

Bossuet was as perceptive as he was forthright; yet his perceptiveness did not go the whole way. "Together with an imperious will, he had a spirit by nature timid."[1] He wanted to maintain forever (though courageously condemning certain faults and criticizing certain abuses) the mental and social world in which his genius found a natural ground for its unfolding. He could not imagine how the faith could survive it— rather like those ancient Romans (among whom were even some Fathers of the Church) for whom the collapse of the Empire could not be anything other than the heralding of the end of the world, so great an impression had the Roman power and majesty made upon the mind of the time.[2] But since Bossuet's dream was of something that was in fact impossible, he found himself involving with the moribund world in question the Church whose business it was to free herself from it in order to bring life to the coming generations. The inadequate defenses he threw up against the oncoming evil buried beyond hope of germination the seeds of the future; he was apparently victorious on every field on which he fought, but it was irreligion that profited from the way in which he won his victories.[3]

---

[1] A. Molien, "Simon (Richard)", DTC, vol. 14, col. 2112.

[2] Thus Tertullian, *Apologia*, chaps. 32, no. 1; 32, no. 2 (pp. 94 and 106 in Waltzing's edition); *Ad scapulam*, chap. 2 (1:541, in Oehler's edition): Melito of Sardis, quoted in Eusebius, *Hist. Eccl.*, bk. 4, chap. 26, no. 11.

[3] One cannot read without profound sadness the reflections of non-believing authors on this subject, however exaggerated they may be; for

In the same way, we are sometimes all the more self-confident and strict in the judgments we pass in proportion as the cause we are defending is the more dubious. It is possible that we sometimes forget in practice something we know well enough in principle—that the intransigence of the faith is not a passionate unbendingness in the desire to impose upon others our personal tastes and personal ideals. A tight-clenched hardness of that kind is fatal to the supple firmness of truth and is no defense to it whatsoever; a Christianity that deliberately takes up its stand in a wholly defensive position, closed to every overture and all assimilation, is no longer Christianity. Sincere attachment to the Church can never be used for the purpose of canonizing our prejudices or making our partialities part of the absolute of the universal faith. It may thus be pertinent to recall that a certain confidence and detachment are part of the Catholic spirit. At the right time, the Church can find in the very shrines of the devil things to beautify her own dwelling; that particular miracle is always something new and unforeseen, but we know that it will happen again.[4] However rooted in history the Church may be, she is not the slave of any epoch or indeed of anything whatsoever the essence of which is temporal. The message she is bound to pass on and the life she is bound to propagate are never integral parts of "either a political régime or a social polity or a particular form of civilization", and she must forcefully remind people of the fact, in opposition to the illusive evidence to the contrary, which, in fact, derives simply from the bonds of habit.[5] She repeats for us, in their widest possible sense, the words of St. Augustine: "Why are

---

example, those of Leon Brunschvicg in his *Le Progrès de la conscience dans la philosophie occidentale* (1927), 1:221–22.

[4] St. Hilary of Poitiers, *In Psalm.* 67, no. 12 (pp. 287–88 in Zingerle's edition).

[5] Bruno de Solages, *Pour rebâtir une chrétienté* (1938), p. 174; see Leo XIII, letter to Cardinal Rampolla, October 8, 1895: "Things human change, but the beneficent virtue of the supreme Magisterium of the Church comes from on high and remains always the same. . . . Established to last as long as time, it follows with a loving vigilance the advance of humanity and does not refuse (as

you dismayed when earthly kingdoms pass away?"[6] for she is founded upon no rock other than that of Peter's faith, which is faith *in Jesus Christ*; she is neither a party nor a closed society. She cannot resign herself to being cut off from those who do not yet know her simply for the sake of the comfortableness of those who make up her traditional faithful. She desires no opposition from the reality in men, since they are all her sons, at least virtually; on the contrary, she will make it her aim to set them free from all evil by giving them their Savior.

We ourselves should therefore get into this frame of mind, which was that of Christ,[7] and we should if necessary impose on ourselves the mortifications fitted to this end. Far from failing in the intransigence of the faith, we shall in this way alone sound its depths. We must not relax in any way our zeal for Catholic truth, but we should learn how to purify it. We must be on our guard against turning into those "carnal men" who have existed since the first generation of Christians and who, turning the Church into their own private property, practically stopped the Apostles from announcing the Gospel to the Gentiles.[8] For if we do that, we lay ourselves open to something yet more calamitous—collaboration with militant irreligion, by way of making it easier for it to carry out its self-assigned task of relegating the Church and her doctrine to the class of the defunct; we provide irreligion with a clear conscience, as it were, for it has no understanding of the actuality of the eternal. Its attitude is: "Let the Church remain what she is" (and one knows what sort of petrifaction such a wish implies)—and then "she will receive all the appreciation always accorded to historic relics".[9] An irreligion of this type mixes up at will the most

its detractors falsely claim) to come to terms with the reasonable needs of the time as far as this is possible."

[6] *Sermo* 105, no. 9 (PL 38, 623).

[7] Phil 2:5.

[8] St. Augustine, *Sermo* 252, no. 3 (PL 38, 1173–74).

[9] Ernest Renan, "Du Libéralisme doctrinal", in *La Liberté de penser* (May 15, 1848).

diverse cases, confusing dogma with opinions or attitudes inherited from situations that have ceased to be, and takes up a firm stand against "concessions" in which it detects "bad faith or irresponsibility".[10] It establishes its own lists of what is suspect—in the fashion of religious authority itself—and is ready to call that authority to order, if need be. Having made up its mind once and for all that there can be nothing reasonable in Christian beliefs, it brands as "liberalism" or "modernism" every effort made to bring out Christianity in its real purity and its perpetual youth, as if this were an abandonment of doctrine. It can never see in the thought of men like Justin or Clement of Alexandria or their modern disciples anything but the concessions of an apologetic that sacrifices the "tough" element in dogma to the desire to please those whom it wishes to win over; Tatian and Hermias are the favorites, and their method alone is regarded as the only Christian one.[11] It maintains that "the Church can never cut loose from her past. . . . Religion is a whole that must not be touched. . . . As soon as you reason about it, you are an atheist." [12] The principle is "All or nothing"—provided that the "all" is understood in the terms dictated—which are not those of the Church; thus, for example, Renan, making the Catholic faith involved forever with the historicity of the Book of Daniel and other things of the same kind.[13] And it is a day of rejoicing in this quarter when voices are raised within the very heart of "this poor and aged Church" [14] that sound like approval. A false intransigence can certainly cause an enormous amount of harm in this way—quite in opposition to its own intentions.

[10] Renan, letter to the Abbé Cognat of September 5, 1846, quoted in J. Cognat, *M. Renan hier et aujourd'hui* (1886), p. 203.

[11] Renan, *Marc Aurèle*, 3d ed. (1882), p. 109; see also pp. 403–4.

[12] Renan, *Questions contemporaines*, p. 423; *Drames philosophiques*, pp. 279–80 (Act I of *Le Prêtre de Némi*).

[13] Letter to the Abbé Cognat, in J. Cognat, *M. Renan*, p. 203; *Souvenirs d'enfance et de jeunesse*; *Questions contemporaines*, p. 457.

[14] Proudhon, *De la Justice dans la Révolution et dans l'Église*, new ed., 4:332.

The vistas opened up by all this should be yet one more motive for our distrusting ourselves. We should be wary of a certain kind of humility that borders on pride, cultivating a healthy fear of sacrilegious usurpation and taking to heart the exhortation of St. Augustine to his fellow fighters in the thick of the Donatist controversy: "Take your stand upon the truth without pride." [15] We have to bear in mind that our knowledge is always partial and that in this world we only glimpse the divine truth "through a glass in a dark manner".[16] Finally, instead of settling ourselves into the Church as our private property and personal possession and more or less identifying her with ourselves, we should, as Newman did, rather make it our business to identify ourselves with the Church, and without expecting any personal triumph from it.[17]

* * *

But there is another temptation from the opposite direction, which is certainly more frequent today and sometimes more aggressive in the provocation it offers—the critical temptation. This also very frequently advances itself cunningly under the camouflage of the good; it can easily put itself forward to the apostolically minded as a necessary concern for clarity. And for this reason it cannot, in most cases, be avoided, save by a preliminary "discernment of spirits".

The very word "criticism" means discernment, and there is, of course, a kind of criticism that is good—particularly self-criticism. That kind is a striving for realism in action—a determination to bar all that cannot justify its claim to genuineness. It is an examination carried out in humility, capable of recognizing the good achieved, but arising out of an essentially apostolic discontent and a perpetually restless spiritual dynamism. It is born and grows from attitudes such as the inability to be

---

[15] *Contra litteras Petiliani*, bk. 1, chap. 29, no. 31 (PL 43, 259).

[16] 1 Cor 13:12.

[17] *Apologia pro vita sua*, chap. 5.

satisfied with work done and a burning desire for the best; integrity of judgment on matters of method; independence of will to break with customs that cannot be justified any more, to get out of ruts and put right abuses; above all, a lofty idea of the Christian vocation and faith in the mission of the Church. It stimulates an intensified activity, inventive ingenuity, and a sudden outburst of exploration and encounter, which must, doubtless, be brought under control on occasion—and which certainly often disturbs our habits a little too rudely. Criticism of this type is hard on the illusions it tracks down but can induce others, which will soon be in turn the object of similar criticism. Yet how very much better it all is, still, than the naïve self-complacency that admits of no reform and no healthy transformation—that certain comfortableness which gradually digs itself deeper and deeper into its dream world, that obstinacy which thinks it is preserving things when all it is doing is piling up the ruins of them.[18]

We should be wrong if we wished to prevent on principle all public expression of this kind of criticism. When the Church is humble in the persons of her children, she is more attractive than when they show themselves dominated by the all-too-human concern for respectability. Jacques Maritain once said, not without a touch of irony, that many Christians of today find any admission of our deficiencies "somehow indecent". "It will be said", he adds, "that they are afraid of putting difficulties in the way of apologetic. . . . The ancient Jews and even the

[18] See the panegyric on St. Rémi delivered at Rheims by Msgr. Chappoulie, Bishop of Angers; confronted with "the great upheaval which has been going on for more than a century in society", the duty of the Catholic is "to try to understand, and above all to desire to love". Certainly, "there are audacities we may not like, and certain 'discoveries' may seem to us to be naïve", but "when all is said and done, is it really preferable . . . to shut oneself up within a disdainful and immovable refusal, to continue to seek a timid refuge in love of the past?" If we are to succeed in freeing the eternal truth of the Gospel from a crumbling past, "as did St. Remi", we must have "a powerful faith in Jesus Christ and the coming of his Kingdom" ("Semaine religieuse d'Angers", *Témoignage chrétien* [November 14, 1952]).

Ninivites did not stand on ceremony in that way." [19] No more did the saints in the past. Think of St. Jerome's famous address to Pope Damasus,[20] or St. Bernard's broadsides against bad pastors[21] and the program of reform he outlines in his *De consideratione*,[22] or diatribes like that of St. Catherine of Siena against certain highly placed ecclesiastical dignitaries: "O men who are no men but rather devils incarnate, how you are blinded by your disordered love for the rottenness of the body and the delights and bedazzlements of this world!" [23] Or again, remember for a moment people like St. Brigid, and Gerson, and St. Bernardino of Siena, and St. Thomas More; or, to come nearer to our own day, St. Clement Hofbauer. Or think of the struggles of the "Gregorians" to tear the government of the Church free from the system that was enslaving it; or the audacity of a man like Gerhoh of Reichersberg, addressing to Pope Eugenius III his work *On the Corrupt State of the Church*, like St. Bernard; or Roger Bacon, demanding of Clement IV that he should "purge the Canon Law" and cast out of the Church the pagan elements that had been brought into her with the ancient Civil Law;[24] or of William Durandus publishing his treatise *De Modo Concilii Celebrandi et Corruptelis in Ecclesia Reformandis*; of the Carthusian Peter of Leyden exhorting the Roman Pontiff at the opening of the edition he issued in 1530 of the works of his fellow Carthusian Denis.[25] This last example evokes the whole

[19] *Du Régime temporel et de la liberté* (1933), p. 139.

[20] *Epist.* 15 (PL 22, 355).

[21] *In Cantica, Sermo* 77, nos. 1–2 (PL 183, 1155–56).

[22] Particularly in bk. 4 (PL 182, 771–88).

[23] Letter 315.

[24] *Compendium*, chaps. 1 and 4.

[25] Dedication to the *Opuscula* of Denis the Carthusian: "I address myself to Your Beatitude, not in my own name but in the name of many, not to say in the name of all. The act of solicitude which we ask for, we call reform of the Church. . . . What is there in the Church which is not contaminated or corrupted? What is there left of integrity among the clergy, of honor among the nobility, or of sincerity among the people? All is put to confusion, wounded, ruined, mutilated. From the soles of the feet to the crown of the head, there is nothing healthy left."

great movement of Catholic reform, which is all too inadequately described under the name of the Counter-Reformation; an enterprise of that kind could not even have been outlined without an effective determination on self-criticism, of which history shows us more than one brilliant example.

Yet for every constructive complaint and each clear-headed and fruitful analysis there is all too much excess and recklessness. Each really courageous act is counterpoised by a mass of futile agitation. There is all too much purely negative criticism. Sanctity is not common, and the most sincere goodwill has neither the same rights nor the same privileges. And both competence and opportunity may be lacking; even if a given criticism is a fair one, we are, nevertheless, not always justified in making it. In addition, we have to bear in mind this important fact: that today we do not have the same situation as existed in what we call the Christian centuries. Then, everything happened within the family circle, as it were; and irreligion was not perpetually on the lookout to turn this, that, and everything to account in argument. Today, when the Church is in the dock, misunderstood, jeered at for her very existence and even her sanctity itself, Catholics should be wary lest what they want to say simply in order to serve her better be turned to account against her. We have to be on our guard against misunderstandings of a fatal kind; and this is a filial delicacy that has nothing to do with prudery or hypocritical calculation. It is not possible to give a hard-and-fast rule, but the Holy Spirit will not be miserly with the gift of counsel to the really "ecclesiastical" man, as I have tried to depict him above—that is, to the man who cannot but be truly spiritual.

We must in any case make a distinction between healthy self-criticism, even when it is excessive or ill-directed, and all sterile complaining—everything that stems from a loss, or even a diminishing, of confidence in the Church. It would certainly be impious to use one or two unfortunate occurrences as an excuse to run down "contemporary Christianity's excellent and laborious task of diagnosing its own deficiencies and trying to understand, love, and preserve all that has grown up of value outside its own direct influence in order to venture out into the storm to collect the first materials for its new dwelling".[26] But if an attempt of this kind is to be carried out and bear fruit, we have to be careful that it is not contaminated by the breath of a spirit very different from that which is its own principle.

There are certain times when one sees springing up in every direction the symptoms of an evil that catches on like an epidemic—a collective neurasthenic crisis. To those who are afflicted by it, everything becomes matter for denigration, and this is not just a case of the irony, quarrelsomeness, or bitterness that are at all times a perpetual threat to a certain kind of temperament. Everything gets a bad construction put upon it, and knowledge of all kinds, even when accurate, only serves to intensify the evil. Half-digested new discoveries and clumsily used new techniques are all so many occasions for believing that the traditional foundations of things have become shaky. The spiritual life goes but limpingly—so much so that nothing is really seen in the light of it any more. People think themselves clear-headed when all the time it is precisely the essential that they have overlooked. We are no longer capable of discovering, sometimes on our very doorsteps, the fresh flowerings of the Holy Spirit's innumerable inventions, which are always in his own likeness and always new. And thus discouragement creeps in by a thousand and one different ways; things that might have given us a healthy shock simply have the effect of paralyzing us. Faith may remain sincere, but it is undermined here, there, and everywhere, and we begin to look at the Church as if from outside, in order to judge her; the groanings of prayer become an all-too-human recrimination.[27] And by this movement of Pharisaism—a sort of interior falling-away—which may be

[26] Emmanuel Mounier, "Un Surnaturalisme historique", *Georges Bernanos*, p. 113.

[27] See Paul Claudel's letter to André Gide of January 9, 1912: "The true children of God keep silent, suffer, and pray; there are more of them than you think, but one must be on the inside to recognize them."

unadmitted but nonetheless pernicious for all that, we set foot on the road that may end in open denial.

That this should be realized in time and that the appropriate reaction should take place is something devoutly to be hoped for. There is no question of blinding oneself to inadequacies; those are always only too real. And there is no question of not feeling the painfulness of them; indifference can be much worse than excess of emotion. The total and burning loyalty of our holding to the Church does not demand of us a puerile admiration for every possible thing that can be, or be thought or done, within her. Christ wished his Bride to be perfect, holy, and without spot; but she is this only in principle. If she does indeed shine with a spotless radiance, it is "in the sacraments with which she begets and nurtures her children; in the faith she preserves ever inviolate; in the holy laws she imposes on all, and in the evangelical counsels by which she admonishes; and, finally, in the heavenly gifts and miraculous powers by which out of her inexhaustible fecundity she begets countless hosts of martyrs, virgins, and confessors".[28] Her soul is the Spirit of Christ, but her members are men all the same; and we know well that men are never up to the level of the divine mission that is entrusted to them. They are never wholly amenable and submissive to the inspirations of the Spirit of Christ, and if they do not succeed in corrupting the Church—since the source of her sanctifying power does not lie in them—she, on the other hand, will never succeed in stopping completely the source of evil in them—at least, as long as the conditions of this world hold good. Their goodwill is no guarantee of their intelligence, and intelligence is not always accompanied by strength. The best among them will always be setting up innumerable obstacles to the good that God wants to bring about through them;[29] so that we may as well get

[28] Pius XII, encyclical *Mystici corporis*.

[29] This reflection appears several times in the correspondence of St. Francis Xavier, and he impresses it again upon his faithful disciple Gaspard Barzée in his final advice to him; see also Catherine Ranquet's letter to Fr. de Bus of May 4, 1647: "Before God, I am nothing but an obstacle to his designs, and the

it into our heads to start with that nothing they do should surprise us—a lesson that is most healthily rammed home by history.

Yet we are all men, and there is none of us but is aware of his own wretchedness and incapacity; for, after all, we keep on having our noses rubbed in our own limitations. We have all, at some time or other, caught ourselves red-handed in the very act of contradiction—trying to serve a holy cause by dubious means. And we must add that our most serious shortcomings are those very ones that escape our notice; from time to time, at least, we see that we are without understanding in the face of the mystery we are called upon to live out. So that there are scanty grounds for making exceptional cases of ourselves; and none at all for the withdrawal implied in a grimly judging eye. If we behave in that way, we fall into an illusion like that of the misanthrope who takes a dislike to mankind, for all the world as if he himself were not a part of it: "In order to attain to a deep understanding with humanity it is enough to be a part of it, to cleave to the whole mass of it and all the intermingling of its members"—then "we have no more grievances left, no more standing back, no more judgments, and no more comparisons." [30] Then the evident contrast between the human wretchedness of those who make up the Church and the greatness of her divine mission will no longer be a scandal to us; for we shall first have become painfully aware of it in ourselves. Rather, it will become a stimulus. We shall understand how a certain sort of self-criticism, which is always directed outward, may be nothing more than the search for an alibi designed to enable us to dodge the examination of our consciences. [31] And a

---

destruction of his work" (quoted in G. Gueudré, *Catherine Ranquet: Mystique et éducatrice* [1952], p. 168).

[30] *Paul Claudel interroge le Cantique des cantiques*, p. 277.

[31] See Cardinal Wyszynski's letter of November 1952, published in the Cracow Catholic weekly *Tygodnik Powszechny*: "The active presence of Catholics in the universal Church needs a deepening. . . . It ought to be the presence of *domestici fidei*, incorporated in Christ living in the Church. . . . We must

humble acceptance of Catholic solidarity will perhaps be more profitable to us in the matter of shaking us out of some of our illusions. It will perhaps help us to fall in love once more, from a new standpoint, with those elements in the wisdom and the institutions and the traditions and the demands of our Church that we were coming near to understanding no longer.

* * *

Today, however, disquiet often takes forms more precise than this, and the most lowly of active Catholics does not entirely escape it. He may ask himself with painful anxiety: Is the Church's action on our age properly adapted to it? Surely indisputable experience shows that it is tragically ineffective? For some time past at least that kind of question has been asked in many quarters, and we should not underestimate its seriousness or dismiss it hastily as if we refused to look at it. If we do that, we shall only add to the troubles of those who (perhaps because they are more wide awake than we) are at grips with it in a real "dark night". But here again we must make a sober effort at the discernment of spirits.[32]

In many quarters people are asking themselves questions as to the real value, not, of course, of Christianity itself, but of many of the parts that go to make up, as it were, the religious instrument, as the centuries have forged it. They find its efficiency at too low a level and point grimly to the worn cogs and

---

induce men to break with religious individualism, with the facile criticisms of far-off observers who impose on the Church (often conceived of in a highly abstract fashion) great demands and forget that these demands should first be imposed upon oneself, since the Church . . . is ourselves" (*L'Actualité religieuse dans le monde* [April 1, 1953], p. 28). See also de Montcheuil, *Aspects de l'Église*, pp. 77–79.

[32] Here I am not envisaging any of the objective problems that may really present themselves. It is not that I wish to question the importance of such, but that to do so would be to go beyond the bounds of my subject. All I am attempting here is to define the attitude without which such problems would of necessity be mispresented and would bear within their very formulation risks of misunderstanding or error.

tired springs; many practices are put in the dock, and there is talk of out-of-date methods and institutions. It will scarcely be a matter for surprise if there is in all this more than one illusion of the inside-out kind, and if certain errors creep into both the diagnosis of the evil and the choice of remedies for it; a genuine intuition of new needs may be accompanied by inadequate knowledge and a certain lack of grip on reality. It is not always possible to make an accurate distinction between what ought to be preserved and what ought to be changed, at the first shot; sometimes we are over-quick to despair of forms that, though apparently dead, are capable of reanimation. However, if our inspiration is sound, we shall not find it difficult to make the necessary adjustments to a program rather hastily drawn up and to round out a somewhat one-sided effort by others more calculated to balance it.

But it is that inspiration, precisely, which stands in need of control. For here the worst may go cheek by jowl with the best. What is the real source of this concern for adaptation, or—which is very much the same thing—the need felt for what is often called a more effective "incarnation"—a concern in itself wholly justified[33] and frequently encouraged of set purpose by the supreme authority of the Church?[34] Is it a pure overflowing of charity, as in the case of St. Paul, who, following the example of Christ, wanted to make himself all things to all men? Or is there some admixture in it of this illusion, all too natural to the professional man—which every priest must inevitably be to a certain extent—that it is enough to make a change of method, as all human undertakings may do, to obtain results that primarily suppose a change of heart? Realistic views, objective

[33] There is a permanent value in what Fr. Alfred Soras wrote in 1938 in *Action catholique et action temporelle* concerning the "law of incarnation", its depth, scope, and problems.

[34] One of the recent examples of this is the allocution of Pope Pius XII to the superiors of female religious gathered in congress in Rome in September 1952: "Where things which are not essential are concerned, adapt yourselves as reason and rightly ordered charity counsel you."

inquiry, statistics, the elucidation of sociological laws, the drawing up of methodical plans, breaks both big and small with the forms of apostolate belonging to the past, the perfecting of new techniques—all these things may be made use of by zeal that is really pure and upright, and anyone who belittles them puts himself in the right with a somewhat suspect facility by contrasting them with the methods of the Curé d'Ars. Yet all these things have to be kept in their proper place, in the service of the Spirit of God alone.

But—and this is something more serious—it may well be that there is mingled with our disquiet in some more or less subtle way a certain timidity, a certain deep-seated lack of assurance and secret revulsion against the tradition of the Church. We may, when we see ourselves as setting ourselves free from what seems a spirit of senility and as struggling against ankylosis and sclerosis, be putting ourselves in the way of contracting "childish ailments";[35] what we take for an awakening of the personality may in point of fact be the end-product of a blind aberration, and we may set ourselves to judge all things in accordance with criteria that are superficially "modern" and no more. The secular values that the world spreads before our eyes may begin to dazzle us, and in the presence of those who stand for them we may, bit by bit, allow ourselves to be affected by an inferiority complex. Where things that should be most sacred to us are concerned, we may be on the way to accepting ideas about them held by men whose blindness should in fact be matter for our sorrow. We may be stupidly allowing ourselves to be imposed upon by the manifestations of the "pride of life"; to put it in a nutshell, although our faith may not be flagging, we may be beginning to lose our faith in our faith, if one may put it so.[36]

---

[35] See Joseph Folliet, *Présence de l'Église* (1949), chap. 3, "Maladies séniles et maladies infantiles des catholiques français"; and Fr. Louis Beirnaert's invitation "not to entrench ourselves in resentment", in his "Fidélité à l'Église et fidélité à l'homme", *Études*, 151:16.

[36] This temptation will already be in part dispelled if we see how others before us have recognized and overcome it. Newman came close to giving way

This should be an occasion for recalling with greater explic-
itness certain constant truths. "I, when I have been lifted up
from the earth, will draw all things unto me" [37]—those words
of Christ are not, doubtless, an invitation to literal imitation,
and we are not Wisdom personified that we should be able to
be content to say: "Come over to me all that desire me: and be
filled with my fruits." [38] St. Paul, conformed to Christ, traveled
the world over, the precursor of a whole army of apostles, and
the Church will always be missionary. And this is at least the
symptom of a certain spirit; in other words, we are quite right
not to want to be separated from men who are to be led to
Christ—if by that we understand the necessity of breaking
down the barriers that would be put between them and ourselves by forms of living or thinking that are superseded and,
even more so, by ways of behaving whose sole justification is
an ideal of comfortableness or peace and quiet. We are quite
right not to allow ourselves to be shut up in any sort of ghetto,
by ourselves any more than by anybody else. But we have to
be on our guard against misunderstanding both the truly central position our faith guarantees us, to the degree of its own
strength, and that essential condition of being "set apart" from
the world which belongs to every Christian, let alone every
priest. [39]

---

to it during his Anglican period—admittedly, within the framework of a
situation very different from ours. He wrote from Malta: "[T]he Christian
world is gradually becoming barren and effete, as land which has been worked
out and has become sand. We have lasted longer than the South, but we too are
going, as it would seem", quoted by Louis Bouyer, *Newman: His Life and
Spirituality* (New York: P. J. Kenedy & Sons, 1958), p. 137. It has been said of a
certain type of politician: "he both believes in his truths and despairs of them"
(Étienne Borne, TH [October 1952], p. 7). It would be even more illogical for
a Christian to harbor such an attitude of mind with regard to his faith.

[37] Jn 12:32; see also Bengt Sundkler's stimulating study "Jésus et les païens",
Revue d'histoire et de philosophie religieuse (1936), pp. 462–99.

[38] Sir 24:26.

[39] *Sanctus = segregatus*; see Acts 13:2; Rom 1:1: "called to be an apostle,
separated unto the gospel of God".

If we are really "turned to God", we have "abandoned idols" and cannot "bear the yoke" with those who are deceived by them.[40] And if we show real vitality in this sacred operation and the joyful practice of all that it imposes on us, others will certainly be drawn to this source of life and will not want to be separated from us. The miracle of the drawing power of Christ will continue in and through our lives.

We should, then, have no inhibitions about feeling a profound sympathy with the men who surround us. We should be fully human, for we are obliged to that by our duty of interior sincerity as well as of brotherly love; or rather, that disposition should be something so natural and congenital to us that there is no need to go looking for it. We ought not to get our loyalty to the eternal mixed up with an attachment to the past that is small-minded and even morbid. Yet at the same time we should beware of modern self-sufficiency; we should be wary of making our own the weakness and infatuations, the pretentious ignorance and the narrowness of the surrounding milieu, and of giving a welcome to worldliness, whether it be proletarian or middle-class, refined or vulgar. Or rather, we should be always extricating ourselves from it—for, unfortunately, we are always getting involved in it to a greater or a lesser degree. To sum up; we should always be adapted, and that as spontaneously as possible; but we must do it without ever allowing ourselves, either in behavior or thought, to adapt Christianity itself in the least—that is to say, to de-divinize it or lower it, make it insipid or twist it out of shape. We should have a great love for our age but make no concessions to the spirit of the age, so that in us the Christian mystery may never lose its sap.[41]

* * *

For some, this difficulty is made more acute at the intellectual level, and the pain more piercing at the depth of the soul, when

[40] 1 Th 1:9; 1 Cor 6:9–12; 2 Cor 6:14–17.

[41] Rom 12:2: "And be not conformed to this world." I have treated of these questions at greater length in my *Paradoxes of Faith*, chaps. 4 and 6.

it seems that in spite of every possible effort of adaptation the action of the Church remains far from effective, through causes that make all effort powerless. Far from making a perpetual advance, she goes back. Even where she is in apparent control and her influence is recognized and encouraged, she does not bring about the reign of the Gospel, and the social order is not transformed according to her principles. Yet the tree is surely to be judged by its fruits; and that, surely, provides grounds for believing that the Church has had her day? It seems that we must fear that she can never realize other than symbolically what others feel confident of being able to realize eventually in truth; and the conclusion would appear to be that we should transfer elsewhere the confidence we once reposed in her.

There is much equivocation in this process of reasoning, apparently so simple. It is obvious that if each member of the Church were all that he ought to be, the Kingdom of God would progress at a very different rate, though always through a perpetual piling-up of obstacles—as we saw earlier on—and always invisible to eyes that are not enlightened by God. And it is equally true that this or that historical happening and this or that social context can, independently of the will of the individual, create unfavorable conditions, deep-reaching mis-understandings and divergences, and thus set formidable prob-lems. But if we are to have a chance of solving these—or at least of maintaining our confidence, even if we have to concede that some of them are, for the time being, insoluble—then a great many latent equivocations must be exposed. We will leave on one side all considerations of the sociological order, for it is with the preliminary "discernment" that we must concern ourselves to begin with.[42]

When the Church is in question, we must not judge advance and retreat, success and frustration, as we should do in the case

[42] See Jean Clémence, S.J., "Le Discernement des esprits dans les Exercices spirituels de saint Ignace de Loyola", RAM (1951), p. 359: while the danger that threatens souls who are still mediocre is that of cowardliness, "that which threatens generous souls is illusion."

of things that are of time. The supernatural good that the Church serves in this world is something that reaches its totality in the invisible order and finds its consummation in the eternal. The communion of saints grows from generation to generation. And we should not regress into any dream of a Church exteriorly triumphant, for the Church's Head did not promise her dazzling and increasing success. If we say of the Church, as did Pascal, that she is destined to be in her agony until the end of the world, like Christ, this is not a relapse into mere rhetoric or the enjoyment of a romantic emotional luxury. We must not forget the demands of the "redeeming wisdom".[43] We should watch her at work in the life and action of Jesus; that will help us to be patient in even our very anxiety. It will help us to pass through our disquiet and arrive on the other side, rather than drag us back to the hither side of it in a sort of resignation, which may be a fall in itself. The apostolically minded must know how to wait, and the priest has often occasion to know how to accept the sense of being helpless; he *must* accept the fact of being nearly always misunderstood.

Above all, we must not get the wrong idea about the Kingdom of God, which is the end of the Church and which it is her mission to anticipate. Here the whole of the faith is involved; without in any way underestimating the urgency of the urban problem or the irreplaceable part that the Church must play in the solution of it,[44] it is impossible to lose sight of the fact that her desire is to solve a problem no less urgent, but at a higher level and more far-reaching, more constant,

[43] See Alfred Soras, S.J., "Besoin actuel d'une sagesse rédemptrice", in *Masses ouvrières* (March 1952).

[44] The situation with regard to social Catholicism is rather like that with regard to Christian philosophy; it is not and can never be a completed system or a total success. In its most fundamental aspect the action of Catholicism on society is essentially indirect, as is its action on thought. However, during recent times, in which the conduct of societies and states has been so little under the influence of the Church, it is something to wonder at that "social Catholicism" has been able to carry out work, in the sphere of influencing doctrine and leavening society, that is by no means negligible.

and more all-embracing. Like sicknesses that evolve in some germ-breeding environment, waging war on the remedies applied to them and cropping up again under a new form every time we think we have got them under control, the root evil that man carries in his depths flares up again, always the same in itself, under forms that change perpetually as society changes. Psychologies, customs, and social relationships change; man remains, with his evil. This does not mean that we ought not to try everything in our search for betterment; the tenacity of evil can be nothing other than a challenge to a yet more determined and sustained struggle. But suppose for a moment something that we are, unfortunately, far enough away from—a more or less perfect functioning of society; that is, not an economic or political machine more or less adequately powerful, but an exterior order that is as human as possible. With all that granted, the Church's work would not, in a sense, have even started. For her business is not to settle us in comfortably in our earthly existence but to raise us above it. Her bringing to us of the redemption of Christ means that she wants to tear us free from the evil that is in us and lay us open to another existence; and the other side of the same fact is that if she were to give temporal effectiveness top priority, that very thing would not be granted to her. If she were to wait, in order to carry out in the world the work of salvation, for temporal conditions to undergo an eventual improvement (whatever the terms in which the ideal state of affairs were actually conceived), she would be playing false to her mission, which is to bring safely home, not a future humanity at some time to come, but the whole of humanity throughout time—not a mythical humanity, but the actual men of each generation.

If, then, we want to be realistic, it is nonetheless indispensable that our realism should not mistake its object. And if we are anxious to be effective, it is essential that we should not build our foundation on means that are too extrinsic and thus calculated to turn us aside from our end. If we rightly may, and sometimes should, be strict with those who call themselves

Catholics—with ourselves—it is essential that we should understand what we do and do it with reference to valid standards. We must not lose sight of the essential.

This essential, which cannot remain as even a distant objective on our horizon if we do not find a place for it in the heart of our present activity, is not something that can be judged from a quantitative point of view. God brings about the saving of us according to laws that are hidden from us as far as their concrete application is concerned but that are imposed on our faith in principle—the mysterious laws of the community of salvation. And today the prayer of intercession and the sacrifice of charity have lost none of their secret power; moreover, the existence of one saint alone would be sufficient witness to the divine value of the principle by which saints live. But the question is whether our sight is clear enough and whether we have sufficient knowledge of where to look, to discern among ourselves, in this order of sanctity, the effectiveness of the Church. Let us at least try to catch a glimpse of it. Massive appearance should not hide from us the central reality, nor noisy ideological debate prevent us from hearing the silent breathing of the Spirit. At a time when he was the head of a community made up of none but the poor and uneducated and was without appreciable influence on the destinies of the Empire, the great St. Cyprian said: "As for us, we are philosophers not in word but in act; we do not say great things, but we do live them." [45] And that saying remains true, in all its proud humility. The essential is very rarely something that can be much talked about; Christian vitality is in every age very much less dependent on all that is discussed and done and picked to pieces on the world's stage than we are often led to believe. There is a life it is almost impossible to judge of from the outside; and that life keeps itself

<hr />

[45] St. Cyprian, *De bono patientiae*, chap. 3: "Nos autem . . . qui philosophi non verbis sed factis sumus . . . , qui non loquimur magna sed vivimus" (1:398, in Hartel's edition); Minucius Felix, *Octavius*, chap. 38, no. 6 (PL 3, 359a); St. Antony, according to St. Athanasius (cf. Moehler, *Athanase le Grand*, French trans., 2:102).

going, passes itself on, and renews itself under all the turmoil of politics, all the swirl of public opinion, the currents of ideas and the controversies, far removed from the scene of public debate, unsounded and untabulated. The blind see, the deaf hear, the dead are raised to life, and the poor have the Gospel preached to them;[46] the Kingdom of God shines in secret. Here and there there are sudden glimpses; patches of light break through, widen, and join up with others. A point of light or two in the night suddenly shines more brightly; sometimes there will be patches of blood, to draw our attention. All are so many heralding signs.

Today, when there is so much discussion about Christianity and so much complaining about its "ill-adaptedness" or "ineffectiveness", we should always be returning again and again to these very simple considerations. The best Christians and the most vital are by no means to be found either inevitably or even generally among the wise or the clever, the intelligentsia or the politically minded, or those of social consequence. And consequently what they say does not make the headlines; what they do does not come to the public eye. Their lives are hidden from the eyes of the world, and if they do come to some degree of notoriety, that is usually late in the day, and exceptional, and always attended by the risk of distortion. Within the Church herself it is, as often as not, only after their deaths that some of them acquire an uncontested reputation. Yet these are responsible, more than anyone else, for ensuring that our earth is not a hell on earth. Most of them never think to ask themselves whether their faith is "adapted" or "effective". It is enough, for them, to live it, as reality itself, and reality at its most actual; and because the fruit of all this is often enough a hidden fruit, it is nonetheless wonderful for that. Even if such people are themselves not engaged in external activity, they are the source of all initiative and action, all spadework that is not to be fruitless. It is these people who are our preservation and who give us hope,

[46] Lk 7:22.

and it would be a bold man who said that they are less numerous and less active today than in the past.[47]

We should not become blind to the real *fruitfulness* of our Mother the Church for the sake of a dream of *efficiency* that may be no more than a mirage.

* * *

But there is another temptation yet. This again is not that of the simple soul, and it is the most serious of all.

It has been creeping in ever since the observation made by St. Paul to the Christians at Corinth: "For consider your vocation, brethren; there are not many wise according to the flesh, not many mighty, not many noble."[48] The wise, the powerful, and the noble were to come, certainly, but the Apostle's words retain their profound and many-sided truth nonetheless for that. Like her Master, the Church cuts in the eyes of the world the figure of a slave; on this earth she exists "in the form of a slave".[49] And it is not only the wisdom of this world, in the crude sense, that is lacking in her; it is also—in appearance at least—the wisdom of the spirit. She is no cenacle of sublime spiritual geniuses or gathering of supermen, any more than she is an academy of the learned; in fact, she is the very opposite. The warped, the sham, and the wretched of every kind crowd into her, together with the whole host of the mediocre, who feel especially at home in her and everywhere set the tone of things. Her most magnificent advances merely serve to accentuate this characteristic, both in the average run of her members and in the stuff of her day-to-day existence; to show how, in detail, would be only too easy. And as a consequence it is hard, not to say entirely impossible, for the "natural man" to find in such a phenomenon the

[47] See my *Paradoxes of Faith*, chaps. 7 and 8 (on the subject of efficacy). The reader should also consult Henry Dumery's *Les Trois Tentations de l'apostolat moderne* (1948); Yves Congar, *Jalons pour une théologie du laïcat* (1953), chap. 9, "Au Monde et pas du monde".

[48] 1 Cor 1:26.

[49] Phil 2:7.

consummation of the saving *kenosis* and the awe-inspiring traces of the "humility of God" [50]—that is, insofar as his innermost thoughts have not been turned around. [51]

The Church has always drawn down on herself the contempt of the élite. There are many philosophers and devotees of the spiritual life, much concerned about the sources of spiritual vitality, who refuse her their adherence; some of them are openly hostile to her, disgusted, like Celsus, by "this pack of ignorant, uneducated, foolish people", [52] and they turn aside from her, either with the Olympian serenity of a Goethe or in the Dionysiac fury of a Nietzsche. It is as if they said: "So you claim to be the Body of Christ, do you?—the Body of God? Could the Body of God really be made of such coarse stuff as that? And to start with, how can Divinity have a body anyhow?" [53]

There are others among these sophisticated men who feel that they are doing the Church full justice and protest when

[50] That is, insofar as there has not been a *metanoia*; see Mk 1:15; Rom 12:2; Eph 4:23.

[51] St. Augustine, *Enchiridion*, chap. 108: "ut humana superbia per humilitatem Dei argueretur ac sanaretur" (PL 40, 283); *Sermo* 184, no. 1: "Teneant ergo humiles humilitatem Dei" (p. 74 in Lambot's edition of 1940); *Sermo* 51, nos. 4–5 (PL 38, 336); *Sermo* 117, no. 17 (PL 38, 671); *Sermo* 123, no. 1 (684); *Sermo* 142, no. 2 (778); *De doctrina christiana*, bk. 1, chap. 14, no. 13 (PL 34, 24); *Confessiones*: "Non enim tenebam Jesum, humilis humilem"; *In Joannem*, tract. 2, no. 4; tract. 25, no. 16 (PL 35, 1390–91 and 1604); *De Trinitate*, bk. 4, chap. 2, no. 4, and bk. 8, chap. 5, no. 7 ((PL 42, 889 and 952); *De agone christiano*, chap. 11, no. 12 (PL 40, 297); *De Div. Quaest.* 83, q. 69, no. 9 (PL 40, 79); St. Leo the Great, *De ascensione Domini sermo* 2, chap. 1: "Sacramentum salutis nostrae . . . per dispensationem humilitatis impletum est" (PL 54, 397a); St. Gregory the Great, *Moralia in Job*, bk. 2, chap. 35, no. 58: "Dum ipse humilitatem carnis suscepit, in se credentibus vota humilitatis infudit" (p. 224 in the edition of de Gaudemaris); see also Fr. Adnès, "L'Humilité, vertu spécifiquement chrétienne, d'après saint Augustin", RAM (1952). Henri Bergson speaks of the "divine humility", in *Deux Sources*, p. 249.

[52] Celsus, *True Discourse*, I (quoted in Origen's *Contra Celsum*, bk. 3, chap. 44; see also chaps. 55 and 60); and compare Goethe's "a narrow-minded mass, ready to cringe and be lorded over", in a letter of March 11, 1832.

[53] Celsus, *True Discourse*, I; see St. Hilary of Poitiers, *Tractatus in Psalm.* I, no. 5: "sacramentum Dei corporati" (p. 22 in Zingerle's edition).

they are described as her adversaries. After all, they would stand up for her if need be; they think she plays a very useful part. "What!" says one of them, replying to some friends who considered him too favorable to the Christian schools. "Do you want me to explain *Parmenides* to my cook?"[54] But they keep their distance; they do not want for themselves a faith that would make them one with all the wretched creatures above whom they rank themselves in virtue of their aesthetic culture, their powers of rational reflection, and their concern with the things of the spirit; they are an aristocracy who do not see themselves mixing with the herd. In their view, the Church leads men by ways that are altogether too well-trodden. They willingly concede her skill in presenting higher truths under the veil of imagery;[55] but they distinguish themselves, as those who know, from the mass of "those who believe", and they claim to know the Church better than she knows herself. They "place" her, condescendingly, and grant themselves the power of disentangling the deeper meaning of her doctrines and actions—without her consent—by virtue of a "metaphysical transposition".[56] They place their own intuition above her

[54] Victor Cousin, quoted by Franck in his *Nouveaux Essais de critique philosophique* (1890), pp. 43–44: "He regarded it as sheer cruelty to deprive of their twilight those whose eyes were closed to light of another kind." And Proudhon mocked the philosophers of his day who "on the strength of having unpicked one or two metaphysical tangles" considered themselves superior to the Church (*De la Justice dans la Révolution et dans l'Église*, 1:275).

[55] See Victor Cousin, *Fragments philosophiques*, 2d ed. (1833), preface: "Religion, which addresses itself to all men, would be wide of its aim if it were to present itself under a form that could be grasped by intelligence alone. . . . It is different with philosophy. Philosophy speaks to intelligence alone, and in consequence to a very small number of men; but that small number is the élite and vanguard of humanity. . . . It takes a bad philosophy and a bad theology to quarrel. Christianity is the cradle of modern philosophy; and I myself have pointed out more than one lofty truth hidden under the veil of Christian imagery" (5th ed. [1866], pp. lxxi–lxxii).

[56] René Guénon, *Autorité spirituelle et pouvoir temporel* (1930), p. 36; *L'Homme et son devoir selon le Vedanta* (1925), p. 51; *Introduction générale à l'étude des doctrines hindoues* (1921), p. 151; etc. See also Schuon's *De l'unité transcendante des religions*

faith, as they would place the absolute above the relative, or
direct and active participation in the divine knowledge above
indirect and passive participation. One might describe them as
"specialists of the *logos*"[57]—but specialists who have not read, in
St. Paul, how the Logos repulses "every height that exalteth
itself against the knowledge of God".[58] They are the wise—but
not wise enough to see how for twenty centuries the prophecy
has been worked out: "I will destroy the wisdom of the wise." [59]
They are the rich who have never taken in the first beatitude.
Some of them, setting themselves up as the leaders of schools or
sects, add to the attraction of the promise of knowledge that of
the secret—like Valentinus in the early days, or that Faustus
under whose influence St. Augustine suffered for a time,[60] or, to
quote an example from our own day, René Guénon—for the
mirage of initiation has a fascination for minds at every level.
Yet others remain in their solitude; and that is not always in
virtue of a diabolical refusal—sometimes, and much less mysteriously, it is quite simply an absurd pretentiousness. It may be
merely a case of the disgust felt by a lofty intelligence for ways of
thinking and living that would get him mixed up with the
common crowd; or the shivering recoil of the "sensitive soul".
And thus there develops a "distinguished individualism that is,
however, a closed one, admitting at most only a few chosen
beings to a friendly sharing in interior experience".[61] There is
a fear that, just as the Church would hamper the freedom
of investigation and put the curb on the adventurousness of
spiritual impulse, so also strict adherence to her would surely

---

(1948), pp. 61, and also pp. 10–22, where there is an attempt to persuade us to
isolate the "naked truth" from the symbol or form that encloses it in faith and
transcend dogma through penetrating to its "internal dimension".

[57] See Marcel Mery, *La Critique du christianisme chez Renouvier* (1953), 2:498.

[58] 2 Cor 10:5.

[59] Is 29:14; 1 Cor 1:19.

[60] St. Augustine, *Confessions*, bk. 5, chaps. 3–7.

[61] Dom Odo Casel, O.S.B. (he is talking about the hermetic books), *Le
Mémorial du Seigneur*, trans. Henri Chirat (1945), pp. 59–60.

involve something like regimentation and forced association with the vulgar masses.

A faint echo of these objections and this repugnance can come to strike the Christian consciousness itself. Faith may not be shaken by them, but all the same they sometimes have the effect of straining the bonds that bind us to the Church and lessening their strength and holding power. Without going so far as making an actual break, we can come to forget the close correlation of ecclesiastical faithfulness and religious faithfulness, for the fact is that Christianity may, at the level of truth, emerge triumphant from the challenge, and the Church yet not appear correspondingly justified; at least, the theoretical justification may not win a downright victory over an experienced repugnance. Impartial inquiry may indeed establish that the wisdom she offers and infuses does not, in fact, consist of that collection of "puerile futilities" which St. Augustine believed it to be before the preaching of St. Ambrose opened his eyes.[62] It may lead a man to discover the solidity of her dogma, even to get a glimpse of the depth of her mysteries, and the orthodox interpretation of them given by the great Doctors of the Church. It may bring him to admire the artistic splendors and the cultural riches that have glorified the human aspect of her, at certain periods at least. But all that does not change the obvious commonness of the binding medium that all Catholic living has to use from day to day and in which we must ourselves be set.

André Malraux, confronted with the pictures in the Roman catacombs and their first graphic expression of the Word that was heard in Christ, was driven to exclaim: "How badly these poor figures answer to that voice and all its depths!"[63]—a reaction we may develop further. Will it not be so, and fatally so, with every expression of the Catholic reality, whatever its mode

<hr />

[62] *Confessions*, bk. 6, chap. 4, no. 5: "Confundebar et convertebar et gaudebam, Deus meus, quod Ecclesia, tua unica, corpus Unici tui, in qua mihi nomen Christi infanti est inditum, non saperet infantiles nugas."

[63] André Malraux, *La Monnaie de l'Absolu*, p. 160.

and its nature? What, in fact, does happen to revelation in current preaching—what becomes of the summons of God in the popular mind, or of the Kingdom of God in many an imagination among the devout or the theologically minded? What becomes of the holy love of unity in hearts that are all too inadequately purified of human passion, or of mystery— all too often—in our textbooks? Pascal was much impressed by the fittingness of maintaining two extremes while covering the whole space that lies between, and thus uniting so many truths "which seem repugnant and yet all subsist in a wonderful order"[64]—yet in practice this dynamic synthesis is very often transformed into some flat-footed formula of the happy medium. The wonderful *complexio oppositorum* held out to us by every aspect of Catholicism does, in point of fact, cause considerable alarm and despondency in a great many believers. The Church herself does not as a rule encourage overbold thought or excessively sublime spirituality; for the forms she approves most willingly must be such as can be accepted by the average Catholic environment—and that, one must admit, is always "something rather insipid and rather mediocre"[65]—which all provides perpetually rich matter for the *irrisio infidelium*, even from among the educated. And in truth, if we look at it realistically, not in the rarefied atmosphere of pure ideas but in concrete reality, "What is the Church"—as Newman pointed out—"but, as it were, a body of humiliation, almost provoking insult and profaneness", sharp revulsion, or, at best, an indulgent reserve, "when men do not live by faith".[66]

There is no question of simply suffering in silence the really destructive elements in all this, or of accepting it wholesale as something to be desired; it is a matter of *assuming* it, of taking it

---

[64] Pascal, *Pensées*, ed. Jacques Chevalier, pp. 169 and 518–19.

[65] *Paul Claudel interroge le Cantique des cantiques*, p. 362; also his letter to Gabriel Frizeau, *Correspondance* (Claudel-Frizeau-Jammes), ed. Blanchet (1953), p. 35.

[66] Newman, "Christ Hidden from the World", sermon 16 of vol. 4, in *Parochial and Plain Sermons* (San Francisco, 1997), p. 893.

all upon ourselves, and that with a loyalty that will not deserve the name if it is of the surface only. There is no "private Christianity",[67] and if we are to accept the Church, we must take her as she is, in her human day-to-day reality just as much as in her divine and eternal ideality; for a separation of the two is impossible both in fact and by right. Loving the Church means loving her in the full massiveness of her tradition, all repugnance overcome, and burrowing deep, so to speak, into the massiveness of her life, as the seed goes deep into the earth. Equally, it means giving up the insidious drug of religious philosophies, which would take the place of our faith or offer to transpose it. For such is the Catholic way of losing oneself in order to find oneself. The mystery of salvation cannot reach us or save us without this final mediation; we have to push to its conclusion the logic of the Incarnation, by which Divinity adapts itself to human weakness. If we are going to have the treasure, then we must also have the "earthen vessels" that contain it[68] and outside which it evaporates. We have to accept what St. Paul, who knew all about the contrary temptation, called "simplicity in Christ".[69] We must be "the common people of God" with no reservations made. To put it another way: the necessity of being humble in order to cleave to Christ involves the necessity of being humble in order to seek him in his Church and add "brotherly love" to the submission of the intellect.[70]

> He alone participates in Christ who keeps himself united to all the members of his body. Insofar as he is rich, he does not say to the poor man: "You are not necessary to me." Insofar as he is

---

[67] Compare E. Kaesemann, quoted by C. Spicq in his *L'Épître aux Hébreux*, p. 277: this Epistle "makes no mention of private Christianity, and faith, like obedience, is characteristic of the community as such."

[68] See 2 Cor 4:7.

[69] 2 Cor 11:3.

[70] 1 Pet 1:22, "with a brotherly love, from a sincere heart"; 2:17, "Love the brotherhood"; and 3:8, "being the lovers of the brotherhood". See also 1 Th 4:9.

strong, he does not say that to the weak: insofar as he is wise, he does not say it to the foolish. . . . He is a part of the Body of Christ, which is the Church. And it is necessary that he should know that those who, in the Church, appear weak, poor, foolish—like the sinners—should be surrounded with all the greater honor and watched over with all the more exacting care. On that condition he will be able to say to himself: "I am one of those who fear the Lord." It is necessary that he should have compassion on men of this kind, as opposed to showing himself embarrassed by them; that he should suffer with those who suffer, in order to learn by experience that we are all one Body with many different united members.[71]

Such is the price of a good thing, which cannot have any price set upon it—Catholic communion. The point was made as early as by St. Clement of Rome, one of the earliest among Peter's successors, who thus went at one stroke to the very heart of the meaning of the Church: "Christ belongs to all those who have a humble attitude and not to those who set themselves above the flock."[72]

As far as the superior type of man can see, everything in the Church is low-grade. But "power gets along well with this poor quality"[73]—in fact, it gets along well with it alone. The idealized forms in which that kind of man finds such satisfaction seem higher and purer to him only because they are the product of his own thought. It does not matter whether he is seeking in them an instrument for the fashioning of a rich personality that is both integrated and forceful; or a frame of reference with which to interpret the universe; or a springboard from which to project himself beyond the limits that enclose the human condition. In each and every case they are equally powerless; they cannot even begin to change his own heart. For all its apparent sublimity, the thought of the superior man is no more than a mirror in which he admires himself and which in consequence

---

[71] St. Ambrose, *In Psalm.* 118, *sermo* 8, no. 54 (PL 15, 1317c–d).

[72] Epistle to the Corinthians, chap. 16.

[73] Pascal, *Pensées*, p. 267.

holds him hypnotized in vanity. It sets up an idol in his heart,[74] and when he throws himself into the arms of it, his embrace finds nothingness—the One which is pure only if it is not being, or the Universal Possibility from which the multiple states of being are derived: "Id vanitate sentit humana non veritate divina." [75] We know all too well—unfortunately—that the profession of Catholicism, even militant Catholicism, does not automatically confer sanctity, and we must admit that among us (and even in surroundings distinguished by fervor and freedom from contamination) much human narrowness often places obstacles in the way of the action of the Spirit. Yet we also know well that the humblest of our saints is freer, interiorly, than the greatest of our masters of wisdom. The former speaks modestly of salvation while the latter is all ready to talk about deliverance; but it does not take long to see which of the two is, in point of fact, "delivered". The noblest and sincerest efforts, thrown awry by an initial *hubris*, end up in the hollowest of pretensions; the only depths that are not deceptive are those that the Spirit himself hollows out within a man,[76] and they presuppose the ground of the common faith, accepted without second thoughts and never abandoned.[77] There, and there only, is the royal road.

"O humility, O sublimity! House of clay and palace of the king, body of death and temple of light! A thing of scorn to the

[74] Ezek 14:3 and 7; Eph 4:18. See also Newman: "[T]hey made their own minds their sanctuary, their own ideas their oracle, and conscience in morals was but parallel to genius in art, and wisdom in philosophy", quoted by Fernande Tardivel, *La Personalité de Newman* (Paris: Gabriel Beauchesne et Ses Fils, 1937), p. 140.

[75] St. Augustine. The vanity of all that which is *figmentum mentis* as distinguished from the truth that comes from God is a frequently recurring theme in his thought; see, for example, *De Trinitate*, bk. 4, no. 1: "Satiavit illos phantasma eorum, non veritas tua, quam repellendo resiliunt, ut in suam vanitatem cadunt" (PL 42, 887); see also Rom 1:18–22.

[76] 1 Cor 2:10.

[77] William of Saint-Thierry, *Aenigma fidei* (PL 180, 407–8); cf. Origen, *In Levit.*, hom. 12, no. 5, concerning the faith that "perseveres in its simple confession as in virginal integrity".

proud, and spouse of Christ."[78] In all her apparent crudity the Church is the sacrament—the true and effective sign—of these "depths of God". And by the same token there are opened to us the depths of man—"deep calls to deep".[79] That is why the passage from St. Paul commented on earlier is at one and the same time the statement of a scandal to the "natural man" and a cry of triumph to the believer—"For consider your vocation, brethren; there are not many wise according to the flesh, not many mighty, not many noble. But the foolish things of this world hath God chosen, that he may confound the wise: and the weak things of this world hath God chosen, that he may confound the strong. And the base things of the world and the things that are contemptible, hath God chosen; and things that are not, that he might bring to nought things that are: that no flesh should glory in his sight."[80]

It takes a miracle of grace to enable us to see things so; without it, the most edifying sentiments and the richest spiritual gifts are merely obstacles, making men like the cedar of Lebanon that has not yet been broken by the Lord—they feed pride and close the heart to charity. And as we have said, they can become a temptation even in the heart of the Church herself. If something of the sort ever becomes the case with us, perhaps we shall benefit from recalling to mind the example of men who have heroically overcome such a situation, together with the concrete circumstances under which they did it.

When Newman, driven by an interior logic that was something much more than a "paper logic", knelt at the feet of Father Domenico Barberi and asked him to receive him into

[78] St. Bernard, *In Cantica, sermo* 27, no. 14 (PL 183, 920d).

[79] See St. Ambrose, *De Isaac et anima*, chap. 8, no. 67: "Philosophi curulia illa animarum in suis libris expressere certamina, nec tamen ad palmam pervenire potuerunt; quoniam summitatem Verbi et altitudinem illorum animae nescierunt, quam cognovit haec anima, in qua erat Verbi conversio" (PL 14, 528b); also St. Bernard, *In Cantica, sermo* 80, nos. 2–3: "Celsa creatura, in capacitate quidem Majestatis. . . . Eo anima magna est, quo capax aeternorum" (PL 183, 1167c–d).

[80] 1 Cor 1:26–29.

the Church, it was not just that he sacrificed a situation, and habits dear to him, and delightful friendships, and a spiritual home loved with a certain melancholy but always tenderly, and a reputation that was already a glorious one. The situation was even more unfavorable than that. It was an autumn evening in the year 1845, toward the end of the pontificate of Gregory XVI; to Newman, Catholicism had everywhere the appearance of a thing beaten by life, and all the sorrier a figure because it trailed after it so many ironic relics of a recent splendor. It could have no human attraction whatsoever for the one-time Fellow of Oriel; as he wrote later:

> Ours is not an age of temporal glory, of dutiful princes, of loyal governments, of large possessions, of ample leisure, of famous schools, of learned foundations, of well-stored libraries, of honoured sanctuaries. Rather, it is like the first age of the Church, when there was little of station, of nobility, of learning, of wealth, in the holy heritage; when Christians were chiefly of the lower orders; when we were poor and ignorant, when we were despised and hated by the great and philosophical as a low rabble, or a stupid and obstinate association, or a foul and unprincipled conspiracy. It is like that first age, in which no saint is recorded in history who fills the mind as a great idea, as St. Thomas Aquinas or St. Ignatius fills it, and when the ablest of so-called Christian writers belonged to heretical schools. We certainly have little to show for ourselves; and the words of the Psalm are fulfilled in us: "They have set fire to Thy sanctuary, they have defiled the dwelling-place of Thy name on earth. Our signs we have not seen; there is no prophet." [81]

Indeed, Newman found nothing attractive about Roman Catholics; he admitted that he did not find himself attuned to them, that he expected little from them, and that in becoming one of their number he had made himself an outcast—he had, as he put it, turned his face to the wilderness. And, of course, at that time he could not know of all the other thorns that were to

[81] *Present Position of Catholics in England*, lecture 9.

tear at him in the course of his long trek across that wilderness. Yet to his soul, full of faith, the step was inevitable, and he was never to regret it for a moment.[82]

Again, we may read what St. Augustine has to say in the eighth book of the *Confessions*. He had the story from his friend Simplicianus, and it is well known how deep an impression it made upon him at the moment when he also was in the process of making a similar decision. The aged Victorinus was a philosopher, "skilled in all the liberal disciplines"; yet he, who had taught so many noble senators and who, as a famous thinker, had seen his own statue set up in the Forum, eventually "thought it no shame to make himself the slave of Christ and bend his neck beneath the yoke of humility and his brow under the shame of the cross". But that did not come about without a long resistance, strengthened by a superb incomprehension— for which the example is nonetheless fine:

> O Lord, Lord, who dost bow down thy heavens and descend, dost touch the mountains and they smoke, by what means didst thou find thy way into that breast? He read, so Simplicianus said, Holy Scripture; he investigated all the Christian writings most carefully and minutely. And he said, not publicly, but to Simplicianus privately, and as one friend to another: "I would have you know that I am now a Christian." Simplicianus answered: "I shall not believe it, nor count you among Christians unless I see you in the Church of Christ." Victorinus asked with some faint mockery: "Then is it the walls that make Christians?" He went on saying that he was Christian, and Simplicianus went on with the same denial, and Victorinus always repeated his retort about the walls. The fact was that he feared to offend his friends, important people and worshippers of . . . demons; he feared their enmity might fall heavily upon him from the height of their Babylon-dignity as from the cedars of Lebanon which the Lord had not yet brought down. But when by reading in all earnestness he had drawn strength, he

[82] Newman, letters to Coleridge (November 16, 1844), Keble (November 21, 1844), and his sister Jemima (March 15, 1845); also see Louis Bouyer, *Newman*, pp. 298–314.

grew afraid that Christ might deny him before his angels if he were ashamed to confess Christ before men. He felt that he was guilty of a great crime in being ashamed of the sacraments of the lowliness of your Word, when he had not been ashamed of the sacrilegious rites of those demons of pride whom in his pride he had worshipped. So he grew proud toward vanity and humble toward truth. Quite suddenly and without warning he said to Simplicianus, as Simplicianus told me: "Let us go to church. I wish to be made a Christian." Simplicianus, unable to control his joy, went with him. He was instructed in the first mysteries of the faith, and not long after gave in his name that he might be regenerated by baptism.[83]

If the elderly Victorinus had not made up his mind to take this decisive step and lose himself among the humble flock of the "practicing" faithful, we should doubtless still remember him as a distinguished philosopher. Perhaps we should be able to admire him still as the thinker who first conceived the elements of that internal theory of the Trinity for which St. Augustine was to provide the West with the definitive formulae. We may even imagine that he would have been capable, without entering the Church, of composing his hymns to the Trinity, in which case his name would also live among those of the poets of dogma.[84] But if all that were so, he would still have no better title than the one he has, for he would not have deserved to be called by a name that is common indeed and in the eyes of many without distinction, yet is the finest of all when its significance is understood: he would not have been a "Catholic".[85]

[83] *Confessions*, bk. 8, chap. 2, nos. 3–4. Concerning Simplicianus, who was to follow St. Ambrose in the See of Milan, see G. Bardy's *Oeuvres de saint Augustin* (1952), 10:383–89.

[84] In point of fact, these hymns, like the other Christian works of Victorinus, come after his public conversion. On Marius Victorinus, see P. Sejourne, "Victorinus Afer", DTC, 15:2887–2954. The three hymns to the Trinity are in PL 8, 1139–46.

[85] A more far-reaching examination of some of the problems discussed in this chapter will be found in Fr. Karl Rahner's *Die Chancen des Christentums heute* (Cologne, Erzbischofliche Seelsorgeamt).

IX

THE CHURCH AND OUR LADY

IT is a remarkable fact that the same hesitations that we come across with regard to the Church are often to be found in certain of the faithful with regard to our Lady. And it is clear that the fundamental criticisms the Reformation directed against the Catholic conception of the Church correspond with those it directed against the Catholic cult of our Lady. The same sort of sacrilegious usurpation was feared alike in the role that the traditional faith accorded to Mary and to the Church; in it the Reformers saw, and denounced, the same calling-in-question of the unique mediation of Christ and the absolute sovereignty of God. Whether it were the justification of each one of the faithful or the coming-down of the Word among us that was in question, it seemed to them equally clear that we should believe that everything takes place "by the grace of God alone and the sole working of the Holy Spirit, without any human action".[1]

Those are Luther's words, and one finds the equivalent of them still today among his spiritual descendants. The Catholic answer to them is that a demand of this kind is "more Christian" in appearance only. In reality, neither the gratuitousness

[1] Luther, *Dictata super Psalmos, in Psalm.* 71, in *Opera*, ed. Weimar, 3:468. Fr. Congar, quoting this text, rightly says that "there are disturbing things in it. Luther wholly passes over both the role of our Lady and that of the Church" (*Le Christ, Marie et l'Église*, pp. 24–25). John Henry Newman, *Mary, the Mother of Jesus* (New York: Catholic Book Exchange, 1894), p. 43, observes that the early Fathers "do not speak of the Blessed Virgin merely as the physical instrument of our Lord's taking flesh, but as an intelligent, responsible cause of it." Froud had inculcated in him love of the Virgin Mary hand in hand with admiration of the Catholic Church.

of the divine initiative nor the transcendence of the divine action has anything to suffer from an economy of salvation that was set up by God himself. In our eyes neither our Lady nor the Church in any way whatsoever replaces the humanity of Christ, as is feared even among those who make the most sincere of efforts to understand the matter.[2] The twofold mystery misunderstood by the Reformation is, on the contrary, the indispensable guarantee of the importance of the Incarnation[3] and, by the same token, bears witness to the divine plan of associating God's creatures with the work of their own salvation:[4] "For the Lord will give goodness: and our earth shall yield her fruit." [5]

These two Catholic truths thus play an analogous role in the defense and exposition of the whole Christian mystery. They delimit exactly the part—subordinate but real and vital—played therein by human action. There is a profound truth in Karl Barth's statement that Marian dogma is the central dogma of Catholicism—the clearest exposition of the Catholic heresy, as he puts it—not in the sense that it eclipses the dogma of the Word Incarnate, but in this sense, that it is the "crucial" dogma of Catholicism, that in relation to which all its cardinal propositions are elucidated:

---

[2] See Max Thurian, "Le Dogme de l'Assomption", *Verbum Caro* 5 (1951): 2–41.

[3] See St. John Damascene, *The Orthodox Faith*, bk. 3, chap. 12: "The name of the Mother of God alone contains the whole mystery of the 'economy'" (PG 94, 1029c).

[4] Louis Bouyer, *Le Culte de la Mère de Dieu dans l'Église catholique*, in the series Irénikon (Chevetogne, 1950), pp. 12–13; Y. Congar, *Jalons pour une théologie du laïcat* (1953), p. 97; E. Mersch, *La Théologie du Corps mystique*, 1:212; E. Druwe, S.J., "Position et structure du traité marial", in the *Bulletin de la société française d'études mariales* (1936); Newman also remarked, in *Mary*, p. 96, that "just those nations and countries have lost their faith in the divinity of Christ who have given up devotion to His Mother."

[5] Ps 84:13; Is 45:8: "let the earth be opened and bud forth a Savior"; see also Is 4:2; Ps 66:4–7; Gen 2:6: "But a spring rose out of the earth"; Bossuet, *Sermon for the Feast of the Conception*: "So necessary was it that Mary should desire their salvation" (*Oeuvres Oratoires*, 5:603).

It is in Marian doctrine and the Marian cult that the heresy of the Roman Catholic Church is apparent—that heresy which enables us to understand all the rest. The "Mother of God" of Roman Catholic dogma is, quite simply, the principle, prototype, and summing-up of the human creature cooperating in its own salvation by making use of prevenient grace; as such, she is also the principle, prototype, and summing-up of the Church. . . . Thus, that Church in which there is a cult of Mary *must* be itself understood as at the [First] Vatican Council; is of necessity that Church of man who, by virtue of grace, cooperates with grace.[6]

Setting on one side the value judgments that go with it, we can accept the Barthian analysis. Catholic faith regarding our Lady sums up symbolically, in its special case, the doctrine of human cooperation in the Redemption and thus provides the synthesis, or matrix concept, as it were, of the dogma of the Church.[7] Thus it has been said that both these doctrines should be maintained or allowed to crumble away together.[8] It is not, therefore, astonishing that history shows us the two constantly associated and that their development in the common Christian consciousness should often go hand in hand. Our own day offers a fresh example of that. But as long as we stop short at positing a functional analogy between the two, and a more or less exterior one at that, we have not fully grasped the reason for it. The links between our Lady and the Church are not only numerous and close; they are essential and woven from within.[9]

[6] Karl Barth, *Die kirchliche Dogmatik* (1938), vol. 1, 2, pp. 157 and 160.

[7] J. Hamer, O.P., "Mariologie et théologie protestante", *Divus Thomas* (Freiburg, September 1952), p. 359; see also Pierre Maury, "La Vierge Marie dans le catholicisme contemporain", in *Le Protestantisme et la Vierge Marie*, p. 47: "Within the Roman system, everything holds together with the utmost logicality. In virtue of a profound internal necessity the Church of Rome is at one and the same time the Church of human cooperation in the Redemption, the Church of merit, the Church that dispenses salvation—and the Church of Mary."

[8] Charles Journet, *L'Église du Verbe incarné*, 2:392.

[9] Clément Dillenschneider, C.S.Sp., *Le Mystère de la corédemption mariale* (1951), p. 79: "Between the two there is no mere similarity. It is in virtue of

These two mysteries of the faith are not just solidary; we might say that they are "one single and unique mystery".[10] At any rate, they stand in such a relation one to the other that each is enriched when elucidated by its fellow; more contemplation of the one is indispensable if the other is to be understood.

In the Church's tradition the same biblical symbols are applied, either in turn or simultaneously, with one and the same ever-increasing profusion, to the Church and our Lady. Both are the New Eve;[11] Paradise;[12] the tree of Paradise, whose fruit is Christ;[13] the great tree seen in his dream by Nebuchadnezzar,

---

an intimate and objective connection that what is fitting in the Church—the mother of the collective Christ—is realized first of all in the personal existence of Mary."

[10] Ruperto Maria of Manresa, quoted by R. Laurentin in the conclusion of his *Marie, l'Église et le sacerdoce.*

[11] The patristic texts are given by S. Tromp, S.J., in his *Corpus Christi quod est Ecclesia* (1946), 1:35ff.; Newman, *Mary*, pp. 39–51; Cardinal Dechamps, *La Nouvelle Ève* (*Oeuvres complètes*, vol. 5); J. B. Terrien, *La Mère de Dieu et la Mère des hommes*, pt. 2, vol. 1, bk. 1, pp. 3–49; A. M. Dubarle, "Les Fondements bibliques du titre marial de Nouvelle Ève", in *Mélanges Lebreton*, 1:49–64. The long comparison drawn between Eve and our Lady by St. Irenaeus in his *Adversus haereses* (bk. 3, chap. 22, no. 4) left its mark on the whole of tradition; see Sagnard's edition in the series *Sources chrétiennes*, no. 34 (1952), pp. 378–83, and appendix B, pp. 422–28; Guerricus, *In Assumptione*, bk. 5, no. 2 (PL 185, 188b).

[12] Origen, *In Cant.*, bk. 3: "Ecclesia Christi, quae est paradisus deliciarum" (p. 193 in Baehrens' edition); St. John Damascene, *In Dormitionem*, 4, 1, no. 8 (PG 96, 712); Theophanes, *Sermo in ss. Deiparam* (pp. 39–45 in Jugie's edition); Anastasius the Sinaite, *Contempl. in hexaem.*, bk. 7 (PG 89, 971–76); St. Augustine, *De Gen. ad litt.*, bk. 11, chap. 25, no. 32 (PL 34, 442); Pseudo-Bede (PL 93, 276a); St. Peter Damian, *Sermo in nat. Mar.* (PL 144, 753); Haymo, *In Apocal.* (PL 117, 968c); Honorius of Autun, *In Cant.* (PL 172, 425a); Richard of Saint-Victor, *Allegoriae in Vetus Testamentum* (PL 175, 639a); Hermann of Saint-Martin, *Tractatus de incarnatione Christi*, chap. 8 (PL 180, 28–31); Philip of Harveng, *De silentio clericorum*, chap. 26 (PL 203, 986d), etc.; also Fr. Poire, S.J., *La Triple Couronne de la Mère de Dieu* (1849), 2:96–103. With the Fathers, the question arises whether the New Eve is not more often the Church and Paradise our Lady (see Yves Congar, RSPT [1951], p. 625).

[13] St. Bernard, *De adventu Domini, sermo* 2, no. 4 (PL 183, 43a); Richard of Saint-Victor, *In Cantica*, chap. 39 (PL 196, 517); St. Amadeus of Lausanne, *De*

planted in the center of the earth.[14] Both are the Ark of the
Covenant,[15] Jacob's Ladder,[16] the Gate of Heaven,[17] the House
built on the mountaintop,[18] the fleece of Gideon,[19] the Tabernacle of the Highest,[20] the throne of Solomon, the impregnable
fortress. Both are the City of God, the mysterious City of
which the psalmist sang;[21] the valiant woman of the Book of

---

laudibus Virginis, hom. 1 and 8 (PL 211; see also the references to our Lady in
cols. 755–56); Adam of Perseigne, *In Annunt.*, s. 1.

[14] G. Reismyller, *Corona stellarum duodecim* (1652), pp. 544–51.

[15] Dechamps, *La Nouvelle Ève*, pp. 359–60.

[16] St. Andrew of Crete, *In Dormitionem sanctae Mariae, sermo* 3 (PG 97, 1105);
Akathistos Hymn (PG 92, 1337c); St. John Damascene, *In Dormitionem*, hom. 1
(PG 96, 714); St. Paschasius Radbertus; *Expositio in Psalmum* 44, 1, 1 (PL 120,
1009a); St. Laurence of Brindisi, *Sermo* 1 *in Assumptionem*, chap. 10 (*Opera
Omnia* [1928], 1:583), etc. See also the Roman Office for the Dedication of a
Church: "Vidit Jacob scalam, summitas ejus, caelos tangebat, et descendentes
angelos." When our Lady is compared with the top of the ladder, the symbol
gets mixed up with that of the gate of heaven, as in Rupert of Deutz's *De
divinis officiis*, bk. 3, chap. 18 (PL 170, 75–77); St. Anastasius of Antioch, *In
Annunt.*

[17] Rhabanus Maurus, *In Genesim*, bk. 3, chap. 14 (PL 107, 593d), etc.; see the
Lauds hymn to our Lady (by Venantius Fortunatus) in the Roman Office: "Tu
Regis alti janua / Et aula lucis fulgida"; St. Jerome, *In Ezech.*, bk. 13 (PL 25,
416–20); *Epist.* 48, no. 21 (PL 22, 510).

[18] St. Bonaventure, *In Assumptione B. M. V.*, *sermo* 1 (ed. Quaracchi, 9:687–
91); see also Is 2:2.

[19] Gloss on Judges 6:36–40; St. Bernard, *Super Missus est* (PL 183, 63).

[20] Origen, *In Exod.*, hom. 9, no. 3; *In Psalm.* 18, v. 6 (PG 12, 1243–44); St.
Andrew of Crete, *In Nativitatem Beatae Mariae, sermo* 4 (PG 97, 877d); *In
Dormitionem Sanctae Mariae, sermo* 3 (PG 97, 1090); Richard of Saint-Victor,
Allegoriae in Vetus Testamentum (PL 175, 661c); Garnier of Rochefort, *Sermo* 37
(PL 205, 807–8).

[21] Helinand of Froidmont, *Sermo* 19 (PL 212, 638–39), etc.; Poire, *Triple
Couronne*, 2:103–16; St. Laurence of Brindisi, *Super fundamenta ejus, sermones
sex*, in *Opera omnia* (1928), 1:333–80; Office of Our Lady; Ps 147, etc. Whatever our views on the celebrated *Life of the Most Holy Virgin* of Maria
d'Agreda, it must be agreed that its alternative title is very apt—*The Mystical
City of God*; see also Alain of Lille, *In Annuntiatione* (PL 210, 200–202); and,
on the Marian interpretation of Ps 86, see Passaglia, *De Ecclesia Christi*, pp.
435–39, 743–54.

Proverbs,[22] the Bride arrayed for her husband, the woman who is the foe of the serpent[23] and the great sign in heaven described in Revelation—the woman clothed with the sun and victorious over the Dragon.[24] Both are—after Christ—the dwelling place of wisdom,[25] and even wisdom herself;[26] both are "a new

[22] St. Augustine, *Sermo* 37 (PL 38, 221–35); St. Bede the Venerable, *De Muliere forti libellus* (PL 91, 1039–52); St. Bernard, *Super Missus est*, hom. 2, no. 5 (PL 183, 63b); Helinand of Froidmont, *Sermo* 20 (PL 212, 646–52); Adam of Perseigne, *In Assumpt.*, s. 5 (PL 211, 733–44).

[23] St. Methodius of Olympus, *Banquet*, bk. 8, chaps. 5–11 (PG 18, 145–57); St. Bruno of Segni, *Expositio in Genesim* (PL 164, 169d, concerning the Church).

[24] Berengard, *In Apoc.* (PL 17, 874–78); St. Andrew of Caesarea, *In Apoc.* (PG 106, 320): Arethea of Caesarea, *In Apoc.* (PG 106, 660–61); St. Bede the Venerable, *Explanatio Apocalypsis*, bk. 2 (PL 93, 165–66); Pseudo-Alcuin, *In Apoc.*: "Mulier amicta sole beata virgo Maria est, obumbrata altissimi virtute; in qua etiam genus, id est Ecclesia intelligitur, quae . . . mulier dicitur, quia novos quotidie populos parit, ex quibus generale Christi corpus conformetur" (PL 100, 1152d); Haymo, *In Apoc.*, bk. 3: "Ipsa autem beata Dei genetrix in hoc loco personam gerit Ecclesiae" (PL 117, 1081a); St. Bernard, *Sermo in dominica infra octavam Assumptionis*, no. 3 (PL 183, 430d); Rupert of Deutz, *In Apoc.*, bk. 4, chap. 12 (PL 169, 1043a); cf. Newman, *Mary*, pp. 61–68; Terrien, *La Mère de Dieu*, pt. 2, 2:59–84; R. M. de la Broise, "Mulier amicta sole: Essai exégétique", *Études* 21 (1897), pp. 300–306; A. Rivera, "Inimicitias ponam . . . ", *Verbum Domini* 21 (1941); Henri Rondet, S.J., in BSFEM (1949), p. 84, and in *Assomption de la T. S. Vierge* (1950), p. 171; J. J. Weber, *La Vierge Marie dans le Nouveau Testament* (1951), pp. 113–22.

[25] St. Bernard, *Sermo* 52 *de diversis* (PL 183, 674–76), etc.; Prov 9:1.

[26] Mass of the Immaculate Conception (Prov 8:22–31), and the Mass of Our Lady Queen of All Saints (Sir 24); St. Bernard, *Sermo* 52, no. 2 (PL 183, 674–75); Alain of Lille, *Sententiae* (PL 210, 262); Olier, as quoted by C. Flachaire in his *La Dévotion à la Vierge dans la littérature catholique au commencement du XVIIe siècle* (1916), p. 128; Helinand of Froidmont, *Sermo* 19 (PL 212, 638c–d). On the subject of the Church, see chapter 2, above. See also St. Anselm, *Homilia* 1, in which he applies Sir 24 to the humanity of the Word (PL 158, 585–95). In his *Institutions liturgiques*, Dom Guéranger criticizes "the remarkable audacity which led the revisers of the Harlay Missal to suppress all the Epistles which the Roman Church had drawn from the sapiential books for the Masses of Our Lady. . . a similar scandal had already occurred where the Breviary was concerned", and thus "One of the sources for the mystical interpretation of the Scriptures" was "blocked for a long time" (2d ed. [1880], 2:57).

world" and "a prodigious creation";[27] both rest in the shadow of Christ.[28]

There is in all this something much more than a case of parallelism or the alternating use of ambivalent symbols. As far as the Christian mind is concerned, Mary is the "ideal figure of the Church",[29] the "sacrament" of her,[30] and the "mirror in which the whole Church is reflected".[31] Everywhere the Church finds in her her type and model, her point of origin and perfection: "The form of our Mother the Church is according to the form of his Mother."[32] Our Lady speaks and acts in the name of the Church at every moment of her existence—"she shows forth in herself the figure of the holy Church"[33]—not, of course, in virtue of some decision that is an afterthought nor, obviously, because of an explicit intention on her part, but because she already carries the Church within her, so to speak, and contains her, in her wholeness, in her own person. She is "the whole of the Church", as M. Olier puts it, "the Church, both kingdom and priesthood, gathered into one single person".[34] All that is prophesied by the Old Testament concerning the Church receives a new application, as it were, in the person of our Lady, whose type the Church thus becomes: "How

[27] St. John Damascene, *In nativ. Mar.*, hom. 2 (PG 96, 684a–b).

[28] Denis the Carthusian, *In Cantica* (*Opera omnia* [1898], 7:329, 345); St. Gregory the Great, *Moralia in Job*, bk. 18, nos. 32–33 (PL 76, 55).

[29] Dillenschneider, *Le Mystère de la corédemption mariale* (1951), p. 79.

[30] Hymn *Mariae praeconio*, thirteenth cent. (*Analecta hymn.*, 54:391).

[31] Pierre Ganne, S.J., "La Vierge Marie dans la vie de l'Église", in *Dialogue sur la Vierge* (1950), p. 152; see also A. M. Henry et al., "La Saint Vierge figure de l'Église", in *Cahiers de la vie spirituelle* (1946); Ambrose Autpert, *In Apoc.*, 12: "Ipsa beata ac pia Virgo hoc loco personam gerit Ecclesiae, quae novos quotidie populos parit" (*Max. Bibl. Patr.* [Lyons], 13:530–31); Alain of Lille, *Elucidatio in Cantica*: "Virgo enim Maria similis est Ecclesiae Dei in pluribus" (PL 210, 60a); Rupert of Deutz, *De Spiritu Sancto*, bk. 1, chap. 8.

[32] Pseudo-Ildephonsus (PL 96, 269d).

[33] St. Ambrose, *In Luc.*, bk. 2, no. 7 (PL 15, 1555a); St. Augustine, *De symbolo ad cat.*, chap. 1 (PL 40, 661); *Sermo Denis* 25, no. 8 (p. 163 in Morin's edition); Pseudo-Augustine, *Sermo* 121, no. 5 (PL 39, 1989), etc.

[34] Laurentin, p. 111 (he is commenting on Pseudo-Bernard).

beautiful are those things which have been prophesied of Mary under the figure of the Church!" [35] And conversely, the things told us by the Gospels about our Lady are a prefiguring of the nature and destiny of the Church: "As with Mary, so also with the Church." [36] "The sacraments of the Church lie hidden" [37] in everything they say about her: "Thus the Virgin Mary, who was the best part of the old Church before Christ, merited being the Bride of God the Father in order to become also the pattern of the new Church, the Bride of the Son of God." [38] And this is equally true of either of the two fundamental aspects that we have distinguished in the Church earlier on in this book—that under which she appears as sanctifying and that under which she appears as sanctified.[39]

* * *

According to the first of these two aspects, our Lady is in all ways the image of the maternity of the Church: "The Church brings forth daily him whom the Virgin Mary brought

[35] St. Ambrose, *De institutione virginis*, chap. 14, no. 89 (PL 16, 326); Driedo, *De regula et dogmat. S. Scripturae* (Louvain, 1556), 1:121 (quoted by Terrien in *La Mère de Dieu*, pt. 2, 2:18): "Everything we find in the sacred books concerning the magnificence, splendor, and sanctity of the Church is justly appropriated to the glorious Virgin in all parts of the universe; for she is the most holy of all the members of the Catholic Church; she whom God our Lord has laden with as many graces as he has distributed among all the other members together. And that is why—in accordance with old custom—we sing in honor of our Lady those passages of Holy Scripture which, in their natural sense, should be interpreted with reference to the Church of Jesus Christ." See also the *Liber mozarabicus sacramentorum* and the text from it quoted below, p. 335, n. 112.

[36] Ivo of Chartres, *De nat. Domini* (PL 163, 570c).

[37] Ambrose Autpert, *Sermo de lectione evangelica* (PL 89, 1302b; cf. 1304d).

[38] Rupert of Deutz, *De Spiritu Sancto*, bk. 1, chap. 8.

[39] There is a critical bibliography concerning our Lady and the Church compiled by R. Laurentin in "Études mariales: Marie et l'Église, I", BSFEM 9 (1951): 1953. In the same volume there are studies by M. J. Nicolas, H. Holstein, A. Muller, G. Frenaud, and, especially, H. Barré, from which I have borrowed the quotation of several texts.

forth." [40] "The glorious Virgin Mary", wrote Honorius of Autun, "stands for the Church, who is also both virgin and mother. She is mother because every day she presents God with new sons in baptism, being made fruitful by the Holy Spirit. At the same time she is virgin because she does not allow herself to be in any way corrupted by the defilement of heresy, preserving inviolate the integrity of the faith. In the same way Mary was mother in bringing forth Jesus and virgin in remaining intact after bearing him." [41] "The one gave salvation to the peoples, while the other gives the peoples to their Savior. The one carried Life in her womb, while the other carries him in the wellspring of the Sacrament. What was once granted in the flesh to Mary is now granted spiritually to the Church; she conceives the Word in her unfaltering faith, bears him in a spirit freed from all corruption, and contains him in a soul overshadowed by the power of the Most High." [42] In fact, the likeness has a perfection even greater than that, for it lies not merely between the order of the flesh and that of the Spirit; before she conceived the Word of God in her flesh, our Lady conceived him in her spirit when she listened to the words of the angel: [43] "And she

---

[40] Berengard, *In Apoc.*, 12, 3–5; Pseudo-Augustine, *In Apoc.* (PL 100, 1152d), etc.

[41] *Sigillum beatae Maria* (PL 172, 499d).

[42] *Liber mozarabicus sacramentorum, Missa de nat. Domini*: "Illa salutem populis creavit, haec populos: illa utero vitam portavit, haec lavacro. . . . Quod praestitum est carnaliter sed singulariter tunc Mariae, nunc spiritaliter praestetur Ecclesiae; ut te fides indubitata concipiat, te mens de corruptione liberata parturiat, te semper anima virtute Altissimi obumbrata contineat" (col. 54 in Férotin's edition of 1912); Ivo of Chartres, *Sermo* 8: "Iste agnus sine macula et ruga virginem sibi sociavit, sicut ibi matrem virginem antea sanctificavit. Unde nativitas, qua temporaliter natus est Christus, non dissimilis est nativitati, a qua spiritualiter nascitur christianus. Sicut enim Christi mater virgo concepit, virgo peperit, virgo permansit, sic mater Ecclesia Christi sponsa, lavacro aquae in verbo christianos populos quotidie generat, ut virgo permaneat. In illa carnis integritas, in hac commendatur fidei puritas" (PL 162, 570b–c).

[43] Rodez Missal (1540), Sequence for the Assumption: "Benedicta tu fuisti / Quae per fidem concepisti / Redemptorem hominum!" (Misset and Weale, *Thesaurus hymnologicus supplementum* [1880], 2:291); Saragossa Missal (1485),

conceived, believing, him whom she bore believing." [44] Which is why, adds Honorius, "everything that is written of the Church may also be read as applying to Mary"—to which we may add that what is written of our Lady can also—as to essentials—be read as applying to the Church; a general principle to which we shall return very shortly.

As early as in the second century, in the famous letter that has been preserved for us by Eusebius, the Christians of Vienne and Lyons spoke of the Holy Church as "our virginal Mother",[45] with a clear though implicit allusion to our Lady. An inscription in the Baptistery of St. John Lateran says, similarly, that "at this spring the Church our Mother bears in her virginal womb the sons whom she has conceived under the breath of God." [46] Patristic preaching frequently celebrates "the mysteries of the virgin Church",[47] and St. Zeno of Verona gives the further definition that this mother who bears us without travail is still virgin after the birth.[48] In St. Ambrose the equation becomes explicit; like Christ's Mother, the Church is wed but virgin; she conceives us virginally by the

---

Sequence for the Assumption: "Ut jam nec in subcalcari / Possit robur infirmari / Virginalis fidei!" (ibid., 2:375).

[44] Pseudo-Ildephonsus, *In Assumptione*, 1, s. 7 (PL 96, 266c); see also St. Augustine, *Sermones* (PL 38, 1019 and 1074; 46, 937–38); *De sancta virginitate*, chap. 3 (PL 40, 398); St. Leo the Great, *Sermo* 21, chap. 1 (PL 54, 191b), etc.

[45] Eusebius, *Ecclesiastical History*, bk. 5, chap. 1, no. 45 (PL 20, 240).

[46] See also Tertullian, *De monogamia*, chap. 11 (PL 2, 943c); St. Paulinus of Nola, *Epist.* 32, no. 5 (PL 61, 332); St. Ambrose, *In Lucam*, bk. 2, chap. 57 (PL 15, 1573a); Rufinus, *In symbolum*, chap. 39 (PL 21, 376); St. Leo the Great, *Sermo* 24, chap. 3: "Omni homini renascenti aqua baptismatis instar est uteri virginalis" (PL 54, 206a), and *Sermo* 63, chap. 6 (356b–c).

[47] Gregory of Elvira, *Tractatus* 12 (p. 123 in the Batiffol-Wilmart edition); St. Epiphanius of Salamis, *Expositio fidei* (PG 42, 776a–b; 781c–d), etc. See also the 1516 *Missale Morinensis*: "Gaude, virgo mater Ecclesia!" (Misset and Weale, *Thesaurus*, 1:347).

[48] *Tract.* 4, no. 1 (PL 11, 290–91); *tract.* 30 and *tract.* 32 (cols. 476 and 477–78); *tract* 33: "Fontanum semper virginis Matris dulcem ad uterum convolate" (col. 479a); St. Pacianus, *De baptismo*, chap. 6 (PL 13, 1092–93).

Holy Spirit, and she bears us virginally without travail.[49] The theme becomes a frequent one in St. Augustine: "For the Church also is both mother and virgin"[50]—and in both he marvels at the same fertile virginity, the same virginal fertility.[51] In order to praise the perpetual virginity of the great "Mother of all the living",[52] who makes him "imitate the Mother of his Savior",[53] Augustine recalls, like others before him,[54] her ever-whole faith, her firm hope, and sincere charity.[55] He also

[49] *In Lucam*, bk. 2, chap. 7: "Bene desponsata, sed virgo, quia est Ecclesiae typus, quae est immaculata, sed nupta. Concepit nos virgo de Spiritu, parit nos virgo sine gemitu" (PL 15, 1555b); *De virginibus*, bk. 1, chap. 3, no. 12 (PL 16, 192a); cf. chap. 6, no. 31 (col. 197c); *De institutione virginis*, chap. 14, vv. 88–89 (PL 16, 322c–d; cf. 344a–b); also St. Bonaventure, *In festo omnium sanctorum, sermo* 2 (ed. Quaracchi, 9:603), etc.

[50] *De sancta virginitate*, chap. 2: "Maria corporaliter caput hujus corporis peperit, Ecclesia spiritualiter membra illius capitis parit" (PL 40, 397); chap. 6: "Oportebat enim caput nostrum propter insigne miraculum secundum carnem nasci de virgine, quo significaret membra sua de virgine Ecclesia secundum spiritum nascitura" (col. 399); *Sermo* 138, no. 9 (PL 38, 768); see also Fritz Hofmann, "Die Mariologie des hl. Augustinus im Lichte seiner Soteriologie", in *Festschrift für Karl Adam* (1952).

[51] *De sancta virginitate*, chap. 2 (PL 40, 397); St. Paschasius Radbertus, *In Ps.* 44 (PL 120, 1101c); Ivo of Chartres, *De nativ. Domini* (PL 162, 570b–c).

[52] *De nuptiis et concupiscentia*, bk. 2, chap. 4, no. 12: "Nam in hoc, quod appellata est vita materque viventium, magnum est Ecclesiae sacramentum" (PL 44, 443); *In Joannem*, tract. 120, no. 2 (PL 35, 1953); *In Ps.* 40, no. 10 (PL 36, 461).

[53] *Enchiridion*, chap. 34 (PL 40, 249); *De symbolo*, chap. 8 (p. 447 in Morin's edition); St. Paschasius Radbertus, *De partu virginis* (PL 120, 1384b); Hervé (PL 181, 1097b).

[54] Thus St. Hilary of Poitiers, *Ad Constantium* (PL 10, 558); Origen, *In Matt., series*, 33: "ecclesiasticam castitatem" (p. 62 in Klostermann's edition); *In Levit.*, hom. 12.5.

[55] *Sermo* 191, no. 2 (PL 38, 1010); *In Ps.* 147, no. 10: "Virginitas cordis, fides incorrupta" (PL 37, 1920); *Contra Julianum*, bk. 2, chap. 10, no. 37 (PL 44, 700); *In Joannem*, tract. 13, no. 12 (PL 35, 1499); *Sermo Denis* 25, no. 8 (p. 164 in Morin's edition), etc.; see also St. Bede the Venerable, *In Joannem* (PL 92, 675b); St. Peter Damian, *Liber qui dicitur Dominus vobiscum*, chap. 12: "sanctae Ecclesiae quae procul dubio virgo est, quia fidei integritatem inviolabiliter servat" (PL 145, 241c); Philip of Harveng, *De continentia clericorum*, chap. 59 (PL 203, 741d);

depicts this "holy virgin" and "spiritual mother" [56] who is "wholly like unto Mary" in her act of birth.[57] And in addition to this he underlines and delineates more clearly this likeness between the two Virgins by pointing out that, though the Church bears multitudes, she makes of all her children the members of one body and that similarly, just as our Lady became the mother of many through the birth of One, so also the Church, by bringing to birth many, becomes the "mother of unity".[58]

There are innumerable texts that, after this, repeat the teaching and develop it with the addition of new features—for example, this sermon on Easter, which has been attributed to both Eusebius of Gaul and St. Caesarius of Arles:

> Let the Church of Christ rejoice in this day—she who, in the likeness of blessed Mary, finds herself enriched by the operation of the Holy Spirit and becomes the Mother of a divine progeny! See how many brothers her virginal and fruitful womb gives you in this one night, to be added to all the rest! Let us, if you will, compare these two mothers, whose motherhood is to fortify our faith. . . . The Spirit overshadowed Mary,

---

Alain of Lille, *Elucidatio in Cantica*, 9 (he is talking about our Lady): "Terribilis ut castrorum acies ordinata, id est ita fide, spe et dilectione munita, ut nullis tentationibus inimici valeat penetrari" (PL 210, 95a).

[56] *Epist.* 34, no. 3 (PL 33, 132); *De sancta virginitate*, chap. 6 (PL 40, 399).

[57] *Sermo* 213, no. 7: "Mariae simillim" (PL 38, 1064); *De sancta virginitate*, chap. 12 (PL 40, 401); St. Caesarius of Arles, hom. 3 (PL 67, 1048b); St. Isidore of Seville, *Allegoriae*, 138: "Maria autem Ecclesiam significat, quae, cum sit desponsata Christo, virgo nos de Spiritu sancto concepit, virgo etiam parit" (PL 83, 117); St. Bede the Venerable, *In Lucam* (PL 92, 330d).

[58] *Sermo* 192, no. 2: "Populos [Ecclesia] parit, sed unius membra sunt, cujus est corpus et conjunx; et etiam in hoc similitudinem gerens illius virginis, quia et in multis mater est unitatis" (PL 38, 1013). Cf. the explanations given by Terrien, *La Mère de Dieu*, p. 10, n. 2, and by Friedrich, *Die Mariologie des hl. Augustinus* (Cologne, 1907), p. 255. See also the *Enchiridion*, chap. 34: "Imitans ejus [Christi] matrem, quotidie parit membra ejus, et virgo est" (PL 40, 249; cf. 397), and, among the sermons: PL 38, 1005, 1012, 1018, 1064.

and his blessing does the same to the Church at the baptismal fountain. Mary conceived her Son without sin, and the Church destroys all sin in those whom she regenerates. By Mary there was born he who was at the beginning; by the Church is reborn he who perished at the beginning. The first brought forth for many peoples, the second brings forth these peoples. The one gave us her Son, remaining a virgin; through this Son, who is her virgin Bridegroom, the other continually brings forth children.[59]

Or consider again the old preface in the Gelasian Sacramentary: "As Mary thrilled with joy at the birth of God, so the Church thrills with joy in the mystery of the birth of her children."[60] Or again, this sequence from a Rouen missal:

Gaude, Mater Ecclesia, filiorum adoptione fecundata,
Quos Spiritus almiflua cooperante Sancti parturisti gratia![61]

The Mozarabic liturgy loved to draw a parallel between the virginal childbearing of our Lady and the unfailing faith and fruitful chastity of the Church,[62] who without corruption conceives children of light and brings them to birth in joy.[63] It is very fond of describing both as "at once wedded and intact" and of praising at one and the same time her whom all generations have called blessed and her by whom all generations are

---

[59] *Hom.* 3 (PL 67, 1048b–c); cf. Morin, 1:921: "Caesario sine causa attributa."

[60] In Mohlberg, *Missale gothicum*, p. 88: "ut exultet, Ecclesia de congregatio populo, sicut Maria meruit gloriari de fructu" (p. 33 in Bannister's edition).

[61] Missal of 1499, *Feria sexta post Pascha* (Misset and Weale, *Thesaurus*, 1:178).

[62] *Missa in diem sanctae Mariae, Post pridie*: "Te totis visceribus deprecantes, ut qui Genetrici praestitisti ut mater esset et virgo, tribuas Ecclesiae tuae ut sit fide incorrupta et castitate fecunda" (*Liber mozarabicus sacramentorum*, ed. Férotin [1912], col. 53).

[63] *Missa in vigilia Paschae, Inlatio*: "In aeternam modo vitam filii lucis oriuntur, quos matutino partu per gratiam spiritalem hac nocte progenerat mater Ecclesia, sine corruptione concipiens, et cum gaudio pariens; exprimens in se formam Virginis genitricis, absque ullo humanae contagionis fecunda conspectu" (ibid., col. 250).

made blessed.[64] Lanfranc explains that "it is the same Word which the one conceives in the Holy Spirit and the other believes in that Holy Spirit."[65] "The body of the Church", writes Guitmond of Aversa, "is, like her Head, born of the Holy Spirit and a virgin Church, and forms itself into one new man from all the nations and all the different members."[66] Isaac of Stella says that our Lady and the Church "both give to God the Father a posterity; Mary, sinless, gave the body its Head; the Church, in the remission of all sins, gives the Head its body. Both are thus Mother of Christ, but neither of the two bears him wholly, without the other."[67] Guerricus says that Mary, offering her Child, is the Church delivering the Word of God.[68]

Rupert of Deutz—referring to Cana—explains that for the celebration of a spiritual marriage the Mother of Christ must always be present—that is, Mother Church.[69] The following hymn of the Church of Sens refers to our Lady, but the whole of Tradition authorizes us, even invites us, to apply it to the other Virgin Mother:

> Arca Novi Testamenti,
> in qua nostri sacramenti
> continetur veritas;
> Vas repletum vino mero,
> cella plena pane vero,
> sub quo latet Deitas.[70]

Among modern theologians Scheeben (following Cardinal Dechamps), Msgr. Laurent, and certain others were particularly

---

[64] See Vives, *Oracional Visigotico* (1946), p. 70.

[65] *De celanda confessione* (PL 150, 6266).

[66] *De corporis et sanguinis dominici veritate*, bk. 2 (PL 149, 1459).

[67] *Sermo* 61 (PL 194, 1683); cf. *Sermones* 27 and 45 (cols. 1778–79 and 1841).

[68] *Sermo* 3, no. 2 (PL 185, 72–73).

[69] *In Joannem*: "Illic tantummodo harum caelestium nuptiarum solemnitas celebratur, ubi est mater Jesu, id est ubi est mater Ecclesia" (PL 169, 285c), and "Mater Ecclesia, quae illas parturit donec Christus formetur in eis" (col. 285d).

[70] Misset and Weale, *Thesaurus*, 1:218.

aware of this first aspect—at any rate, Scheeben brings it into greater prominence in his published work, though not without certain restrictions and precisions that are debatable.[71] Writing in 1870, he noted "a fertile and striking analogy between the dogma of the Immaculate Conception, the absolute purity of the *Sedes Sapientiae*, and the dogma of the infallibility of the Holy See, the absolute purity of the *Cathedra Sapientiae*".[72] Between these two motherhoods he sees a relation so intimate and universal that the terms "correspondence" and "analogy" do not seem to him adequate to do it justice. It is, rather, he says, a "perichoresis";[73] indeed, he might have made use of the most expressive formula of Serlo of Savigny: "Mary is figured in the Church, and the Church is figured in Mary." [74]

There is, in fact, a constant exchange of attributes and mutual interpenetration between the two, which provides the basis for a certain "communication of idioms". Tradition offers us examples of this—St. Bede the Venerable, for example, drawing his inspiration from St. Augustine in his salutation of the Church under the title of *Dei Genetrix*[75]—or, correlatively, Gilbert Foliot calling Christ "Son of the Church":[76] for today, still, and indeed every day—*usque hodie*—the Church brings into the world him whom Mary bore long ago. Each time a man

---

[71] Scheeben did not work out his teaching on this subject fully. At the end of his treatise on our Lady, he refers us to his future treatise on the Church, which was in fact never written.

[72] *Periodische Blätter* (1870), pp. 508ff.; cf. *Dogmatik*, bk. 5, p. 629.

[73] Scheeben is, of course, much more than a mere academician; he is a real theologian—a fact made plain here yet once again. As was his way, he gets at the depth of the meaning of the doctrine, going beyond the academic schematization.

[74] *In nativitate B. M.* (p. 117 in Tissier's edition).

[75] *In Lucam*, 1, no. 2 (PL 92, 330); St. Augustine, *De sancta virginitate*, chap. 5: "Mater ejus est tota Ecclesia" (PL 40, 397); *Sermo Denis* 25 (ed. Morin, p. 163—the phrase is in the glossary on St. Luke). See also Serlo of Savigny, *Dei Genetrix*: "Est enim Ecclesia mater ejus, verbi praedicatione ipsum generando" (p. 115 in Tissier's edition).

[76] *In Cant.* (PL 202, 129a).

becomes a Christian Christ is born again,[77] and a new virgin birth gives him a new childhood.[78] The two motherhoods turn on the animation of the Holy Spirit by virtue of the handing on of a sacred life;[79] the Canticle of Tobias is in reality addressed to both these mothers alike when it says to Jerusalem:

> Thou shalt shine with a glorious light . . .
> And thou shalt rejoice in thy children
> Because they . . . shall be gathered together to the Lord.

Just as the maternal function of Mary is to give the God-Man to the world, so the maternal function of the Church, which culminates, as we have seen, in the celebration of the Eucharist, is to give us Christ, "the Head, Sacrifice, and Food of the members of his mystical body":

> As Mary bore the earthly Christ, so the Church bears the eucharistic Christ. As the whole life of Mary is centered upon the bringing up and protecting of Christ, so again the deep life and solicitude of the Church are centered on the Eucharist. As Mary gives the earthly Christ to the world . . . and from this gift are born the children of God, so also the eucharistic flesh and blood produced by the Church should form living children of God. As Mary offered up Christ together with him at the foot of the Cross, so the whole Church, at each Mass, offers the sacrifice with him. As Mary received at the foot of the Cross the whole treasury of grace in order to administer it spiritually, so the Church received it and in a certain sense receives it anew at each Mass for its ministerial administration and distribution. As Mary is in heaven, at her Son's side, a true suppliant, so also the Church makes effective prayer for her children. . . . Where subjective redemption is concerned, the Church signifies what Mary stood for in the accomplishing of objective redemption.[80]

[77] St. Bede the Venerable, *In Apoc.* (PL 93, 165–66); Berengard, *In Apoc.* (PL 17, 877a), etc.; see also Barré, pp. 74–75.

[78] St. Paschasius Radbertus, *In Matt.* (PL 120, 104c).

[79] Tob 13:17.

[80] Carl Feckes, "Maria als Vorbild, Mutter und Herz der Kirche", in *Das Mysterium des hl. Kirche*, 2d ed. (Paderborn, 1935), pp. 270–71.

The prerogatives of the one thus pass into the other and vice versa: "Insofar as there are in this world the faithful, the members of Christ, Mary contains them in some sense and carries them in her womb" [81]—just like the Church; if, in virtue of her submission to the Word, the Church thrusts aside all heresies, Mary has conquered them likewise by believing in the word of the Angel. [82]

In the midst of sorrow the Church brings forth with joy, and our Lady, who brought forth her Firstborn into the world without pain, now only bears Christ in our hearts in the martyrdom of her compassion. [83] So that the maternity of Mary with regard to Christ involves for her a spiritual maternity with regard to all Christians: "She bore One according to the flesh, but spiritually she bore the whole human race" [84]—while the spiritual maternity of the Church with regard to all includes that power over the Eucharist by the exercise of which the Church, we may say, carries out a sort of maternal function with regard to Christ himself. [85] Hence those comparisons, sometimes rather daring, between our Lady and the priest and those speculations on our Lady's priesthood, the history of which has been traced for us in such detail by the Abbé Laurentin. It was natural enough to consider, after the gift of life in baptism, and that of

[81] Salazar, In Prov., p. 684d.

[82] "Cunctas haereses sola interemisti in universo mundo."

[83] Rupert of Deutz (PL 169, 170), etc.; cf. F. M. Braun, La Mère des fidèles: Essai de théologie johannique (1935), pp. 100–105.

[84] St. Bonaventure, De nativitate B. V. M., sermo 1 (ed. Quaracchi, 9:706); see also De Purificatione B. V. M., sermo 1 (ibid., pp. 634–35); St. Epiphanius of Salamis, Haeres. 78, chap. 18 (PG 42, 728–29); St. Peter Chrysologus, Sermo 117, "Virginei fontis uterum caelestis Spiritus arcana luminis sui admixtione fecundet, ut quod origo limosae stirpis profuderat sub misera conditione terrenos, caelestes pariat et ad similitudinem sui perducat auctoris" (PL 52, 521b).

[85] Scheeben, Dogmatik, bk. 5, no. 1818. See also Dom Augustin Kerkvoorde's introduction to the French translation of Scheeben's Die Mysterien des Christentums, pp. 59–60; Olier, Traité des saints ordres, 3, chap. 2; St. John Eudes, Memorial, v. 17 (Oeuvres, 3:216).

the Word in the preaching that gives birth to faith,[86] the sacramental sentence that makes present the body of Christ, as did Mary's *fiat* at Nazareth. From the twelfth century onward we repeatedly come across the exclamation: "O truly to be venerated is the dignity of priests, for in their hands, as in the womb of the Virgin, Christ is incarnated anew!" [87] In the seventeenth century the French School in particular dwelt upon the wonderful "alliance", "conformity", and "liaison" that link the priest to the Mother of Christ. St. John Eudes was to see in him "the image of our Virgin Mother", since by him "Christ is formed, given to the faithful, and sacrificed to God." [88] But if we overparticularize the great traditional view, we run the risk of robbing it of its force and at the same time getting entangled in the details of a theology that is as yet in many ways tentative. It is thus best to restrict ourselves to the general reciprocity and interlacing of function between Mary and the Church—something witnessed to by the Gospel according to St. John when it shows us Christ on the Cross giving us his Mother—*discat ergo hic esse mysterium*[89]—and soon afterward his wounded side

[86] Helinand of Froidmont, *In Purif.*, chap. 1 (PL 212, 543b–c), etc.

[87] See Laurentin, p. 43. Scheeben also says—using a terminology that might perhaps be disputed—that it is given to the priesthood "to engender the God-Man in his sacramental existence". For the reciprocal role of our Lady with regard to the Eucharist, see Terrien, *La Mère de Dieu*, pp. 41–45; Pseudo-Bernard: "Tu protulisti frumentum electorum, quod est etiam angelorum cibus" (PL 184, 1075).

[88] *Oeuvres*, vol. 3, p. xxv; also Laurentin, "Marie et le sacerdoce", pp. 346–59.

[89] St. Ambrose, *In Luc.*, bk. 10, no. 134; bk. 6, no. 5 (PL 15, 1838a–b, 1700c); Origen, *In Joannem*, bk. 1, no. 6 (PL 14, 12); Gerhoh of Reichersberg, *Liber de gloria et honore Filii hominis*, chap. 10: "Omnes illa beata Mater stans juxta crucem parturivit, quando pro his liberandis et salvandis Unicum suum pati sciens, gladio compassionis pertranseunte ipsius animam cruciebatur ut pareret" (PL 194, 1105c); Rupert of Deutz, *In Joannem*, bk. 13 (PL 169, 789–90); St. Bernardino of Siena, *Opera* (1745), 1:257: "Mystice intelligimus in Johanne omnes animas electorum quorum per dilectionem Beata Virgo facta est mater"; Ubertino of Casale, *Arbor vitae crucifixae Jesu*, bk. 4, chap. 14: "In Quo exemplariter omnes electos fecit et constituit legitimos filios caritatis aeternae"; Bossuet, *Sermon pour la fête de la compassion*, in *Oeuvres oratoires* (1914), 2:483–86—he is talking about our Lady's two childbirths.

giving to the Church, together with the water of baptism, the blood of sacrifice.[90] Whatever the conscious intention of the Evangelist may have been, that is the way in which Christian meditation has taken the matter, by virtue of a profound twofold symbolism that is authorized by the analogy of faith:[91]

> At the moment when Mary appeared to have brought to perfect completion her life as Mother of Christ, she became, in reality, the Mother of all Christians. And then was realized for the second time the angel's greeting—"all generations shall call thee blessed." There will be no further mention of Mary in the Gospels, but the Acts of the Apostles are to show her to us as the great art of the West is to paint her later—reunited with the disciples at Jerusalem to await the outpouring of the Spirit. At the foot of the Cross Mary realized for the second time the blessing of the Gospel salutation; on the morning of Pentecost she was visited for the second time by the Holy Spirit. The Mother of Christ became the great maternal figure of the Mother Church.[92]

But by that very fact the initial significance of the figure is surpassed. Here it is Mary's maternity of grace with regard to men that is evoked; and that is something that can already be heard in the wondering words of St. Ambrose on the birth of Christ: "A virgin has given birth to the world's salvation, a

[90] See Oscar Cullmann, *Les Sacraments dans l'évangile johannique* (1951), chap. 14, à propos the episode of the lance-thrust (Jn 19:34): "He has not kept this feature in his Gospel for its own sake, but because it constitutes a particularly striking sign of the relation presented by the two sacraments with the death of Christ. We have met with this thought all through the Gospel" (p. 81). See also Gregory of Elvira, *Tract.* 9: "Caro, inquit, Christi, quod est Ecclesia, ex qua omnes credentes in Christo generati sumus" (p. 99 in the Batiffol-Wilmart edition).

[91] Hermann of Saint-Martin, *Tractatus de incarnatione Christi*, chap. 9 (PL 180, 34b–c); St. Hildegard, *Scivias*, bk. 2, vision 5 (PL 197, 507–9); St. Albert the Great, *Super Missus est*, q. 29, a. 3 (37:67, in Borgnet's edition), etc.

[92] Gertrud von le Fort, *Die Ewige Frau* (p. 149 in Boccongibod's French trans.); Guerricus, *In Assumpt.* (PL 185, 188c), etc.

virgin has brought forth the Life of all men!"[93] And St. Peter
Damian, at the extremity of a parallelism that draws upon the
classical formulae—*utraque nimirum mater*—expresses himself in
a clear-cut image we must be careful not to overmaterialize:
"Great and happy mother, from whose womb was drawn the
flesh of Christ and from whom the Church stems anew today in
water and blood!"[94] Thus is affirmed the superiority of Mary
over the Church, as Scheeben points out:

> In this precisely we see the superior and more fundamental
> character of Mary's maternity when compared with that of the
> Church, together with the organic union that connects the one
> and the other. The maternity of the Church acts on the basis
> and by the virtue of that of Mary, and that of Mary continues to
> act in and by that of the Church.[95]

If then in a sense Mary belongs to the Church, inasmuch
as it has been said—no doubt with some exaggeration—that
she is the Church's daughter, it is also true, and at an even
deeper level, that she can be called the Mother of the Church.[96]
Since she is the "daughter of Jerusalem, who is our mother
from on high",[97] she is mother of the Church we constitute.
She is "the mother of the new people",[98] "the earth in which
the Church was sown".[99] In one passage St. Augustine does,

[93] *Epist.* 63, no. 33 (PL 16, 1198b).

[94] *Sermo* 63 (PL 144, 861a–b).

[95] *Dogmatik*, bk. 5, no. 1819.

[96] Berengard, *In Apoc.*, on the subject of the *mulier amicta sole*: "Haec mulier
Ecclesiam designat. . . . Possumus mulierem in hoc loco et beatam Mariam
intelligere, eo quod ipsa mater sit Ecclesia, quia eum peperit qui Caput est
Ecclesiae, et filia sit Ecclesiae, quia maximum membrum est Ecclesia" (PL 17,
875–76); Cornelius a Lapide, *In Apoc.* (21:235, in the Vivès edition of 1866); Leo
XIII, encyclical *Adjut. Popul.* (September 5, 1895), etc.

[97] Bruno of Segni, *De laudibus B. M. V.* (PL 165, 1021b); *In Levit.* (PL 164,
421a); Philip of Harveng, *Moral. in Cant.* (PL 203, 571d); also *Distinctiones
monasticae*, 3:174: "Mater igitur Ecclesia Mariae, et Maria mater Ecclesiae"
(Pitra, *Spic. Solesm.*, 3:130–31).

[98] Bossuet, *Quatrième Sermon pour l'Annonciation* (*Oeuvres oratoires*, 2:6).

[99] St. Ephrem the Syrian, quoted in A. Muller, *Ecclesia-Maria*, p. 148.

admittedly, put the Church above her; but that is because he is thinking of the whole Mystical Body together with its Head.[100] Mary is a member of the Church,[101] but she is the first, principal, and highest member,[102] and this uniquely and in so eminent a sense that we may also say—and perhaps with even more reason—that the Church belongs to her. Christ, of course, is always the one and only Head of his Church. and it is not in any sense our Lady's work to guide it.[103] And it is also true (it is probably a good thing to recall this as a precaution against certain possible exaggerations) that she, like all the rest of us, is one of the vast family of the redeemed and that all her greatness comes to her—as greatness comes to all men—from "the redemption which is in Christ Jesus".[104] As far as she is concerned "there is no less a need of salvation and grace than there is in all the rest of us";[105] she is in need, like all the rest of us—"he hath filled the hungry with good things"—and she owes everything to the mercy of God: "And his mercy is . . . to them that fear him." Our Savior is her Savior too; "Christ", writes Arnold of Bonneval, "included his Mother herself among the others for whom he offered to the Father the sacrifice of his blood".[106] For she is wholly a daughter of our

---

[100] *Sermo Denis* 25, no. 7: "Sancta Maria, beata Maria, sed melior est Ecclesia quam virgo Maria. Quare? Quia Maria est portio Ecclesiae, sanctum membrum, excellens membrum, supereminens membrum, sed tamen totius corporis membrum. Si totius corporis, plus est profecto corpus quam membrum. Caput Dominus, et totus Christus caput et corpus" (p. 163 in Morin's edition). See also *De Div. quaest.* 83, q. 69, no. 10: "Christum universum, quod est Ecclesia."

[101] See Dom A. Stolz, O.S.B., *Scheeben et le mystère de l'Église*, p. 121; Haymo, *In Apoc.*, bk. 3: "Ecclesia, cujus et mater Domini membrum est" (PL 117, 1081a).

[102] Ambrose Autpert, Geoffrey of Saint-Victor, Serlo of Savigny, etc. Also St. Augustine, *Serm. ined.*, 25, no. 7 (PL 46, 938).

[103] This point is made by Fr. Dillenschneider in his *Le Mystère de la co-rédemption mariale*, p. 164.

[104] Rom 3:24.

[105] Bouyer, p. 22.

[106] *De laudibus Virginis* (PL 189, 1731c); Lk 1:47: "My spirit hath rejoiced in God my Savior."

race; her privilege was not come by "through a right older than the world", nor is it the effect of a decree that lies outside the dimension of the Redemption.[107] But although she is redeemed like ourselves, she is redeemed in a manner altogether different—"redeemed by a more singular salvation[108] and in a way more sublime".[109] "She was included, together with the whole race, in Adam's sentence; . . . she incurred his debt, as we do; but . . . for the sake of Him who was to redeem her and us upon the Cross, to her the debt was remitted by anticipation." [110] From the instant of her conception, God, by preserving her from sin and sin's slavery, forestalled her, as it were, by his grace and "prepared her so that his only Son might be born of her and, with him, the Church in her wholeness". For it was in her—that is, in her womb—"that the whole Church was betrothed to the Word and united to God by an eternal alliance";[111] *Partus Mariae, fructus Ecclesiae*.[112] When, in the mystery of the Incarnation, "the heavenly King celebrated the wedding of his Son, giving him the Holy Church as his companion, Mary's womb was the bridal bed for this royal Spouse." [113] It

[107] See Msgr. J. B. Malou, *L'Immaculée Conception de la B. V. Marie* (1857), 1:9–11.

[108] Pseudo-Augustine, *De Assumpt.*, 5 (PL 40, 1145).

[109] Pius IX, bull *Ineffabilis Deus*: "Omnes norunt quantopere solliciti fuerint sacrorum antistites palam publiceque profiteri, sanctissimam Dei genitricem Virginem Mariam, ob praevisa Christi Domini Redemptoris merita . . . , praeservatam omnino fuisse ad originis labe, et idcirco sublimiori modo redemptam." See also Suarez, *Opera* (Venice, 1746), 17:6–22; Louis Billot, S.J., introduction to *Marie Mère de grace: Étude doctrinale*, by R. M. de la Broise and J. V. Bainvel (1921), pp. v–ix, and *L'Ami du clergé* (June 15, 1939). Fr. Dillenschneider (*Le Mystère de la corédemption mariale*, p. 134) uses the expression "privileged preredemption".

[110] Newman, *Mary*, p. 55; see the *Akathistos Hymn*, v. 230 (in the ninth-century Latin translation): "Ave, princeps redemptae plasmationis!"

[111] Pseudo-Ildephonsus, *Sermo 2 de Assumptione B. M. V.* (PL 96, 252).

[112] Christmas Mass in the Mozarabic Rite, *Inlatio* (*Liber mozarabicus sacramentorum*, ed. Férotin [1912], col. 56; cf. *Post pridie*, col. 57); Pius X, encyclical *Ad diem illum* (February 2, 1904).

[113] St. Gregory the Great, *Hom. 38 in evangelia*, no. 3 (PL 76, 1283).

was a unique and privileged position for Mary—*singulariter eminet in corpore*[114]—and a number of writers express it aptly by means of an image that has long had classical status, but the usual symbolism of which they have modified. Guided, apparently, by the letter of the Song of Songs, which compares the neck of the Bride with the Tower of David, they see in the neck something more than an image of Christ the Mediator,[115] or the Church, or the Church's preachers and teachers, or even Scripture itself, which brings to us both doctrine and the indication of the divine will;[116] they compare Mary to the neck, which connects the Head to the other members of the body.[117] Others, following St. Bernard, depict her crowned with the sun and holding the moon under her feet—that is, as the living link between the two stars, the Church and Christ.[118]

This relationship of subordination should, however, be neither made merely external nor allowed to harden into something mechanical. We should, rather, look upon it as a sort of mystical participation or identity, which is the fruit of the "perichoresis" spoken of by Scheeben. This is what Clement of Alexandria was doing when he wrote: "There is only one Virgin Mother, and I am glad to call her the Church";[119] Pseudo-Methodius also took great delight in "making as one the Virgin

[114] Helinand of Froidmont, *In Assumptione*, s. 1 (PL 212, 406a).

[115] Gilbert of Hoyland, *In Cant.*, s. 26, no. 7 (PL 184, 138b).

[116] So also Gilbert of Hoyland (PL 184, 157a); St. Bruno of Segni (PL 164, 1240c); Gilbert Foliot (PL 202, 1198d); St. Bonaventure, *De donis Spir. sancti.*, col. 5, no. 1 (ed. Quaracchi, 5:479), etc. Also Alcuin, *In Cant.* (PL 100, 651c).

[117] Hermann of Saint-Martin (PL 180, 30a); Helinand of Froidmont (PL 206, 122c; 212, 640a, 667a–b), etc.; Amadeus of Lausanne (PL 188, 1311d); Philip of Harveng (PL 203, 260b).

[118] *Sermo de duodecim praerogativis B. M. V.*, *In dominica infra octavam Assumptionis*, no. 5 (PL 183, 431–32); Newman, *Mary*. Sequence in the Missal of the Teutonic Knights (1499): "Vellus interrorem et aream, Christum et Ecclesiam, Solem et lunam, limes est Maria" (Misset and Weale, *Thesaurus*, 2:585); Richard of Saint-Victor, *In Cant.* (PL 196, 517b–c); also, above, p. 333, n. 96.

[119] *Paedagogus*, bk. 1, chap. 6 (PG 8, 300); cf. Tertullian, *De carne Christi*, chap. 20 (PL 2, 787b).

and the Church",[120] and a similar intention was doubtless in the mind of St. Cyril of Alexandria when he sang the praises of "Mary the ever-virgin, the Holy Church".[121] St. Leo the Great, having shown "in the generation of Christ the origin of the Christian people",[122] goes on to show how the actual mystery of our being brought to birth by the Church is the conclusion of the historical birth of Christ through Mary—its continuation, as it were, under the influence of the same Spirit.[123] The Middle Ages thought likewise: "Mary and the Church, the one and manifold Mother".[124] But there are some who receive an intuition of this that is vital and direct and anterior to any thought-out theology and do this without any recourse to the guiding lines provided by the ancient texts. There was, for example, the young man of twenty-five who once followed the Office in Notre Dame with a mind still crammed with objections and a heart full of repulsion. One Christmas Eve, during the singing of the Magnificat, the whole faith of the Church burst in upon him. From then onward he came again and again to the old cathedral to take his theology course—his teacher being "the Holy Virgin herself, patient and majestic". With his face "pressed

[120] PG 18, 381a–b; see also Laurentin, pp. 22–23.

[121] *Hom. Div.*, 4, *in fine* (PG 77, 996); in the Latin translation: "Mariam semper virginem, sanctum videlicet [Dei] templum"; see also St. Epiphanus of Salamis, *Panar.*, 78, 19 (3:469–70, in Holl's edition).

[122] *Sermo* 26, chap. 2: "Generatio enim Christi, origo est populi christiani" (PL 54, 213b).

[123] *Sermo* 63, chap. 6: "Omnia igitur quae Dei Filius ad reconciliationem mundi et fecit et docuit, non in historia tantum praeteritarum actionum novimus, sed etiam in praesentium operum virtute sentimus. Ipse est qui de Spiritu sancto ex matre editus Virgini incontaminatam Ecclesiam suam eadem inspiratione fecundat, ut per baptismatis partum innumerabilis filiorum Dei multitudo gignatur" (PL 54, 356b–c). There is more than one parallel between the womb of our Lady and the baptismal font—see *Sermo* 20, chap. 5: "Originem quam sumpsit in utero virginis, posuit in fonte baptismatis; dedit aquae quod dedit matri; virtus enim Altissimi et obumbratio Spiritus sancti quae fecit ut Maria pareret Salvatorem, eadem facit ut regeneret unda credentem" (PL 54, 211c).

[124] Isaac of Stella, *In Assumptione beatae Mariae, sermo* 1 (PL 194, 1863a).

against the grille of the choir" he watched the Church living, and through that sight, which leaves the minds of so many in an apathetic inertia, he understood all. For, as he explained, "when Paul spoke to me, and Augustine made things clear to me, and Gregory broke bread for me with antiphon and response, the eyes of Mary above me were there to explain it all to me." The "maternal and reassuring majesty" that enveloped him was at one and the same time that of Mary and that of the Church, and indissolubly so. All he had to do was to find his support in that unique twofold Mother, without any further making of distinctions; the Mother "who brings together in silence in her heart and reunites in one single hearth all the lines of contradiction".[125]

* * *

It is not only in her sanctifying maternity that our Lady is like the Church. When we think of the Church under her second aspect—that is, as the community of the saints, the community of the sanctified—the analogy is no less profound.

If it is true that the Church, through the extension and the sufferings of temporal existence, reconstitutes bit by bit the first paradise, then our Lady is the first cell of the organism of that restored paradise, which is more glorious than the original one.[126] If it is true that the world was made for the Church, then the world was no less made for our Lady.[127] If it is true that the

[125] Paul Claudel, *L'Épée et le miroir*, pp. 198–99; cf. pp. 202–3; also the letter to André Gide of December 7, 1911: "The Church of the Councils, the wonderful Theotokos", and to André Suarez, December 3, 1911. Also the following: "For me, the Holy Virgin Mary is the same thing as the Holy Church, and I have never learned to distinguish the one from the other." See also *Paul Claudel interroge l'Apocalypse* (1952), p. 80.

[126] Rupert of Deutz, *In Cantica*, bk. 4 (PL 168, 895–97); Congar, p. 21; Louis Bouyer, *Vie monastique*, p. 57; Olier, *Grand' messe de paroisse*, p. 231: "The holy religion of Jesus Christ had its beginning in the secrecy of the heart of the most holy Virgin."

[127] Pseudo-Bernard: "Ut breviter concludam, de hac [Maria], ob hanc et propter hanc omnis Scriptura facta est, propter hanc totus mundus factus est, et haec gratia Dei plena est" (PL 184, 1069).

Church is founded on faith in her Lord, during the Passion, our Lady, through the strength of her faith, sustained and carried the whole edifice of the Church, like a frame built of wood that cannot decay; when she stood before the Cross, it was the whole Church who stood there in her;[128] on the evening of Good Friday, when the faith of all the others had been at least darkened, she alone constituted, through her ever-unshaken faith, the Church of Jesus;[129] and in the long Saturday vigil, when Christ slept in the sepulcher, the whole life of the Mystical Body withdrew, taking refuge in her as in its heart. If the Church is a Virgin Bride[130] of unswerving faithfulness, then Mary, "the most faithful soul in the Church, is that Bride par excellence".[131] If the Church, in her saints, deserves to be called—in the spiritual sense—the Mother of Christ (in accor-

---

[128] Nicholas of Biard, quoted by Barré, p. 84; see also Gen 6:14; Richard of Saint-Laurent: "In sola Virgine stetit Ecclesia . . ." (Barré, p. 63).

[129] Servasanctus of Faenza, *Mariale*; Jacopo de Voragine, quoted by Barré, p. 84; Odo of Ourscamp, *Quaestiones* (ed. Pitra, *Anal. noviss.*, 2:63); St. Bonaventure, *In III Sent.*, d. 3, q. 1, a. 2, q. 3 ad 3: "Ipsa fuit in qua fides Ecclesiae remanserat solida et inconcussa"; St. Albert the Great, *Mariale* (37:119 and 213, in Borgnet's edition); St. Thomas Aquinas, *In III Sent.*, d. 3, a. 2, q. 2 ad 1; Durandus of Mendes, *Rationale divinorum officiorum* (Naples edition, 1857), p. 145, etc. We know that it was this belief that was at the origin of Saturday's being a day dedicated to our Lady, a custom either abandoned or qualified as a consequence of the Protestant controversies; see Congar, "Incidence ecclésiologique d'un thème de dévotion mariale", MSR (1950), pp. 287–91.

[130] St. Jerome, *In Jer.*, 1, 44; *In Matt.*, 1, 15 (PL 26, 57a); *Adversus Jovinianum*, bk. 1, chap. 31 (PL 23, 254).

[131] *Vie intérieure de la Sainte Vierge: Ouvrage recueilli des écrits de M. Olier* (Rome, 1866), 1:241. It is known that this book, which was edited from the stylistic standpoint and furnished with a commentary by M. Faillon, only just escaped being placed on the Index on account of certain exaggerations; see C. Flachaire, *Dévotion à la Vierge*, p. 104; Henri Bremond, *Histoire littéraire du sentiment religieux*, 3:494–95; C. Dillenschneider, *Marie au service de notre rédemption* (1947), p. 190. According to Fr. Congar, these exaggerations were perhaps the result of "a certain monophysicist tendency". See also Franzelin, *De verbo incarnato*, p. 331. An abridged version, authorized by the Congregation of the Index, was published in 1875 by Icard; an edition that is at once more critical and less limited is much to be desired (cf. Laurentin, p. 362).

dance with what he himself said of her on one occasion),[132] then our Lady, in virtue of her perfect obedience to the will of the Father, is the first to deserve that title.[133] If the Church is united to the Holy Spirit to the extent of being figured, as he is, by the symbol of the dove, then our Lady shares that privilege with her.[134] She, too, is a "Sacrament of Jesus Christ",[135] and her heart is a "living Gospel".[136] Both are "faithful virgins" and both are "immaculate";[137] whether as Woman or as City, both are surrounded with angels:

> Sponsaeque ritu cingeris
> Mille angelorum millibus.[138]

[132] Pseudo-Chrysostom, *De Caeco et Zacchaeo*, 4 (PG 59, 605–6); Richard of Saint-Victor, *In Apoc.*, bk. 4 (PL 196, 799a–b); St. Gregory the Great, *In Evangelia*, bk. 1, hom. 3, no. 2: "Sciendum nobis est, quia qui Christi frater et soror est credendo, mater efficitur praedicando; quasi enim parit Dominum, quem cordi audientis infuderit; et mater ejus efficitur, si per ejus vocem amor Domini in proximi mente generatur" (PL 76, 1086d); Haymo, *In Apoc.*, bk 3: "Ipse dicit in evangelio: Si quis fecerit voluntatem quia dum quoslibet ad fidem adducit, mater est . . . , in illis autem qui accedunt ad baptismum et confitentur se in Christum credere, filius est" (PL 117, 1082a).

[133] St. Augustine, *De sancta virginitate*, chaps. 5–6 (PL 40, 399).

[134] St. Justus of Urgel, *In Cantica* (PL 67, 980a); St. Paschasius Radbertus, *Expositia in Matthaeum*, bk. 2, chap. 3 (PL 120, 172–74); *Expositio in Psalm.* 44, bk. 1: "Haec est igitur Ecclesia una et perfecta columba Dei, veraque catholica mater, et sponsa et virgo. Mater, quia generat; virgo, quia fide incorrupta perseverat. Nec enim fecunditate virginitas corrumpitur, nec virginitate fecunditas impeditur" (1001b–c); St. Bruno of Segni, *In Cant.* (PL 164, 1263c); Rupert of Deutz, *In Cantica* (PL 168, 912b); Adam of Perseigne, *Fragmenta mariana* (PL 211, 750–52; cf. 774–76); Scheeben, *Dogmatik*, bk. 5, no. 1612; St. Germanus of Constantinople, *In Praesentione Deiparae*, hom. 1: "Mary is the golden dove who shines under the reflection of the Spirit" (PG 98, 297); *Liber mozarabicus sacramentorum*, ed. Férotin, cols. 75–78.

[135] Olier, *Recueil de la Sainte Vierge*, pp. 134–38 (Flachaire, *Devotion à la Sainte Vierge*, p. 117).

[136] St. John Eudes, *Oeuvres*, 8:431.

[137] Origen, *In Cantica*, prol.: "immaculata Ecclesia" (p. 74 in Baehrens' edition); St. Ambrose, *De virginitate*, bk. 1, chap. 6, no. 31 (PL 16, 197); *In Lucam*, bk. 2, chap. 26 (PL 15, 1562a); St. Augustine, *Sermo* 191, no. 3: "ut sibi immaculato immaculatam consociaret Ecclesiam" (PL 38, 1010).

[138] Hymn for the Dedication of a Church.

"Garden Enclosed", "Sealed Fountain", "Hidden Treasure", "Tower of David",[139] "House of Gold", "Blessed Earth", "Sanctuary of the Paraclete",[140] Throne of God, Mystical Vine, Gate of the East, Venerable Treasure of the Whole World, Never-Extinguished Light, Crown of Virginity, Scepter of Orthodoxy,[141] "New Heaven and New Earth", "Dawn" heralding salvation[142]—the litanies of our Lady are often the litanies of the Church, and the litanies of the Church are often the litanies of our Lady.[143] Through the ages there has been a whole series of borrowings of each from other—or rather, it has more often been a case of possession in common.

> Ut aurora, Virgo, progrederis;
> Solem tenens, caelum efficeris. . . .
> Tu columba simplex et humilis,
> Tu columna fidei stabilis,
> Porta Sion inexpugnabilis. . . .[144]

In short, our Lady "comprises in an eminent degree all the graces and all the perfections" of the Church;[145] all the graces of

[139] From the Mozarabic *Liber ordinum*, ed. Férotin (1904).

[140] "Terra benedicta" (Rupert of Deutz, *In Cantica*, bk. 4 [PL 168, 899a–b]); "Maria templum Domini—Sacrarium Pacliti" (*Rythmus ad sanctam Mariam* [PL 158, 965]); "Gratissimum Dei templum, Spiritus sancti sacrarium, janua regni caelorum" (St. Anselm, 53rd prayer [PL 158, 959b–c]); and *Psalterium Dominae nostrae* (PL 158, 1042, 1045, 1050).

[141] St. Cyril of Alexandria, *Hom. div.*, 4 (PG 77, 992), etc.

[142] Song 6:9. For the interpretation in terms of the Church, see St. Gregory the Great, *Moralia in Job*, bk. 18, chap. 29, no. 46 (PL 76, 62a), etc. See also Garnerius, *Gregorianum*, bk. 12, chap. 3 (PL 193, 365–66).

[143] St. Bede the Venerable, *In Cant.*, bk. 4 (PL 91, 1148–50); Pseudo-Isidore, *In Cant.* (PL 83, 1124d); Thomas Gallus and Joannes Algrinus, *In Cant.*, bk. 7 (PL 206, 452–58); Adam of Perseigne, *Mariale, sermo* 5: "Hanc itaque Ecclesiam sanctorum, sive hortum conclusum, sive signatum fontem, sive thesaurum in agro absconditum, sive regnum caelorum, sive pudoris claustrum, sive mulierem fortem nomines" (PL 211, 741b); St. Jerome, *Epist.* 9, chap. 9 (PL 30, 132a–b).

[144] *Parnassus Marianus*, ed. Ragey, *Hymnarium quotidianum B. M. V.*, pp. 19 and 165.

[145] *Vie intérieure de la très sainte Vierge*, 2:75.

the saints flow into her, as all the rivers flow into the sea.[146] "It is from her, forever in place before his gaze, that the Eternal takes the measure of all things";[147] in her the whole Church is outlined,[148] and at the same time already completed; she is simultaneously the "seed" and the "pleroma" of it.[149] She is the perfect form of the Church:[150] "In plenitudine sanctorum detentio mea." Our Lady is "in the Church what the dawn is in the firmament",[151] and in her "youthful splendor" she is already that new universe which the Church is to be;[152] the long panorama of the People of God climbs slowly and painfully to the peak that our Lady occupies at a stroke. At the end of time the Church, "which is the beauty of the individual soul",[153] will be "all fair"; our Lady is all fair from the instant of her springing into existence, for her response to the divine forestalling is total and immediate, and her Beloved can say to her at once: "There is not a spot in thee." [154]

"How wonderful a sight, to see in this soul, alone and from its beginning, all that the Spirit of God will spread abroad one day over the whole Church!" [155] When Mary was presented in the Temple as a young child, her total self-offering to God was

[146] Conrad of Saxony, *Speculum B. M. V.*, lect. 3 (ed. Quaracchi, p. 27).

[147] *Paul Claudel interroge le Cantique des Cantiques*, p. 23.

[148] Gerhoh of Reichersberg, *Liber de gloria*, chap. 10: "post filium suum Ecclesiae sanctae nova inchoatio" (PL 194, 1105b).

[149] Semmelroth, p. 40; C. Journet, *Les Sept Paroles du Christ en croix*, p. 63: "In the Church, our Lady alone is the Church more than the whole Church herself."

[150] Pseudo-Ildephonsus, *De Assumptione, sermo* 3: "Ita ut in ea esset forma non solum virginum, sed etiam omnium Ecclesiarum Dei" (PL 96, 257a).

[151] Bérulle, *Vie de Jésus*, chap. 6.

[152] Charles Péguy, *Tapisserie de Notre-Dame*; see also the homily by Nicholas Cabasilas, ed. Jugie, *Patrologia orientalis*, vol. 19, col. 495.

[153] Gilbert of Hoyland, *In Cant.*, s. 47, no. 3 (PL 184, 247a).

[154] *Cant.*, 4, 7. See the office for the feast of the Immaculate Conception and the fourteenth-century canticle's phrase, "Tota pulchra es"; also Pius IX, bull *Ineffabilis Deus*: "Pulchritudine pulchriorem, venustate venustiorem, sanctiorem sanctitate"; George of Nicomedia (PG 100, 1437b).

[155] *Vie intérieure de la très sainte Vierge*, 1:3.

an offering of the Church too; and when the Word, becoming flesh in her womb, poured out all his treasures upon her, he was already wedding and endowing his Church in the person of his Mother.[156] Mary's *fiat* was an acceptance of the full realization of promises on her own account but also for all—collectively[157]—and that *fiat* was awaited as coming from all.[158] And when she exulted in her joy before Elizabeth, it was again in the name of the whole Church that she cried out prophetically: "My soul hath magnified the Lord." [159] When she placed her newborn child in the arms of old Simeon, the gesture was also the beginning of the Church's offering to the Father of the sacrifice for our sins. And when she looked on the Son in Nazareth and worshipped him in silence, she was anticipating the worship he was to receive from all the saints to come and thus held the place of the whole Church, which she represented before him.[160] When, as the "silent Mother of the silent Word",[161] she held blindly to the mysteries of God, watching all things and keeping them and pondering them in her heart, she prefigured that long train of memory and intense meditation

---

[156] Thomas Gallus, *In Cant.*, bk. 4: "In utero Virginis factae sunt nuptiae divinae et humanae naturae, sive Christi et Ecclesiae" (PL 206, 380a); Olier, *Mémoires autographes*, 2:338 (quoted in Flachaire, pp. 113, 115).

[157] Edmond Ortigues, S.M., "Note théologique sur la révélation et l'Écriture à propos du dogme de l'Assomption", *Cahiers universitaires catholiques* (December 1950), p. 140. See also Dom E. Pichery, *Le Coeur de Marie Mère du Dieu Sauveur* (1947), p. 116: "The whole Church-to-come was mystically present in her so as to say yes to the Lord who came to take her as his Bride."

[158] St. Thomas Aquinas, ST III, q. 30, a. 1; Ruysbroeck, *L'Ornement des noces spirituelles*, trans. Saint-Paul de Wisques, p. 36.

[159] St. Irenaeus, *Adversus haereses*, bk. 3, chap. 10, no. 2: "Propter quod et exultans Maria clamabat pro Ecclesia prophetans."

[160] Ambrose Autpert, *In Purif.*: "Non sit vile illud spectaculum . . . , in quo multa Ecclesiae sacramenta declarantur" (PL 89, 1294–1304); Guerricus, *In Purif.*, s. 3 (PL 185, 72d); *Vie intérieure de la très sainte Vierge*, 1:373, 2:20. See also Paul Claudel, *L'Épée et le miroir*, p. 25, on the subject of our Lady's feeding of her Child: "this tender lactescent Church".

[161] Santeuil, *Hymn for the Purification*; see also Rupert of Deutz, *In Cantica*, bk. 1: "Religiosum silentium Virginis . . . circa secretum Dei" (PL 168, 844a).

which is the very soul of the tradition of the Church.[162] And finally, on Calvary, through the three long hours, holding the Church's place at the foot of the Cross, she received from her Son the definitive teaching—a teaching not of words but of act, through which all words are illuminated.[163] In the name of the whole Church and on behalf of every generation of Christians, she contemplated that Cross which is the principle of all understanding, the living and painful synthesis, the "resolution of forces" in which all contradictions are taken up; "the concordance of the Scriptures, the frontier and junction of both the

[162] H. Paissac, O.P., "Théologie, science de Dieu", LV 1 (1951): 47: "Only the Church—like our Lady—can say what she keeps in her heart."

[163] Paul Claudel, *L'Épée et le miroir*, pp. 73–75. There is probably no better passage to quote in order to prove that great Marian literature is not extinct in our age: "On Calvary our mother Mary has something better to do than cry; she has to learn her catechism lesson in the name of the whole Church that has just been instituted in her person. 'O foolish and slow of heart', Christ was to say later to the disciples at Emmaus, 'to believe in all things that the prophets have spoken. Ought not Christ to have suffered these things and so to enter into his glory?' The teaching that he gave in minute detail and line by line, as it were, to those slow-witted men, he gave in a broad sweep and stripped of all veiling to the Valiant Woman. It is she who has for so long pondered all things in her heart who now says: 'Ecce adsum!' The fusion has taken place. The page that explains everything is turned, like that big illustrated page in the missal which priests know when they are preparing to read the Canon, for is it not said that 'at the head of the whole book it is written concerning me'? There, dazzling and painted in red, is the great page that separates the two Testaments. All that the Virgin learned at the lap of Anne, all the scrolls of Moses and the prophets that are gathered in her memory, all the generations since Adam whom she bears in her womb, the promise to Abraham and David, the wisdom of Solomon and Daniel, the incandescent desire of Elias and John the Baptist, and all those at prayer in limbo—all that has begun to breathe, to understand, to see, and to know in her heart under the life-bringing ray of grace. All is in motion, and there is reunion from all sides: 'Be ye lifted up, ye everlasting doors.' All the doors open at once, all oppositions vanish, all contradictions are resolved. She presses into the service of her seeing all the powers of looking that are possessed by the generations with her. Mary sees all; contemplates. She is face to face with that three hours' elevation."

Testaments".[164] And at the same time as she fulfilled in herself the prophecy of Simeon, "involved in the whole of the mystery" that was consummated by the death of Christ,[165] she also inaugurated that perpetual compassion of the Church, who will remain pierced with a sword until the end of time.[166] She began it; but she was also its limit and its surpassing.

All this the Church knows; and that is why, instinctively, she makes all things come by way of our Lady. She "flies to her protection", shelters under her mantle, and utters her own praise under the lead of Mary's.[167] In the total and incessant victory of the grace of Mary she sees the heralding of her own victory—a victory now already won at her own apex of purity. In the mystery of the Assumption—which marks, in our Lady, the complete and definitive triumph of the divine action upon her, right up to its consequences in the bodily order—she sees no mere wonderful exception to the common destiny, which

---

[164] St. Peter Damian, *Sermo* 48 (*De exalt. sanctae crucis*, hom. 2): "Crux igitur est concordia Scripturarum, et limes quidam atque confluvium veterum et novorum" (PL 144, 771b–c).

[165] Bossuet, *Sermon sur la compassion* (*Oeuvres oratoires*, 2:465).

[166] St. Bede the Venerable, *In Lucam*, bk. 1: "Et tuam ipsius animam pertransiet gladius. . . . Hoc est dolorem dominicae passionis ejus animam pertransisse . . . sed et usque hodie et usque ad consummationem saeculi praesentis Ecclesiae animam gladius dirissime tribulationis pertransire non cessat" (PL 92, 346–47); Ambrose Autpert (PL 89, 1301); Pseudo-Bede (PL 94, 340); Haymo (PL 118, 86d), etc.

[167] Cf. the *Sub tuum praesidium*, the oldest prayer to our Lady, discovered in 1938 on a third-century papyrus. See also the *Vie intérieure de la très sainte Vierge*, 2:329–32: "Like a living temple, Mary alone contains to an eminent degree all the praises that Jesus Christ can receive from his true worshippers. And above all that she turned herself into perfect praise. . . . [T]hat is why the Church, incapable of honoring Jesus Christ as he is worthy of being honored, does not offer to him any praise . . . without being united to the Most Holy Virgin. . . . Before all the canonical hours, after the quietly intoned *Pater*, which is the praise and prayer of Jesus Christ, the Church makes her children say the *Hail Mary*—conforming to the movement of the spirit of Christ himself, in order to teach them that the way of uniting oneself to Jesus and the praises he offers God is to unite oneself with his Most Holy Mother and thus partake in the perfect prayer that she herself offers him."

(therefore) can have nothing to do with us; rather, she hails in it the pledge and anticipation of her own triumph.[168]

> Haec assumpta nos assumat in caelis cum Filio,
> ut antiqua sic assumptis reddatur promissio! [169]

Thus the feast of the Assumption is a day of wonderful hope for all her members—"the first fruits of Mary"; *Praevia dux est Ecclesia*.[170] "Today the flamelike choirs of the angelic spirits see our human nature, which was drawn out of the dust of the earth; and they tremble." [171] Just as our Lady was the model of Christian hope on the day of the Annunciation, so on the day of her Assumption she became the guarantee of that hope. As the great sculptured portico at Rheims so ingeniously teaches us, her coronation in heaven is already the Coronation of the Church,[172] and the kiss she then gives our Lord is given in her by the Church:

---

[168] See Jean Daniélou, S.J., "Le Dogme de l'Assomption", *Études* (December 1950), pp. 301–2: "The mystery of the Assumption teaches us that in Mary the transfiguration of the cosmos, the principle of which lies in the Resurrection of Christ, has already begun to produce its effects. The Assumption is the dawn of the new creation whose first rays filter through into the darkness of this world. The divine energy is already at work."

[169] Sequence for the feast of the Assumption according to the use of Aix (ed. Misset and Weale, *Thesaurus*, p. 79). See also the thirteenth-century hymn: "Exaltatur hodie / hominis natura / in Maria virgine / Dei matre pura" (*Anal. Hymn.*, 14:199); Serlo of Savigny, *In Assumpt.* (p. 115 in Tissier's edition).

[170] Honorius of Autun, *Sigillum*, 4 (PL 172, 506a).

[171] A quotation from the early Armenian liturgy, given by M. Jugie in his *La Mort et l'Assomption de la sainte Vierge*, p. 309.

[172] Pseudo-Ildephonsus, *De Assumptione, sermo* 3: "gratia qua illustratur non tantum beata ipsa Virgo, verum et etiam per eam omnis Christi Ecclesia" (PL 96, 254c); and "Collata quippe est gratia et beatitudo in specie, ut diffunderetur in omne genus Ecclesiae; unde nec immerito beata et venerabilis hodie praecellit in genere totius corporis, quae ultra omnes fecundata est in specia prolis" (256c); *Vie intérieure de la très sainte Vierge*, 2:290–91. See also Joseph Duhr, S.J., "Le Dogme de l'Assomption de Marie" (supplement to the French translation of Msgr. Bartmann's *Lehrbuch der Dogmatik*, p. 20).

Christum, Os virgineum
Osculatur hodie,
Ut sit pax Ecclesiae! [173]

In her the whole Church henceforward takes part in the
"celestial liturgy of the eternal High Priest, and his permanent
intercession before the Father"; in her, decked out as she is with
the signs of compassion, the "royal priesthood" of the whole
People of God is brought to a glorious consummation.[174]

Since the Church of the Saints is, in the last analysis—insofar
as she is already one with the Kingdom of Heaven—nothing
other than the assembly of faithful souls,[175] the relation of our
Lady to the Church is thus, for each one of us, the relation of
our Lady to our own soul. Mary, the Church, and the soul—on
that threefold and unique theme Tradition gives us some of the
finest among its dogmatic compositions[176]—for example, the
sermon of Isaac of Stella, from which I quoted briefly earlier on.
In accordance with a usage that became the rule from then
onward, Isaac manages the union-through-distinction of the
three subjects of his composition through the coordinated use
of three adverbs; that which is said "universally" of the Church,
he says, is said of Mary "specially" and of the faithful soul
"singularly"—that is to say, individually.[177] These three adverbs

---

[173] Ratisbon Missal, *In Assumptione Beatae Mariae Virginis*, in *Sequentiae ex
missalibus . . . collectae*, ed. J. M. Neale (London, 1852), p. 20.

[174] H. Hirschmann, S.J., quoted by Laurentin, p. 738.

[175] Origen, *In Cantica*, bks. 1 and 3 (pp. 90 and 232 in Baehrens' edition); St.
Jerome, *Tract. de Psalm.* 86 (*Anecdota Maredsolana*, bk. 3, 2, p. 104); St. Augustine,
De sancta virginitate, chap. 24 (PL 40, 409); Haymo, *In Cantica*: "Sponsa Christi
Ecclesia est, quae ex singulis fidelium animabus constat"(PL 117, 335c). The
point should, of course, be considered within the framework of the precisions
already made in chapter 3, above.

[176] See *Paul Claudel interroge le Cantique des cantiques*, p. 12: "Who should this
woman be whom the great Forty-Fourth Psalm counsels to leave the house of
her father, if not the human soul, if not Mary, if not the Church?"

[177] "The same thing is said universally of the Church, specially of Mary and
singularly of the faithful soul. . . . In the universal sense the inheritance of the
Lord is the Church; in the special sense, it is Mary; in the singular [individual]

were not chosen haphazardly; as Fr. Barré has shown, we must, if we are to understand them, go right back to Ticonius, whose fourth "rule for interpretation of Scripture"—*de specie et genere* —was taken up by St. Augustine and commented upon by the whole Latin tradition. Scripture, said Ticonius, is in the habit of concealing the species under the genus—for example, the whole body under a member.[178] This principle may be applied to the relation of the Church to our Lady. In the Gospel texts where she is mentioned we may see, performed *in specie*, what was to be realized later on *in genere*, and the genus anticipatorily concentrated, so to speak, in the species.[179] There are, of course, only two terms involved here, which prevents us from forming a definition in terms of the threefold relation with which we are at present concerned. And in addition, there is not exactly a "hierarchy" between the "genus" and the "species", but a simple relation analogous to that of the part to the whole, so that in the inverse sense we apply to the individual soul *specialiter* what is said of the Church *generaliter*. Hence the need to introduce a third term, which will allow us to give our Lady her proper place of preeminence—without, however, in any way straining the bond of reciprocal inclusion witnessed to by tradition. *Specialis* or *specialiter* was thus reserved for our Lady, while the individual faithful soul was allotted the adjective *singularis* or the adverb *singulariter*. This new usage was never wholly standardized, for the transfer it demanded was a break with a custom of long standing; and it left room for many

sense, it is each faithful soul" (PL 194, 1865). The sermon of Isaac of Stella gives cause for regret that the commentary on the Song of Songs (which, according to the *Histoire littéraire de la France*, is also by him) has not been published. See also Haymo, *In Apoc.*, bk. 3 (PL 117, 1080); St. Peter Damian, *In Assumptione*; Odo of Cluny, *In Assumptione*; Philip of Harveng, *Moralitates in Cantica* (PL 203).

[178] Ticonius, *Regulae* (PL 18, 33–46); St. Augustine, *De doctrina christiana*, bk. 3, chap. 34, nos. 47–49 (PL 34, 83–86); St. Bede the Venerable, *In Apoc.*, preface (PL 93, 131–32), etc.; see also Barré, pp. 114–15 and 118–24.

[179] St. Paschasius Radbertus, *In Matt.*, bk. 2 (PL 120, 103d, 104c–d, 106c).

variants. It was nonetheless in accordance with the logic of language and, in particular, provided a happily chosen and simple form for the expression of the faith on this point.

There would thus seem to be a fundamental difference between *specialiter* and *singulariter* when these two words are used in opposition one to another, as in the example from Isaac of Stella. In this case *singulariter* does not specify any being in particular or denote any particular excellence; it may be set quite straightforwardly against *pluraliter*[180] and applied in succession to any number of examples. It is applicable to every faithful soul: "What the prayer of all is to the Church, his own individual prayer can be to any faithful soul whatever."[181] *Specialiter* is, on the contrary, unique, and it should be translated on the lines of "out of the ordinary, par excellence, preeminently, incomparably". The nuance was sharply realized by St. Paschasius Radbertus when he explained in the commentary on the Forty-Fourth Psalm, which he wrote for dedicated virgins, that the titles "virgin" and "spouse", which are given by Scripture in general to the whole Church—that is to say, to all Christian souls—are proper to them in a special way.[182] The same holds good, of course, to an even greater extent, in the case of our Lady, where *specialis* corresponds exactly to *singularis et unica*, and *specialiter* to *singularis et superexcellenter*.[183] For example, if the heavenly Bridegroom celebrates in the womb of his Mother his wedding with the whole of human nature, our Lady, nonetheless for that, rejoices in a "special glory"[184] and

[180] St. Bruno of Segni, *In Cant.* (PL 164, 1238c).

[181] Gilbert Foliot, *In Cant.* (PL 202, 1268a; see also col. 1172a): "Singulis et universis"—that is, to all and to each.

[182] *Expositio in Ps.* 44 (PL 120, 996b, 1001a and d, 1005a, 1053a).

[183] Rupert of Deutz, *In Cant.* (PL 168, 941d); Raoul Ardent, *Hom.* 30, *In Assumptione* (PL 155, 1423a and c, 1425a); cf. St. Peter Damian's phrase "proprium et singulare" (PL 144, 747b).

[184] Sequence from the *Missale Trecensis* of 1497: "Laudes Christo decantamus / Matris ejus qui gaudemus / Specialis gloria" (ed. Misset and Weale, *Thesaurus*, 2:337).

"special power"[185] because she is and will be the "special bride",[186] the object of a "special dilection".[187] She is "specially united to the Holy Spirit",[188] and from this "special privilege" she, and she alone, draws a "special excellence".[189]

Here we are dealing with an expression of an idea the same as Olier's. With the aim of pointing toward the unique perfection of our Lady, he makes her say, in a lyrical passage where he achieves the quality of real poetry: "In my Spouse I and I alone have gone about the great heavens that are to be the reward and dwelling place of the elect."[190] In the same way it may be said that each holy soul is the city of God but that the description of this city applies to our Lady *specialiter*.[191] *Ave, Virgo specialis!* sing the medieval sequences, "our special glory, the special flower of women in the court of heaven".[192] And an Anselmian prayer says: "Special and incomparable virgin";[193] or again, an anonymous eleventh-century poem, praising our Lady in terms of Wisdom (or, if you prefer, Wisdom in terms of our Lady), says: "Unique Queen, special virgin".[194] In the twelfth century Adam of Saint-Victor wrote:

[185] St. Peter Damian, *Sermo* 40, *In Assumptione* (PL 144, 732c).

[186] Denis the Carthusian, *In Lucam*, commenting on the words "Dixit autem Maria".

[187] Godefroy, *Hom.* 31, *In Annunt.*, 5 (PL 174, 768a); *Hom.* 66, *In Assumptione*, 3 (972a).

[188] St. Peter Damian, *Sermo* 40, *In Assumptione* (PL 144, 719b); and "Illorum verborum enodanda proprietas, quae Virgini Matri sunt specialiter dedicata" (719a).

[189] Peter Cellensis, *Sermo* 6, *in Adventu* (PL 202, 649d); Philip of Harveng, *In Cant.* (PL 203, 355b).

[190] Olier, *Recueil de la Sainte Vierge*, p. 119 (quoted in Flachaire, p. 128).

[191] Joannes Algrinus, *In Cantica*: "Haec ergo descriptio urbis beatae Virgini specialiter convenit" (PL 206, 458c); Garnier of Rochefort, *Sermo* 40, *De arca spirituali*: "specialis et singularis arca" (PL 205, 828a); *Sermo* 37 (808a): "Specifice Virgo Maria".

[192] Ed. Misset and Weale, *Thesaurus*, 1:351.

[193] *Oratio* 53 (PL 158, 959b).

[194] Ed. Mlle M. T. d'Alverny, "La Sagesse et ses sept filles: Recherches sur les allégories de la philosophie et des arts libéraux du IXe au XIIe siècle", in *Mélanges Félix Grat* (1946), 1:275.

Haec est sponsa spiritalis,
Vero sponsa specialis.[195]

The relation of the adverb *universaliter* to the two others has, however, a certain element of ambiguity in it. In a sense it covers both, since universality includes all instances, and our Lady is as much a member of the Church as each one of us is; but in another sense it is excluded from the "special" case, the unique case, the genuine universal concrete, which includes to an eminent degree and in a pure state the sum of perfection of all the other members: "Ecclesiae totius portio maxima, portio optima, portio praecipua, portio electissima." [196] For Mary may be said to be "the universal creature";[197] God has placed in her "the fullness of all good" [198] and has filled her "to an eminent degree with the substance of which the Church is formed"; he has conferred on her "in wonderful preeminence all the majestic qualities" with which he endows "his Bride the Holy Church".[199] His word is born in each one of the faithful,[200] as in the Church as a whole; but this is in the likeness of his birth in the soul of our Lady, and in addition, if faith is to bear its fruit, there must be in each of us the soul of our Lady, who magnified the Lord, and the Spirit of our Lady, who rejoiced in God.[201] The three figurative senses of Scripture—allegory, which refers to the Church, tropology, which concerns the

[195] Sequence for the Epiphany, quoted in Léon Gautier, *Oeuvres poétiques d'Adam de Saint-Victor: Texte critique*, 2d ed. (1881), p. 23.

[196] Rupert of Deutz, *In Apoc.*, bk. 7, chap. 12 (PL 169, 1043a); Gerhoh of Reichersberg, *Liber de Gloria* (PL 194, 1105d).

[197] Olier, *Traité des saints ordres*, pt. 3, chap. 6.

[198] Leo XIII, encyclical *Supremi apostolatus* (September 1, 1883): God has placed in Mary "totius beni plenitudinem".

[199] Olier, miscellaneous ms., pp. 107 and 130, in Laurentin, p. 371.

[200] Origen, *In Cant.*, hom. 2: "Et in te, si dignus fueris, nascitur sermo Dei" (Baehrens, p. 51).

[201] St. Ambrose, *In Lucam*, bk. 2, chap. 26: "Sit in singulis Mariae anima, ut magnificet Dominum; sit in singulis spiritus Mariae, et exsultet in Deo" (PL 15, 1561d).

soul, and anagogy, which looks above—all converge at a peak
that soars above them all in order to describe this unique marvel.[202] If it is true that God gathered together all the excellence
scattered throughout the universe to put into his masterpiece,
man, the same holds true in the case of our Lady and all the
excellence in the spiritual universe, which is the Church.[203] If
the Church is the Temple of God, Mary is the Sanctuary of
that Temple;[204] if the Church is that sanctuary, Mary is within
it, as the Ark was.[205] And if the Church herself be compared to
the Ark, then our Lady is the Propitiatory, more precious than
all else, which covers it.[206] If the Church is paradise, our Lady
is the spring from which flows the river that waters it;[207] the
river that makes glad the City of God,[208] the cedar on the top

---

[202] St. Bonaventure, *De nativitate B. V. M.*, *sermo* 5, on the subject of the
symbol of the Ark (Rev 11:19) (ed. Quaracchi, 9:715).

[203] St. Laurence of Brindisi, *Super fundamenta ejus*, *sermo* 4, chap. 1: "Sicut
enim Deus totius majoris mundi nobilitatem collegisse visus est et posuisse in
homine, ita totius Ecclesiae et militantis in terra et triumphantis in caelo
nobilitatem collegit in Virgine."

[204] With the Greek homilists, "if she is compared to the temple, she is less
likely to be called *hieron*—the outer temple—than *naos*, the sanctuary reserved
for the priests" (Laurentin, p. 77; see also pp. 57 and 78).

[205] St. Andrew of Crete, *In Dormitionem*, *sermo* 2 (PG 97, 1101); St. Paschasius
Radbertus, *Sermo in Assumptione*: "Apertum est templum Dei in caelo, et arca
testamenti ejus visa est. Quae profecto arca non illa Moysi fabricata, sed beata
Virgo Maria est, quae hinc jam transposita erat. . . . Quia in caelo visa est,
monstratur species in genere, sicuti et genus per speciem declaratur. . . . In
templo Dei visa est, scilicet in Ecclesia Dei; Ecclesia vero in ejus virginitatis
fructu penitus Domini dedicatur; ac per hoc . . . in templo ejus non immerito
visa est, quia Ecclesia et ipsa virgo est" (PL 96, 250a): "Pulchrior [Maria] quam
luna, quia in ejus specie genus omnium Ecclesiarum resplendet" (241–42);
Honorius of Autun, *Sigillum Beatae Mariae* (PL 174, 498a–499c); Garnier of
Rochefort, *Sermo* 32: "Ista enim arca in templo Domini, id est in honore
Ecclesiae Dei posita est" (PL 205, 776c); Rev 11:19.

[206] Philip the Chancellor, *In Annunt.*, 3 (ms.; given in Barré, p. 135, n.
276).

[207] Hesychius, *De Deiparae laudibus*; St. Modestus of Jerusalem, *In dormit. B.
M.*, 6; cf. St. Peter Damian, *Sermo* 11 (PL 144, 558d), etc.

[208] Ps 45:4; Quirinus of Salazar, *In Prov.* (1619), p. 671. Cf. Song 4:15.

of Libanus, the rose in the midst of Jericho. She is like the
royal quarter of Sion, the Tower of David, which dominated
the whole city;[209] "Thou art the glory of Jerusalem." [210]

* * *

This way of looking at the matter involved a principle of exegesis that was not only fruitful but also, from the viewpoint of
faith, perfectly objective. And this is the principle that—more
or less consciously and completely realized (to say nothing of
more or less happily!)—is the inspiration of the many mario-
logical commentaries on the Song of Song.

Exegetes are still discussing the antecedents of this enigmatic
little composition and its original meaning. We may note that
those who will not admit any "mystical" interpretation do not
merely strike at "the most sacred fibers of the heart and the
deepest theological roots of our faith";[211] their naturalist exegesis, even when it does not stop short at the incredibly plati-
tudinous, is no more able than any other to avoid all use of
allegory.[212] And it is hard to know what to say of an example
like that of Luther, when he sets aside the whole previous
exegetical tradition as "untimely and exaggerated", presupposing "an inconceivable ignorance and blindness", and "incapable
of bearing any fruit" and substitutes the "simple and natural"
idea of a passionate eulogy of the wise government of Solomon![213] Interpretations of this kind, and many others whose

[209] Song 4:4; Rupert of Deutz, *In Isaiam*, bk. 2, chap. 31; Joannes Algrinus, *In Cant.* (PL 206, 415c).

[210] Judith 15:10; see also Honorius of Autun, *Sigillum B. M.* ("Rose of Jericho"); Absalom, *In Assumptione, sermo* 4 ("Tree of Paradise").

[211] *Paul Claudel interroge le Cantique des cantiques*, p. 13.

[212] P. Vulliaud, *Le Cantique des cantiques d'après la tradition juive*, pp. 19–29; A. Feuillet, *Le Cantique des cantiques: Étude de théologie biblique*, in the series Lectio divina (1953), p. 248.

[213] *In Cantica canticorum brevis enarratio* (1538; in *Opera* [Jena, 1583], vol. 4, fols. 268–90). The *flos campi* and the *lilium convallium*, for example, become the upper and lower classes of magistrates (fol. 274 verso). In his more reasonable moments, Luther comes closer to the usual interpretation: "Est enim totus

more modern and more scientific nature still clothe a similar arbitrariness, are really not worth forsaking the traditional paths for.

In any case, one thing is certain to begin with (and everything else follows logically from it throughout the Christian era): the Song of Songs was admitted to and retained in the Jewish canon of the Scriptures because the Jews saw it as a symbolic expression of the love between Israel and Israel's God —in accordance with a scriptural theme that goes back to the prophet Hosea,[214] is to be found in the books of Isaiah, Jeremiah, and Ezekiel,[215] and is worked out in the Forty-Fourth Psalm:[216]

> And the bridegroom shall rejoice over the bride
> And thy God shall rejoice over thee.[217]

It must also be pointed out that by driving us to withdraw the ascription of this poem to Solomon and view it instead as a composition dating from after the Exile, the critical work done on the Song of Songs has made more plausible—from one aspect at least—the traditional belief that saw in it a sacred

---

liber, quasi colloquium inter Deum et populum suum, seu inter conscientiam et Verbum" (fol. 275).

[214] Hos 2.

[215] Jer 2:2, 31:17–22; Is 51:17–22, 52:1–12, 54:4–8, 61:10–11, 62:4–5; Ezek 16, 17, 34, etc.

[216] A. Robert, *Le Cantique des cantiques* (*Bible de Jerusalem* edition, 1951), introduction, pp. 8 and 15: "The Jews have always taken the Song of Songs in an allegorical sense. The theme that it suggests to them from the very start, and which they are to maintain unchangingly, is that of the love of Yahweh for the Chosen People, and his union with the people in a mystical marriage. . . . The author of this book is closely dependent on the wonderful prophetic tradition stemming from Hosea." A. Feuillet, "Le Cantique des cantiques et la tradition biblique", NRT (1952), p. 732: "This love poem is bound in every strand to the prophetic literature; from the theological standpoint, to those passages that deal with Yahweh's marriage with Israel; from the psychological and historical standpoints, to the prophetic writings that are contemporaneous with the Exile or the early days of the Return."

[217] Is 62:5; and 54:5: "For he that made thee shall rule over thee."

poem from the very beginning. Coming after the allegories of the prophets, which are in some cases both extremely bold and developed to a high degree, the allegory of the Song is not quite so startling. It is, simply, taken farther than those allegories on which it is modeled and perhaps leads us into a deeper penetration into the plan of God. Considerations of this nature made the Rabbi Akiba say: "All the books of Scripture are holy, but the Song of Songs is holy among the holy!" [218] Later, the author of the Zohar was to write that it gives us "a compendium of all the Scriptures", and Rabbi Akiba, again, goes so far in his enthusiasm as to say that the whole world is less precious than the day when Israel received the Song from God.

But, in the second place, it is no less certain that, within the framework of the history of salvation, the Church, after the Incarnation of the Word, carried on the role of Israel—hence the christological and ecclesial character of the first Christian commentaries on the Song. They are not—as Renan so superficially put it—the offspring of an "embarrassment", from which an attempt was made to escape "by means of pious subterfuge".[219] At the beginning of the third century St. Hippolytus provided what was to be their unchanged foundation

---

[218] In the twelfth century, Ibn Ezra was to describe it as "This majestic book, wholly worthy of love" (cf. Song 5:16). See also Louis-François d'Argentan, *Conférences théologiques et spirituelles sur les grandeurs de la très sainte Vierge Marie la Mère de Dieu* (Rouen, 1680), vol. 2, 3d conference, no. 2 (pp. 336–37): "The Church would never have reckoned this Canticle among the sacred Scriptures if it had been a thing on the natural level alone; and even if it be true that (as some have thought) he [Solomon] wrote this book at the end of his life, when he was wholly depraved by his love of women, and that in it he talks like a man out of his mind and wholly intoxicated with the passion of a blind love—even if this be true, at least it cannot be doubted that the Holy Spirit, who has so often caused wholly divine truths to issue from the mouths of the most scoundrelly (as with the false prophet Balaam, in the Book of Numbers, and Caiaphas, in the Gospel), dictated all the words with which he composed this marvelous Canticle, and that he concealed within it a wholly spiritual and divine sense."

[219] *Le Cantique des cantiques*, 2d ed. (1861), pp. 105, 125, 146. Similarly, E. de Faye, *Origène* (1928), 3:145.

through all the centuries. His work appears to have been composed especially with a view to a Jewish public, in order to lead them to the Gospel;[220] and without having to make any of the "despairing efforts" conjured up by the imagination of Renan, he uses a new interpretation—which is in no way improvised but, on the contrary, presupposes and continues that current in the synagogues—to illustrate the teaching of St. Paul and St. John concerning the union of Christ and his Church.[221] Now this was something very much more than an ingenious illustration or even a "particularly apt application";[222] all the more, therefore, was it *not* a violence done to the Jewish origin of the poem—as if the Jewish race, rejecting all mystical symbolism in the very name of its faith, had wished to preclude forever the possibility of "all reciprocity between heaven and earth".[223] As far as its relation with the tradition of Israel went, it was effected by a transposition not only legitimate but necessary and implying a real continuity; and in virtue of that very fact it was also a penetration to a greater depth. It was the discovery of the true sense at its deepest—the sense willed by the Holy Spirit. To use the old terminology of the Fathers (in a sense long accepted by all but no longer that of current usage), it was the necessary

[220] L. Mariès, *Hippolyte de Rome sur les bénédictions d'Isaac, de Jacob et de Moïse: Notes sur la tradition manuscrite, texte grec, versions arménienne et géorgienne* (1935). See also St. Methodius of Olympus, *Banquet*, bk. 7, chap. 7 (PG 18, 133); St. Ambrose, passim; St. Epiphanius of Salamis, *Expositio fidei* (PG 42, 776–85, 809, 821); St. Augustine, *Sermo* 46, no. 35 (PL 38, 290); *Sermo* 138, no. 9 (PL 38, 768); *Speculum* (PL 34, 925); St. Jerome, *Epist.* 53 and *Epist.* 107 (PL 22, 547 and 876).

[221] Eph 5:25–33: 1 Cor 6:16–17; 2 Cor 11:2; Rev 19:7, 21:2; Jn 3:18–29. Cf. Bossuet, *Préface sur le Cantique des cantiques*: "This figure is to be found in all the sacred books, in which nothing is come across more frequently than the eternal alliance of God with the Church, and that most ardent love and inviolable fidelity which are its accompaniment, all represented under the image of a husband and wife" (*Oeuvres*, ed. Lachat, 1:610).

[222] Jouon, no. 21, p. 19; no. 15, p. 16.

[223] See Renan, *Le Cantique des cantiques*, 2d ed. (1861), p. 121. For the Jewish origins of the image of the Spouse, see "Joachim Jeremias" in G. Kittel's *Theologisches Worterbuch zum Neuen Testament*, vol. 4, cols. 1092–99.

transition from "history" to "allegory"; in other words, one of the consequences of the great real *transitio*, the great and unique and decisive "passing-over" from the Old Testament to the New.[224] It is not impossible that St. Paul himself was already explicitly aware of this. When in the Epistle to the Ephesians he writes that Christ wished to provide for himself in the Church a Betrothed "glorious . . . , not having spot or wrinkle", or when he speaks to the Corinthians of the divine jealousy, it is possible that he was in fact recalling the appropriate verses in the Song and desirous of showing their implications.[225] It is at any rate certain that the exegesis which has become the rule since Hippolytus does no more than apply this doctrine. Those who go all the way in admitting the allegory of the relationship between Israel and Yahweh but still want to exclude from the interpretation of the Song "all the fantasies of Christianity" [226] do not realize what they are asking; they want us to renounce our "passover" in order to Judaize afresh.

But this transposition was not the whole of the story. By virtue of a sort of transference, which this time was not in any way a substitution but rather an extension, the "allegory" was in its turn to flower (as elsewhere) into "tropology" and the "mysticism" into morality. And here again there was a genuine element of inevitability, for "what happens to the Church in general happens to the Christian in particular" [227]—a constant law, and one we have run across more than once. Or again, to put it in the words of a modern commentator on the Song,

[224] See "La Doctrine du quadruple sens", in *Mélanges F. Cavallera* (1948), pp. 347–66; Philip of Harveng, *Moralitates in Cantica*, preface: "Si ergo apud illos figura fuit, apud nos veritas esse debet" (PL 203, 491d).

[225] See A. Feuillet, *Le Cantique des cantiques*, pp. 104, 113.

[226] See E. Reuss, *Le Cantique* (1879), p. 6.

[227] See my *Histoire et Esprit* (1950), pp. 142–50, and my *Catholicism*, pp. 206–16; also Charles Moeller, "Simone Weil devant l'Église et l'Ancien Testament", CS (June 1952), p. 120: "The progressive educational process carried on by God with regard to his people is an image of that which he carries out in the government of his Church and the spiritual education of the individual soul."

Fr. Martin del Rio: "The plan of the whole is to be found in each part singly." [228] A third way of putting it would be to say that the spiritual life reproduces in the soul the mystery of the Church herself, since it is there that, in the last analysis, this mystery is consummated by becoming interiorized: "Either the Church or the soul".[229] Here, in the heart of the Christian faith, we have again, transfigured, the old analogy of the microcosm and the macrocosm:

> Just as man is called in Greek "microcosm", which means "little world", because in his material essence he is composed of the same four elements as the universe, so also each one of the faithful has the appearance of a Church in miniature, when in the mystery of the hidden unity a man receives all the sacraments of human redemption that are conferred by God on the universal Church herself.[230]

The relation of Christ and his Church, symbolized in the Song, should also, therefore, become the relation of the Christian soul and the Word of God—"the soul in the Church is a faithful soul, a wise soul, an elect soul, a holy soul, a soul

---

[228] Martin del Rio, S.J., *In Canticum canticorum Salomonis* (Paris, 1604), p. 9: "Arbitror sic agi de amore Dei erga totum coetum fidelium, qui Ecclesia vocatur, ut multa quoque singulis conveniant Ecclesiae membris. . . . Fatemur ergo rationem totius a singulis partibus non esse alienam."

[229] Origen, *In Cantica comm.*: "Sive anima . . . sive Ecclesia" (ed. Baehrens, p. 61); *Excerpta Procopiana* (PG 13, 207c); St. Ambrose, *De Isaac*, chap. 1, no. 2: "Descendit itaque ad Sapientiae fontem, vel Ecclesia, vel anima" (PL 14, 503a); chap. 2, no. 8: "Quid est igitur, *Osculetur me*? Considera vel Ecclesiam . . . , vel animam" (505–6); also chap. 6, no. 56 (522d); *In Lucam*, bk. 8, chap. 10 (PL 15, 1768a–b); *De sacramentis*, bk. 5, chap. 2, nos. 5–8; St. Jerome, *Tract. de Psalm.* 86: "Quae interpretati sumus de Ecclesia, potest intelligi et in anima nostra. . . . Vera Ecclesia, verum templum Christi non est nisi anima humana"; St. Cyril of Alexandria, *Fragmenta in Cantica* (PG 69, 1284c); St. Bernard, *In Cantica, sermo* 58, no. 3 (PL 183, 1056d); Gilbert of Hoyland, *In Cantica, sermo* 40, no. 5: "Hortum sponsae, statum animae vel Ecclesiae" (PL 184, 210c), etc.

[230] St. Peter Damian, *Liber qui dicitur Dominus vobiscum*, chap. 10 (PL 1145, 239d); cf. the timely reflections of Fr. Lucien-Marie de Saint-Joseph, *Le Cantique des cantiques* (trans. Chouraqui, 1953), pp. 27–29.

enchurched". Made Man in Mary, the Word goes forth from her: "Tanquam sponsus de thalamo suo, amaturus novam Ecclesiam, et in ea quamlibet fidelem personam tanquam sponsam ornatam viro suo." [231] The kiss he has for the Church is a kiss in which every one among the faithful will have a part "inasmuch as a member of the Church", [232] for while each soul is loved individually, none is loved separately. And thus what was originally written for the Chosen People "may be transposed for each soul that is espoused by God. Through the mediation of Christ the love of God for his people is extended to every soul." [233] St. Paul was talking to each one of the Corinthian Christians and through them to every member of the great Christian community when he wrote: "For I have espoused you to one husband, that I may present you as a chaste virgin to Christ." [234] Those words are meant for all of us: "The Song is a book for all, rediscovering and retracing as it does the whole pilgrimage of love." [235]

It was not necessary for a long time to elapse before this second step could be taken;[236] the thing is fully grasped from the time of Origen—that is, the middle of the third century. Origen's explanation of the Song is one of his masterpieces;[237]

[231] Gerhoh of Reichersberg, *Liber de Gloria* (PL 194, 1105b).

[232] Michele Ghisleri, *Commentarii in Canticum canticorum Salomonis*, 4th ed. (1617), preface, chap. 3: "quin et pia quaelibet anima, ut Ecclesiae membrum."

[233] Guy Sauvard, "Saint Jean de la Croix et la Bible", CS (June 1952), p. 138; cf. p. 136: the experience of the People of God, Israel, and the Church is the foundation and guarantee of that of each one of its members.

[234] 2 Cor 11:2.

[235] A. Robert, *Le Cantique des cantiques*, p. 25.

[236] It is somewhat astonishing to read, in as well-informed a historian as Anders Nygren, that in the Middle Ages, in order to convey the communion established between the soul and God, men turned gladly to the image—already current in the mystery religions of antiquity—of a spiritual marriage (*Eros and Agape*). As if that particular image were unknown to Christian antiquity and its Jewish origins were of no account!

[237] See my *Histoire et Esprit*, pp. 142–50 and 192–94. St. Jerome's verdict is well known (*Praefatio in Or. Cant.*): "Origen, having surpassed all other interpreters in all the books of Scripture, surpassed himself in his interpretation of the Song." That is an opinion which has been confirmed by succeeding centuries.

he provides both the mind and the heart of Christianity with authentic expression. Now, it becomes plain in his works, as in those of the rich tradition that he begins and presides over, that the nuptials of the Church and those of the soul are not set side by side in a system of mutual interchangeability. It is true that sometimes (as in Theodoret, Gregory of Elvira, or St. Justus of Urgel) it is the espousal of the Church that is chiefly in question, whereas sometimes (as in St. Gregory of Nyssa, St. Nilus, or, more recently, St. Ludwig von Bruck, Cathius, St. Robert Bellarmine, and St. John of the Cross) our attention is directed chiefly to that of the soul, so that the "mystery of the Song" reveals itself as tracing for us the way of perfection.[238] But just as the first group does not exclude further application in the spiritual plane from its ecclesial exegesis, so the second group always takes that exegesis as given. William of Saint-Thierry explains the matter in one of his prefaces with all the clarity one could wish for.[239] With St. Gregory the Great, St. Bernard (who owed so much to Origen),[240] and others as well, the two aspects get equal attention, and thus we can see more clearly how they are fitted together in an organic exegesis. The two constitute, not two keys that can be used alternatively, but one—"*idem est*"—and the kingdom to which that key gives us access is no illusory one. For as St. Ambrose says, it is indeed "in souls that the Church is beautiful",[241] and, on the other hand, as St. Peter Damian writes, "through the mystery of the sacrament each soul is in some sense the Church in her fullness." [242] We can translate *anima ecclesiastica* as "that soul which is the Church" without forcing the primary sense of the phrase,

[238] St. Gregory of Nyssa, *In Cantica*, hom. 1 (PG 44, 764–65 and 765d; 769–72).

[239] *Expositio altera in Cantica* (PL 180, 476a).

[240] The work of Dom Jean Leclercq, O.S.B., has elucidated the influence of Origen on St. Bernard in the matter of interpretation of the Song.

[241] *De mysteriis*, 7, 39.

[242] St. Peter Damian, *Liber qui dicitur Dominus vobiscum*: "ut et omnis universalis Ecclesia non immerito una Christi perhibeatur sponsa, et unaquaeque anima per sacramenti mysterium plena esse credatur Ecclesia" (PL 145, 235).

and Blessed Mary of the Incarnation is saying nothing that is not in line with the most solidly based tradition when she writes, speaking of her prayer: "It has seemed to me that the soul which is destined to dwell in this holy city should be like that city and have some relation to that city itself, for it is the Kingdom of God by virtue of the beautiful qualities with which the Bridegroom of the heavenly Jerusalem—who is also her own—has been pleased to adorn it." [243] We need only add, as does St. Bernard, following Origen, that if the Church "is the unity of souls, or, rather, their unanimity", in actual fact no individual soul does more than participate, more or less imperfectly, and in accordance with its degree of spiritual advancement, in the privileges that are in principle the Church's own.[244] Everything is always applied "principally" to the Church.[245]

In all these commentaries the allegorical detail is, of course, often gratuitous, and the literary canonization that authorized its repetition through century after century is not in any way to be confused with the authority of a doctrinal tradition. We are quite free to agree with Renan that it indicates, as far as its inventors are concerned, "an exuberance of the imagination that is sometimes truly astonishing".[246] We may even grant that it is often as tedious as it is gratuitous. The works in which it unfolds itself are often almost unreadable, as far as we are

[243] *Relations d'oraison*, 1, 10, 2 (*Écrits*, ed. Jamet, 2:66).

[244] *In Cantica, sermo* 12, no. 11: "Ipsa [Ecclesia] audaciter secureque sese nominat sponsam. . . . Quod etsi nemo nostrum sibi arrogare praesumat, ut animam suam quis audeat sponsam Domini appellare, quoniam tamen de Ecclesia sumus, quae merito hoc homine et re nominis gloriatur, non immerito gloriae hujus participium usurpamus. Quod enim simul omnes plene integreque possidemus, hoc singuli sine contradictione participamus" (PL 183, 833c–d); *Sermo* 61, no. 2 (1071c); see also Richard of Saint-Victor, *In Cantica canticorum expositio*, prologue: "Toti simul sponsa sunt, quia toti simul Ecclesia sunt" (PL 196, 410).

[245] Martin del Rio, S.J., *In Cantica canticorum*, p. 9: "non debere sic de quavis anima justi intelligi, ut non id praecipue de Ecclesia universa dictum putemus."

[246] *Le Cantique des cantiques*, p. 123.

concerned, and the beauty of certain features in them is not enough to bring the whole to life. It is also quite true that we cannot follow many of the old writers "through the dizzy paths of their fantastic interpretations" or "imitate them when, in their desire to get down to their task more quickly, they graft the texts of the Old Testament onto the Christian tradition of their time, all in one mass". Indeed, I think that St. John of the Cross (for example) was wise when he "did not attempt to make his *Spiritual Canticle* correspond point by point" with the biblical text.[247] Yet if we want to do justice to these early writers and at the same time not deprive ourselves of something really valuable, then we must be on the watch that we do not become the victims, in our judgments, of too analytical an approach. As far as one can see it does not seem that their legitimate conviction of obtaining "the understanding of the Scriptures" through the contemplation of loving faith made them accord uncritically an absolute value to each and every one of the allegories, tropologies, and anagogies that they distinguished and worked out in their exegesis; there are many scattered remarks and nuances of meaning that make that evident. They did not have in mind the strictness of scientific objectivity in this particular field—which is not one that calls for it—and they did not disown the very large part played in it by the personal factor—a part perhaps all the larger in proportion as it was at the service of a deeper truth. As far as they were concerned, it was enough to get inside and remain inside the faith and—always working in accordance with its "analogy"—to bring the "understanding" desired to a greater pitch of clarity, thus obtaining a grasp of it that was more reflective and more communicable. They were content to feel in their hands the instrument that would allow them to convert, for preaching purposes, the mystery that was everywhere latent in the sacred text. And that implies, on their part, both a very strong sense of the unity of the Bible and a synthetic way of thinking—despite

[247] A. Feuillet, *Le Cantique des cantiques*, pp. 129 and 241.

the appearance to the contrary created by the mass of detail. The multiplicity of their figurative explanations, whether it be properly ordered or no, does not break up their concept of the spiritual meaning. For them, each detail is meaningful only within the whole—that is, as a partial sign and not a detachable piece—and they well knew that the mystery of the Scriptures, whether signifying or signified, is one.[248] Hence it comes about that "by the roundabout way of an exegesis that seems to us, and so often is, somewhat fantastic" (that is, if one looks only at the detail in an artificial state of isolation) they got at "the true sense" [249] and that very much in depth. "See, brethren, how great is the unity of the Scriptures!" [250] "See how deep calls to deep, how the different chapters of Scripture fit one with another!" [251] If the search for mystical senses is not to become a snare or a mere pastime, it is certainly essential that there should be a real link between the passage under comment and the fact of Christ; and they were as firmly convinced of that as we are. It is simply that the principle of the analogy of faith enabled them to understand this link in a freer sense; and this principle itself cannot operate at full power save when there is clear awareness of the unity of revelation.

In the sometimes strange growths—today often somewhat faded and withered—preserved for us in the old commentaries on the Song of Songs, we should get used to seeing simply a freely devised method designed to bring out in its full worth the essential idea[252]—whatever may be the truth concerning the

[248] See Rupert of Deutz, *In Matthaeum*, bk. 2: "omne Scripturarum sacramentum" (PL 168, 1348c).

[249] P. M. Standaert, "La Doctrine de l'image chez saint Bernard", *Ephemerides theologiae Lovanienses* 23 (1947): 134.

[250] St. Bernard, *In festo omnium sanctorum*, s. 2, no. 4 (PL 183, 467a).

[251] Gilbert of Hoyland, *In Cant.*, s. 18, no. 4 (PL 184, 94a).

[252] Michele Ghisleri (*Commentarii*, preface, chap. 11) endeavors to show (having, like del Rio, admitted to the parabolic character of the Song) how it is nonetheless permissible for the exegete to look for a mystical sense in each of its words.

literary genre, more or less rooted in parable or allegory, originally adopted by the sacred poet. The method will, of course, seem all the freer the more we uphold the allegorical character of the original text—it being obvious that the two situations are different in matters of detail. Now, this essential idea is in no way arbitrary; no more has it given birth to "a whole forest of interpretations", as Renan seems to believe, that are divergent and take their rise from different systems.[253] If we consider it at source and from the aspect of its permanent intention, the traditional interpretation of the Song of Songs—one in its duality— rests on an inheritance that is historically witnessed to and upon a profound symbolism that Christ himself chose to use[254] and that we may consider as rooted in the actual being of things.[255]

* * *

The Marian interpretation was, as we know, to be of later origin, though some scattered traces of it are already to be found in the age of the Fathers.[256] St. Paschasius Radbertus gives it as

[253] *Le Cantique des cantiques*, p. 123. Reuss had achieved a more balanced view when he wrote (*Le Cantique*, p. 7): "If these differ among themselves to some extent, that is only where the interpretation of detail is concerned."

[254] Mt 9:15, 22:1–10; cf. Mt 25:1–33, Jn 3:29.

[255] See Louis Beirnaert, S.J., "La Signification du symbolisme conjugal dans la vie mystique", in *Mystique et continence* (1952), pp. 381–84; Bossuet, *Préface sur le Cantique des cantiques*: "If anyone meditates attentively upon these words, separating from the work of God (which is holy and chaste) the shameful operation of concupiscence, which is caused by sin, he will easily grasp how Solomon was justified in representing the chaste love between the Church and faithful souls by conjugal love and society" (*Oeuvres*, ed. Lachat, 1:610–11); Jean Chatillon, IK 194, p. 135: "This nuptial symbolism is without doubt that which best expresses the inmost nature and destiny of the Church"; Richard of Saint-Victor, *In Cantica canticorum expositio*, prologue: "Debemus ad has nuptias sponsi et sponsae cum intellectu intimae caritatis, id est, cum veste nuptiali, venire, id est, digna caritatis intelligentia; qua si non induimur, ab hoc nuptiali convivio in exteriores tenebras, id est, ignorantiae caecitatem, repellimur" (PL 196, 405–6); St. Teresa, *Conceptions on the Love of God*, chap. 1.

[256] Notably in Hippolytus, Epiphanius, Andrew of Crete, Theodore the Studite, George of Nicomedia, Ephrem; also St. Jerome, *Epist. ad Paulum et Eust.* (PL 30, 134–35); St. Ambrose, *De inst. virginis*, 87–89 (PL 16, 326–27).

normal in the ninth century,[257] and it was exploited by men such as Ambrose Autpert in the eighth century and St. Peter Damian in the eleventh, in their sermons for the feasts of our Lady,[258] while the liturgy also contains certain anticipations of it;[259] but all the same it is not until the twelfth century that it becomes systematized in the West, beginning with Rupert of Deutz.[260] In the East, in the fourteenth century, the Emperor Matthew Cantacuzenus, who became a monk of Mount Athos, joined the ranks of its contributors, and in a commentary that is not without its beauty he hails in "the fairest of women" the holiest and by far the most glorious soul in the whole Church, the "Virgin Immaculate"; in the call given her in the spring by the Bridegroom he recognizes the voice of the Word in that spring-time moment of history in which the Incarnation was to take place.[261] However, he did not go so far as to link up interpretations of this kind into a consistently pursued exegesis; according to him, the Song should sometimes be interpreted as applying to our Lady and sometimes to the Church of the Gentiles,[262] and his contemporary Theophane of Nicaea, who was in contact with

[257] *In Matthaeum*, bk. 2, proemium: "Ubi nimirum universalis Ecclesia praesignatur, tandem de Spiritu sancto replenda, per quem in cordibus credentium et ipsa Christum quotidie non solum parit, quia mater et virgo est, sed etiam sponsa in omnibus appellatur. . . . Quod de hac [Maria] specialiter dictum est in Canticis, quamvis generaliter de Ecclesia significatum intelligamus" (PL 120, 103–4, 106).

[258] PL 89, 1275–76; 144, 508a, 510d, 561c, 717–22, 754, 760–61; also the sermons of Pseudo-Ildephonsus on the Assumption (PL 96, 239–82)—in this case the author may be St. Paschasius Radbertus.

[259] Some ninth-century texts are given by G. Frenaud in *Marie et l'Église*, 1:54–56. Dom Célestin Charlier, O.S.B., writes in his *Bible et vie chrétienne* that the liturgy "made the Song of Songs into the source of its Marian inspiration, and that with a sureness in interpretation which is far from being a mere accommodation, as it is commonly described".

[260] PL 168, 1387b, 1603b, etc. See also the wonderful prologue in which he expounds the nature of his undertaking (PL 168, 837–40). He also makes use of the Song in order to interpret his own experience (col. 1453); see also Philip of Harveng, *Moralitates in Cantica*, preface (PL 203, 491–93).

[261] *In Cantica canticorum* (PG 152, 1008, 1020, 1024, 1051).

[262] Matthew Cantacuzenus, *In Cantica canticorum* (PG 152, 1021a–b).

him, also turned the Song to account in praising Mary.[263] The Latins had already shown themselves bolder, and the Marian interpretation seemed to them to cover everything. In point of fact it does not constitute a new key, properly speaking, any more than the others. It is not just that the Marian interpretation is not "that garland of poetic fabrications woven by the Christian imagination around the object of its favorite dreams";[264] I think it is not even enough to describe it as "entirely legitimate".[265] Far from making us stray away onto the fringe of things, it plants us, on the contrary—if we grasp its meaning properly—at the very center of the mystery prefigured by the revelation made to Israel and enshrined in the Song; for the Song is, according to the very intention of its authors, a hymn to the Incarnation. Its intention is to celebrate the first union of the Word with human nature in the womb of our Lady—the first kiss of the Word, which is the pledge of the final union.[266]

Even if we limit ourselves to considering in greater detail the relation of the Word and our Lady, this interpretation was destined to develop sooner or later by virtue of that same logic, inherent in the Christian mystery, that we have already seen at work.[267] If that logic is to be allowed to run its course freely, all that is necessary is a number of unfoldings cast in the traditional mold, concerning the transition from the Synagogue to the Church of the Gentiles or individual conversion from the state of sin.[268] It is still not entirely certain that even at the earliest

[263] Jugie, *La Mort et l'Assomption de la sainte Vierge*, pp. 25, 133–35, 163, 171, 179, 181.

[264] Renan, *Le Cantique des cantiques*, p. 141.

[265] See Jouon, no. 23, p. 20.

[266] Cf. the title of Rupert of Deutz's commentary: *In Cantica canticorum de Incarnatione Domini*; and the opening of bk. 1 (PL 168, 839–40).

[267] See Philip of Harveng, *Moralitates in Cantica*, bk. 6: "Dignum est ut ad beatae Mariae Virginis personam stylum nostrum dirigamus, quia in ejus laudem et sanctae Ecclesiae honorem totum librum istum a Spiritu sancto editum per os Salomonis non dubitamus" (PL 203, 571d).

[268] Cf. A. Robert, *Le Cantique des cantiques*, pp. 24–25; A. Feuillet, *Le Cantique des cantiques*, pp. 110–11 and 128.

level of its meaning the Song accords a part to sin in the life of the Bride, and it is possible that, if we interpret it too strictly in accordance with the previous prophetic tradition, we may run a risk of losing sight of its originality from this point of view.[269] Is the primary subject of the book, in point of fact, the pardon granted by God to his guilty and repentant people, so that the Shulamite's invitations to "return" may be understood as invitations to *conversio*? Or should we see rather in the "going up by the desert" an allusion to the leaving of the wasteland of sin? It would seem that the point is at least debatable.[270] On the other hand, however, the union between God and his people here appears in a state of striving and desire rather than in terms of accomplished fact; its full realization is depicted only in anticipation, and for this reason we may maintain that its direct application is less to the perfection of our Lady than to our own souls in their state of pilgrimage. In his preface to his commentary, Gilbert Foliot remarks (à propos "I will seek him whom my soul loveth. I sought him, and I found him not"): "Here we have to do with the Church or the soul inflamed with love and seeking God, but not yet laying hold upon him", and that is doubtless why he decided against any Marian interpretation.[271] Whatever the truth may be about all this, the two opinions that confront each other today had already made their appearance, as tendencies at any rate, in the Middle Ages. Thus Rupert of Deutz held that everything in the Song could be read as applying to our Lady;[272] according to him, the texts concerning the search of the Bride for the Bridegroom were more fitting when referred to her than to other souls less advanced, since she

[269] This is the view of D. Buzy, *Le Cantique des cantiques* (1949), pp. 24–25: "The Song breaks with the prophets' conception. . . . We must eliminate from the Song the very shadow of unfaithfulness." Fr. Lucien-Marie de Saint-Joseph holds the same view (*Mystique et continence*, pp. 15, 22–23, 37, 38).

[270] See St. Justus of Urgel, *In Cant.*, nos. 147 and 178 (PL 67, 986b–c and 990b).

[271] *Expositio in Cantica* (PL 202, 1150b).

[272] PL 169, 1550.

realizes the perfection of all striving and desire.[273] Denis the Carthusian was to say, similarly, that the Word of God "is sought for with far greater perfection, affection, and fruitfulness by those who have him than by those who do not",[274] and later on yet Michele Ghisleri was to adhere to this viewpoint from the very beginning of his own great commentary.[275] Philip of Harveng has no hesitation about seeing in the Song "a whole allegory of the Virgin", and he presents it as a "dramatic dialogue" between the Word and our Lady, the Word being escorted by angels and our Lady by the Apostles and the faithful.[276] But Guerricus, taking a slightly different standpoint, wrote that in this kind of symbolic exegesis "we may—while respecting the substance of things—allow ourselves a certain liberty in matters of detail", and according to his way of thinking it was solely on grounds of this kind that the words of the Song could be applied to the Assumption of our Lady.[277]

---

[273] *In Cantica*, bk. 3 (PL 168, 874–76). Matthew Cantacuzenus avoids the difficulty by an exterior interpretation: Our Lady cannot find her Son any more on earth when he is in the sepulcher, or after the Ascension (PG 152, 1052).

[274] *In Cantica*, a. 11: "Ab habentibus cum quaeritur, multo perfectius, affectuosius et fructuosius, quam a non habentibus" (*Opera omnia* [1898], 7:359).

[275] *Commentarii*, p. 12: "Cum beatissima Virgo Maria supra omnem creaturam (unica excepta humanitate Christi) divino amore flagravit, necessario illud consequitur, ut super omnes antiquos patres divinae Incarnationis languere desiderio, per quam tanto prae aliis Deo dilecto suo arctius uniretur, quanto prae caeteris universis una electa esset, ex cujus, carne Deus ipse humanam assumeret carnem . . . [If then the Fathers longed for the Incarnation, saying, 'Osculetur me osculo oris sui'], . . . quanto congruentius eadem a Beatissima Virgine dicta asseremus?" Cf. p. 439, where, commenting upon Song 3:2 ("I sought him, and I found him not"), he speaks of our Lady searching for her Son during the *triduum mortis*.

[276] See N. L. Renviaux, in *Maria*, 2:718. We may note that the curious and very Dionysian commentary of Thomas of Verceil, which does not make mention of our Lady, sees the Spouse, not as an imperfect Church or a soul still in the state of sin, but the *deiformis anima* (see B. Pez, *Thes. anec. noviss.* [1721], vol. 2, pt. 1).

[277] PL 185, 190d. See also Msgr. Malon's *L'Immaculée Conception*, pp. 310–11: "The interpretation of the mystical sense of Scripture does not follow along the

In point of fact, the Marian exegesis retains a certain freedom right down to the period of its "silver age".[278] Nevertheless, by the nature of things it was destined, once worked out, to become the privileged explanation, last in order of time and discovery but logically first. It speedily wins a place with the commentators and becomes the theme of liturgical poetry.[279] And there is no contemplative fantasy here—matters of detail excepted (which is, certainly, to except a good deal). In point of fact it is impossible not to consider Mary as being the beloved Bride par excellence of the Bridegroom: "inter omnes sponsas prae omnibus fuit ac permanet ornata".[280] The Bride's privileges are accorded to her "more amply and in greater perfection".[281] She is the *anima decora* above all others; the soul of dazzling beauty, whose chaste union with the Word was celebrated by Origen.[282] She is called *mons montium*, *virgo virginum*, *sancta sanctorum*,[283] and the song of love, which the Song of Songs is above all things, is preeminently—*specialissime*—the song of Mary.[284]

---

strict and cautious lines of the interpretation of the literal sense; its style is altogether freer and more liberal, and its point of application is not so much the word as the thing."

[278] Thomas Gallus, for example—although he had no hesitation in frequently applying one and the same text in threefold fashion—writes in his *In Cantica*, bk. 10: "Per sponsam diximus quod aliquando designatur Virgo Maria, aliquando anima ambulans in justitia, aliquando militans Ecclesia" (PL 206, 697c).

[279] See the long sequence *infra octavam Nativitatis Beatae Mariae* in the Tournai Missal for 1498 (ed. Misset and Weale, *Thesaurus*, 2:166–68).

[280] Gerhoh of Reichersberg, *Liber de gloria*, chap. 10 (PL 94, 1105b); see also Bossuet, *Préface sur le Cantique des cantiques*, p. 677.

[281] Several references are given in Barré, nos. 72, 73, 74 bis, 116.

[282] *In Cant.*, hom. 1, no. 1. Dom Olivier Rousseau, in his edition of these homilies of Origen (*Sources chrétiennes* (1953), believes he has grounds for perhaps detecting in homily 2, no. 2, the first allusion—even though it be both a distant and an indirect one—to a relation between the Bride of the Canticle and our Lady.

[283] Rupert of Deutz, *In Cantica*, bk. 7 (PL 168, 962a).

[284] Alain of Lille, *Elucidatio in Cantica*: "Cum canticum amoris, scilicet epithalamum Salomonis specialiter et spiritualiter ad Ecclesiam referatur,

Which was most excellently explained in the seventeenth century by the Capuchin Louis-François d'Argentan:

> Since it is true that the Holy Church is the well-beloved Spouse of Jesus Christ, who speaks to her in the sacred Song, and similarly that all the souls who make up a part of this Church may speak to him as the whole does of which they are a part, it is most certain that the most Holy Virgin, who is first and noblest among the souls that make up the Church, and she who has the highest worth in herself alone, and who is more beloved by God and more favored with his graces than all the Church together, is truly that dear Spouse, that dove, that unique and incomparable one to whom the whole holy Song is addressed; and that is why the commentators usually give three senses to all its words; the one concerning the Church in general, the other concerning each soul in particular, and the third—which is apparently the principal one—concerning the person of the most holy Virgin.[285]

Although "all the mysteries of this book", says Godefridus of Admont, "fit perfectly either the universal Church, or each faithful soul in the bosom of the Church, conveying in a spiritual manner (thanks to the mystical sense) the mutual love of the Bridegroom and the Bride, they nevertheless seem to fit more 'specially' the Blessed Virgin Mary, who, above all souls, was singularly full of a 'special' dilection and deserved above all to be 'specially' loved by the Bridegroom.[286] "We see thee with no first like to thee and none second."[287] St. Francis de Sales says that she is "a dove so uniquely unique in dilection that all

---

tamen specialissime et spiritualissime ad gloriosam Virginem reducitur" (PL 210, 53). Martin del Rio says: "Quodam specialis praerogativae jure" (*In Cantica*, p. 9).

[285] D'Argentan, *Conférences sur les grandeurs de la très sainte Vierge*, 2:337–38; also Malou, *L'Immaculée Conception*, 1:297–312.

[286] PL 174, 972.

[287] Sedulius, *Carmen paschale*, bk. 2; Rupert of Deutz, *In Cantica* (PL 168, 854a, 935a): "Una et electa est, quia nec inter angelos, nec inter homines, similem vel primam habet, vel sequentem habitura est" (936b).

others are, when placed in comparison with her, rather deserving of the name of crows than of doves".[288] And thus the daughters of Sion give place to her when they proclaim her blessed; the followers of the Bride and the companions of the Bridegroom—that is, the perfect as well as the beginners, and angels as well as men[289]—show to her the respect due to a unique mystery. Or, rather, we may here recall the "perichoresis" invoked by Scheeben, for here there is no place for anything that is merely of the surface; strictly speaking, there is no more question of going from one system of interpretation to another when we pass from the individual soul to Mary than there is when we pass from the Church to the soul—we are all the time moving along the same network of correspondences. Mary is the first-beloved; but in her all saintly souls, and primarily the Church, whose "form" she is, are loved also.[290] The Christian mystery is one: it is the same thing in our Lady, in the Church, and in each individual soul. Here—as Fr. Barré has recently reminded us—everything should be understood "within the more general framework of the perpetuity of the mysteries of Christ, which was so strikingly emphasized by St. Leo and reemphasized by Bede, Ambrose Autpert, and Haymo: 'But until today, and until the consummation of the world, the Lord ceases not to be conceived in Nazareth, born in Bethlehem. . . .' The mystery of the Church is the continuation of the mystery of our Lady rather than the prefigured replica of it; the same mystery deepens and unfolds." [291] "In specie genus intelligitur. Gratia in specie collata, in omne genus diffunditur." [292]

[288] *Traité de l'amour de Dieu*, bk. 10, chap. 5.

[289] Richard of Saint-Victor, *In Cantica* (PL 196, 409).

[290] See Jean de Saussure, "Méditation sur la Vierge", in *Dialogue sur la Vierge* (1950); Paul Claudel, *L'Épée et le miroir*, pp. 42 and 73; St. Ambrose, *De virginitate*, chap. 4, no. 20: "Est enim anima quae spiritualiter parit Christum" (PL 16, 271b).

[291] Barré, p. 114; cf. my *Histoire et Esprit*, pp. 206–17.

[292] See Pseudo-Alcuin, *In Apoc.* (PL 100, 1152d); Pseudo-Ildephonsus, *Sermo 3, de Assumptione* (PL 96, 256c).

In the sacrament of these nuptials "the Virgin Mary becomes the Church and every faithful soul", or again the Church and all faithful souls "become the Virgin Mary" by virtue of "integrity of will and purity of faith". A sermon by Peter Lombard assures us of this,[293] and Rupert of Deutz gives us a firm hold on the idea when he shows us everything said of the great scattered body of the Church as unified and drawn together as to its center or its peak in the unrivalled soul of Mary, the uniquely beloved.[294] St. Thérèse of Lisieux, without scholarship or philosophical training as she was, nevertheless grasped this point with all her instinctive Christianity of the heart when she said to her sisters in religion: "There is no need to believe (as I have often heard it said) that by virtue of her prerogatives the Blessed Virgin will eclipse all the glory of the saints, as the sun, on its rising, makes the stars disappear. *Mon Dieu*, what a strange idea! A mother who makes her children's glory disappear! I think exactly the opposite—I think that she will very much increase the glory of the elect." [295] St. Bonaventure before had made a point of showing the same thing by means of two carefully chosen words. When discussing "the excellence of the glorious Virgin with reference to the universal Church", he says: "As the sun *excels* and *makes glorious* all the bodies of the world, so the Blessed Virgin *excels* and *makes glorious* the members of the whole Church." [296]

---

[293] *Sermo* 55, *In Annuntiatione*: "In hoc conceptu [Christi] magnum et mirabile sacramentum, conjunctionis scilicet Christi et Ecclesiae, seu Verbi et animae. Virgo enim Maria facta est Ecclesia, vel quaelibet anima fidelis, quae in corruptione voluntatis, castitate et sinceritate fidei virgo est" (PL 171, 609).

[294] *De glorificatione Trinitatis*, bk. 6, chap. 13: "adunando et congregando voces tam magni tamque diffusi corporis Ecclesiae in unam animam singularis et unicae dilectae Christi Mariae" (PL 169, 155). See also Honorius of Autun, *Expositio in Cantica* (PL 172, 494c–d); Guerricus, *In Assumptione sermo* 3, 3: "Si quis tamen curiose inquirere vellit, cujus potissimum vox illa sit, *in omnibus requiem quaesivi*, vox est utique sapientiae, vox Ecclesiae, vox est Mariae, vox est cujuslibet sapientis animae" (PL 185, 195a).

[295] *Novissima verba*.

[296] *De nativitate B. M. V.*, *sermo* 3 (ed. Quaracchi, 9:712); cf. Sir 26:21; see also *In Purif.*, 4: "Plenitudo enim quae fuit in virgine Maria redundavit in totam Ecclesiam" (ibid., 9:651).

Thus the whole Church "rejoices in the blessed Virgin",[297] and the whole Church participates in her privilege. Together with her the whole Church hears the call of the Bridegroom in the Song: "Come from Libanus, come", and with her replies: "Come, my beloved, let us go forth"[298]—the cry that she still utters across the centuries toward the consummation, as the last page of the Bible tells us: "Come, Lord Jesus!"[299] There is, in fact, a wonderful parallelism between the Song and Revelation, for there the whole of revelation and the whole story of salvation are summed up in one and the same song of love, which is the prelude to one and the same song of eternity.[300] The majestic and tender gesture of Christ in the mosaic at Santa Maria in Trastevere—who embraces our Lady while his left hand holds the inscription *Veni electa mea*—is at the same time the gesture with which he summons and embraces the Church;[301] by a miracle that lies at the very heart of that universe into which we are introduced by grace, the Word of God can say without the slightest implication of exclusivism: "One is my dove; my perfect is but one."[302] "On one side and the other a marvelous lover, on one side and the

[297] St. Ephrem the Syrian, in a hymn to our Lady translated by E. Amann in *Le Dogme catholique dans les Pères de l'Église*, pp. 221–23; N. Grou, S.J., *L'Intérieur de Jésus et de Marie*, p. 493: "At Pentecost the Holy Spirit pours down on all the disciples the rays of his holy fire; but he unites them all over Mary."

[298] Song 4:8, 7:11, 8:13–14.

[299] Rev 22:17 and 20: St. Bede the Venerable, *In Apoc.* (PL 93, 206c); see also Rupert of Deutz, *De divinis officiis*, bk. 7, chap. 25.

[300] Some commentators have tried to find parallelisms of the external variety between these two books, as if the same events of Church history were predicted in both in symbols. This is, of course, a blind alley; though this reservation does not mean that there are no historical allusions whatsoever in the Song. See Feuillet, *Le Cantique des cantiques*, p. 83, but also Fr. Lucien-Marie de Saint-Joseph, *Mystique et continence*, pp. 23–25, 67.

[301] There is a similar fresco, though less well known, at Subiaco. For the Marian iconography of the Song in France, see Émile Mâle, *L'Art religieux de la fin du moyen âge en France*, pp. 220–26.

[302] Song 6:8; also Thomas Gallus and Joannes Algrinus, *In Cantica*, bk. 9 (PL 206, 638a–b and 643a).

other a lover like none." [303] Thought of that kind is always alive, and its essentials did in fact pass over into Scholasticism, particularly in the case of St. Thomas, who retains the two-fold ecclesial/Marian interpretation;[304] with later authors, in whose writings the theory reaches a pitch of precision verging on the mechanical, a fourth term is sometimes added as well, and it becomes scarcely possible to discern any longer a sense of the vital correspondence between the various levels of the explanation.[305]

Yet the systematized form it assumes in the hands of later authors does not—for all that—crush all the sap out of it; for its roots are in the enduring soil of the Christian *mystique*. And the liturgy of our Lady continues to make it flourish, just as the recent developments of Marian dogma are helping to revive it: "The soul and the Church—the twofold aspect of one single

[303] Hugh of Saint-Victor, *De Assumptione* (PL 177, 1211a–b); Peter Cellensis, *In Assumptione*, s. 6 (PL 202, 863–64), etc.

[304] His commentary has been studied by M. Grabmann in his *Die Lehre des hl. Thomas von Aquin von der Kirche als Gotteswerk* (1903), pp. 296–300.

[305] Denis the Carthusian, *In Cantica*, proemium: "Triplex est sponsa Christi, videlicet: tota universalis Ecclesia, quae vocatur sponsa . . . generalis; et quae libet anima fidelis et amorosa, quae dicitur Christi sponsa particularis; item-que beatissima Virgo Maria Christifera, quae Christi sponsa singularis censetur. . . . Sed et quaecumque particularis Ecclesia sponsa est Christi, et respectu animae potest dici sponsa communis" (*Opera omnia* [1898], 7:201); cf. *In cap.* 1, a. 5: "Sponsa singularis et singulariter unica atque ineffabiliter praedilecta sponsi caelestis est . . . mater ipsius" (ibid., 7:321). In his tenth "canon", Cornelius a Lapide thus distinguishes the three traditional senses: "Totalis et adaequatus sensus litteralis hic est de connubio sive conjunctione Christi et Ecclesiae per fidem et amorem; partialis litteralis est de con-junctione Christi cum anima sancta, praesertim quae studet perfectioni: haec est enim pars et membrum Ecclesiae; partialis principalis est de Christo et beata Virgine: haec enim est praecipua pars, primumque membrum Eccle-siae" (p. 2); and he has, for each verse, a threefold commentary divided into three separate paragraphs. The same thing is to be found with Ghisleri, who mentions in turn "prima Sponsa, Ecclesia Christi", "secunda sponsa, anima justi", and "tertia sponsa, Beata Maria", etc. See also Salazar, *Canticum canti-corum Salomonis allegorico sono et prophetica: Mystica et hypermystica expositione productum* (Lyons, 1643).

lover, whose ceaseless flux of changing countenance is tinted with the rays of the Immaculate One." [306]

"Oh, that thou wouldst rend the heavens and come down!" [307] But the Word of God has rent the heavens; and he came down into the womb of a virgin; and a virgin still bears him in her womb today—the Church, the Tabernacle of God.[308]

> Ave Sion, in qua Deus
> Habitavit, homo factus.[309]

"Let us marvel at this great mystery! The Son of God, whole and in his integrity, has passed from the heart of the Father into the womb of Mary and from Mary's womb into the bosom of the Church. What is in the Father is in the Virgin; and what is in the Virgin is in the unity of the Church. . . . Thus the heavens have rained mercy, thus the Word of God has been poured out to us, thus he without whom there is nothing is to be found spread abroad everywhere. . . . He, our God, our King, is substantially enclosed within the confines of a virgin's womb, for 'he hath wrought salvation in the midst of the earth'—of that earth concerning which it is written that there was no one to till it (Ps 73:12; Gen 2:5). And he is also in the

---

[306] Paul Claudel, *L'Épée et le miroir*, p. 213.

[307] Is 64:1; cf. Song 8:1–2 and the commentary in Feuillet, *Le Cantique des cantiques*, pp. 42–44; Ps 17:10.

[308] Isaac of Stella, *In Assumptione B. M.*, sermo 1: "*Et in haereditate Domini morabor*. Haereditas enim Domini universaliter Ecclesia, specialiter Maria, singulariter quaeque fidelis anima. In tabernaculo uteri Mariae moratus est Christus novem mensibus; in tabernaculo fidei Ecclesiae usque ad consummationem saeculi; in cognitione et dilectione fidelis animae in saecula saeculorum morabitur. . . . Qui creaverat eam novam creaturam in seipso, requievit, in utero suo Christus" (PL 194, 1865c and 1866a); Methodius of Olympus, quoted by Niessen in his *Die Mariologie des hl. Hieronymus* (Munster, 1913), p. 32. Cf. Sir 24:8: "He that made me rested in my tabernacle"; St. Ephrem the Syrian, *Sixth Hymn on Paradise*, 7–10: "[Deus] in medio Ecclesiae fixit Verbum. . . . Habitavit in Paradiso quem plantavit" (trans. Dom Edmond Beck, O.S.B., *Studia anselmiana* 26 [1951]: 51 and 53); St. Bonaventure, *De nativitate B. M. V.*, sermo 5 (ed. Quaracchi, 9:715).

[309] Pseudo-Anselm, *Psalterium*.

midst of the Church, as the Psalmist says: 'The Most High hath sanctified his tabernacle; he hath stood in the midst, and shall not be shaken.' " [310]

> Haec est arca continens manna delicatum,
> Haec sancti sacrarium Spiritus sacratum.[311]

The peoples who have not heard the word, those who have rejected him, the unbelieving, the worldly, the politicians, the sociology specialists, the "private" mystics—all these do not know him; but then we do not know him either—we who are his children and speak in his name. All over the world we encounter the lack of understanding of his mystery. We are never done with the work of clearing away the misunderstandings that hide him and letting a glimpse of his glory break through; but equally we have to put right the ideas about him that the merely human element in us leads us to hold ourselves. Here a deeper penetration is not enough; our very faith and love and our very zeal to defend and extend the Church demand of us a ceaseless effort of purification. And in all this there is no surer help than contemplation of our Lady.

At the solemn moment in which he proclaimed her triumph, thus setting the seal of approval on a movement of popular piety that caused a certain amount of offense to some who had constituted themselves the defenders of God's privileges, the Holy Father said: "The great benefit that mankind will draw from this definition [that of the Assumption] lies in the fact that it will turn men toward the glory of the Most Holy Trinity." [312]

Soli Deo gloria—everything in Mary proclaims that; her sanctity is wholly theological, for it is the perfection of faith, hope, and charity. Our Lady is the consummation of "the religion of

[310] St. Peter Damian, *Sermo* 43, *De sancto Victore confessore* (PL 144, 733–34).

[311] Quoted in Ragey, *Hymnarum quotidianum B. M. V.*, p. 425.

[312] Pius XII, constitution *Munificentissimus Deus* (November 1, 1950). See, previously, Pius IX's phrase in the bull *Ineffabilis Deus* (1854): "ad honorem Sanctae et Individuae Trinitatis".

the humble"; the handmaid of the Lord effaces herself before him who has regarded her lowliness,[313] marvels at his power, praises his mercy and faithfulness, and rejoices in him alone;[314] she is his glory.[315] The whole of her maternal role as far as we are concerned consists in her leading us to him.

That is Mary; and so also is the Church our Mother—the perfect worshipper; there lies the focal point of the analogy between them, for there the same spirit is at work in both. But whereas this humble and lofty perfection shines dazzlingly in supreme purity in Mary, in ourselves (who are as yet barely touched by the Spirit) it scarcely struggles to the light at all. The Church-as-Mother is never at the end of her labor to deliver us to the life of the Spirit, and the greatest danger we are to the Church, the most subversive temptation, the one that is ever and insiduously reborn when all the rest are overcome, and even strengthened by those victories, is what Abbot Vonier called the temptation to "worldliness of the mind . . . the practical relinquishing of other-worldliness, so that moral and even spiritual standards should be based, not on the glory of the Lord, but on what is the profit of man; an entirely anthropocentric outlook would be exactly what we mean by worldliness. Even if men were filled with every spiritual perfection, but if such perfections were not referred to God (suppose this hypothesis to be possible) it would be unredeemed worldliness."[316]

---

[313] Lk 1:46–48; see Newman, *Mary*: Mary is not the rival of her Son but his servant; cf. Rupert of Deutz, *In Cantica*, bk. 2: "In quo facies tua decora? In eo videlicet, quod magna est fides, magna humilitas" (PL 168, 869d).

[314] Lk 1:47–53. Cf. St. Bernard, *Sermo de duodecim praerogativis*, nos. 12–13 (PL 183, 436–37); St. Ambrose, *De Spiritu Sancto*, bk. 3, chap. 11, no. 80: "Maria erat templum Dei, non Deus templi. Et ideo ille solus adorandus, qui operatur in templo" (PL 16, 795a); *De laudando in Maria Deo*, a work by the Protestant Johann Oecolampadius (1521); see also Laurentin, p. 168.

[315] Léon Bloy was struck by this idea, which he expressed in his own fashion. In *Mon Journal*, p. 308, he writes: "There came back to me the idea, formerly so familiar, that the glory of God is our Lady"; see also M. J. Lory, *La Pensée religieuse de Léon Bloy*, p. 178.

[316] *The Spirit and the Bride*, p. 168.

If this spiritual worldliness were to invade the Church and set to work to corrupt her by attacking her very principle, it would be something infinitely more disastrous than any worldliness of the purely moral order—even worse than the hideous leprosy that at certain moments in history inflicts so cruel a disfigurement on the Bride; when religion seems to set up the scandalous "in the very sanctuary itself—represented by a debauchee Pope, hiding the face of Christ behind jewels, rouge, and beauty spots".[317]

None of us is wholly immune to this sort of evil. A crafty humanism that is the enemy of the living God (and in secret equally the enemy of man) can find its way into our hearts by a thousand and one paths; our original *curvitas* is never put straight for good and all. The "sin against the Holy Ghost" is always possible. But none of us is the Church herself, and none of our treacheries can deliver over to the devil that city which is watched over by God. "The Magnificat was not said once and for all in the garden at Hebron; it was put into the mouth of the Church for all the centuries",[318] and it has kept all its power. Like our Lady, the Church magnifies the Lord from age to age, for "pouring into our darkness the Light of the Godhead";[319] the idea of divine

[317] Auguste Valensin, S.J., "Le Sourire de Léonard de Vinci", *Études*, 274:47.

[318] Paul Claudel, letter to Gabriel Frizeau, September 25, 1907, in *Correspondance*, ed. Blanchet (1953), p. 111; cf. also Jean de la Saussure's words: "The poverty of thy Mother is the sole riches of the Church; the humility of thy Mother is the sole greatness of the Church" (*Méditations sur la Vierge: Figure de l'Église*).

[319] Adam of Perseigne, *Epist.* 17, *Quomodo Maria Dominum magnificaverit*: "Magnificas ergo . . . lumen verae deitatis incognitum mundanis tenebris inferedo" (PL 211, 643b). Thus we may say to the Church, as we say to our Lady: "At tu, Mater misericordiae, quia sum sicut lapis in acervo Mercurii, et quasi plumbum in aquis vehementibus, et ponderosus sum, quia me movere non possum: trahe me post te, ut currere post te valeam, in odorem unguentorum tuorum . . . , et postea, tecum amando et justitiam operando, magnificare Deum, cui est honor et gloria" (PL 211, 643–44). See also St. Cyril of Alexandria's acclamation to our Lady at the end of the Council of Ephesus: "The Trinity is glorified by you!" (PG 77, 1032–33); the whole passage is translated by Bossuet, in the explanation of the Litanies of our Lady, in his *Catéchisme des prières ecclésiastiques*.

praise is forever associated with her name.[320] And in spite of all
the resistance we put up, the Spirit of Christ goes on being
her life; she is the House of God built on the summit of the
mountains and above all the hills, and all the nations shall come
to her and say: "Glory be to thee, O Lord." [321] Even today, and in
spite of all we can do to obscure the fact, she is—again, like our
Lady—the Sacrament of Jesus Christ. All our faithlessness put
together does not stop her being "the Church of God" and "the
handmaid of the Lord"; she begins the great eternal liturgy in
time.[322] And with a voice whose power nothing will ever be able
to silence she utters the great call to freedom:

> Come, O peoples, let us adore the Divinity in three Persons—
> the Father in the Son and with the Holy Spirit. For the Father
> engenders from all eternity a Word who is co-eternal and co-
> regnant, and the Holy Spirit is in the Father, glorified with the
> Son, a unique power, a unique substance and a unique divinity.
> It is it whom we adore saying: Holy God who hast created all
> things by the Son with the cooperation of the Holy Spirit: Holy
> Strong One by whom we have knowledge of the Father and by
> whom the Holy Spirit is come into the world: Holy Immortal
> One, Consoling Spirit, who proceedest from the Father and
> restest in the Son: Holy Trinity, glory be to thee! [323]

IPSI GLORIA IN ECCLESIA. AMEN.[324]

---

[320] See Heb 2:12, quoting Ps 21:23; St. Augustine, *Sermo* 252, no. 11: "Ecclesiam futuram, ubi semper laudabitur Deus" (PL 38, 1178).

[321] Cf. the Roman Pontifical: "Fundata est domus Domini super verticem
montium, et exaltat est super omnes colles, et venient ad eam omnes gentes, et
dicent: Gloria tibi, Domine!"

[322] Rev 5:6–14, 7:9–12.

[323] Idiomelon of Leo the Despot at Great Vespers (Byzantine Rite), trans. Mer-
cenier, 2:365. This text is nonetheless irreproachable in its positive tenor with regard
to the Catholic teaching because it does not give expression to the doctrine of the
filioque, which is of course rejected by the Eastern dissidents. See St. Cyril of Alexandria, *Hom. div.*, 4: "By you he who cometh in the name of the Lord is blessed in
the Holy Gospels. . . . By you the Trinity is glorified. . . . By you the light of the only
Son shines on those who are in the shades and the shadow of death" (PG 77, 992).

[324] Eph 3:21; cf. Rev 1:6; Ps 67:27; Rom 11:36.

ABBREVIATIONS

AAS	*Acta apostolicae sedis*
BLE	*Bulletin de littérature ecclésiastique*
BSFEM	*Bulletin de la Société française d'études mariales*
CS	*Cahiers sioniens*
DR	Denzinger-Bannwart, *Enchiridion symbolorum*
DTC	*Dictionnaire de théologie catholique*
DV	*Dieu vivant*
EJ	*Eranos Jahrbuch*
GR	*Gregorianum*
IK	*Irénikon*
JTS	*Journal of Theological Studies*
LV	*Lumière et vie*
MD	*Maison-Dieu*
MGH	*Monumenta Germaniae Historica*
MSR	*Mélanges de science religieuse*
NRT	*Nouvelle revue théologique*
OA	*Oecumenica*
PG	Migne, *Patrologia Graeca*
PL	Migne, *Patrologia Latina*
PS	*Patrologia Syriaca*
RAM	*Revue d'ascétique et de mystique*
RB	*Revue biblique*
RBN	*Revue bénédictine*
RSPT	*Revue des sciences philosophiques et théologiques*
RSR	*Recherches de science religieuse*
SA	*Studia anselmiana*
ST	St. Thomas Aquinas, *Summa theologiae*
TH	*Terre humaine*
VI	*Vie intellectuelle*
VS	*Vie spirituelle*
ZAM	*Zeitschrift für Asceze und Mystik*
ZKT	*Zeitschrift für Katholische Theologie*